American Workers, Colonial Power

American Workers, Colonial Power

Philippine Seattle and
the Transpacific West, 1919–1941

Dorothy B. Fujita-Rony

UNIVERSITY OF CALIFORNIA PRESS
Berkeley · Los Angeles · London

University of California Press
Berkeley and Los Angeles, California

University of California Press, Ltd.
London, England

© 2003 by The Regents of the University of California

Library of Congress Cataloging-in-Publication Data

Fujita-Rony, Dorothy B.
    American workers, colonial power : Philippine
Seattle and the transpacific west, 1919–1941 /
Dorothy B. Fujita-Rony.
        p.   cm.
    Includes bibliographical references and index.
    ISBN 0-520-23094-9 (alk. paper).—
    ISBN 0-520-23095-7 (pbk. : alk. paper)
    1. Filipino Americans—Washington (State)—
Seattle—History—20th century.   2. Filipino
Americans—Washington (State)—Seattle—Social
conditions—20th century.   3. Immigrants—
Washington (State)—Seattle—History—20th
century.   4. Immigrants—Washington (State)—
Seattle—Social conditions—20th century.
    5. Seattle (Wash.)—Ethnic relations.   6. Seattle
(Wash.)—Social conditions—20th century.
    7. Philippines—Emigration and immigration—
History—20th century.   8. Seattle (Wash.)—
Emigration and immigration—History—20th
century.   I. Title.
    F899.S49 F85   2003
    979.7′7720049921—dc21   2001052279

Manufactured in the United States of America

12   11   10   09   08   07   06   05
10   9   8   7   6   5   4   3

For Tom

Contents

Illustrations

Acknowledgments

In the process of writing this book, I incurred many debts. First and foremost, I thank the Filipina and Filipino American community members of Seattle for opening up their lives and sharing their knowledge with me. For their time and patience, I thank the following individuals and their families: Mariano Angeles, E. "Vic" Bacho, Peter Bacho, Leo Bautista, Rufino Cacabelos, Anthony Colinares, Timoteo P. Cordova, Belen Braganza DeGuzman, Frank H. Descarger, Cindy Domingo, Emiliano Francisco, Ben Gonio, Juan F. Gulla, Alejandro Halabaso, Emiliano Madrid, Carl Manalang, Rosalina V. Mendoza, Pedro "Pete" M. Pedronan, Antonio Rodrigo, Trinidad Rojo, Magno Rudio, Bengie Santos, Robert Santos, Dolores Sibonga, Ciriaco "Jerry" S. Solar, Sylvestre A. Tangalan Sr., and Austin "Tony" Vilonza. I also thank Jacqueline Lawson, Hanae Matsuda, M. F. Numoto, Yukiko Sato, and Josephine Patrick for their memories. For the many informal conversations, dance lessons, and food that I received from the staff and participants at the International Drop-In Center, *maraming salamat po* to Zenaida Guerzon and the rest of the special community there. Special thanks go to historians and community workers Fred Cordova and Dorothy Laigo Cordova for encouraging me to do this project in the first place, and for their continued guidance and help in conducting my research. It was their book, *Filipinos: Forgotten Asian Americans,* that started me thinking about Filipina/o American history more than ten years ago, and I owe them a great deal. I also must thank the rest of the Cordova family, in particular

Timoteo Cordova, Damian Cordova, and Joan May Cordova, for their great insight and support. Thanks are due as well to the Seattle chapter of the Filipino American National Historical Society (FANHS) for the knowledge that I gained, especially to Cynthia Mejia, Melissa Flores, and Jackie Bergano. The labor of love also known as the National Pinoy Archives deserves recognition for the fine collection of materials that it houses, which greatly facilitated my research. While completing this project, I also became a life member of the FANHS and a member of its board of trustees—and I thank my fellow trustees and FANHS members as well.

I am further indebted to Norma Timbang Kuehl, Gabrielle Kuehl, Natasha Kuehl, and Gigi Peterson and her daughter Marina Urrutia-Peterson for sharing the warmth of their homes and their constant encouragement with me. These generous people not only provided me with intellectual support but also gave me an endless supply of lodging and home-cooked meals, as well as many of the furnishings in my Seattle apartment. Norma also patiently shared hours upon hours of insight into the Filipina/o American community with me, as well as her commitment to community service. Linda Revilla provided me with encouragement in Seattle and later in Honolulu.

The Department of History at the University of Washington deserves special thanks for sponsoring me as a Visiting Scholar during my time in Seattle. Having a home base at the department enabled me to have easy access to the university's resources, and I thank the faculty of that program, particularly Richard Kirkendall, Richard Johnson, Laurie Sears, and Richard White, as well as Gigi Peterson and Steve Marquardt, who were graduate students when I conducted my research. My affiliation at the University of Washington led me to think about the importance of that institution for Filipina/o Americans in the city, which resulted in the conceptualization of chapter 2. Thanks also to Margaret Levi and James Gregory for inviting me to speak at a labor studies conference at the University of Washington, which provided a valuable opportunity for me to talk about some of the issues in this book. Thanks are due, too, to the helpful staff members of the Manuscripts, Special Collections, University Archives Division, and the staff members of the Periodical Room. I am also grateful to the staffs of the Pacific Northwest regional branch of the National Archives, the Seattle Municipal Archives, and the Seattle Public Schools Archives and Record Management Center.

In Honolulu, I acknowledge Teresa Bill for her critical yet kind support throughout the entire tenure of my graduate-school career and her patient reading of my drafts. In New York City, I thank the former and present staff members of the Museum of Chinese in the Americas for training I received in Chinese American studies and community history. In particular, I acknowledge John Kuo Wei Tchen and Charles Lai, who took me on board as a staff member in 1986, and whose lessons in political organizing and community history I will always use. Thanks, too, to the rest of the staff and board members, past and present, and especially to Fay Chew Matsuda, Mary Lui, and Michael Frisch. I also thank Bernadita Churchill and the organizers of the International Conference on the Centennial of the 1896 Philippine Revolution in Manila, Philippines, for giving me an opportunity to present part of my research during that program.

In Ithaca and New York City, special thanks are due to Gary and Libby Okihiro and Anita and Jim Affeldt for their support of my husband, Tom, and me during our year at Cornell University. Gary Okihiro has been a crucial mentor in many ways, and I thank him for his constant help and for his comments on an earlier draft of this project. For their encouragement of this project at various stages, I thank many people who consider Asian American studies to be one of their academic homes. Thanks in particular to Franklin Odo, Davianna MacGregor, Martin Manalansan, Alice Hom, Barbara Posadas, Sucheta Mazumdar, Judy Yung, Gail Nomura, Steffi San Buenaventura, Yen Le Espiritu, Madeline Hsu, Eric Reyes, Gregory Mark, Robert Lee, Stephen Sumida, and K. Scott Wong. I also thank Chris Friday, a fellow traveler in the study of Asian American labor history, for sharing his research with me and for his comments on an earlier draft of this project. Dana Frank, whom I have known since taking one of her seminars as an undergraduate at Yale, has also supported my work in Seattle, and I thank her for her helpful advice and collegiality, and also for her keen insights throughout various stages of this book. Thanks, too, to Monona Yin, Rosie Reardon, Rebecca Noel, and Linda Lynch for their personal encouragement during my long years as a graduate student. For their inspiration and advice, I thank George Sánchez and George Lipsitz.

My committee members from my graduate-school days at Yale University were exemplary academic and political role models. My deep thanks to my chair, David Montgomery, for his guidance and incisive comments throughout the dissertation process and in the drafting of this book manuscript. Thanks as well to my other committee members, Hazel Carby and Michael Denning, for their challenging comments and continual support. These three people helped to show me the political and intellectual vision that I needed not only to better understand my project but to share it with others. I cannot imagine having a better or more supportive committee, especially in my attempts to link my community work outside of school with my academic projects inside Yale's walls. Thanks also to other faculty and staff at the Department of American Studies at Yale University, and in particular to Ann Fabian and Jean-Christophe Agnew. I also thank Howard Lamar and William Cronon for introducing me to the field of the history of the American West in a graduate seminar. They gave me great encouragement during graduate school when I switched from doing a dissertation on New York City to beginning a project on Seattle, Washington, a city that I never had visited prior to that time. To my fellow graduate-student community, many thanks to everyone, and to Debbie Elkin and Susan Johnson in particular. I also thank Amy Kaplan and Elizabeth Blackmar for their early inspiration for my work when I was an undergraduate, as they, too, influenced my career as an academic.

I am further grateful to the Graduate School of Arts and Sciences at Yale University for providing me with a graduate fellowship and a dissertation fellowship. Thanks are due to James Scott and the Southeast Asian Studies Program for a grant that greatly assisted me in my initial research in Seattle. Thank you as well to the Southeast Asian Studies Summer Institute for providing me with a fellowship to study Tagalog for a summer. From the University of California, Irvine, I have been fortunate to receive Faculty Career Development Awards, a Cultural Diversity Studies Faculty Research Grant, and research and travel grants, additional support that greatly helped me to conclude this project.

At the University of California, Irvine, I thank Ketu Katrak and R. Bin Wong for their guidance and exemplary mentorship; thanks also to everyone else in the Department of Asian American Studies there: John Liu, Mary Ann Takemoto, Claire Jean Kim, Yong Chen, Karen Leonard, Glen Mimura, and Linda Trinh Võ. Ketu Katrak has been unstinting in her support of my research and career, and I am greatly in her debt. As always, special thanks to June Kurata, whose hard work and generous spirit are critical in making Asian American studies at UCI such a special place. Many thanks are also due to the faculty and staff of the Department of History. Thanks to Vicki Ruiz, Vinayak Chaturvedi, Charles Wheeler, Karl Hufbauer, Steven Topik, and Kenneth Pomeranz for their support. Thanks as well to Anna Gonzalez and the other members of the Cross-Cultural Center for their help to me as a faculty member. For their insights, I thank Theo Gonzalves, John Rosa, Charlene Tung, Jocelyn Pacleb, Patrick Karlsson, Augusto Espiritu, and Jose Alamillo. Jocelyn Pacleb also assisted with newspaper research, and I give her special thanks for that, in addition to our conversations on Filipina/o American history. Thanks also to the Focused Research Program in Southern California Labor Studies at UCI for community and support, with special thanks to Gilbert Gónzalez and Raul Fernandez. A big thank-you to the staff at the UCI libraries, and in particular to Daniel Tsang and Anne Frank for their leadership in Asian American studies both on and off campus. Many thanks, too, to N. Lavada Austin for her generous support and for the clarity of her vision. At the University of California Press, I thank Monica Mc-Cormick for her guidance and wisdom in shepherding this manuscript through the process of becoming a book. I also thank Laura Harger, my production editor, and Susan Ecklund, my copyeditor, for their gracious help in this project.

My family, above all, deserves thanks for helping me to reach my goals. Thank you to my parents, Minar Tobing Rony and Abdul Kohar Rony, for their love and support and for their example of hard work, especially as I took on this very ambitious project. In particular, they helped me to understand the complexity of the immigration experience, which had profound influence on my work as a scholar. In Honolulu, I thank my step-mother-in-law, Pamela Fujita-Starck, for her love and support and her always-wise counsel, as well as Sydney and the Boyz: Crock, Pup E., Wilbur Wilbur, and Skooter. I also thank my aunts and uncles, especially Ismail Rony, Chadidjah Rony, Zainel Rony, Saleh Zen, and Salmiah Zen, and all my "siblings": Fatimah Rony, Akira Boch, Mark Fujita, Rheta Kuwahara, Pam Fujita-Yuhas, Tim Fujita-Yuhas, Paul Fujita, and Nobuko Fujita. There are also five special people who were not able to see this project to its completion. My grandmother Hermina Lumban Tobing and my mother-in-law, Terry Shimazu Fujita, both passed away in the last year of the writing of my dissertation, which forms the core of this study. My father-in-law, George Fujita, passed away as the dissertation was being turned into a manuscript. I thank them all for teaching me about the importance of commitment to one's work and the love, care, and honesty that we should show other people. I also remember my uncle Apul Tobing and my aunt Demak Tobing Mark, who both passed away before this project was fully realized, and I thank them for their love and generosity of spirit. Last but not least, my beloved partner, Thomas Fujita-Rony, is due many thanks for taking time from his own academic and political work to assist me in my labors as a historian and, most of all, for sharing his life on a daily basis with me. I thank him for his constant support, especially for his insisting that I take on the tough questions and then standing beside me when I did so. Aside from me, he has lived with this project longer than anyone, and I dedicate this book to him for the joy and the love that we share.

Note on Terminology

While writing this book, I had to make a decision about whether to use *F* or *P* when referring to the Filipina/o American community. Although most older immigrants who arrived in the United States before the post-1965 emigration use the *F* spelling, many other community members refer to themselves as *Pilipino* and *Pilipina*. The formative 1976 anthology *Letters in Exile*, in which the term *Pilipino* was used, explains its choice of terminology as follows: "'Pilipinos' is used here instead of 'Filipinos' technically because there is no phonetic 'ph' or 'f' sound indigenous to the Philippine language. However, 'Pilipinos' is more than 'Filipinos' spelled with a 'p' instead of an 'f.' The term represents a recognition of the identity and the history of the Pilipino people in America."[1] Because many Filipina/os in this country grew up with the *F* spelling, though, the change has met with some controversy. A decade after *Letters in Exile* was published, the editors of *Amerasia Journal*, in a special issue entitled "Filipinos in American Life," discussed how the *P/F* controversy represents the struggle over community self-definition:

> In the late 1960s, activists emerging from the struggle for ethnic studies advanced the spelling "Pilipino" as part of a redefinition of the Filipino American experience. They argued that the Tagalog language did not contain an "F" sound and that the imposed spelling "Filipino" was a remnant of colonized mentality. However, more recent immigrants have contended that other languages in the Philippines do contain "F" sounds and that the spelling "Filipino" is consistent with their cultural heritage.[2]

In this book, I have chosen to use *Filipino* and *Filipina* in deference to the regular usage of these spellings by the community members from the period under study. I have, however, chosen to make these terms more inclusive of gender. Traditionally, *Filipino* is used to refer to Filipino men as well as Filipina women, while *Filipina* refers only to Filipina women. Many people feel that the term *Filipino* serves to reinforce the historical absence of women because of the use of the male ending, *o*. Hence, as with the term *Chicana/o*, I have opted to use *Filipina/o* to refer to both men and women.[3] In this book, I use *Filipina/o American* to refer to Filipina and Filipino Americans inclusively, and *Filipino American* or *Filipina American* when I discuss the experience of one gender alone. I chose to use *a/o* as opposed to *o/a* because of my desire to argue for the centrality of women in the community's history. Women, like men, are at the core of the community history I tell, and because of their marginalization in many recountings of pre–World War II Filipina/o American history, as an intervention I have chosen to place the feminine ending, *a*, first.

Addressing these kinds of categories leads to even more questions. Sometimes, deciding when to use the *a/o* ending versus using *o* or *a* has not been easy. Since the experience of Filipina/o Americans in the pre–World War II period was so skewed toward men, many of the people featured in my story are males. At the same time, it is quite possible that despite gender discrimination, a few women pioneers were present in any given occupation or experience, whether or not they were identified in the historical record. On another level, since gender and sexuality are such fluid categories, the binary opposition represented by *Filipina* and *Filipino* seems problematic. These issues indicate how much more there is to pursue in terms of understanding and documenting the experience of Asian Americans in American culture.

Finally, I also want to note that much of the documentation about Filipina/o Americans in the era before World War II used *Filipina* or *Filipino* instead of *Filipina American* or *Filipino American* when referring to Filipina/o Americans, as did many of the interviewees themselves. Hence, at times I use *Filipina* or *Filipino* when referring to Filipina/o Americans because this is how people would identify themselves. Similarly, when I address the Chicana/o experience, I sometimes use *Mexican* if this was the term used in the historical evidence. Similar issues exist for other groups, such as Chinese Americans and Japanese Americans.

The Role of Colonialism

Most discussions of Filipina/o American history in the 1920s and 1930s focus on the role of young men like Carlos Bulosan, who migrated to the United States in search of opportunity. Margaret Duyungan Mislang's life suggests a different way to approach this history. Mislang met her first husband, Virgil Duyungan, at a church social in the Pacific Northwest. Duyungan was, according to Mislang, from a "very high class" background. They married when she was twenty-three. Interviewed in an oral history project in 1975, Mislang remembered that Duyungan worked in a smelter, and then as a contractor "over east of the mountains," where he would find male workers for crops such as hops, apples, and peaches, a reflection of the extractive and agricultural economy of the region. The children came quickly. Mislang gave birth to a daughter a year after she was married, and she eventually had six others. Raising a Filipina/o American family was a struggle because they encountered discrimination from people in the area. Mislang remembered the serious problems they faced in securing housing. As she recalled, "One year alone we moved 13 times. And if we get into a house and the landlord likes us then the neighbors would kick, and the next thing I knew we were asked to move."[1] Mislang's family was relatively fortunate, though, because Virgil Duyungan was able to get jobs that were considered relatively prestigious for Filipina/os (racial and social segregation faced by the group during the time often barred them from such positions). During the Great Depression, her husband had a series of "higher class" jobs, which in the context of the time meant that he was able to be a cook in downtown establishments.[2]

In the history of the community, Mislang's husband, Duyungan, became famous and was most remembered as one of the founders and presidents of the Cannery Workers' and Farm Laborers' Union, organized in the 1930s. Duyungan's tenure as president, however, was not long, as he and vice president Aurelio Simon were tragically slain in 1936. Afterward, Mislang went to the Philippines with her children for three years under circumstances that are somewhat unclear. Mislang reported that people in the union thought "that it would be good to send his body back to the Philippines." But then she added, "So, as I had been working in the union, I knew maybe a little bit too much. They want[ed] to get me out of the way, so they sent me back with my seven children." Mislang also related to an interviewer, "My husband told me how much money they had in the union and then they killed him and stole the money."[3] It is not clear to whom Mislang is referring when she mentions "they," but her oral history does suggest that she was largely excluded from the organizational process of the union following her husband's death.

To this day, the circumstances around Duyungan's and Simon's deaths are still murky. Their deaths occurred in the midst of considerable turmoil around the status of the union. At the time, both the American Federation of Labor (AFL) and the Congress of Industrial Organizations (CIO) were trying to recruit Filipina/o Americans and their unions. The AFL, in keeping with its organizational philosophy and historical practices, wanted to support separate, ethnic locals, which was why Duyungan's union was the AFL, whereas the CIO was trying to recruit across class.[4] Referring to the growth of the CIO, Mislang reported that "they wanted to take it out of the AFofL [sic] because the AFofL wouldn't stand for radicals [sic] movement in their union."[5] These "radicals" would later emerge as victors in the union movement, which is perhaps one reason this story of Mislang is seldom discussed.

When Mislang went to the Philippines with her seven children, ranging in age from four months to eleven years, she had no money because it was believed that her late husband's family in the province of Negros would aid her. According to her testimony, this did not happen. Mislang had to work as a tutor to support the family in Manila, and she also received money from her godmother. She took care of her children for three years in the Philippines, then returned to Seattle when she was subpoenaed for a court case regarding the union and was ordered by the high commissioner in the Philippine Islands to go to the United States. She testified for three weeks. She was allowed to take only two of her children with her to the United States; the others had to stay behind in the Philippines.[6]

Mislang eventually pressed a case against the union in the Washington State Superior Court to gain more funds for her children, through which she received almost two thousand dollars. From this sum, however, she also had to pay the costs of the trial.[7] Through connections, she found support from Catholic Charities and then was able to get money from the Aid for Dependent Children program.[8] A year later, she married Joe Mislang, another Filipino, fulfilling a request made by her late husband before his death. Joe Mislang was the children's godfather and had been picked by Duyungan to raise the children if he himself was killed.[9]

But there is yet another level at which Mislang's story might seem surprising to the reader. Margaret Duyungan Mislang, who went to the Philippines as a widow with seven children and eventually returned to Seattle to marry one of her husband's colleagues, was actually not Filipina by ancestry. Mislang was a European American of Scottish descent, born in Seattle in 1901. Both of her parents were immigrants who came to the States in the late nineteenth century. As Mislang recalled in her 1975 interview, they were "really oldtimers here," indicating how new the European American community was in Seattle, and also how quickly European immigrants became integrated into the city's culture. Mislang's father had a job in Rainier Valley as a freight clerk on a streetcar line, later working on a shipping line as a freight clerk and a mechanic; Mislang's mother worked at home.[10]

Mislang's story, positioned as it is within the formation of American culture as well as Philippine culture, delineates some of the major interventions that this book will undertake, including emphasizing the primary role of colonialism in the development of the American West and the fluid transpacific culture and economy that resulted. It thus operates within the context of a number of interdisciplinary fields, including American studies and Asian American studies. This book lies within the political projects of both of these disciplines through its investigation of American culture and its relationship to the Filipina/o community in Seattle. To more fully delineate this book's analytical framework, the next sections explain how this study addresses concerns in three related areas: American social history, immigration studies, and the New Western history.

AMERICAN SOCIAL HISTORY:
RECLAMATION AND COMMUNITY STUDIES

First, my work on the Filipina/o American community in Seattle can trace its lineage to the "new social history," now over three decades old. In contrast to previous historians, who focused on "great men" and political institutions, historians in the 1960s and 1970s sought to expand the field, in part in response to the social movements sweeping American culture at that time. David Montgomery and Herbert Gutman, two leading figures in this regard, argued for the importance of history "written from the bottom up." Everyone had a part to play in history, these writers contended, and the fact that ordinary people's stories were not yet written was a function of a society in which only the elite were seen as spokespeople. The new social history privileged the voices of people articulating their own experiences and particularly looked at groups that were typically marginalized in American history.[11] As part of this movement, the "new labor history" also sought to expand its sites of investigation. For example, scholars pointed out that "private" sites such as the household were also important spaces for social and political activities and that the new labor history needed to look past the traditional scope of trade unions to analyze labor activity beyond that sphere.[12] Christine Stansell's finely detailed study of the lives of women in New York City in the eighteenth and nineteenth centuries is one illustration of this approach.[13] Historians such as Stuart Blumin sought to integrate not just the working class but also the middle class in these new views of history.[14]

Attempts to address these previously less-documented groups transformed the nature of studies of American culture and did not go uncontested. Critics argued that the new paradigm was fragmented and unwieldy, pointing out the difficulty of assembling these new histories into a coherent whole. Dana Frank, in her study of the Seattle labor movement, *Purchasing Power,* countered these charges in her examination of how both gender and race are central to labor mobilization. As she noted, "Integrating race and gender into the 'main' story of labor history does not 'splinter' class analysis. The skilled white male workers who constructed the movement and claimed to speak for the whole working class did that."[15]

Like a good number of these works, this book draws its rationale in part from the political project of American social history and ethnic studies to record the histories of communities that have rarely been examined. This introduction began by highlighting Mislang's story in an attempt to place people in the picture, or to underscore the role of individual agency in the face of the hegemonic structures that dominated and continue to dominate the political and economic landscape of Filipina/o America. In this sense, it is an attempt to build upon studies such as sociologists Lucie Cheng and Edna Bonacich's landmark work on labor immigration under capitalism, which emphasizes the political and economic forces that brought Asian immigrant workers to this country, but does so at the expense of a fuller discussion of the individual agency of these immigrants.[16]

In the new social history, methodological concerns also shifted as the role of oral history took on greater importance, particularly because of the general lack of documentation on the working class, women of all backgrounds, and people of color. Ethnic studies, which was emerging as a distinct field at the same time, produced many works that were part of this movement, especially because people of color have been among the most historically marginalized groups in American culture, a fact reflected in the historiography. Community studies dominated much of the early work of Asian American studies, and it continues to play a prominent role, such as in the field's focus on San Francisco Chinatown. Scholars such as Him Mark Lai, Judy Yung, Genny Lim, Ruthanne Lum McCunn, Wei Chi Poon, and John Kuo Wei Tchen and organizations such as the Chinese Historical Society of America were instrumental in reclaiming community history, particularly that of San Francisco Chinatown. For example, *Island,* a study of Angel Island, a longtime detention center for Chinese immigrants similar to Ellis Island on the East Coast, features poems written by detainees. The original poems had been carved into the walls of the immigration detention barracks, and the site was narrowly saved from destruction when an alert park ranger realized that the Chinese characters on the walls were more than simply graffiti.[17] Reclamation was also a critical project for Filipina/o American community history, as demonstrated by Fred Cordova's pictorial history *Filipinos: Forgotten Asian Americans* (1982), which portrays the pre-1965 period through oral history excerpts and photographs. It was also realized on an institutional level with the founding of the Filipino American National Historical Society (FANHS) in the early 1980s.[18]

My study builds on previously unavailable sources that have allowed a more nuanced and expansive U.S. history to be written. In the late 1970s and 1980s, there was a tremendous increase in the production of public history, including oral history collections, exhibitions, and documentaries. Some of the core materials for my book were assembled in response to this upsurge in democratic historical production. For example, more than fifty interviews of Filipina/o Americans were created as part of the Washington State Oral/Aural History Program, through the auspices of the Demonstration Project for Asian Americans, in commemoration of the American bicentennial year, 1976. The staff of the Demonstration Project also completed several other interviews through a grant from the National Endowment for the Humanities.[19] Through their dedication and hard work, researchers now have a stunning array of oral histories, artifacts, and other materials available for use. These sources form the basis of my work, along with scholarly studies, archival documents, and materials from newspapers and magazines from diverse places. In particular, I gleaned information from records about the Philippines and Filipina/o Americans at the National Archives in Washington, D.C., and College Park, Maryland; the Pacific Northwest regional branch of the National Archives in Seattle, Washington; and library collections at Yale University, Cornell University, UCLA, and the University of California, Irvine. Fortunately, I was also able to gain access to diverse public and private collections in Seattle, Washington, especially at the Manuscripts, Special Collections, University Archives Division of the University of Washington; the National Pinoy Archives at the FANHS; the Demonstration Project of Asian Americans; the Museum of History and Industry; the Seattle Municipal Archives; and the Seattle Public Schools Archives and Record Management Center. I name these sites to emphasize that while oral history forms an important means of documenting the past, it is crucial to use its insights in conjunction with other existing sources, since people's voices and perspectives are available to us through "official" histories as well. For example, one rich source for my study was the Bureau of Insular Affairs records at the National Archives in College Park, which contained considerable correspondence from American colonials articulating their demands on the United States government.[20]

Like many other scholars, I believe that the history I seek to tell should go beyond mere celebration of previously "invisible" or "forgotten" people, to mention two adjectives commonly used by reclamatory projects. Michael Frisch cautions historians against "using historical intelligence as a commodity whose supply they seek to replenish, whether by bringing down illuminating fire from elite heights or by gathering gold in mineshafts dug from the bottom up."[21] Frisch reminds us that this reclamation, however well-intentioned, is also fraught with potential problems, like documentation of any community. As Renato Rosaldo demonstrates in his discussion of imperialist nostalgia, or "a particular kind of nostalgia, often found under imperialism, where people mourn the passing of what they themselves have transformed," an array of power relations informs reclamation of Filipina/o American history, whether from inside or outside the community.[22]

Let me illustrate the complex politics and narratives that surround reclamation of Filipina/o American history with two related examples. In Asian American studies, the narrative that is perhaps used most often in charting the pre-1965 history of Filipina/o America is that of Carlos Bulosan, whose stirring autobiographical novel, *America Is in the Heart,* is considered one of the classics of the field. The novel begins by describing the impact of American colonialism and the resulting economic and political unrest in the Philippines, a situation that leads to Bulosan's migration to the United States and an extended journey among working-class communities in the American West. Like many fictionalized narratives that come to represent the whole of an experience, Bulosan's novel is powerful and dramatic, and it represents a deeply problematic record for historical use because of its particular blend of fact and elaboration. Bulosan's story is often told and retold in community settings such as public history programs, in plays, and in academic classrooms.[23] I am less interested, though, in critiquing the writings of Carlos Bulosan per se than I am in understanding why this particular image of the past has had such an impact on how pre-1965 Filipina/o American history has been understood.[24] How have cultural nationalism and gender privilege guided who and what are reclaimed? Why does the single male hero resonate so much with these definitions of Filipina/o American history? The emphasis on the working class, and also on Filipino-ness, greatly influences who is highlighted in Filipina/o American historiography. Mislang's story, which was collected in 1975, has been available for several years, yet it has been little discussed by scholars in the field of Asian American studies. Instead, the narrative of the single male hero has continued to hold sway, as suggested by the iconic figures of Carlos Bulosan and, more recently, Philip Vera Cruz, who holds a similar place in this pantheon of male leaders who are held up to represent Filipina/o American history.[25]

A second example of the complexity and political contingency of the existing Filipina/o American narrative, connected to the first, is the way in which women's labor typically is marginalized within pre–World War II Filipina/o Seattle, especially because of the demographic majority of men. My study underscores what can be gained when students of American social history explore not only paid labor in public spheres but also unpaid labor in the home, especially as that labor helps us to see the integral position of women in community formation, even in communities that were overwhelmingly male. Scholars have demonstrated that reproductive labor, often taken for granted, was vital to household economics and within families. One way in which my study departs from other portrayals of Filipina/o American labor, such as Chris Friday's discussion of cannery workers, is in my attempt to show more fully how the private and public spheres were linked. Both in Hawai'i and on the mainland, for example, public sphere labor unions provided one of the few outlets for Filipina/os to gain political resources and recognition, as well as to make political connections with other groups.[26] However, unions were often male-dominated public space, despite the many contributions made by women, as demonstrated by Margaret Mislang's story, and women's labor is regularly rendered "invisible."

Moreover, unions were not the only venue for activity. In the course of the interviews I performed with Filipina/o Americans in Seattle in the early 1990s, I was typically told about people's union membership in the context of their several other identities and affiliations, including kinship ties and membership in churches, secret societies, and ethnic organizations. Once more, without a full accounting of both public and private activities, much is lost or obscured. As a result, although the public space of the Cannery Workers' and Farm Laborers' Union is a primary area of focus in my book, I try to place it within the larger set of frameworks indicated by informants that includes both public and private arenas.[27] Because the critical struggle over workers' control took shape not only inside the workplace but also outside it, a good portion of this book follows people's lives beyond places of wage labor—for example, I demonstrate that popularity contests and other social activities were sites for contests over class power.[28] In this way, I have attempted to make stories such as those told by Margaret Mislang more visible and to demonstrate their centrality to the growth of Filipina/o America, showing them to be as integral to its history as that of her first husband, union president Virgil Duyungan.

American social history, along with other disciplines, has helped to open a space for formerly less documented peoples, and our understanding of the past is far richer for it. Now we not only have more sources to draw upon in writing these histories but also have radically reshaped where we look for information and what we see when we do so. As a result, my project analyzes how power and privilege have informed which stories are preserved and told, a selection process that is familiar to anyone who documents the history of groups that do not typically form the mainstream of American culture or to anyone who has ever listened to family members recount contested versions of "what really happened." One of my main motivations for this book is to better understand the dominant narratives that inform Filipina/o American history and to find counternarratives that recontextualize, if not challenge, this history.

IMMIGRATION STUDIES

The second body of studies that I address is a related field that often overlaps with the others I have named: immigration studies. If an account of Mislang's life seems a surprising way to approach the formation of the Filipina/o American community in Seattle in the pre–World War II era, the surprise is also illustrative of the narratives in popular American culture that regularly structure our approach to the history of Asian American communities. In American history, we often document how Asian Americans come to be included in the mainstream European American whole and how those who are more "marginalized" are incorporated into the "center" and thus "become American." The phrase *to become American*, I would contend, is somewhat loaded when it implies that people are assimilated to a mainstream "norm." In the mythic tale of becoming American, immigrants go to school to receive American civic lessons, nonmainstream accents are lost, and national loyalties are irrevocably shifted to the United States. The locus of power thus remains centered in an American culture that is oriented to a white, male, heterosexual norm.

The traditional focus in immigration studies, exemplified by William I. Thomas and Florian Znaniecki's classic work on the Polish community from Chicago, has been on how immigrants fit themselves within the dominant culture and in doing so suffer fragmentation and loss. Thomas and Znaniecki's analysis of social values and attitudes in the Polish immigrant community and the role of ethnic ties, social disorganization, subjectivity, and qualitative research materials provided models of inquiry for Robert Park and his students in the development of the Chicago school of American sociology in the 1930s.[29] Later, Oscar Handlin would also characterize the immigration process as one of alienation, writing, "The immigrants lived in crisis because they were uprooted."[30] This story of assimilation was long the dominant trope in characterizations of immigrants, and it continues to have prominence in popular culture.[31]

Even within this dominant framework, however, Asian Americans have occupied a peripheral position. One result of the dominance of the

Chicago school narrative, as Henry Yu has explained, was that the "marginal man" theory developed by Robert Park had enormous impact on how Asian Americans were perceived. According to this theory, those who migrated were caught between two cultures and embodied the conflict and hardship of negotiating two worlds. Since they were not truly members of either world, however, Asian Americans also demonstrated the possibilities of bridging this gap.[32] Because of this pervasive framework, Asian Americans, although they reside in the United States, have been regularly characterized as being outside the American culture, as "perpetual foreigners" with a transplanted "traditional" culture from Asia.[33] Over the decades, the emphases of these immigration studies have changed—they once focused on dysfunction and assimilation into American culture but now more fully address immigrant strategies in the transformation of American culture. However, until well into the 1980s, it remained difficult to escape the common notion that Asian Americans were somehow lost foreigners, particularly because general recognition of Asian American history has occurred only relatively recently, despite the many decades of scholarship documenting their experience. Notably, the two books considered primary general histories of Asian Americans, Ronald Takaki's *Strangers from a Different Shore* and Sucheng Chan's *Asian Americans*, were published only in 1989 and 1991, respectively.[34]

John Bodnar, in his aptly named book *The Transplanted*, calls for a more complex and nuanced analysis that takes into account the diverse ways that immigrants addressed life in the United States. As he writes, "Immigrant adjustment to capitalism in America was ultimately a product of a dynamic between the expanding economic and cultural imperatives of capitalism and the life strategies of ordinary people."[35] He argues that relations with the homeland have to be seen in this far more complicated context.[36] Tracing the ways that migratory Filipina/os both worked within and resisted first Spanish and then American rule, for example, provides insight into the class dimensions of the migrants who journeyed to the United States and how these individuals might have been affected by events "back home."[37] This process further reminds us that many who came were among the more privileged, and they need to be considered in that wider context.[38] Thus, when we examine the life of Mislang, we must note that she married into a Filipina/o American world and thus occupied a space in both the Philippines and the Seattle area.

Other members of this newer generation of scholars, such as Robert Orsi and George Sánchez, have further documented the rich life of immigrant communities in major urban centers, particularly in New York

City and Los Angeles.[39] Sylvia Yanagisako's study of the Japanese American community in Seattle, written more than four decades after Miyamoto's classic study of that same community, for example, identifies a much more fluid sense of kinship and identity, one in which the past is informed by current understandings.[40] Despite these important advances, Asian Americans up until the present have still been identified as alien to the American culture, and their ability to assimilate remains contested.[41]

Mislang's story also points us away from the dominant reliance on American exceptionalism, in which the United States was seen as the most favored destination for immigrants, and toward the fluidity of migration experienced by many, as suggested by Frank Thistlewaite's early characterization of migration.[42] Mislang's journey across the Pacific to the Philippines for a few years further emphasizes the role of transpacific networks and empire, and her decision to go to the Philippines as a place with more viable options for her and her children contests the dominant characterization of the United States as the "land of opportunity."[43]

The recent emphasis on diaspora studies, driven particularly by the expansion of scholars studying transnationalism in Filipina/o American studies, has redirected our attention to the critical role of the Philippines and Asia as a whole, helping us to move beyond American nationalist perspectives. Theories of transnationalism further enable us to contest nationalist boundaries, to understand, as Linda Basch, Nina Glick Schiller, and Cristina Szanton Blanc have described in their classic text *Nations Unbound,* "the processes by which immigrants forge and sustain multistranded social relations that link together their societies of origin and settlement."[44] Such studies urge us to pay close attention to the multiple sites of interaction for Filipina/o American communities both in the United States and in the Philippines, and to the contested nature of cultural practices and community formation as illustrated by Mislang's experience.

MODELS OF ASIAN AMERICAN MIGRATION

Charting the development of Filipina/o Seattle is further complicated by the regular reliance on Chinese American and Japanese American models to tell the history of Asian America, especially because of the strong position of both of these fields within Asian American studies.[45] Certainly, several ties linked Filipina/o Americans to various racialized communities, and to other Asian Americans in particular. Among these were the United States' long-standing interests in the Pacific economy and the perception of the Philippines as a base for American interests, interests that developed out of the United States' prior interaction with China and Japan. Furthermore, because Filipina/os are classified as "Asians," their experience is also shaped by this racial context. Dana Frank and Carlos A. Schwantes have argued that race relations were at the core of Seattle's labor movement, dating back to the exclusionary anti-Chinese movement in the 1880s.[46] By the time the great waves of Filipina/o Americans arrived in the Seattle area in the 1920s, the city's history had already been shaped by exclusionary movements against Chinese and Japanese immigrants, and Filipina/o Americans encountered a legacy of racial discrimination and segregation. Along with Chinese Americans and Japanese Americans, they often occupied areas such as Chinatowns, and the groups regularly labored together in racialized spaces in the American West, for example, in the salmon canning industry and agriculture.

In other ways, though, the experience of Filipina/o Americans was unlike that of other groups from Asia, and it is important to question their "fit" within the dominant model that describes successive waves of Asian immigrants coming to the United States. In the popular model, the "Chinese came first" to California during the gold rush, and their experience set the path that would be followed by groups such as Japanese Americans, Korean Americans, and others.[47] This model has been contested for several reasons. First, Filipina/os have now been recognized as having developed the oldest permanent community of Asian Americans in this country through the Manila galleon trade. These workers came to North America aboard merchant vessels, beginning in the 1500s, and took up residence in what is presently Mexico and Louisiana. While they might have come on ships along with Chinese workers, and while it is likely that many of these individuals had Chinese ancestry and also intermarried with the Chinese, it is important to acknowledge that the community established in Louisiana is considered "Filipina/o," thus challenging the dominant California gold rush narrative of Chinese settlement.[48] The model is also contested because it reinforces entrenched ethnic hierarchies in which Chinese Americans and Japanese Americans are placed at the center of analysis, and so inhibits our ability to see how experiences might have varied across different groups.

Another common assumption about Asian American migration is that, in keeping with the narrative of American exceptionalism in which the United States is seen as the primary destination, the United States was the only place to which Asians migrated, when in fact large numbers entered this country after initially migrating elsewhere.[49] Finally, because our emphasis is typically on the wage workers who come to U.S. shores, we usually focus on the men in the community, rather than fully considering the transpacific communities that men and women created on both sides of the ocean.[50]

For an example of how these models shape Filipina/o American history, it is helpful to consider the phrase *bachelor society*, typically used in a Chinese American context in relation to the pre–World War II era. This term is often applied to the Filipina/o community during the same period, and, similar to Jennifer Ting's argument in the Chinese American case, it confines our analysis in the case of Filipina/o Americans during this period.[51] The fact that heterosexual nuclear family formations were not the dominant mode meant not the absence of "family" but that the circumstances of pre–World War II Filipina/o Seattle privileged other kinds of familial relationships. Both men and women in Filipina/o Seattle operated within kin networks that were constructed, if not through immediate family connections, then through extended families or fictive kinship links that were typically reinforced by ties to the same village, town, or region of origin. In response to the dominance of the "bachelor society" model, I hope to contribute to a more expansive understanding of the familial nature of these male-male relationships. Because of the gender imbalance among Filipina/os migrating to the United States, "brothers" and "uncles" emerged as two dominant forms of social relations, rather than the more familiar nuclear family formation.[52]

Another reason that it is important to critique popular Asian American migration models is the reliance on studying Chinatowns to delineate Asian American community studies. "Chinatowns," the study of which emphasizes the urban experience of Asian Americans, are critical sites to examine because they represent a space of interaction between the mainstream American public and the immigrant communities that blossomed in major cities such as San Francisco. However, because these neighborhoods are typically studied as bounded communities within the context of a single site, emphasizing these urban centers has led to what Gary Okihiro calls the "tyranny of the city" in Asian American studies.[53] There has not been enough research on people's movement in and through these demarcated spaces, or on the economic, social, cultural, and political relationships that connected these urban sites to rural ones. Most crucially, in the case of Filipina/o Americans during the pre–World War II period, permanent residence in an urban, ethnic space was less typical, since most Filipina/o Americans were not only nonurban but also nonstationary.

In conclusion, whereas earlier immigration studies emphasized the assimilation of immigrants within the United States, scholars have now begun to show how American culture was a contested space and that assimilation was not merely the replacement of a foreign culture with an American one. Far from being secondary participants, Filipina/o Americans were integral players in the Pacific Northwest cultural matrix, as well as in other parts of the country. Those documenting Filipina/o American history, though, have been especially constrained by the general use of Chinese American or Japanese American models to represent Asian Americans in American culture. These models might conceal more than they reveal for the Filipina/o American case. My intent here is not to overstate the differences among the communities but to point out that the experiences of Filipina/o Americans were often very dissimilar from those of other groups because of legislation or the period of migration, to name two factors among many. Even using the term *immigrant* for the pre–World War II period is problematic because Filipina/os came to Seattle during this era as American colonials who were not entering a foreign country but "returning home" to the United States. Thus, understanding how the U.S.-Philippines relationship was built upon force is critical, which leads to a consideration of the importance of conquest in the story of the American West.

THE NEW WESTERN HISTORY

The third body of studies with which this book is in dialogue is the history of conquest and the American West, particularly the recent conversations established by scholars working within what is known as the "New Western history."[54] The experience of being colonized by the United States is one that Filipina/os share with Hawaiians, Chicana/os, and others. The United States' occupation of the Philippines at the turn of the century occurred in close conjunction with other endeavors in places such as Puerto Rico, Guam, and Samoa and followed the conquest of Alta California by roughly half a century. Hence, discussions such as Richard Drinnon's in *Facing West,* which links the United States' oppression of Native Americans with its overseas campaign and articulates the nation's grappling with manifest destiny, helps us understand how the Philippines fell under American influence. Patricia Nelson Limerick's *Legacy of Conquest,* which suggests that Frederick Jackson Turner's frontier thesis is better replaced by a narrative of conquest, offers important ways to rethink the United States' expansionist project, as well as its relation to other countries. This field further reminds us of the importance of examining the interactions between the various indigenous peoples of the American West and the different "settlers" who entered the region over the course of centuries.[55]

The American West, far from being the mythical open space the frontier thesis would have us believe, was populated, occupied by others, and taken by European American settlers through force in a series of conquests. This expansion is often downplayed because of the regular reference in our culture to the "American Dream," which tends to privilege individual migration and success as well as idealize the opportunities represented by the United States. When the Philippines was colonized, it became the most western part of this American empire and entered into the realm of the American West. It was precisely this imperial expansion that brought Filipina/o Americans across the Pacific Ocean to Seattle. From their perspective, Seattle was a colonial metropole, and a "frontier city" in a very different sense than the one promoted by the narrative of European American settlement across the American mainland from the East Coast. My work underscores the vital role of Seattle in the United States' transpacific interests, as well as the importance of Asian trade and Asian workers in the development of its image.[56] In the same way that urban centers such as New York City and Boston were affected by their role as entry ports for passenger and cargo traffic from Europe, West Coast ports such as Seattle, San Francisco, and Los Angeles also were significant because of their proximity to Asia. Part of my work is to demonstrate that in the pre–World War II period, transpacific endeavors had a vital impact on the formation of cultures in the Pacific Northwest.[57]

American West studies also remind us to consider carefully the role of region in relation to race. Another reason that Filipina/o Seattle is rendered less visible is the city's particular racial configuration. Unlike in other parts of the American mainland, most people of color in this region prior to World War II were not African Americans or Chicana/os but Asian Americans and Native Americans. In 1940, for example, there were twice as many Asian Americans as African Americans in Seattle, and many of the jobs performed by African Americans elsewhere in the country were filled by Asian Americans.[58] However, not only has there been a historical focus on relations between African Americans and whites on a national level, reflecting the demographics of the United States as a whole, but until recent decades there also has been a lack of established studies on Asian Americans. Both of these factors have influenced the historiography of people of color in Seattle. As scholars such as Tomás Almaguer remind us, race shaped the history of all the communities in the American West, whether they were European Americans or people of color.[59] Furthermore, racial categories, infused as they were with multiple hierarchies of power, were further complicated and informed by the colonial relationship between the United States and the Philippines. Filipina/o Americans thus faced exclusionary responses from an American culture of which they were an integral part.

In Seattle and the immediate region, racial hierarchies took on a unique configuration. Among people of color, all of whom faced discrimination as racial minorities, Filipina/o Americans tended to occupy a position on the social hierarchy generally below that of Chinese Americans and Japanese Americans, although above that of Native Americans, an indication of the oppression of indigenous peoples relative to other groups. African Americans and Chicana/os, though forming politically and culturally significant populations in the city, were not present in large numbers, and their communities also encountered extreme racial discrimination. These demographics sharply distinguished Seattle from cities in the Northeast or the Southwest, including sites in California. Filipina/o Americans in Seattle also shaped the racial dynamics of that city in alternate ways because of their considerable presence outside of Chinatown, where Asian Americans traditionally congregated because of economic and racial discrimination. Many were employed as service workers in Seattle's downtown, for example, or attended educational institutions such as Broadway High School or the University of Washington. Unlike in other parts of the country where they might have been labeled as "Chinese" or "Mexican," their identity was not subsumed into that of other, more recognized populations in Seattle at the time. Their racial presence was thus qualitatively different than in sites such as Los Angeles, a larger metropole, where attention was more focused on the relationship of Chicana/os to the European American population.

American West studies also direct our attention to the geographic use of space. As Sarah Deutsch's regional study of Chicana/os in the Southwest asks, how does one deal with a largely migratory population that continually crosses various borders? What do these issues mean for the Filipina/o Americans under study, for whom "home" might mean many different places and many different things?[60]

In fact, mobility would become a distinctive feature of the Filipina/o American experience not just because of the fluidity of the transpacific economy but also because of the growth of the regional economy of the American West. Unlike the Chinese Americans and Japanese Americans who earlier faced exclusion (the Chinese in 1882 and the Japanese in 1907), Filipina/o Americans had easy access to the United States until the passage of the Tydings-McDuffie Act in 1934, for until that point, they were "nationals" and were not required to possess passports to enter the United States. There was no Angel Island immigration station to screen out potential arrivals, for example, as with the Chinese Americans.[61] It was only with the onset of the Great Depression that their transpacific movements were slowed. Because of the availability of transportation systems developed on international, national, and regional levels through American military and economic expansion, these workers could take advantage of an unprecedented ability to travel cheaply and easily by ship, train, and automobile.

Examining the link between the rural and the urban experiences of Filipina/o Americans is another way in which my study departs from many others. Patricia Limerick notes that one of the contributions the history of the American West might make to Asian American studies is to underscore the connection between urban and rural spaces. Urban spaces took on different significance in largely rural regions, a significance made possible because of the resources they offered and their position as a hub in transportation networks mentioned earlier.[62] Furthermore, workers in Seattle need to be contextualized in a range of sites because of their migration from industry to industry, from the Alaska canneries to urban occupations in Seattle to the fields of California's agricultural industry.[63]

In sum, then, studies of the American West, particularly those that form the New Western history, are vital to uncovering the histories of Filipina/os in Seattle. For one thing, they better enable us to see the role of U.S. militarism and the connection of events in the Philippines to what happened in other military campaigns. They help us to discern the role of region and the specific historical context of Seattle, Washington State, and the Pacific Northwest. Furthermore, because racial and ethnic identities developed from a different demographic base and set of political realities than in many other places in the American West, these studies indicate how we can better contextualize the choices made by community members in Filipina/o Seattle. By doing so, they underscore the regular contrast that Filipina/o Seattle offers to similar communities in New York or California, the common sites of comparison for immigrant populations.

DEPARTURES

The various issues suggested by these three fields of study—American social history, immigration studies, and the history of the American West—
lead me back to my reason for beginning with Mislang's story. While these
fields profoundly influenced my work in the context of American studies and Asian American studies, in other ways my project takes a different path. As Amy Kaplan and others have argued, studies of American
culture have tended to focus on the production of categories like race,
gender, and class on an internal level, in part because of the emphasis on
American exceptionalism. American "multiculturalism," then, is usually
defined within the United States' national boundaries and is often described within the context of the contiguous forty-eight states of the American mainland. This myopia has confined our analysis of the role of the
United States abroad, as well as the impact of imperialism at home.[64]

As opposed to focusing on European migration and the passage across
the Atlantic, I want to draw attention to what the United States might
have looked like to those who traveled back and forth across the Pacific
Ocean to the American West Coast. What did the United States represent for Filipina/o workers who, in coming to ports such as San Francisco and Seattle, were actually journeying toward colonial metropoles?
Even beyond its significance for the extended Filipina/o American community, this story of Filipina/o Seattle also sheds important light on the
workings of American culture as a whole, for how Filipina/os were named
and contained says much about American culture itself.[65] Part of the challenge in providing a history of Filipina/o Seattle is that studies of Asian
American communities, particularly those less well known in mainstream
American culture than Chinese Americans or Japanese Americans, are
seen as "particular" or "specific." In contrast, studies of native-born European American men form the "norm" for measuring people's experiences.[66] Beyond documenting the formation of Filipina/o Seattle on its
own terms, an important task in itself and one in which I join others in
undertaking, my study also poses questions about the marked and unmarked categories that shape our understanding of American culture.[67]

What if we reverse the gaze to imagine what it meant for a community to "face America" instead of the other way around? What if those
typically excluded from the dominant narratives become the primary
players, and we tell the story of American culture from a far different
perspective, but one that is nonetheless central to the development of
American culture? Frederick Cooper and Ann Laura Stoler argue in a

recent anthology about colonialism that "Europe was made by its imperial projects, as much as colonial encounters were shaped by conflicts
within Europe itself."[68] Similarly, my project seeks to understand how
the Filipina/o American community in Seattle was in itself formed by the
colonial relationship, not just how American colonials from the Philippines created a space for themselves in the colonial metropole of Seattle, but also how Seattle, in turn, was changed by its Filipina/o American residents. While the role of British colonials traveling to the colonial
metropole of London is relatively well known, for example, this has typically not been the case for American nationals traveling to colonial metropoles on the American mainland in the era before World War II.[69] What
was at stake in the shifting definitions available to Filipina/o Americans
in Seattle culture, and how did they affect the European American culture as well as others with which they came into contact?

Hence, by telling the tale of Mislang's relationship to the Filipina/o
American community, and her transpacific options in both the Philippines and the United States, I want to suggest the powerful reach of colonialism in Philippine-American relations. Seattle, I argue, was a much
more fluid space for transpacific encounter than we have generally acknowledged, and one in which Margaret Duyungan Mislang's story portrays many of the central dynamics of a rapidly moving economy of
people and resources. In the late nineteenth century and the first half of
the twentieth century, the United States' interests in the Pacific region
would transform its economic and military relationship to the area and,
because of its relationship as colonizer to the Philippines, stimulate the
flow of economic products and peoples in the transpacific region. By the
end of the nineteenth century, the importance of coaling stations in the
Pacific in part drove the United States' positioning in the area, a critical
factor in U.S. interests up until World War I. As David Montgomery comments, the United States' major shipping lines developed in the Pacific,
not in the Atlantic, and the United States Navy rapidly established a presence in the transpacific region.[70]

But power did not reside with the colonizers alone. I also want to underscore how members of the Filipina/o American community, both men
and women, chose their own destinies, despite their status as racialized
colonial subjects and workers, and the harsh social and political barriers they encountered. Whether openly in confrontation, or using the "hidden transcripts" discussed by James Scott, Filipina/o Americans did not
simply acquiesce to American culture.[71] Thus, my analysis will focus on
how these people reacted to colonialism and actively chose options, re-

making the world around them, despite the often debilitating forces of colonialism, capitalism, sexism, racism, and class conflict. They were not passive objects of colonial domination but people who developed complex and sometimes contradictory strategies to deal with the barriers and hardships they faced.

Focusing on the colonial experience of Filipina/o Seattle, for example, makes it far easier to understand why education had such a profound impact on community members, whether or not they themselves were able to secure a formal education, and why institutions such as the University of Washington were so critical to the expanded Filipina/o American community. Education, I will argue, was a crucial part of the United States' mission in the Philippines, and Filipina/os who came to the American mainland had typically been exposed to American colonial educations "back home." Their pursuit of education on the American mainland, then, was an extension of their prior experience and an integral part of the production of colonial intelligentsia for the Philippines. American colonialism also had a tremendous impact on the development of the Filipina/o American community because education prompted many people to go to the United States and profoundly shaped social formations on both sides of the Pacific Ocean. As would-be students streamed to colonial metropoles such as Seattle, particularly to take advantage of the United States' universities, this affected both the physical mobility and the class mobility of Filipina/os on the U.S. mainland and in Hawai'i. Thus, another contribution that I hope to make is to examine more fully the profound impact of education on community formation and its continuing effect on the laboring class, many of whom were former students or workers who aspired to gain more education.[72]

In my opening story, Mislang thus succeeds in contesting many long-held "truths" in her discussion of pre–World War II Filipina/o American history. As with all the community members I studied, her history resolutely defies any attempts to put it into neat categories of race, class, and gender. As anyone who has ever done a life history well knows, race, class, gender, ethnicity, sexuality, nation, and place are all central to the lived experience of informants. Mislang's part in the story of the labor union shifts the "male" story typically presented about this period. She demonstrates that women played an important role and that the "bachelor society" concept often used to describe the pre–World War II period of Asian America is misleading, at best.[73] Her story also suggests the wide arena that Filipina/o Seattle members occupied. Thus, Mislang's complicated story of family and marriage, of gender discrimination, racism, and economic segregation, of labor organization and murder, of the strength and limits of family and political networks, and of the United States' sustained role in the Philippines, illustrates the complexity of the formation of Filipina/o America and many of the main themes that I will articulate in this project.

This book unfolds as follows. Chapter 1 provides a background context for Filipina/o Seattle by describing the impact of Spanish and American colonialism in the Philippines. I explain how these developments resulted in the mass migration of Filipina/o workers to the U.S. mainland, and specifically why the Port of Seattle emerged as a favored destination. Chapter 2 analyzes the role of colonial educational policy in stimulating the passage of Filipina/os to high schools and universities in the United States. In particular, I examine the pivotal role of the University of Washington in producing the Filipina/o intelligentsia and the impact this would have on class consciousness both in Seattle and back home in the Philippines.

The next two chapters move the geographic emphasis to the American West as a region and focus on the relationship of these predominantly male societies to the region's frontier economy and to urban sites such as Seattle. Chapter 3 explores the regional labor migration of Filipina/o laborers in this period in sites such as Alaska, California, and Washington State. Chapter 4 analyzes the pivotal function of Seattle and the immediate area around the city for the extended Filipina/o American community.

The final two chapters explore how the centrality of these workers affected political aspirations and community formation in Filipina/o Seattle. Chapter 5 examines the political resistance of Filipina/os, particularly during the unrest of the Great Depression, and the enactment of the Tydings-McDuffie Act, which closed Filipina/o migration to the United States, as well as promising eventual independence to the Philippines. The last chapter evaluates how competing and overlapping interests resulted in a complex class consciousness in the late 1930s, particularly with the rise in power of the community's union members. I conclude the book with a brief discussion of present-day Filipina/o Seattle and its significance for our culture as a whole.

Susan Johnson writes, "The West is historically a place of disrupted gender relations and stunning racial and ethnic diversity, a diversity structured by inequality and injustice."[74] This book is an attempt to chart those inequalities and injustices and, by doing so, to pay tribute to the strength and spirit of these pioneers who contributed so much to Seattle and the American West. At the same time, however, although this book owes a great debt to close examinations of communities in the United States, in other ways it has a different political focus. This book analyzes the role of colonial power in the lives of a group of American workers within the United States empire. It examines how these people sought to address inequities, sometimes by creative resistance and challenge, and other times by perpetuating those very same oppressions, particularly in the area of gender relations. At its heart, it is a story about the United States and what American conquest meant not just "over there" but also "over here." I hope that it will contribute to the body of literature reassessing American culture and its colonial relationships, and highlight the vital role of Filipina/o Americans in shaping and transforming American culture.

PART ONE

Charting the Pacific

Empire and Migration

A popular portrayal of pre–World War II Asian American history is that of Asian workers, almost always men, coming to the United States in search of opportunities. This portrayal, which tends to privilege people's individual motivations for journeying to the United States, usually downplays the United States' interest in gaining control of lands and resources in the Pacific. The realities were far more complex, as suggested by Rufina Clemente Jenkins's story, which spans both Spanish and American colonization of the Philippines. Rufina Clemente Jenkins was born in Naga, Nueva Caceres, in the Philippines, in 1886. Her father was "Castilian Spanish"; her mother was Filipina. Although her family planned to send her to Spain for school, her education was interrupted by the Spanish-American War. Following the American conquest, the United States sent different troops to the Philippines, first white soldiers, then men of color. Jenkins's future husband, Frank Jenkins, belonged to the latter group; he was a Spanish interpreter in the Eighth Troop, Ninth Cavalry, of African American and Mexican American background.

Although Rufina Clemente Jenkins was engaged to a European American named Lindsay, and Frank Jenkins was courting Rufina's cousin Matia, the two decided to marry when Lindsay was on a trip to Manila. Jenkins's narrative suggests both emotional and practical reasons for this decision. Rufina was fifteen years old at the time, and without family upon whom she could rely. Her father had died when she was fourteen, and an aunt who was looking after her had died as well.

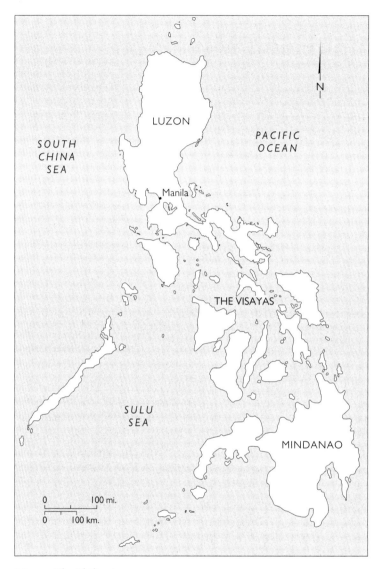

Map 1. The Philippines.

The Jenkinses' daughter Francesca was born in the Philippines in 1902, and six months later, when Frank was posted to California, they moved to the United States. As a Filipina, Rufina encountered some discrimination there, although Francesca recounted that "the colored soldier wives were very nice to her." A son, Frank Jenkins Jr., was born in 1903 at the

Presidio (which was later annexed to Fort Ord, California), and then the family went to Fort Riley, Junction City, Kansas, where another son was born. In 1907, the family returned to the Philippines for two years, then came back to the United States and settled in Fort Lawton, Washington, becoming one of the first Filipina/o American families in the Seattle area. When I conducted my research for this project, descendants of Rufina Clemente Jenkins and Frank Jenkins still resided in the Seattle area.[1]

Rufina Clemente Jenkins's story graphically illustrates the impact of empire and the world economy, in which colonialism not only shaped new nations and governments but also transformed transportation, communication, and migration patterns in several parts of the world.[2] In many ways, the formation of Filipina/o America has striking parallels to the formation of communities of Indians who traveled to London, Algerians who left for Paris, or Indonesians who settled in Amsterdam, as all were traveling to colonial metropoles.

Studies of these communities offer us a way to understand more about the role of urban metropoles in colonial empires. They underscore how colonial spaces created new opportunities and sites around the globe, dramatically changing the realm of the possible for people around the world. But, as this chapter will underscore, these routes were also a manifestation of colonial power. Most centrally for my story here, during the era between World War I and World War II, cities such as Honolulu, Seattle, Los Angeles, and particularly San Francisco took on new significance in the formation of the United States, its transpacific economy, and the rise of Asian America. These cities emerged as regional centers and urban metropoles, to which both immigrant and native-born workers flocked. This is partly why, for example, San Francisco emerged as such a pivotal site of study for scholars of Chinese American communities.

EARLY HISTORIES

The Philippines that Rufina Clemente Jenkins experienced while growing to adulthood had sustained several hundred years of diverse cultural influences by the time of American conquest. In addition to indigenous groups like the aboriginal Negritos, Malay peoples moving up from Indonesia also began widespread settlement, displacing the native peoples at a regular rate. Prompted by the search for gold, political ambitions, and religious aims, Spain began building its colonial empire in the Philippines in 1521, ushering in more than three centuries of domination by that country.[3] During this period, the first Filipina/os made their way across the Pacific to the American mainland. The galleon trade led to sustained contact between Filipina/os and other residents of North America. The Manila galleon sailed every year from the Philippines to Acapulco, Mexico.[4] Employed as laborers on the Spanish galleon, Filipina/os abandoned ship in Acapulco as early as the sixteenth century, migrating to other parts of Mexico. One observer even referred to Acapulco degradingly as the "sepulchre of Mexicans and Filipinos," reflecting the racial biases of the time. By 1763, Filipina/os had settled in Louisiana, establishing what would become the longest-running permanent settlement of Asians in this country.[5]

In addition to the Filipinos who served as crew members, it is likely that Filipina/os were also brought on board as prostitutes, and that they later made new homes in the Americas. William Schurz reports that a law from 1608 prohibited the use of "slave women" as prostitutes on the galleons and enabled "the confiscation" of these women by colonial authorities at Acapulco, indicating that prostitution was probably common. One administrator allegedly brought fifteen women with him, many of whom bore children during the trip or arrived in Acapulco already pregnant.[6] The children of these unions, along with the children of Mexican women and Filipino men, likely ranked among the first American-born Filipina/os in the Americas. As an indication of the importance of this settlement, the Sociedad de Benefiecencia de los Hispano Filipinas de Nueva Orleans (Hispano-Filipino Benevolent Society of New Orleans) was founded in 1870.[7]

Filipina/os came to what would become United States territory not only from the south but also from the northwest. During his travel in that region in 1788–1789, Captain Douglas of the *Iphigenia Nubiana* reported that he had a servant who was "a Manilla man." Another captain discussed the presence of someone in a Native American visiting party in the Northwest who may have been "a native of the New Spain, who might possibly have deserted from some of the Spanish vessels."[8]

Rufina Jenkins entered the world stage when the Philippines was undergoing dramatic change, at the close of Spanish control. By the end of the nineteenth century, the five main social groupings were the *peninsulares,* who were from Spain; the *insulares,* or creoles, who were of Spanish descent and born in the Philippines, and the Spanish *mestizos;* the Chinese *mestizos;* the "common people"; and the Chinese.[9] Changes in land tenure and an increasingly commercial economy promoted the development of a business class of Spaniards, Chinese *mestizos* and Chinese, and natives in the cities. The Chinese *mestizos* and others obtained properties so that they could participate more in the export crop economy, thus competing with the *principales* who held land.[10]

The years 1855–1872 had brought a brief period of social change to the Philippines, with expanded educational opportunities and a climate that allowed greater debate and exchange of ideas. This situation encouraged a thriving intellectual environment at home and promoted the movement of Filipina/os to Europe.[11] As a result, by the last decades of the nineteenth century, Filipinos from wealthy families who had gone to Spain and other parts of Europe brought home the political ideals of the French Revolution. Advocating nationalism and democracy, they began organizing against Spanish colonialism and for the nucleus of what would become the Propaganda Movement. Spain clamped down on these resisters, including their leader, Jose Rizal, who was executed by Spanish authorities in 1896. Resistance by Filipina/os continued, however, evolving in the final years of the nineteenth century into armed struggle through a new organization, the Katipunan, led first by Andres Bonifacio and later by Emilio Aguinaldo.[12]

By the close of the nineteenth century, Filipina/os were well on their way to defeating their Spanish colonizers. But in 1898, as Filipina/os struggled to free themselves, the United States was victorious in the Spanish-American War and annexed the Philippines, joining other nations in the race for lands. In the last decades of the nineteenth century and through 1914, colonialism took on a greater importance; in this "Age of Empire," France, Germany, Great Britain, Belgium, Italy, the Netherlands, Japan, and the United States claimed areas of colonial control, gaining dominance over the former powers of Spain and Portugal. In fact, roughly one-fourth of the world's land mass from 1876 to 1915 was controlled by these eight countries. Cities such as Chicago, Richmond, Toronto, Warsaw, and Berlin took on new prominence as industrializing centers, and less developed countries increasingly sent their exports to countries besides Great Britain, shifting the focus of international trade. These changes benefited the United States—after World War I, New York took London's place as the financial center of the world.[13]

While the United States had long been attracted to the Pacific, its interest expanded tremendously as the region became another site for contestation. The United States had been drawn to the Pacific for more than two centuries, particularly because of the China trade, and it had already established economic and religious connections with Hawai'i. Through an 1854 treaty, Japan was required to open its ports to the United States; by 1882 the United States gained entry to the Korean economy after Japan

secured a treaty with Korea. Then, in a few short years around the turn
of the century, Guam, Cuba, Puerto Rico, Hawai'i, and the Philippines
came under U.S. rule.[14] The United States was not alone in its imperial
ambitions. In establishing itself in the Pacific, the United States, like
Germany, was contesting the expansive British Empire. German plantations in Samoa, utilizing workers from the Marshalls, New Britain, and
the Gilbert and Ellice Islands, were one manifestation of this jockeying
for position. By 1899, the United States would divide up Samoa with
Germany.[15]

These global developments sent workers around the emerging United
States empire, and the marriage of Frank Jenkins to Rufina Clemente was
a reflection of the United States' increasing power overseas. Frank Jenkins's service record also indicates the politics of empire. Frank Jenkins
was a corporal and a drum major in the cavalry when he came to the
Philippines, and his battle experience in the United States Army also included the recent Sioux wars and military intervention in Cuba.[16] By the
time the United States reached the Philippines, the nation had already
exerted control over a substantial part of the globe.

CONQUEST AND "THE WHITE MAN'S BURDEN"

Despite the United States' stated mission of "uplifting" the Philippines,
the reality of American militarism was quite harsh.[17] The United States
brutally overcame the resistance of Filipino rebels led by Aguinaldo to
institute an American-style colonial government. Although one barrio
reported that the American occupying forces gave out candies, cigarettes,
and clothing to win over the residents, the overwhelming majority of
Filipina/os met with severe military repression.[18] War from 1899 to 1902
devastated the countryside, resulting in famine, disease, and pestilence.
Loss of life was enormous, with estimates ranging from two hundred
thousand for the entire country to six hundred thousand for Luzon alone,
particularly around central Luzon and Manila.[19] Some areas were oblit-
erated. For example, the town of Batac, Ilocos Norte, founded more than
three centuries earlier by the Spanish, was "burned to ashes" on April 16,
1900.[20]

The American military suppressed Philippine resistance with often extreme measures. One barrio in Ilocos Sur reported in detail about the
torture of alleged suspects:

> At the dawn of American victory over the Spaniards on the islands, the
> "Kwentasan" (American soldiers) came to the barrio and summoned all

able bodied men together. When all men of the barrio were gathered, they were placed under a heavy guard. The captain of the Kwentasan ordered someone to prepare strong good size pieces of rattan and a wooden bench. Each of the civilians was ordered to lie on the bench with his back up. The captain ordered one of the strongest soldiers or one of the good natives to whip him many times until the skin of his back burst.[21]

Samar and Batangas were places of death. In 1901 in Samar, when Filipino soldiers led by General Vincent Lukban killed fifty-four Americans and wounded others, the Americans meted out harsh retaliation. General "Howlin' Jake" Smith told his men, "Kill and burn, kill and burn, the more you kill and the more you burn the more you please me." "Everything over ten" was considered fair game. All island residents, numbering a quarter of a million, were told to come to detention camps or risk being shot.[22] That same year, Major General J. Franklin Bell established concentration camps in Batangas and gave residents two weeks to relocate to them. Those who refused were labeled as rebels. Inside the camp, Filipina/os faced malaria, dengue fever, and other diseases and were denied adequate clothing and food. Outside the camp, many did not survive the onslaught of the American military. United States government sources counted a minimum of one hundred thousand dead, about a third of the island's population.[23]

Americans were not uniformly behind their country's militarism overseas, and many criticized the activity, from Jane Addams to Mark Twain to former presidents Benjamin Harrison and Grover Cleveland, the latter two from opposing parties.[24] There was also significant anti-imperialist activity by African Americans, who saw parallels in treatment of people of color at home and overseas. In fact, some African American soldiers fighting as American troops in the Philippines deserted, and a few actually changed allegiance to fight with the Filipinos.[25] In one letter published in the *Wisconsin Weekly Advocate* in 1900, an African American soldier wrote concerning Filipina/o resistance to American troops, "I must confess they have a just grievance. All this never would have occurred if the army of occupation would have treated them as people."[26]

Americans at home also criticized their country's policies. For example, in 1899 an African American group in Boston adopted a resolution condemning the United States' military intervention in the Philippines, "while the rights of colored citizens in the South, sacredly guaranteed them by the amendment of the Constitution, are shamefully disregarded."[27] The position of American labor regarding the conquest of the Philippines was mixed. Although labor leaders initially supported the war because it bolstered the economy and because they did not want to be perceived as unpatriotic, afterward they again took an anti-imperialist stance. This concern about overseas matters, in part, was due to the perceived competition with labor.[28]

Despite these protests, American conquest continued. After the Americans asserted control, Philippine resistance continued, from everyday measures to more protracted campaigns. In 1913 one observer in Cebu noted in an article in the *Manila Times* that "when the strains of the [Aguinaldo] march are struck up, every Filipino rises, uncovers and stands at attention, but as soon as the American national air is played, they put on their hats and insolently strut away."[29] This casual disregard for the new regime represented one level of resistance. Some nationalist leaders posed an open challenge to the colonial government. Artemio Ricarte, a leader in the Philippine Revolution and an Ilocano, fled to Japan after the American conquest. Nevertheless, he maintained a following in the Philippines despite doubts by Francis Burton Harrison and other colonial authorities about Ricarte's ability to mobilize against the United States. In 1915 Harrison wrote of Ricarte, "As you know, his deluded followers in the Islands have always been led to believe that when the 'revolution' came Ricarte would get help from Japan."[30] Despite this negative characterization by a figure in the colonial administration, historian David Sturdevant reports that Ricarte was "the only prominent nationalist" who would not recognize the results of the American conquest.[31] He was also remembered by other Filipina/os. For example, naval worker Severo Fontanares Flores recalled meeting Ricarte when his ship stopped in Japan: "I was with four other Filipino musicians. As we were saying goodbye, the general gave a parting shot, 'Now that you are in the United States Navy, I wish you all the best of luck.' Then he added in Tagalog, 'You are still Filipinos. Do not forget your own country.' It was so sad the way he said it. I shall never forget."[32]

ECONOMIC CHANGES

Like other colonial powers in the wake of conquest, the United States restructured the Philippine economy to benefit American capitalist interests, especially through the domination of exports and production and the regulation of labor.[33] After the Civil War and increasingly toward the close of the century, the United States economy developed into a mode of monopoly capitalism, focusing capital in a select number of bigger business concerns. This development was also tied to the growth of imperialism. Typically, the United States shipped manufactured products overseas and shipped in raw materials and other goods that required heavy inputs of labor from abroad. However, the Philippine economy was so dependent on the United States economy that it even had to bring in goods traditionally produced in the Philippines. As a measure of how thoroughly the Philippine economy was geared to the American economy, even access to food and clothing was altered by American rule. Formerly an exporter of rice, the Philippines had to regularly import the grain after the 1870s, as well as the textiles needed to make clothing for its people, in contrast to the commonly held rule that the flow of raw materials and goods is always from the colony to the colonizer. From 1930 to 1935, the Philippines relied on the United States for 65 percent of its imports and 83 percent of its export trade. In contrast, the United States had only 1 percent of its total foreign investment in the Philippines. During this period, foreign capitalists focused on the Philippine export sector as opposed to manufacturing.[34] During the 1899–1937 regime, the main exports were sugar, abaca, copra, coconut oil, and tobacco. Through 1918, trade in *abaca,* or Manila hemp, dominated Philippine exports. Then, as in Hawai'i, the sugar trade began to dominate. In 1920, sugar became the leading export commodity, and by 1932–1934 it was the most valuable export in the market.[35]

Trade agreements promoted further dependency on the United States, blocking industrial development in the Philippines. There was little incentive to invest in Philippine industry when American imports could be brought into the country for little beyond the shipping costs. Low tariff schedules designed by the United States Congress regulated commerce between 1902 and 1909. In 1909, the Payne-Aldrich Tariff Act further consolidated trade relations between the Philippines and the United States with few restrictions, developments that were continued by the Underwood Tariff of 1913.[36] Philippine and American capitalists who wanted to expand and protect the Philippine market for American goods had their interests at stake. Furthermore, both the landed elite of the Philippines, which tied its fate to the American export economy, and American private corporations that favored the development of sugar benefited from the colonial regime.[37]

The new accessibility of the American market and the growth of internal transportation stimulated the movement of commodities and people. Manila, established as a central city under Spanish colonization, continued to be a vital hub in this process. After the galleon trade concluded in the early 1800s, Manila became the crossroads where more de-

veloped domestic regions and foreign countries could obtain raw materials, and where manufactured goods could be sold to the Philippine population. The development of rail systems as well as roads facilitated
Manila's connection to the rice and sugar areas of central Luzon. Other
areas were also served by shipping along the coast and between islands,
allowing products to flow more directly to Manila and permitting goods
from America and Japan to enter the Philippine economy. As Daniel
Doeppers notes, however, the trade relationship of the Philippines and
the United States protected both parties from outside competition, particularly by the levying of tariffs. For example, by the end of the 1920s,
the Philippines received the greatest amount of cotton cloth exported by
the United States. When Japan's superior textile manufacturing proved
threatening to the United States' interests in the 1930s, taxes were imposed on Japanese imports into the Philippines. This regular trade contributed to the growth of metropolitan Manila, whose population increased four times, to over nine hundred thousand, by 1941.[38]

As the elite groups were able to make some economic gains with the
American colonial government, many Filipina/os grew even poorer. Although Chris Mensalvas's family was "fortunate" to own their own land
in Pangasinan, other people's land "belonged to the big landlords."[39] Felicisimo E. Corsino remarked that the caciques maintained economic and
political power because of their capital: "Since all these wealthy 'caciques'
own the largest portion of cultivated lands in Ilocos Sur, naturally they
have absolute control over their farmers. The tendency is the development
of aristocracy. The 'caciques' look upon the laboring class as inferiors and
they often harshly treat them."[40] Josefina Tongson reported that the people
who farmed subplots for the wealthy were known as *catalonan* and were
"sort of vassals."[41] These disparities not only resulted in labor agitation
in the late 1920s and especially the 1930s in the Philippines but also would
contribute to the widespread migration of Filipina/os to the United States.

THE RISE OF PORT SEATTLE

The popular emphasis on the American West as a frontier, particularly
because of the continuing legacy of Frederick Jackson Turner's famous
thesis, has tended to constrain our perceptions of port cities in the American West. We often focus less on these cities as colonial metropoles or
downplay how cities such as Seattle eagerly sought connections with
Asia in their development as urban centers.[42] In doing so, it becomes
difficult to see how the migration of different groups was part of the

larger developing relationship between the United States and Asia, promoted by city and regional boosters, as well as on state and federal levels. Asia was essential to the formation of Seattle and the American West as a whole not only in terms of trade but also because of its labor supply.

This history can be discerned through U.S. militarism. Military ties knit the Philippines to the United States as American forces expanded their power in the Pacific Rim.[43] The United States was not alone in this regard. For example, the British were interested in developing a transpacific steamship line because of the military advantages of having a completely British-controlled route in that region.[44]

Furthermore, Pacific coast port cities such as San Francisco, Los Angeles, and Vancouver, Canada, were also soliciting connections with Asia. On the opposite side of the globe from Manila, Seattle competed with these other sites for the emerging Pacific commercial trade. In fact, Seattle's growth at the turn of the century resulted in part from the United States' involvement in the Philippines. Richard C. Berner argues, for example, that Fort Lawton—where Rufina Clemente Jenkins and Frank Jenkins's family would eventually settle—was built by the United States Army as a point of departure for forces leaving for the Philippines. Economics and military ambitions for Seattle went hand in hand, as transport ships bringing foodstuffs and other supplies for the soldiers and even hay and oats for horses left for the Philippines from the city's shipyards. They returned with hemp, thus contributing to the manufacture of cordage in Seattle's maritime economy.[45]

After the United States colonized the Philippines, new demands led to further consolidation of the transportation routes between the two countries. In 1903, one Seattle company agreed to ship "vagrants and others" at fifty dollars per person from Manila to the United States for the colonial administration.[46] The labor pool for U.S. projects also expanded through colonization. According to Thelma Buchholdt, at the beginning of the twentieth century, the United States Army started building communication cables in both the Philippines and Alaska, and Filipino crew members actually went to Alaska to apply knowledge they had acquired in the Philippines. From 1903 to 1904, the U.S. cable ship *Burnside* lay cables linking Seattle to parts of southeast Alaska. Eighty of its 175 crew members were Filipino.[47]

The expansion of the United States' empire also created labor opportunities through the military, much as British imperialism promoted military service for Punjabis throughout England's empire.[48] As Sammy

Lopez reported regarding the recruitment of Filipinos, "any young man who is available" could join the American armed forces.[49] Many Filipinos found work in the U.S. Navy, particularly because its racial and gender restrictions favored the employment of men of color in service positions. Like African American sailors, Filipinos were restricted to labor in the galleys and mess halls, however, lower-rank employment that on dry land was typically considered "women's work." Two thousand Filipinos served in the navy by 1917. Their numbers grew rapidly, in part in response to the banning of African Americans from service in the navy, a reflection of how different groups might be played off against each other by military and economic interests. Following World War I, Filipinos averaged about 4.5 percent of the navy population, contributing about four thousand men. However, they still faced discrimination in promotions or movement to other kinds of jobs, as well as in securing shore leave.[50]

In the first decades of the twentieth century, Seattle actively built up its facilities to take advantage of the foreign goods and passengers passing through the West Coast, particularly as Asian trade was perceived as a key component to the port's eventual success.[51] The rate of transpacific trade in 1920 was over five times that in 1914, due to the massive construction of new ships, the resumption of European trade in the Pacific, and the opportunities offered by the Panama Canal.[52] From 1922 to 1931, commerce with Japan and China constituted over half of Seattle's total foreign trade.[53] Japan emerged as a crucial trade ally because of its geographic and commercial status, as well as its industrial and maritime power within Asia. Indeed, much of Seattle's early growth in shipping derived from the silk trade from Japan.[54]

In addition to developing into a center for international trade, Seattle became known as the capital for the Northwest region, most notably Alaska. The shortest route from North America to Asia was along the Great Circle through Alaska, along which were located the major cities of Seattle and Vancouver on the Pacific Coast, and Yokohama, Osaka, and Kobe in Japan (see map 2).[55] Because the coastlines of North America and Asia were almost straight, ships typically traveled along the coasts until cutting across the northern part of the Pacific Ocean. Of the West Coast ports, Seattle had the shortest crossing to Yokohama on the Great Circle route: 4,257 miles. From San Francisco to Yokohama, passage measured 4,536 miles by the Great Circle route and 5,485 miles by the Hawaiian Islands. Thus, Seattle edged out other West Coast cities in proximity to the major cities in eastern Asia by a few hundred miles.[56]

The preeminence of Seattle's port was also the result of aggressive

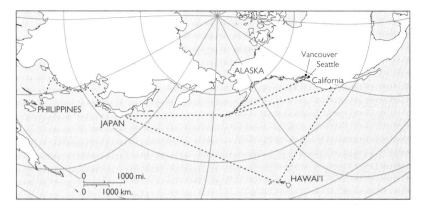

Map 2. The Great Circle route.

management by the Port of Seattle, a municipal corporation created in 1911. The Port of Seattle substantially developed its port facilities and was better prepared than San Francisco to accept the traffic flow generated by the crisis of World War I. At that point, Seattle undercut rates to become the least expensive port on the West Coast. By 1916, it was the most important West Coast port in terms of "dollar volume," a position it held for the next five years. Eight years later, heavy advertising by the Washington Customs District helped Seattle regain its position as the premier West Coast port in terms of the value of imports and exports moving through its facilities after business had declined because of competition from other ports and the conclusion of shipping contracts from World War I.[57]

Seattle's growth was also intimately connected to its position as a transportation center for both water and land routes. Although short-lived, the first transpacific line from Seattle was the Great Eastern Steamship Company in 1893. Then, Great Northern railroad magnate James Hill recognized the importance of trade with Asia. In 1896, James Hill worked with the Northern Pacific railroad to obtain control of the Chicago, Burlington, and Quincy Railroad, whose tracks left Chicago and went up to the Great Lakes, down to the Gulf of Mexico, and over to the Rocky Mountains. This enabled the Port of Seattle to gain importance not only in southwest commerce but also as a node in the import-export business to Asia. In 1896, under Hill's direction, two large passenger and cargo vessels, the *Minnesota* and the *Dakota*, were built and put on a route between Seattle, Japan, China, and the Philippines. That same year, Hill also developed a relationship with Nippon Yusen Kaisha, a Tokyo steamship

line, to inaugurate regular transpacific service on a monthly basis between
Seattle and Japan in conjunction with the railroad.[58]

Seattle had many natural advantages in building up this Pacific Rim
trade. It had a grain hinterland on the east up to the Rocky Mountains,
a fruit hinterland in the Puget Sound region, irrigated lands to the east
of the Cascade Mountains, a nearby timber hinterland, and a fish hinterland from Puget Sound up to the Bering Sea. Not surprisingly, the biggest
exports in the 1920s were wheat, fruit, lumber, and fish to Asian countries, in rank order, China, Hong Kong, Japan, the Philippines, and others.[59] This productivity enticed potential emigrants. Felipe G. Dumlao
was attracted to Seattle because of its "green" reputation: "Oh, strawberry I heard it . . . [was one of] the products of Washington. Potatoes, . . .
apples, . . . that's what you call a green country. Oh, I said I liked that,
so I tried to get to Seattle, Washington."[60] Seattle was also blessed with
an excellent harbor. With the Pacific Ocean only 125 nautical miles away,
Elliot Bay was a deep and easily accessible harbor for incoming ships.[61]
Furthermore, because it was centrally located in the middle of the coast-
line, Seattle was in a position to command traffic within Puget Sound
and from the Columbia River and Canada.[62] It also was accessible from
the east through the Snoqualmie Pass in the Cascades Range.[63]

Another major boost to Seattle's governing role in the regional economy was its relationship to Alaska. Seattle was the logical big city to assume the main portion of the Alaska trade; along the Great Circle route,
it was only 649 miles away from the port of Ketchikan.[64] Seattle's maritime trade increased rapidly following the 1897 Klondike gold rush.
When the discovery of gold drew would-be prospectors to the Northwest, Seattle overtook San Francisco as a supplier for travelers to
Alaska.[65] Canned salmon later emerged as the main commodity moving
from Alaska to Seattle. Seattle was also able to send a great deal of tin
to the territory and profited from this new boon.[66]

Seattle's popularity was further strengthened by its position as a tran-
sit center. A 1935 publication reported that the city had over one hundred steamship lines coming to its docks.[67] The Empress Lines was another
transpacific shipping company that began landing in nearby Vancouver
in the late nineteenth century in conjunction with the Canadian Pacific
Railway.[68] On a regional level, the numerous railroad lines that used Seattle as a depot further bolstered the city's position as a way station. The
Great Northern, the Northern Pacific, the Oregon-Washington Railroad
and Navigation Company (the Union Pacific), and other domestic railroad lines stopped in the city. To the north, Canadian railroads that used

Seattle's facilities included the Canadian Pacific, the Canadian National, and the Southern Pacific.[69]

Seattle's position as a transportation nexus directly affected the flow of Filipina/os to the city. In addition, because transportation charges were highly profitable, agents from shipping lines would recruit prospective emigrants, thus further promoting migration. A 1931 study reported that the Dollar Line, which regularly docked in Seattle and was then the primary shipping line for Filipino workers arriving in the city, offered recruitment materials in Ilocano and English describing "a healthful, happy and comfortable voyage."[70] When John Mendoza said that he landed in Seattle by coincidence, his words reflected how the transportation systems regulated emigrants' expectations and possibilities. As Mendoza reported, "It was just a chance that I came over here, I didn't select Seattle."[71] Seattle also became an attractive option as an intermediary port. In 1921, Salvador Del Fierro spent six months persuading his father to grant him permission to go to the United States. Finally, en route to New York City to attend Columbia University, he arrived in Seattle and located a cousin. Because Del Fierro was so homesick, he ended up staying in Seattle and never went to New York.[72]

"THERE WAS A MIGRATION MOVEMENT AROUND ME"

During this "Age of Empire," the world economy expanded its geographic base, and the people followed. As the amount of land available for agricultural workers in the Philippines shrank, people went abroad to improve their opportunities, thinking that they might be able to return with capital to the home village. The great majority were Ilocana/o. In a 1971 study, Henry Lewis noted that two-thirds to three-fourths of the Filipina/o immigrants and children in the United States had origins in that region (map 3).[73] As the figures suggest, not all Filipina/o emigrants came from agriculturally based families in the Ilocos; emigrant "Vic" Bacho, for example, came from a family of fishermen in Cebu.[74] Still, why did the Ilocos region produce the great majority of the emigrants to the mainland United States and Hawai'i during the colonial period?

A consideration of the geography and economy of this area provides some answers. The five provinces of Ilocos Norte, Ilocos Sur, Abra, La Union, and Pangasinan all lie along or close to the northwest coast of the Ilocos region.[75] The general economic pattern was of "small-scale producers" who earned their living from "agriculture, home industries, fishing, and trade."[76] However, ownership of land in the Ilocos area was

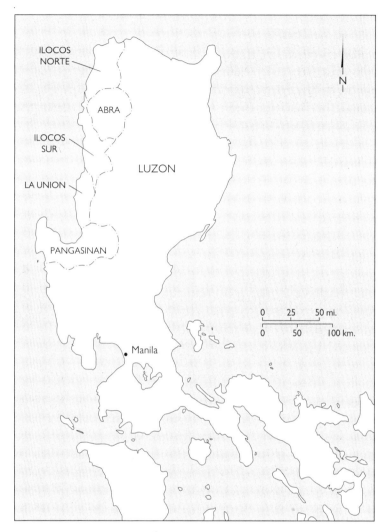

Map 3. Originating areas of most Filipina/o emigrants in Luzon, Philippines.

relatively common as a result of the lack of large landholdings, the ability to grow rice on small, intensive plots, and the *sabong*, a male land dowry that by custom was divided into equal inheritances for men in the family. Miriam Sharma suggests that these factors contributed to a "peasant-proprietor" role and to a reputation for being hardworking.[77] Sylvestre Tangalan recalled the rigorous demands of the rural economy: "Farmers . . . that's the main industry of the Philippines, at that time, northern

part of Luzon. It's really farming country. It's not industrialized, consequently the people have to work hard in the fields . . . and . . . after farming season you have to fish in the rivers and the seas."[78] For most households, life was relatively modest. Ceferíno Purísima characterized a typical
home in a paper published in 1918:

> We ascend the house by a removable ladder of choice bamboo. . . . On
> one end of the room is a table on which are placed things used in religious
> worship such as a candlenut lamp and some images. Against the walls are
> wooden trunks and some bamboo and wooden benches and chairs. . . . In
> the kitchen we find a stove or two at a corner with a pile of firewood beside
> them. . . . For sleeping purposes they have pandan or buri mats which they
> spread on the floor, a pillow made of cotton tree fiber and blanket of home-
> woven cloth of various designs and colors.[79]

Historically, migration was a fact of life for the Ilocos region. With a
dry climate inhibiting development of the area, the region was overpopu-
lated, prompting residents to seek better options elsewhere.[80] The regular movement of workers made Ilocana/os, as described by Mercedes A.
Vega, "the most wide-scattered tribe in the Philippines." Vega continued, "Many of them . . . [have] recognized that labor is not a disgrace
but [an] honorable means of becoming prosperous."[81] Settlement was
rapid. In 1850, the province of La Union was created from a northern
section of Pangasinan and a southern part of Ilocos Sur, and Ilocana/os
became the main group there and more numerous than the Pangasinans.
Ilocana/os also traveled into Abra province and overtook the Tinguians
in population, and they migrated into the Cagayan Valley after 1850.[82]
In the eighteenth and nineteenth centuries, Ilocana/os moved to Pangasinan and Nueva Ecija to establish new homes.[83] In the latter part of
the nineteenth century, they journeyed to Cagayan Valley to labor for
the Compañia General de Tobacos.[84] Additional destinations included
Abra, Nueva Vizcaya, Tarlac, Nueva Ecija, and Zambales.[85]
    Migration for these workers was often temporary. E. B. Christie re-
ported that "not less than a thousand people" left Ilocos Norte each year
to help harvest rice in the south. Most returned home after a three-month
period, while some stayed away for a year before coming back for their
families. Some workers migrated to the northern part of Cagayan to go
fishing, or to Manila to labor as coachmen.[86] Other Ilocana/os traveled
for trade. Josefina Tongson noted in 1918 that hundreds of Ilocana/os
left for regions such as Cagayan and Pangasinan with cloth.[87]
    Several factors pushed Ilocana/os to look elsewhere for opportunities.
The Ilocos region had both monsoons and a long dry season, and it was

susceptible to typhoons.[88] In addition, American capitalists became interested in Ilocana/os as potential overseas workers because business interests did not want to draw away needed laborers from the sugar industry in Luzon and the Visayas. Similarly, Filipina/o sugar investors also had a stake in maintaining a labor force at home.[89] Not surprisingly, the provinces of central Luzon exhibited far lower migration rates outside of the province than did the Ilocana/o areas.[90]

Al Bautista's father was one of those Ilocana/os who left for work in other regions. At age seventeen, he left with a friend for Talavera, Nueva Ecija, 120 miles away. When he did not return for a year, his mother was afraid that he had died. Instead, he was busy homesteading in Nueva Ecija, clearing land and planting crops on public lands opened up by the colonial government.[91]

Al Bautista was born in Luna, La Union, in 1908. By the time he was in second grade, his family was ready to move to Nueva Ecija. Bautista's mother sold some of the family's lands in Luna to pay for train passage. Al Bautista worked in the fields until he was a teenager. His formal education had ended in second grade, after the move to Nueva Ecija, because his family lacked the funds to send him to school, and the school was some distance away. Bautista stayed in Nueva Ecija several years before returning to Luna.[92]

Ironically, migration to these new regions forced migrants into greater dependency. Possessing little capital, migrants borrowed from businesspeople and landlords to raise crops and relied on others to market their harvests. Tenants commonly paid back landlords at high interest rates, a practice that began when rice, not money, was the form of payment. Because rice can be used as seed, it was possible for tenants to return their loans at high rates. With the introduction of a cash economy, conditions became far more exploitative.[93] As a result, Filipina/os began thinking about going overseas. Anastacio B. Gerardo commented:

> The educated classes are still taking advantage of their poor brothers. Their land are grabbed from them. . . . Some of the members of the lower classes had caught sight of the glimmer of progress, could no longer tolerate the oppression they were bearing. This mistreatment accelerated the migration of Ilocano workers to Hawaii, Zamboanga, Mindoro, Nueva Ecija and somewhere else. . . . Reports about these workers seem to show that they are accumulating great fortunes now.[94]

As Gerardo discusses, internal migration was compounded with external migration to the United States. Ilocana/os moved not only within the Philippines but also abroad to Guam, Hawai'i, and the mainland United

States to find better prospects.[95] For example, a barrio in Ilocos Sur reported that while some residents went to the United States, others who were fishermen traveled to Aparri, Cagayan, to fish.[96] One count taken in 1939 revealed there were 709,000 Filipina/os who spoke Ilocana/o in the "home" region and a projected 1.6 million Ilocana/os who had moved away.[97] These figures indicate the expanded opportunities for people elsewhere, and how possibilities for migration were being rapidly reshaped during this era.

Those who left for the United States followed a well-traveled passage. Both men and women were stirred by the stories of opportunities in the United States. Bibiana Laigo Castillano, a teacher in the Philippines, recalled, "My father talked of my coming to America and he asked me if I wished to go. Well thinking about the present salary that the Filipinos were receiving over there, I jumped to my satisfaction and I was so pleased."[98] David Guerrero was the oldest son in a farming family from the Pangasinan province who landed in Seattle as a young man in 1929. In going to Seattle, he followed not only an uncle who had come to the United States through service in the U.S. Navy but also townmates who had previously journeyed to the United States. Already, several of these townmates were in Seattle, and they had written their wives and parents about the United States, enclosing money with their letters. With passage paid by his parents and buoyed by his father's hopes that he go to school, Guerrero also set off for the United States aboard the *President Cleveland*.[99]

The hierarchies of colony and colonizer were also apparent in the choices that people made. Reflecting back on his journey to the United States, Trinidad Rojo reported that if he had stayed in Manila and gone to school, he could have become a high official in the Philippine government. Instead, as for many of his compatriots, the lure of the American mainland was too powerful to resist. As Rojo recalled, "There was a migration movement around me."[100]

It was difficult to dissuade hopeful emigrants in the face of such powerful attractions, especially because of the promise of financial gain.[101] Compared with the salaries available in the Philippines, the wages offered for work in Hawai'i and on the American mainland seemed considerable. Leo Aliwanag recalled, "You know, how very poor was the Philippines in those days. . . . You were lucky . . . if you could get 50 centavos a day."[102] Furthermore, it was easy for Filipina/os to go to the United States. At a time when other would-be emigrants from Asia were barred by exclusionary laws, Filipina/os were able to enter as American nationals. Juan Mina reported, "We can come anytime. . . . We didn't even have passport to come over, as long as we can . . . [pay] to come over."[103]

Some would-be emigrants were directly influenced by Americans stationed in the Philippines. Maria Abastilla Beltran remembered that a medical adviser to Governor General Woods encouraged her to go to the United States so she "could be somebody else."[104] John Castillo also spoke of the role of Americans in his decision to come to the United States: "All of the faculty at the Philippine Normal School were Americans. And they are the ones that encourages us to go abroad, you know, and get more experience, you see. . . . They give us glowing stories about the United States and how they love the Filipinos and . . . there would be no problem whatsoever. But when we get over here, I find it totally different."[105] Contractors were another influence on prospective emigrants. As will be explained in greater depth in chapter 3, Seattle contractors such as Pio De Cano and Valeriano Laigo recruited their relatives directly from the Philippines, helping them come to the United States and thus aiding the extended family.[106] These workers were also desirable employees not only because they shared familial, cultural, and linguistic bonds with the contractors but also because these shared attributes reinforced their loyalty to those who had recruited them.[107]

MIGRATION, FAMILY, AND GENDER

Widespread migration of Filipina/os, particularly to the United States, both reshaped the gendered worlds of Filipina/os in the sending areas in the Philippines and dramatically affected the realities of Filipina/os in the United States. Although both men and women went abroad, migration was stunningly dominated by young, "single" males.

Women on both sides of the Pacific Ocean, however, were instrumental in sustaining this community. Back in Asia, they often had the important job of maintaining the family home. In her 1985 study, Susan Evangelista reported that Carlos Bulosan's sister "Escolastica" remained in the family village of Binalonan, Pangasinan, in lodging constructed from the materials of their original home. Escolastica Bulosan gardened on what was left of the family land, which measured less than a hectare. Other land had been sold off when three of her brothers went to the United States. Although Evangelista did not indicate whether Escolastica Bulosan had ever been able to marry, she did note that Escolastica did not speak English.[108] Although Escolastica Bulosan's older brother Carlos has received far more attention in the American culture, the lives of Escolastica Bulosan and others who remained in the Philippines while so many journeyed to the United States in the 1920s and 1930s provide us with important insights into the formation of Filipina/o America in the period before World War II.

For Filipina/o Seattle and other communities, the standard emigrant profile was that of a young man who was sent to a capitalist economy on behalf of his family. As the barrio Rancho in the province of Ilocos Sur reported: "During the American regime many able bodied men of the place went to Hawaii and America. Some of them were able to cont[i]nue their studies in the United States. Some of them sent money for their families and most of them were able to buy lands in other places and build better homes."[109] Edna Bonacich remarked regarding this phenomenon: "The result was a kind of vicious circle, perpetuating a form of migrant labor or sojourning."[110] The overwhelmingly male migration to the United States, however, had its own economic logic. If someone emigrated alone instead of with a family, expenses abroad would be paid for just one person, while the other family members could support themselves at home.[111] Vincent Mendoza, who originally did not want to go to the United States, was asked to go to provide more resources for his family. He said: "They encouraged me to come because you can earn money and then I can help them. You know, money is very hard to get there. And I can be able to help them . . . bring my brothers to school as far as high school."[112] Having family members abroad potentially meant having a greater pooled income for the family or, at the very least, one less mouth to feed. The worker would also have the security of a home village to which he could return. Ties were maintained by sending money or making rare visits, or even having a wife at home.[113] In Al Bautista's case, his grandfather required him to marry one of his many girlfriends before the grandfather would sell the land to send him abroad. Thirty days after his first son was born, Bautista left for the United States at age seventeen. Although married emigrants were more the exception than the rule because of the general youth of the emigrants, these family ties served to bind the men to families back home. For example, when Al Bautista's grandfather had him marry as a precondition for getting ship fare to the United States, he was helping to ensure the young man's responsibility to the family back home.[114] These kinds of familial strategies can also be read as a form of social control, since they helped to regulate the sexual conduct of both the women who stayed in the Philippines and the men who went abroad.

Although a few women did emigrate to the United States, typically the men left for overseas work, and the women stayed behind. Jose Acena remarked, "I think they [the parents] were too old fashion[ed] . . . conservative, that possible they didn't want their girls [to] get away from their homes."[115] Anthropologist Stephen Griffiths's description of one informant's family illustrates how gender and sibling order dictated a family member's prospects regarding migration. In "Enrique Cruz's" family, "Cruz" was one of seven sons, and the fourth of nine offspring. Because of the limited resources to be shared among his siblings, "Cruz" and three other brothers emigrated to Hawai'i. One brother migrated to Cagayan Valley, and another left for Mindanao. The youngest brother stayed to take care of the parents and was given the family lands.[116]

The two sisters in this family had very different opportunities. Although both stayed in the same village, only one was able to marry and have her own family.[117] Even if the other sister had consciously chosen to be independent, she likely was vulnerable economically and socially. Not all women might have had a heterosexual orientation or wanted to get married, but marriage and the production of children were among the few ways they could secure social status within a rural community. For women who did want to marry, choices were curtailed by the drastic gender imbalance. Writing in 1966 about an Ilocana/o community under their observation, anthropologists William F. Nydegger and Corinne Nydegger remarked of this phenomenon: "At the time of the study there was a disproportionately large number of widows and middle-aged spinsters in Tarong, apparently the result of the California-Hawaii labor migrations during the 1930s."[118] In the village he studied, anthropologist Stephen Griffiths recorded some of these women's options, noting that these single women could travel to the Cagayan Valley to work as paid labor in the rice harvests or be hired locally by others who could afford to pay them.[119]

Although they were in the minority, a handful of Filipina pioneers did cross the Pacific Ocean in the 1920s and 1930s for a variety of reasons. Some traveled for education, like Mercedes Balco, who came to study at the School of Social Work at Catholic University in Washington, D.C., or Maria Abastilla Beltran, who sought further training as a nurse. Others arrived in the United States to join husbands or family members. Like their male counterparts, these early pioneers were lured by the promise of economic and social possibilities in the United States.[120]

For both men and women, these journeys often resulted in great homesickness. Migration to the United States, especially during the Depression years, divided families for long, indefinite periods. Teodolo Ranjo recalled the first time he received a letter from home while working in Cosmopolis, Washington. Ranjo was so lonesome that he cried after reading the letter. Robert Fernando remembered a fellow passenger on a train "losing his mind" because he had left behind his girlfriend in the Philippines.[121]

Members of the home community, particularly the women, shared the burden of separation. Loss of contact was a common part of the emigration experience for many groups before World War II, a point that is driven home by a category of verses from San Francisco's Chinatown labeled by Marlon K. Hom as "Lamentations of Estranged Wives."[122] As the Nydeggers commented about the people who had left the Ilocana/o community they studied, "Many of these migrants, married as well as unmarried, never were heard from and are considered dead."[123] This comment suggests the potential social costs involved in migration. If the absent community members were not among the living, they had indeed left the living world of the village's social reality. Thus, despite the tremendous opportunity represented by travel to the United States for both the emigrant and his or her family, the stakes were very high.

Whether the trip was to Hawai'i or the mainland United States, the boat voyage was long and arduous. Zacarias Manangan recalled about traveling to the United States, "Well it was difficult all right because . . . in those days you have to cross the ocean."[124] Those Filipina/os with more resources had an easier time. Paula Nonacido recalled mingling with white passengers without any difficulties when she came on a second-class fare. She told an interviewer in 1976, "And we ate together, we danced together and we do something on the boat."[125] Nonacido's experience, however, was not typical. Like most Filipina/os journeying to the United States at that time, Toribio Madayag rode in third class, or steerage, for the price of three hundred pesos, or ninety-five dollars.[126] Other people who did not have money would stow away on board.[127] Regardless of the fare paid, the trip could take twenty-one to thirty days from Manila to San Francisco.[128]

Leo Aliwanag had wretched memories of his trip from Manila to Honolulu on a Japanese ship. In steerage, beds were stacked as high as four bunks, and around one hundred people could occupy one compartment. There was no air-conditioning, and food was "mostly stew, rice, you know and fish." Aliwanag recalled that "many of us get sick, you know and even some of us died and buried in the sea."[129] Felipe Dumlao also remembered that there was no ventilation on the boat and that

the sanitation was poor. On his trip to the United States, four passengers died of meningitis and were buried at sea.[130] During one ill-fated
1930 trip on the *President Monroe* of the Dollar Lines, pneumonia swept
through the steerage area, leaving five dead. One "delirious" passenger
jumped overboard, and seventy-three other Filipina/os fell ill.[131]

Still, some passengers devised strategies to make the trip more bear-
able. Felipe Dumlao remembered a Chinese vendor selling food. One
"very clever" passenger would position himself on the top bunk in order to scoop food from the vendor's basket. When Dumlao caught him,
the passenger asked him not to say anything, and invited Dumlao to join
in—which he did.[132] Zacarias Manangan also remembered the shared
knowledge passed by other Filipina/os when they were quarantined in
British Columbia. The "people who come from the north," like the Norte-
nians and Bauangians, were able to catch mussels and octopus, giving
Manangan the chance to taste octopus for the first time.[133] Hence, even
as larger colonial and economic forces swept waves of Filipina/os to the
United States, Filipina/os devised a range of strategies to make the best
of their situation.

Lest I create the impression that the migrations were singularly directed
from the Philippines to the United States, in keeping with the standard
narrative of Asian American male migration to the United States, I will
return briefly to the family of Rufina Clemente Jenkins. The travels of
Francesca Robinson, the daughter of Rufina Clemente Jenkins and Frank
Jenkins, illustrate this new fluidity of movement. Robinson was born in
the Philippines, but soon afterward her parents moved to the Presidio, now
Fort Ord, California, in 1902. In 1907, the family returned to the Philippines because her father was stationed in Parang-Parang. Robinson had
strong memories of her girlhood years in the Philippines—learning needle-
work at a convent, playing with neighborhood children—and even recalled a time when she was in a religious parade and her "veil caught on
fire." The family returned to the United States, settling in Fort Lawton
in the Seattle area in 1909. Robinson remembered, "We talked a little
bit of everything but when we come back we couldn't talk English at all
so we had to stay out of school."[134] Robinson's crossing of the Pacific
between the Philippines and the United States three times while she was
a girl illustrates the growth of the transpacific traffic in the early part of
the twentieth century and the pivotal role of militarism in developing
Filipina/o Seattle.

The formation and migration of the Jenkins family remind us of Frank
Thistlewaite's point, in his pathbreaking essay "Migration from Europe

Overseas in the Nineteenth and Twentieth Century," that to view the populating of the United States by immigrants as a unidirectional process would be a serious mistake. For example, of the Italian emigrants who came to the United States in 1904, 10 percent had previously journeyed to the country. In addition, countries such as Argentina, Brazil, and Canada received a relatively larger proportion of emigrants than the United States.[135] Hence, emphasizing the United States alone as a destination for migration gives us a false perspective on the movement of peoples to other countries. Furthermore, not understanding the role of the U.S. military and government in promoting the formation of Filipina/o Seattle—as well as the growth of the Seattle economy—would be to miss the intricate links of empire, politics, and economy in the development of the city as a colonial metropole to the Philippines.

CONCLUSION

This chapter has explored the relationship of the United States and the Philippines and has demonstrated how going to the United States became an important means of economic success and class mobility for families. Distant places such as Washington, California, and New York took on new significance for aspiring emigrants, particularly following the emigration of fellow townmates or family members. Established traffic from Asia to Seattle created a city that was a crossing ground for people in search of information about work or school. Seattle received a regular influx of new people, especially because it was a shipping and a railroad hub, and also because of U.S. military ambitions in the Pacific, which further promoted movement to the city. This migration dramatically shaped the gender composition of communities both in the Philippines and in the United States, as a mostly male cohort of young migrants left for colonial metropoles abroad.

In analyzing the formation of Filipina/o Seattle, it is important to understand how Filipina/os operated within a political space constructed by colonialism. Take, for example, the recounting of the narrator's first sighting of the mainland United States in Carlos Bulosan's autobiographical novel, *America Is in the Heart*. The protagonist recalls his impressions of the United States as his ship draws closer to the shores of Seattle in June 1930: "My first sight of the approaching land was an exhilarating experience. Everything seemed native and promising to me. It was like coming home after a long voyage, although as yet I had no home in this city."[136] He continues, with words that reveal his idealism: "Every-

thing seemed familiar and kind—the white faces of the buildings melt-
ing in the soft afternoon sun, the gray contours of the surrounding val-
leys that seemed to vanish in the last periphery of light. With a sudden
surge of joy, I knew that I must find a home in this new land."[137]

Bulosan's words portray a central irony. "Everything seemed native
and promising," even though he was actually the colonial "native."
Colonialism in the Philippines, an ocean away, made it possible for young
Filipina/os like Carlos to imagine the United States as home even though
they had never been there before. This sense of home, of familiarity, is
part of what would make the Filipina/o American experience so unique,
as well as a reason why their political efforts would be framed in a different context than those of other groups from countries without explicit
U.S. domination.

It is this expanded arena that I hope to explore in the following chapters. In her study of black laborers in the British global empires, whose
ranks included not only West Indians and Africans but also South Asians
and Arabs, Laura Tabili demonstrates how black seamen in sites such
as London and Manchester challenged and negotiated British imperial
rule and racial meanings.[138] Similarly, Filipina/o Americans contested
and articulated their position in the United States' empire. In the next
chapter, I will examine one group that exemplified Seattle's status as a
colonial metropole: the Filipinos and Filipinas who pursued education
in the city. Colonial ideology vaunted access to colonial education for
"natives," and the eventual return of these Filipina/os to run the government in the Philippines. Hence, Seattle emerged as an alluring destination for these would-be students. Whether the goals of the colonial
enterprise were achieved reveals much about the function of Seattle for
Filipina/o Americans.

CHAPTER 2

Education in the Metropole

Of all the factors that would mark Filipina/os as different from the first generation of other groups who migrated to the American mainland and Hawai'i, the widespread emphasis on university education because of American colonialism in the Philippines would be a crucial distinction. While education was an important value for Asian Americans as a whole, particularly because of its connection to class mobility, it is important to recognize how in the Filipina/o case, education in the United States was seen as an extension of education in the Philippines. Belen DeGuzman Braganza was one such early pioneer who received a university education in Seattle. She was born in 1913 in Manila, the second oldest of five siblings. Her father was an architect, but he died when Braganza was only seven years old. Braganza's mother supported the children by selling jewelry and conducting other small business activities. To extend the family's resources, Braganza lived with her grandmother. Braganza's educational trajectory was unusual for a woman—although she finished grade school and some high school in the Philippines, she left for the United States at age sixteen. Luckily for her, she had an uncle on her mother's side who had first come to the United States in 1903 and who wanted to fund an education for one of his young relatives. Braganza competed with her cousins to get this financial help, winning out over two older male cousins. She arrived in Seattle in 1930, chaperoned by a Filipina teacher named Alpina Zamora, who was looking for employment in the United States. Braganza went to Broadway High School and then enrolled at the University of Washington and Seattle College (later called Seattle University).[1]

As Braganza's story suggests, the contradiction of being both an American colonial traveling to the metropole *and* an immigrant person of color in an American West economy that was segregated by race, class, and gender was part of the regular lived experience of Filipina/os in the first decades of the twentieth century. How they negotiated that contradiction, particularly through education, forms an important part of their experience. Ann Laura Stoler and Frederick Cooper have pointed out in a recent anthology about colonialism, "The most basic tension of empire lies in what has become a central, if now obvious, point of recent colonial scholarship: namely, that the otherness of colonized persons was neither inherent nor stable; his or her difference had to be defined and maintained."[2] Perhaps nowhere is that more apparent in the case of Filipina/o Seattle than among the community members who were involved in the educational process. Those who received education became part of the colonial elite, and even those who never went near a classroom in the United States still were affected by the community's emphasis on education. This is partly why it is so important to analyze the role of Filipina/o students in the context of U.S.-Philippines relations.

The migration of Filipina/os for education was part of a larger phenomenon. As with the Malaysian students who went to study in London or the Vietnamese who went to Paris in the 1920s and 1930s, this education was part of the process of training a colonial elite in the maintenance of imperial rule. Benedict Anderson argues in *Imagined Communities* that education was crucial in promoting the colonial mission. Large empires required native personnel to fill the colonial bureaucracy, hence the need for educational systems to train these would-be bureaucrats.[3] One of the most famous world figures of the twentieth century, Mohandas Karamchand Gandhi, exemplified this process in the British system. Gandhi was born in 1869 in India, educated in England, and then engaged in legal and political work in South Africa. He would become famous, though, for his leadership and mass mobilization against the British. By the time he went back to India in 1915, he was a leader in transforming the Indian National Congress Movement and in contesting British rule.[4] A recipient of colonial education, Gandhi would later make use of some of the resources conferred by this education to lead an anticolonial movement that would become known around the world.

This chapter documents Seattle's position as a colonial metropole in terms of education and describes how the ideology and experience of education affected class formation. Because of colonialism, the educational experience was somewhat different for Filipina/o Americans than for other groups. The first-generation experience was the central focus for the Filipina/o American community in the pre–World War II era, particularly because many Filipina/os, like Braganza, came explicitly for education and utilized the American public school system as a continuation of education they had received in the Philippines. While members of the immigrant generation in other communities also sought education and went to school, much of the educational experience in the American public school system was directed at the second-generation members of most Asian American communities. Furthermore, because the great waves of Filipina/o migration came during times of tight restrictions on other groups, the demographics of these communities by generation varied considerably. Filipina/o college students encountered primarily second-generation Japanese American and Chinese American university students in the late 1920s and early 1930s. The Filipina/os' different identities and opportunities, as structured by generation, also shaped their experiences in school as well as in the job market.

In addition, particularly because those coming from the Philippines were mostly male, student demographics tended to be extremely gendered. Although some educational opportunities were open to women, the bulk of resources were usually directed toward the men, since both Philippine and American cultures emphasized male privilege. Thus, as a woman, Braganza represented the exception more than the rule. The fact that she required a chaperone indicates that women were far more constrained in their mobility than men. However, Braganza's desire to come to the United States, her reliance on family networks (her uncle), and her travel to public and private educational institutions on the American mainland were characteristic of many in her generation.

COLONIAL EDUCATIONS

Braganza's decision to go to the United States reflects the sweeping social and economic changes that occurred in the Philippines in the first decades of the twentieth century. Education was the centerpiece of American colonization in the Philippines, and Braganza's cohort were beneficiaries of these policies. One Filipino, "Vic" Bacho, vividly remembered his first day at primary school: "The sight of the children standing at attention when the American flag was raised and singing 'My Country 'Tis of Thee' will always be with me."[5] Half a world away from the mainland United States, Filipina/o children were diligently learning to be good "Americans." Historian Renato Constantino has commented on the inculcation of American culture: "The new Filipino generation learned of the lives of American heroes, sang American songs, and dreamt of snow and Santa Claus."[6] As a class marker, education offered the possibility of upward mobility to ambitious Filipina/os, with the promise of clerical or even professional work at the end of their time as students.[7] The American system, however, was not the first colonial education in the Philippines; Spain had already instituted educational opportunities prior to U.S. rule. Indeed, Jose Rizal, a famous Philippine nationalist hero, first received education in Spain like many of the elite of his generation. He would later travel to the United States, eventually returning to the Philippines to emerge as a political leader.[8]

Students in the first decades of the twentieth century encountered a rapidly shifting political terrain. In his study of Manila before World War II, Daniel Doeppers discusses the changes brought about by the exit of the Spanish administration, the modernization and consequent restructuring of the economy, and the expansion of social mobility across previous class and ethnic divides. Increased American markets for Philippine goods, better transportation facilities, and new economic and financial policies further increased the speed of development.[9]

Under American colonization, education was a key vehicle in the restructuring of Philippine society.[10] Education followed militarism in the Philippines and was actually conceptualized within a larger system of American domination. As a result, colonial education typically reinforced class privilege and maintained colonial objectives. During American rule, educational opportunities were opened through a national system of public primary schools, promoting change particularly at the rural and barrio (village) level. In this period, colonial education was more accessible than ever before, particularly for men. Although education had been available under the Spanish government, the American system promoted greater access and emphasized a technical and academic curriculum.[11] Within the first ten years, public schools were set up on the primary level in most barrios, on the intermediate level in the *poblaciones* (principal barrios) of municipalities, and on the secondary level in the provinces. Leo Aliwanag remembered, "Gradually they had high schools and then colleges and universities."[12] In Manila, new institutions included an arts and trade school, a nursing school, and the University of the Philippines. To provide teachers for this new system, hundreds of Americans were brought to the Philippines, largely on the transport *Thomas,* earning them the name of the "Thomasites."[13] Other educators were Americans who had remained after the war and become teachers throughout the Philippines.[14]

Physical location, family background, and gender affected one's ability to secure an education.[15] During its heyday in the early twentieth century, the *pensionado* and *pensionada* program, which sent government-sponsored students to study in the United States, also reflected these social biases. By and large, most of these students came from positions of class privilege, especially because prospective *pensionada/os* were required to be high school graduates.[16] Initially, the Filipino governor and the American school superintendent from each province chose the candidates. Later, the *pensionada/o* program set up examinations for prospective students. Other students were chosen by "special sponsors" such as the Jockey Club or tobacco and sugar interests. A final twenty-five students were chosen by Governor William H. Taft, whose emphasis on the privileged was clear. As William Alexander Sutherland recalls in his memoirs of the program: "In the telegram of instructions prepared for the Governor to sign was written, 'Each student must be of unquestionable moral and physical qualifications, no weight being given to social status.' The Governor, more realistic than I, scratched out the word 'no' before the word 'weight.' He saw the importance of this, particularly with those first boys going over."[17] The initial *pensionada/os* embarked on their journeys to the mainland United States in 1903, when roughly one hundred students were sent to California.[18] They first attended high schools in southern California, then went to summer school the following year in Santa Barbara. The irony of their position as colonials was underscored in August 1904 when they spent a month at the Louisiana Purchase Exposition in St. Louis. In this celebration of American nationalism, they spent one month in the Philippine Reservation, acting "as guides in the exhibition halls and as waiters in the mess hall," presaging the position of many Filipina/os as native informants and service workers.[19] The year 1907 saw the highest number of *pensionada/os* being sent abroad: 186 Filipina/os.[20] The *pensionada/o* movement lasted roughly from 1903 until 1910, when most of those who had participated returned to the Philippines.[21] In addition to the *pensionada/os*, other Filipina/o students traveled overseas, especially those from privileged backgrounds.[22]

Hence, the American colonial education system was arranged in tiers. As students ascended the academic hierarchy, they also drew closer to the regional centers, as well as to Manila. However, the pinnacle of colonial education and the mark of the highest prestige was study in the United States.

The majority of Filipina/os who came to the United States in the pre–World War II era arrived during the latter part of the 1920s and early 1930s, after the heyday of the *pensionada/o* program. Many came without scholarships, particularly men, dependent on the resources of family and friends and, most of all, on their own persistence and initiative. By the time of Bruno Lasker's 1931 study, there were "few government fellows." However, the Philippine school system had enlarged the pool of potential students who wanted to go to the United States, including some teachers who chose to continue their study abroad.[23] Not all students went to the United States—one article in the *Philippine Herald* brought to attention the presence of Filipina/o students in Japan who came under the public eye through their social misdeeds.[24] There is also evidence that some Filipina/os studied in Russia, such as Dominador Galvez, who was in Moscow in 1932 and could speak the Russian language.[25] In 1931, Eustaquir Sugintan reported to the Bureau of Insular Affairs that three Filipinos were in Russia "studying communists."[26] Clearly, the development of the Filipina/o community in Russia is a less documented part of the history of the Filipina/o diaspora that needs to be researched more fully.

But by far the heaviest traffic was to the United States. In the 1920s and 1930s, the expectation that young people would go to the United States had already been well established by previous waves of Filipina/os.[27] For example, Maria Orosa, a pharmacy student, first came as a stowaway, an unusual means of passage for Filipina/os and especially for women, and paid her own way through the University of Washington before receiving some funding from the Philippine government.[28]

Because many families did not have enough resources to send all their children to school, parents usually chose to concentrate their resources on assisting their elder sons. Gender and position in the family would prove to be two of the main determinants of who went to school and who did not. Because Rufino Cacabelos was the fifth of six children and the youngest of three sons, he had to wait his turn to go abroad. His mother "mortgaged a piece of land" so Cacabelos's brother Narciso could go to Seattle, as she hoped he would earn "honor and financial help to the family." Rufino Cacabelos, however, had to delay his entrance into fifth grade to help in the family farming. His uncle Fernando intervened and found him a job with Ramon Crisologo, an attorney, for whom Cacabelos did housework in exchange for educational support. Despite Crisologo's offer to provide him with an education at the University of San Tomas in Manila, Cacabelos's "spirit was already in America." His brother Narciso wrote to him about prospects in the United States, and his brother Luis, who labored on a sugarcane plantation in Hawai'i, another part of the American empire, was able to build a large home. Finally, Cacabelos's mother relented and took out one more land mortgage to pay for Cacabelos's passage to Seattle.[29]

Filipinas, even those who received considerable family support, had great difficulty in pursuing their educations, particularly because of gender barriers. Bibiana Laigo Castillano was a twenty-four-year-old teacher when her father asked if she wanted to go to the United States. Traveling with her brother James, she was the only Filipina in a boat of about three hundred Filipinos. Although she intended to continue her schooling in the United States, she was told by Pilar Mendoza, another resident in her boardinghouse, that it was inappropriate for her to go to school because of her age.[30] Castillano's acceptance of Mendoza's pronouncements suggests the lack of support available to women students, similar to what Judy Yung has noted about the difficulties faced by women in San Francisco Chinatown in their attempts to gain a university education.[31]

EDUCATIONAL DREAMS

In the decades around the turn of the twentieth century, when thousands of immigrants and their American-born children transformed the face of major urban centers such as New York City, public education was seen as a critical place where immigrant communities could be introduced to "native" American ways.[32] Progressive reforms during this period opened up educational opportunities for immigrants and people of color, but at the same time, they typically constrained occupational possibilities in order to produce workers who would continue to labor in the existing economy. As Gilbert Gónzalez writes, "In the final analysis, schools became the key institution for socializing the individual to the emerging corporate industrial order."[33] Gónzalez notes that the first five decades of the twentieth century were a period of "de jure segregation" for the Chicana/o community, despite considerable resistance from the community.[34] Similarly, in Hawai'i, Gary Okihiro has commented on the tracking of Japanese American students and others into vocational occupations, particularly into the agricultural industry.[35]

Educational segregation has been regularly contested by Asian American communities. For example, in San Francisco in 1884, Mary and Joseph Tape took the case of their daughter Mamie to court so that she could go to public school, and authorities responded by establishing an "Oriental Public School" the following year.[36] Thus, Chinese Americans, unlike Filipina/o Americans and Japanese Americans during this period, were expected to attend a separate school in San Francisco Chinatown, although they were able to avoid segregated schools in other parts of the West Coast.[37] Only in 1926 were Chinese American students able to enroll in Francisco Junior High, which enabled them to gain public education beyond the confines of the Chinatown community.[38] The Japanese American community also faced segregation until after 1907, when Theodore Roosevelt negotiated with the San Francisco school board to open up places for Japanese American students in public schools to placate Japan, an emerging world power that had greater international influence than China at the time. This concession came at great cost: in allowing Japanese students to enroll in white public schools, the American government required Japan to restrict laborers from gaining passports for the United States through the 1907 Gentleman's Agreement.[39]

The Filipina/os differed from other groups not only because many of them had prior exposure to the English language but also because they tended to enter educational programs in the United States on the secondary and university levels because of the American educational establishment in the Philippines. At an earlier stage, this was also the case for the Japanese American community. Following the Meiji Restoration, as part of its campaign for modernization, the Japanese government sent many young men to the United States and Europe on scholarships. Others also traveled abroad for education, often taking employment in domestic service to support themselves. In fact, from 1882 to 1890, over fifteen hundred student passports were allocated by the Japanese government, constituting over 40 percent of all passports for travel to the United States.[40] For Chinese Americans, too, whereas common laborers were largely barred from entering the United States after the exclusion laws initiated after 1882, students were one of the few classes exempted from this legislation.[41]

But by the time students such as Rojo and Braganza went to school in the late 1920s and 1930s, the other Asian Americans they met there were primarily American-born students who had parents in the United

States. It is not surprising, then, that the Japanese American and Chinese American communities were perceived as more privileged, particularly because they typically received more intergenerational support within the United States. For example, Teodolo Ranjo remembered that the Filipina/o students at the University of Washington wanted a clubhouse, like the Japanese and the Chinese. He commented, "Naturally, they were . . . older immigrants, they have richer parents and all that."[42] Unlike these other communities, the Filipina/o population largely consisted of young adult males with a small but significant number of women, and there were few second-generation community members at the time. Because of the separate waves of migration that resulted from legislative policies, a great many of the Filipina women in Seattle had come from the Philippines. In contrast, during that period in San Francisco Chinatown, 69 percent of the women were of the second generation.[43]

For many aspiring migrants, Seattle institutions were highly influential for a number of reasons. One, of course, was geographic. As both an international and a regional hub, Seattle was an accessible city. Coming on a direct route from Manila, students might have remained in Seattle because they did not have enough money to go elsewhere, and because it was easy to return home from there. Filipina/os, especially men, could maximize their work opportunities in and around the region; by staying in Seattle, they could find summer jobs in Alaska, nearby agricultural employment, or part-time work as domestics or as employees in service establishments around the city.[44] Many student workers were dependent on jobs to make their way through school and may have resigned themselves to exploitative working conditions that they felt were only temporary. The ability to find work, though, was very gendered, with men, who had greater mobility, having far more access to different kinds of jobs.

Area institutions offered special help for working male students. Agustin P. Palacol claimed in the *Filipino Student Bulletin* in 1924, "Self-supporting Filipino students have better facilities for work in this university than any other institution in the Union." For example, Eagleson Hall of the Young Men's Christian Association (YMCA) was an important place for students to find leads on employment.[45] At the same time, Seattle employers could take advantage of a cheap and relatively reliable pool of labor.

Academic reputation was another factor. A degree from the University of Washington was considered prestigious in the Philippines, especially because of the established flow of Filipina/os to the university. The school was promoted by Filipina/o alumni associations in both Seattle and Manila and by newspaper publicity through the three Filipina/o newspapers in the city.[46] The relatively low tuition at the University of Washington, a state school, also made it more accessible; Filipina/os could try to claim status as Washington and Alaska residents and thus qualify for lower resident tuition fees.[47] Prior immigrants who shared their knowledge with newly arriving immigrants also encouraged Filipina/os to take advantage of Seattle. Sylvestre Tangalan's cousin advised him to stay in the city, where Tangalan was able to attend Broadway High and the University of Washington.[48]

As these stories show, Filipina/os in the Seattle region could pursue their educations through a number of local venues. Before going to the university level, many Filipina/os first attended classes at local public secondary institutions such as Franklin High School, Garfield High School, and especially Broadway High School. Some students also pursued postgraduate courses at these institutions.[49] Even though the students still had to pay for their living expenses, the public high schools were free, since they were American nationals. By the 1920s, Filipina/os were already well represented at area high schools. Roman Simbe, who graduated from Franklin High School in 1923, remembered "more than a dozen at least" Filipina/os at Franklin High School.[50] A photograph of the Broadway Filipino Club in the Broadway High School yearbook of 1922 shows more than thirty members.[51]

While high school graduation itself was an achievement, many aspiring students hoped to obtain an undergraduate or graduate school degree. Filipinos could continue their educations at a number of local schools, including Seattle College (later Seattle University), St. Martin's College, or the University of Washington. Belen Braganza's educational record indicates the availability of different educational institutions for aspiring students. She recalled, "I graduated from Broadway High School in 1932[,] then I attended the University of Washington until '34. And when Seattle College (Seattle University) opened its doors to women, I attended the first co-ed class of Seattle U. and went there and took my Theology and Philosophy and Psychology[,] and then I went back to the University of Washington and finish[ed] in the school of Home Economics."[52]

Maria Abastilla Beltran also took advantage of a professional program offered in the Seattle area. She was able to study at Firland Sanitarium for training as a public health nurse, enrolling in a special two-year course at Firland in 1929 in lieu of a nine-month course at the University of Washington. As an intern in the contagious ward, she received the impressive salary of one hundred dollars a month along with room and board.[53] Although vocational training was available for both men and women, women were often found in training programs that led directly to careers rather than in professions that required extended university attendance. Not surprisingly, because women were expected to marry, they were under more pressure to gain quicker returns from their educational investments.

St. Martin's College in Lacey, Washington, was a popular alternative for many male students, particularly because it allowed students to use their earnings to pay for their schooling. Jose Acena went to St. Martin's for one year because, as he said, "Well, we can work out our board and room free."[54] Pete Filiarca recalled another strategy of "Filipino boys" to pay their way through the school: washing dishes for the college after mealtimes. Filiarca later attended Ellensburg Normal School (now Central Washington State College) and then the University of Washington. He was almost a senior when World War II began.[55]

Some Filipina/os had positive memories of their educations. David Guerrero remembered a favorite teacher at night school at Broadway High School. The teacher's husband was a dentist who gave Guerrero free dental care.[56] But Filipina/os were regularly reminded of their status as racial minorities. Felipe Dumlao remembered one joke from Broadway High: "'How you define Chinese, Filipino or Japanese,' he said, and things like that. 'The Japanese bow like this. Filipinos, the eyes go like this. Chinese, they run away like this.'"[57] Filipina/os displayed their resistance to these kinds of negative images in a number of ways. For example, John Castillo had to educate his classmates at St. Martin's College about the Philippines as "one of the greatest countries in the Orient." Castillo played upon his classmates' notions about people from the Philippines: "The first thing that comes to their mind is that Filipinos are nothing but headhunters. You know, yeah. They're savages. I was very much surprised to hear that. They said, 'Did you come from one of those tribes?' I said, 'Yeah, so you better watch out.' (chuckle) One of the best ways to scare them to death."[58]

THE UNIVERSITY OF WASHINGTON

Historically, the University of Washington has been a significant site for Asian Pacific America because of the opportunities it represented as a public state university within an urban center. For example, Gordon Hirabayashi, who would later become famous for his court case regarding the constitutionality of the U.S. government's incarceration of Japanese Americans during World War II, was in his senior year at the University of Washington when he challenged curfew and evacuation rulings in 1942.[59]

The University of Washington experience was not only important to the Seattle Filipina/o community because it was the premier educational institution in the Northwest region, but it was also well known in the extended Filipina/o community in both the United States and the Philippines.[60] For some time, not only were there more Filipina/os than any other "foreign student" population on campus, but there were also more Filipina/os at the University of Washington than at any other institution in the entire country. The *Filipino Student Bulletin* reported in April 1924 that the Filipina/os had been the most numerous "foreign" group at the university for the past four years and that their numbers peaked at almost one hundred during the 1919–1920 school year.[61]

In cultivating a pool of Filipina/o alumni, the University of Washington was addressing its interest in the Pacific Rim, as well as bolstering its role as a colonial metropole. When the Alaska-Yukon-Pacific Exposition was held on its grounds in 1906, the university's president, Thomas F. Kane, lobbied the regents for a course in Asian languages and literature in anticipation of trade with Asia.[62] World War I, however, inaugurated a new phase in the university's self-conscious positioning in global politics.[63] At the same time, the University of Washington was trying to compete as an alternative to more established East Coast schools.[64]

By the beginning of the 1920s, the drive to establish the University of Washington's reputation through an orientation to the transpacific economy was in full swing.[65] In May 1921, a special "Foreign Students' Number" of the school's literary magazine, *The Columns*, made its appearance, vaunting the university's "thorough[ly] cosmopolitan" and international nature. The university's eighty-four Filipina/o students represented the largest enrollment of Filipina/o students in any higher-education institution in the country. As one author noted, "Literally, then, there is the world at our door."[66] Throughout the decade, the university was highly aware of burgeoning trade possibilities with Asia, a reflection of Seattle's interest in the Pacific economy as a whole. As an editorial from 1928 predicted:

> The state of Washington, the Northwest and the nation as a whole will find increasing importance in the trade and commerce of the Pacific Rim. The geographical position and educational standing of the University of Washington make it a logical key which will help unlock the misunderstanding

and prejudice that has existed and does to a certain extent still exist. The acceptance of independent Oriental students here and the admission of American students to Oriental colleges is a healthy situation.[67]

Conferences, YMCA events, and other special programs showcased the foreign student population. The first Pan Pacific student conference was announced in the *University of Washington Daily* in February 1927. On campus, foreign students also met to discuss international issues in debates and club meetings. Filipina/o students often highlighted concerns about Philippine independence or other events happening at home.[68]

Further ties were built because the University of Washington was also a site for recruitment of personnel for Philippine institutions. Dr. W. W. Marquardt, a "Philippine educational agent," arrived at the university in 1921 to investigate the progress of seven students from the Philippines, as well as to recruit teachers.[69] An additional link between the university and the Philippines was provided by European American teachers and missionaries. An article in the *University of Washington Daily* profiled Jean Rothenhoefer, who had traveled seven thousand miles from the Philippines, where her mother taught high school home economics, to attend her mother's alma mater.[70]

Foreign students represented an efficient way to promote American influence overseas, since these American-educated Filipina/os would ostensibly return to the Philippines with deep sympathies to American interests.[71] The Committee on Friendly Relations among Foreign Students, a Christian organization that provided considerable support to Filipina/o students, including financial assistance, was founded by the likes of businessman Andrew Carnegie and was organized by the International Committee of YMCA.[72] Because of their international focus and religious mission, the YMCA and Young Women's Christian Association (YWCA) also supported foreign students. The YMCA played a prominent role among Filipino students, typically serving as the most important social space for foreign students and offering placement for employment.[73] The University of Washington also was diligent in serving its large foreign student population. To better accommodate foreign students, the university offered special advisers, setting a precedent for other schools.[74] In 1926, Elaine Swenson of the school of education reported that the university's prime location and inexpensive tuition gave it "the most acute foreign student problem." Because the big eastern schools had smaller and "select" foreign student enrollment, they had different responsibilities to foreign students. The University of Washington, claimed Swenson, was "the only large university getting at the heart of the foreign student trouble" through counseling and entrance examinations.[75] The university additionally inaugurated an orientation program for students who required further help with the English language.[76] Filipina/o students at the university even had their own alumni club. Vicente Navea, who was a political science graduate and studied for two quarters toward a master's degree in political science, organized the University of Washington Alumni Association in 1929. In 1930, the association held its first banquet for Filipina/o graduates, featuring an Archbishop O'Dea as the guest speaker.[77]

Despite these programs, the rhetoric that welcomed foreign students always had implicit and explicit boundaries. An article from 1919 entitled "Our Cosmopolitan Friends" neatly laid out the position of foreign students as temporary residents and future ambassadors: "It should not be our purpose to Americanize the foreign students, but we should afford them the opportunity to gain an appreciation of the highest ideals of American civilization which they can blend with the best of their own when they return to their home land."[78] As colonials, Filipinos had second-class status, even though new opportunities opened up for them as students in American institutions. Even American-born students of Asian descent were often seen as "foreign students," and thus put into a category that allowed for general exclusion. Judy Yung notes, for example, that the Chinese American women she studied in San Francisco were not able to join sororities and fraternities and were also regularly viewed as "foreign students."[79]

An editorial from 1922 reveals the resentment against foreign students who studied in libraries over the winter break: "Undoubtedly the American takes the only sensible attitude. Undoubtedly the intense and continuous application of the foreign student is a mistake. And yet, it is sometimes disconcerting to look up from the flower we are gathering by the wayside to see the foreigner striding past us into the leadership of his country."[80] Jane Garrot, who ran the International House, where all foreign students were welcome to find housing or company, pointed out that "foreign students are puzzled at the American students' exclusiveness; they don't expect the unfriendliness that they meet." Even James Gould, the dean of men, reported in the same article: "Lately there has been a growth of international feeling and with that somewhat of a breakdown of the antagonism, but there is yet lots of feeling against the foreigners and perhaps there always will be." Charles L. Maxfield, the general secretary of the university YMCA, referred to "the existence of an imaginary color line, which, however unnecessary and repugnant, remains a line of demarcation between Americans and foreigners."[81]

Housing segregation was quite typical in the university experience, as Filipina/os and other "foreign students" faced discrimination. A report by Chinese student Y. Y. Tsang on "Oriental students" found that they were often turned away by being told that the room in question was already taken or was for someone of the opposite gender. Housekeepers who were interviewed by nonforeign students reported preferring "American" students because they were afraid of "loss of patronage of American students" or depreciation of their property. For instance, a lease for the proposed site of the International House was eventually refused by the owner because a university professor did not want to live next to "dark skinned students." Reports were also made about discrimination at barber shops near the campus, most of which would not accommodate Chinese, Japanese, or Filipina/o students for fear of losing "American" students.[82] It is likely that area residents were less threatened by Filipinas. "Foreign" women had greater ease at finding housing than "foreign" men, probably because of their smaller numbers and because they often lived with families.[83]

In 1935, freshman Julius Ruiz provided harsh criticism of the treatment of Filipina/o students in an article entitled "Filipinos Resent Exclusion from Student Affairs." Ruiz claimed, "American university students despise us and look down on us and refuse to allow us the representation our numbers should entitle us to."[84] A few weeks later, a letter from V. Acosta Velasco strongly objected to Ruiz's characterization of the position of Filipino students. Velasco, however, undermined his own argument by carefully citing instances of inclusion that only threw the general rule of exclusion into relief.[85]

Trinidad Rojo claimed that, over time, racism against Filipina/os increased. He reported that sororities used to invite Filipina/os to parties, but then the situation changed. Rojo was likely referring to the increased hostility toward Filipina/os after the Great Depression. He further recalled, "Then still later on brave was a coed that would be seen with a Filipino walking across the campus." This racism should be considered within a wider context, however. Although Filipina/os encountered much racism, other groups such as African Americans faced even more. Rojo recounted, "It was lucky if I could see one Negro . . . studying there, because discrimination against them was even worse than against us at that time."[86]

Despite the barriers they faced, Filipina/os still created a memorable experience for themselves. They had boarding places run by a Mrs. Edwards and a Mrs. Garrett, and then "our Filipino place," a Filipina/o student house, on Brooklyn Avenue and Fortieth Street. A Dr. McAllen, a preacher, would visit on Sundays to minister to the Filipinos. About forty Filipinos lived there in an atmosphere of camaraderie despite economic hardship. Ranjo remembered: "Sometime we helped us a lot, you know, we are all by ourselves. We contribute whatever we can for our food. Sometimes we had to gather go and gather some fern . . . [at] the university campus. That's a good vegetable. Yeah, . . . good salad, depression time."[87] On a day-to-day basis, however, Filipina/o students appear to have been marginalized within a special "foreign student" space. One incident illustrates the character of their interaction with the majority culture, at least in the context of hazing. Roman Simbe remembered:

> In those days hazing was . . . pretty rough. . . . So stupid me, I wear a green cap and you know freshmen aren't supposed to enter Meany Hall then. . . . But you are not suppose to walk on the grass, you're not suppose to go in the front of Meany Hall and you are not suppose to talk to girls or anything like that. Stupid me down there, wearing a cap, we went down there in the front of Meany Hall and the vigilanties [sic] saw me down there, all white guys, they spread eagle me and gave me a good licking.[88]

Although it is not clear whether Simbe might have been targeted as a victim because he was Filipino, the anecdote suggests a university culture that did not readily incorporate Filipina/os. Even if they had time for leisure activities, Filipina/os and other people of color by and large lived a more segregated existence, despite disclaimers to the contrary.

RETURNING HOME

As I have stressed, Seattle was a colonial metropole, drawing men and women with the promises of education and the eventual return to a high-status job in the Philippines. The desire for education was a primary motivation for Filipina/os to emigrate to this country, and education provided a measure of status not only within the Filipina/o community but also in terms of how people perceived their own lives and work.

Typically, educated Filipina/os who returned to the Philippines took up residence in the cities. Benicio Catapusan was in touch with sixty-four Filipina/o student returnees, with 56.3 percent in "invariably responsible" jobs located in Manila, 31.3 percent located in the provinces, usually in teaching, and only 12.5 percent going back to their original communities.[89] In the first decades of American colonialism, educational investments offered ample rewards. New graduates found ready employment in the public school system and clerical field and through an American-created civil service.[90] For example, by 1911, *pensionada/os* might be sent for service to recently opened state educational institutions such as the University of the Philippines in Manila and the agricultural college in Los Banos. These new institutions, in turn, stimulated better educational opportunities in Manila. According to 1939 census data, Filipina/os formed 89.4 percent of the professionals in metropolitan Manila working as doctors, lawyers, accountants, engineers, and professors.[91]

The University of Washington had a good reputation in the extended Filipina/o American community. Enrique Navarro, interviewed in 1928, commented: "We regard it as an honor to carry back to the Islands with us the fact that we have been graduated from a school whose scholastic requirements are as high as Washington's. Then we find a friendly spirit, both teachers and students treating us in a friendly manner."[92] Almost a decade later, in 1937, student Julius Ruiz glowingly confirmed the positive returns of a University of Washington education:

> Most Filipino graduates now in the Philippines were graduated from Washington. Many of them today occupy business positions of high responsibility throughout the country. Others are heads of government posts.
>
> Washington's reputation in the Islands of being one of the best schools brings these Filipinos to its doors. Its educational facilities afford them the essential preparations for life. The students say the faculty members at the University understand Filipino individual problems.

Ruiz also noted the founding of an alumni organization in Manila that assisted fellow alumni in finding "jobs that are in conformity with their American college training."[93] Returning graduates could also seek help from the Committee of Friendly Relations among Foreign Services, which stated that it would "gladly render every possible assistance to Filipinos returning home," including help with tickets, routes, baggage, and letters of introduction.[94]

Numerous examples exist of University of Washington students who returned to the Philippines to land important jobs in teaching and government administration. One "success story" was Pablo Laigo, who came to the university in 1919 and supported himself by working summers in canneries and state factories. Laigo earned a bachelor of science degree in biology with a "certificate of professional training in education" and eventually returned to the Philippines and held a position at the Philippine Bureau of Education.[95] Florencio Tamesis, who earned a master's degree in forestry in 1923, rose to become director of the Bureau of Forestry.[96] Victorio Edades graduated from the school of fine arts in 1928 with a master's degree and became a "most outstanding mural painter in the Islands" and the dean of the fine arts department of the University of Santo Tomas. His wife, Jean Garrot Edades, who had a degree in drama, became a professor of English at the University of Philippines and "won recognition throughout the islands for her work as director of dramatics."[97] Maria Orosa returned to the Philippines after graduating in 1921; she eventually became the director of the Bureau of Science and even had a Manila street named after her.[98]

Nevertheless, not all returning graduates were given a positive reception. When landowner Manuel Tinio passed away in central Luzon in 1924, his son, Manolo Tinio, took control of his father's lands. With a degree in engineering from Cornell University, the younger Tinio was interested in mechanizing the farmland. To the intense dissatisfaction of the workers, Manolo Tinio not only became "stricter" and more socially distant but also stopped offering loans and instituted other practices that went against the perceived social contract. As the patronage system of the early twentieth century gave way to an emerging capitalist economy organized around American colonialism, land and population pressures pushed landless workers into an even more untenable position, eventually leading to the political dissension of the Huk Rebellion.[99] This anecdote illustrates the great changes occurring in the agrarian economy during this period and the disjuncture between the American colonial educations that Filipina/os acquired and the expectations of community members back home.

As time passed, the returns for education also became more meager. Social mobility was dependent on a number of external factors, such as the state of the American and Philippine economies. Growth prior to and during World War I promoted mobility in the "middling ranks," with fewer options toward the end of the 1920s and during the Great Depression.[100] In June 1930, a front-page story in the *Philippines Herald* reported "an acute intellectual unemployment the like of which has never been known in the history of the whole Ilocos region" as graduates from the Philippines and the United States were unable to find jobs.[101] In his 1931 study on Filipino immigration, Bruno Lasker reported that the availability of government, teaching, and private sector jobs had diminished, since many of the original openings had already been filled. As a result, students in the Philippines who had received preparation for white-collar jobs were thwarted in their ambition for upward mobility. This, in turn, led to more emigration to the United States.[102] Technically and vocationally educated graduates, such as engineers, scientists, and aviators, were in demand. United States–educated students who came back to the Philippines also had to compete with Philippine graduates whose vocational and technical education was specific to the Philippines.[103]

DEFERRED REWARDS ON THE AMERICAN MAINLAND

In the United States, most students took on jobs in order to pay for their educations, even if their status was relatively privileged. If Filipina/os were not presently enrolled in school, they likely were trying to save up money or were supporting other people's attempts to achieve education on a regular or intermittent basis. One author noted:

> The representative Filipino in the U.S. is a working man, whether student or not. The student does any kind of work to go to school. If he is not at present going to some school, he has, way down deep in his heart, the intention to finish his studies at some future date. He hunts for a job in order to live. Life to him is but one continuous struggle after another. It is work, work, work![104]

Many Filipina/os went to school not just for themselves but also, as noted earlier, because they were expected to help other family members. Typically, young men were perceived as the most logical investments for a family, with the hope that the family's sacrifices would eventually pay off in terms of the young man's financial contributions after graduation. Even if a family did not directly help to fund a student, its budget might still be affected by the student's lack of contribution. Thus, some Filipina/os, such as Juan Mina, chose to defer their educations so they could provide income for the family back home.[105]

The difficulties of earning an education were widely recognized among community members during the colonial era. Sylvestre Tangalan remembered: "Many of the elderly in Chinatown were really good students, some of them were . . . also teachers back home but because of hardship and then temptations . . . they were not able to go to college."[106]

Would-be students who could not attend school were forced to take "interim" jobs for economic survival. These workers, particularly men, joined others in relying upon a variety of labor opportunities in both the city and its rural surroundings. They found summer employment in

Alaska or sought jobs in agricultural labor, domestic labor, or service work in the cities.[107] Trinidad Rojo, a University of Washington student, spoke of how he supported himself while in school:

> But before I graduated, the routine was, during school days I worked in a Sorority or Fraternity or [with a] family, then I go to school. After three quarters I went to Alaska. Then I worked on the farm for about a month more before I went to school. The money we had in Alaska took care of books. . . . The money we had from the Sororities or Fraternaties [sic] were for monthly expences [sic], also for board and room.

Rojo reported that his salary of fifteen dollars a month, plus room and board, was actually at the top of the pay scale at that time. Regular wages were only ten dollars a month. To fulfill his job duties as an undergraduate, Rojo would go to bed at 9:30 P.M. and wake up at 4:45 A.M. to begin dusting and preparing the table for breakfast.[108] Similarly, Teodolo Ranjo supported himself by working in Alaska and waiting tables at fraternities and sororities. Student workers such as Ranjo who wanted to give their educations priority over their jobs were in a bind. Filipinos had to mesh their job routines with their class schedules even if doing so caused them to miss required classes.[109]

Many student workers turned to domestic work in private homes as another option. This path of employment was familiar to other Asian American groups as well. Chinese male workers had entered domestic service in the mid-nineteenth-century American West, moving into this traditionally gendered labor field because of the shortage of women workers who typically would have done this kind of work. Then, "Japanese school boys" also went into this occupation, their name supposedly derived from Japanese students who earned their educations through household labor in a Belmont, California, boarding school in the 1880s. Later, as Evelyn Nakano Glenn notes, the title "came to refer to any live-in Japanese apprentice servant, whether or not he was involved in formal education."[110] Glenn also notes the concentration of "Nisei school girls" in domestic service; this work was considered appropriate for young women because it was in keeping with the goal of educating them in household skills prior to marriage.[111]

The various names for this form of employment reflect the devaluation of the workers who performed it. In fact, as in the process described by Glenn, Filipino male students who were domestic workers became so associated with this work that they were called "school boys," like other groups before them. Pete Filiarca described a typical schedule: "Well, you have to help in the morning, breakfast. I serve the people that I work for. . . . then you do the cleaning and all the dishwashing and after you do that in the morning, you go to school. Then you come back in the evening again. That's all the job."[112] Other duties might include doing yard work or serving company.[113] The difficulty of the lifestyle depended on the particular employer. John Mendoza worked for one family who were proprietors of a printing company. Although Mendoza received free room and board, he earned only five dollars per month for his expenses. As a postgraduate student at Broadway High School, he brought lettuce and tomato sandwiches to eat at school for a whole year. His life was so difficult that he thought, "I will never go back to school if this is the way I have to earn it, never."[114] Domestic work paid so little that even agricultural work was sometimes preferable.[115]

For male Filipino students, cannery work was a time-honored tradition in the Seattle area, particularly because the bulk of the work was done in the summer, when school was out of session. Teodolo Ranjo remembers that contractor Pedro Santos gave preference to students: "Pedro Santos we call him Panyell, he use to favor the students. . . . [He] would hire students first before he gets somebody else because he knew we were struggling for better education and he believe[d] we were good workers. I had a nice job from Pedro Santos every time I went to Alaska."[116] Unfortunately, labor in the canneries did not guarantee that Filipinos would have enough to pay for their educational expenses. As Ben Rinonos commented, "When you got little money, only seasonal Alaska money, that's not to[o] much to go to school with."[117]

The prior example of successful students might have motivated prospective students, but there were no guarantees that they would achieve the same success, particularly after the onset of the Great Depression. Felipe Dumlao explained about the difficulties of going to school: "Everything, everything you move here is money. You don't have no home so in order that you are not going to suffer of staying outside, sleeping outside under the bridge, why, you have to have a job . . . you have to go to work." Dumlao found a "houseboy job" for ten dollars a month. He also tried going up to Alaska while school was out of session during the summer, as well as farming and picking strawberries and apples. "But," he remembered, "it did not materialize at all, my plan did not materialize at all." Dumlao managed to go to Broadway High School for six months, then he was "short of money." Toribio Martin also explained, "I wanted to go to school, but, you see there was hardly any chance to go to make it." After three or four years of going to school during the day and working at nights, Martin decided, "Well, heck with it. I might as well quit for awhile and make some money and then go back to school." Ponce Torres also left after a semester because he ran out of money and, as a newcomer, only knew about cannery work.[118] The challenge of realizing educational ambitions was not confined to the Filipina/o American community. In the period before World War II, many American-born Chinese Americans hoped to go into teaching and engineering, although the reality that they faced was segregation into the same economic venues to which their parents were confined.[119] A Stanford University study found that, similar to these Chinese Americans who wanted more choices in their future work, second-generation Japanese American adults sought jobs as engineers, doctors, and other professionals, thus hoping to move out of the agricultural labor that had confined earlier generations.[120]

Whether or not they attended school, Filipina/o community members were profoundly affected by the ideology of education. Lorenzo Pimental succinctly explained the reasons that he decided not to go back to the Philippines when he did not complete his schooling: "I was ashame[d] that my classmates in the Philippines, they thought I'm gonna be somebody when I go home."[121] Particularly because of the Depression, many immigrants were unable to fulfill their dreams of obtaining an American education. Eddie Acena remembered wanting to attend the University of Washington in 1929, but he recalled the difficulty of raising the fifty-dollar tuition.[122] One desperate Filipino, Buena "Benny" Lagpacan, made the front pages of the *University of Washington Daily* when he was caught hocking overcoats taken from university buildings at different pawnshops. On his fourth try, he was apprehended by the police and given a jail sentence of ninety days.[123] Even contractor Pio De Cano, who had not completed high school, gave funding to University of Washington Filipina/o students and registered as a special student at the university.[124]

As these stories indicate, pursuing an education was an investment, with very delayed returns. Felix Narte opted not to continue his studies because he arrived in the United States with a limited education: "So since I was only still in a low grade when I come to . . . this country, it makes no sense to go to school. It . . . [w]ould have been different if I was in high school when I come up here but, no, I didn't intend to go no more."[125] Even if the dream of earning a degree and returning to the Philippines seemed increasingly remote, it was still a measure of status and a longed-for ambition for many community members. Ray Edralin Corpuz decided to go "all over America on my own" and took on a series of jobs. Still, he always remembered his original ambitions: "I worked in the farms, I work in the city and sometimes I don't work either. But I never lost the sight of the fact that some day I would finish my studies and then I would go back to the Philippines."[126]

As the pool of educated Filipinos within the Seattle community grew, and many of these graduates did not return to the Philippines, the shift in numbers also affected local social and political relations. Some graduates were forced into the same kinds of menial labor that they had done on a "temporary" basis as students. Fred Floresca noted that "there were several college graduates from the University of Washington who were graduates in [the] college of education, and . . . they don't want to go to the Philippines [so] they stayed in the restaurant as dishwasher[s], washing dishes in the Olympic Hotel and some other restaurants."[127]

Despite the lack of opportunities because of racial and gender discrimination, former students still possessed status within the community. Because students tended to have highly developed communication skills and knowledge about the American educational and legal system, they were often quite valuable for other community sectors, particularly if they were men. Labor leader Chris Mensalvas spoke about his experience in California during this period:

> I thought I was going to complete my education here. I went to school in L.A. to be a lawyer. But I finally found out that Filipinos cannot practice law in this country. They cannot even own farms, nothing we can do. I got so disgusted I said, "Why am I studying law when I can't practice law in the States.["] So I quit. I spent three years in college. And then I went to organize our people on the farms.[128]

In addition to organizing, some students chose to use their talents in the field of journalism. The *Filipino Forum* was run by Victorio A. Velasco, and the *Philippine Review* was led by Vicente O. Navea, both University of Washington graduates. Later, Velasco and Navea combined forces to produce the *Philippine Advocate,* a contractor-dominated newspaper.[129] In this way, male students could use at least some of their academic training and attain influence within the community. Women, however, faced greater social barriers and family obligations, and thus had fewer options.

CONCLUSION

Education was a central aspect of the American colonial policy in the Philippines, and its promises drew many people to the American mainland. Yet, because of social and economic discrimination, even the most successful students were regularly forced into menial positions or common labor. An illuminating incident happened in the summer of 1934, when one Filipino community member was working in an Alaskan cannery. Partnered with a Native American high school student for a task, he began a conversation with the young man. He later recalled:

> Now I advised him to work hard so that once he graduate in the high school, he can get a degree in the college. You know the answer? The answer was very revealing. He said, "Look, . . . you have a master's degree and you are working with me. And I am only a high school kid." There was something in what he was saying. That even if he graduated from the university, there would be prejudice against him. That is what he was driving at.

When asked how he felt about the experience, this man replied that it was "all right because I am adjustable, I usually triumph over my immediate surroundings."[130] His "adjustable" position reveals the tension of being part of the intelligentsia in Filipina/o Seattle. He and other university graduates had much at stake in justifying the hard work and sacrifice required to send a family member to the United States for an education. Unfortunately for most Filipina/os, the hope of pursuing an education or even finding work commensurate with their training would remain an elusive dream.

Belen Braganza's story, which opens this chapter, further suggests the extent of barriers to education, particularly for women. Although she was able to attend school, her scholarly program was cut short because she was a woman. When Belen Braganza attended the University of Washington, she was the sole woman among 150 or 200 Filipino men. Despite her ambitions to become an architect like her father and to learn about math and architecture, she ended up studying home economics. She reported, "It was the choice of my uncle. A woman had to take [home economics] or Nursing. I didn't want to take Home Economics but it was preordained. I was told to take Home Economics."[131] Braganza also studied typing, accounting, bookkeeping, and shorthand even before she graduated from the university. This enabled her to make some money, and she was able to provide for her brother's and sister's educations "back home."[132]

As Braganza's story suggests, the impact of education upon the Filipina/o American community would be profound not only in terms of the resources available to community members but also in how it would reshape class aspirations and leadership opportunities. These individuals' stories demonstrate the promise of social mobility through education in the United States, as well as the double-edged sword represented by education in colonial metropoles because of continued social and political segregation. These hierarchies would be further compounded by issues surrounding social positioning within the Filipina/o American community, depending on factors such as gender.

Gary Okihiro writes about the Japanese American community in Hawai'i in the era through World War II: "The contradiction was that the tools provided by education and sharpened by dedicated teachers within classrooms infused with the ideals of democracy would eventually unyoke the bonds of planter rule and transform the political order."[133] Education also transformed the Filipina/o American community, but with other kinds of resources and experiences, these issues would be resolved very differently within Filipina/o Seattle.

PART TWO

Working the American West

CHAPTER 3

Region and Labor

The link between migration and labor formed a fundamental part of the reality of almost all Filipina/os in the American West. For example, Paula Nonacido, another early pioneer to the Seattle area, made several choices shaped by the experience of migration and the pull of job opportunities. Born in the Bicol province, Nonacido was the second of five children. She "took nursing" at a hospital in Manila and then decided to continue her education in the United States. She came with a woman friend in 1926, working first in a hospital in Cleveland for three years, then in New York. Nonacido remembered that there were around fifteen Filipina nurses in New York. In fact, they had their own group—the Filipino Nurses Association. While in New York, Nonacido also attended Teachers College at Columbia University for six months.[1]

Nonacido came to Seattle in 1932 because her friend had a baby, probably to provide companionship and support. She found a job as a private nurse. On the suggestion of contractor Pio De Cano, Nonacido also contributed to the local community, assisting inebriated Filipinos at the police station by vouching for them to help them get released.[2] Seven years after arriving in Seattle, Nonacido returned to the Philippines because of the outbreak of World War II and her concern for her mother. The following year, however, she came back to the United States to do more professional research in Seattle, Tacoma, and other sites. She then crossed back to the Philippines in 1941, although, because of the war, she had to argue to a Commissioner Elizade that she would "be responsible for my life" so she would be allowed to go.[3]

Like many other Filipina/o American pioneers in the United States in the pre–World War II era, Nonacido was extremely mobile, following both educational and professional opportunities around the country, and back and forth across the Pacific Ocean. Her migration and employment choices were also very much determined by a variety of social and political networks. Nonacido first went to Seattle in 1932 because the friend with whom she had journeyed from the Philippines had a baby. She returned to the Philippines in 1939 because she was worried about her mother. She was integrally involved in the Filipina/o community, even helping out Filipino men in her community when they got into trouble. Nonacido's story also illustrates political networks. She was part of a Filipina nurses group in New York and secured government funding to return to the United States. Her trips back and forth indicate the political connections between the United States and the Philippines and her strategic use of these ties in her professional career and her personal responsibilities.

Nonacido's tale thus points to the intimate connection of migration and labor in the lives of Filipina/o Americans in the pre–World War II era. Virginia Scharff has written in a recent essay, "I think it is time we stopped envisioning women's history as a narrative chiefly about attempts to establish geographical stability (what might be called 'home on the range'), and begin to accord itinera[n]cy the historical importance in western women's lives that the record suggests is necessary."[4] My task in this chapter is to explain how migration and labor shaped Filipina/o Seattle, as the community not only was formed as a result of its strategic locations for those coming to the United States but also was informed by the regular movement of workers to and through its site. As suggested by Nonacido's story, these issues have always been historically linked for Filipina/o workers. In fact, one of the notable issues that Carlos Bulosan's *America Is in the Heart* documents about Filipina/o life in the Philippines and the United States prior to World War II is that migratory labor in the United States was an extension of the displacement and the search for work in the Philippines.[5]

By focusing on migration strategies and their connection to labor opportunities, my research points to the pivotal role of region in defining and shaping the position of Filipina/o Seattle. Sarah Deutsch argues about the Chicana/o experience, "But a group with as large a migratory element as Chicanos calls out for a study that will go beyond the bounds of a single geographically defined community, a study that will link, as the migrants themselves did, the disparate sites of Chicano experience: the home village, the city, the fields, and the mining camps." She reminds us that analyzing only one community or one site "distorts not only the picture of Chicano experience in the region, but even the Chicano experience at that site."[6] Similarly, the goal of this chapter is to place Filipina/o Seattle within that expanded context called for by Deutsch. To focus on Seattle without looking at what happened in California, Alaska, and other parts of the American West would be to miss vital dimensions of what Filipina/o Seattle represented for the primarily migratory Filipina/o American population at that time. Seattle was a crucial site precisely because the community was so fluid, not only in travel between the Philippines and the United States but also within the United States itself. Rather than looking only at the established community set up by year-round residents and focusing on a single place within Seattle, it is important to widen our gaze to understand the position of this community within multiple migrations to and through the city, migrations organized by economic and transportation networks, U.S. capitalism and colonialism, and the complex social networks that so determined the lives of Filipina/os there. Thus, understanding the role of Filipina/o Seattle helps us, in turn, to understand the workings of American imperial culture and also provides insight into what it meant to be a worker in the American West.

MIGRATION AND LABOR

On the American mainland, since well before Dorothea Lange's famous images of the dust bowl migration brought the issue of migrancy to the general public's attention, migrancy has been an essential part of the American culture.[7] Migration, for example, has always been pivotal to the shaping of the American West, particularly with the influx of so many different groups to the region. One reason was that migration was usually a job requirement for those who engaged in common labor, often performed by traveling men. David Montgomery describes these workers:

> They moved continually, and unlike the iron puddler or railroad machinist who might also rove about in search of work, laborers belonged to no particular industry. On the contrary, they were necessary to nearly all forms of manufacturing, transportation, and commerce. Even an effort to distinguish between industrial and agricultural laborers is thwarted because most of

them were of rural origin, and consequently they persistently quit steel
mills or road construction in the heat of summer to harvest sugar beets,
wheat, or cotton.[8]

For many communities, the movement of adults in a family in search
of work was one way to counter lack of employment opportunities for
the family as a whole, in addition to offering other advantages such as
allowing these family members to see new sights.[9] Furthermore, the travel
of workers in the pre–World War II era was tied to the improved transportation systems and the expansion of corporate businesses in the American West. Dennis Nodín Valdés notes in his study of Mexican agricultural workers in the Great Lakes region that Detroit automakers were
able to bring the cost down of cars in the 1920s, making them more accessible to industrial workers and also increasing the pool of available
used vehicles.[10]

Like many of his generation, Carlos Bulosan, the most famous Filipina/o
American writer chronicling the pre–World War II era, had an extended
and mobile relationship with Seattle. Bulosan first arrived there in 1930,
spent time in the city in the last years of his life in the 1950s, and was
buried in a Seattle cemetery. Bulosan and other Filipina/os repeatedly returned to Seattle to find out about employment elsewhere or in the city
itself. Located between California and Alaska, Seattle was a logical and
convenient stopping place for workers in their travels across and through
the whole of the West Coast. It was the midpoint in the regional search
for work, particularly for men, and usually the site where people would
return following a seasonal stint elsewhere. As the interface between agricultural and cannery work, Seattle represented a temporary but reliable
reprieve in the ceaseless grind of labor for many. In the same way that
Los Angeles was a touchstone for the Mexican American community,
and Chicago was a central site of labor for Polish Americans, Seattle
formed an integral space to the mapping of Filipina/o workers. George J.
Sánchez, for example, has noted concerning Mexican migration to Los
Angeles, "Unlike foreign newcomers to other parts of the United States,
Mexicans who settled in Los Angeles were often seasoned sojourners who
chose this city after careful exploration of other options."[11] Like their
Chicana/o peers, Filipina/os also utilized urban sites, attaching different
kinds of associations to each place based on personal networks and the
ability to secure resources.

The Filipina/os who came to the American West were heeding the siren
call of the global economy. Similar to many other groups during this pe-

riod, Filipina/os provided a convenient labor force for employers because they were subjugated by racial oppression and were vulnerable to legal and political restrictions. Hence, they were easily expendable and easily replaceable. As part of their marginal status, Filipina/o workers were an exceptionally mobile group, ready to take on nearly any kind of work to make ends meet. Even Filipina/os who were doctors back home in the Philippines were confined to agricultural labor or other kinds of menial work.[12]

Gender had great impact on what people could and could not do, and this is partly why women who were not part of family households in agricultural areas were often concentrated in urban sites. The experience of Bibiana Laigo Castillano is instructive in this regard. While she was staying with her uncle in a boardinghouse, he became concerned about all the attention she was receiving from men. Even though her uncle was six months younger, he still had greater authority within the family in terms of determining Castillano's options. She remembered:

> "You know," he said, "we have to move from this place to another place." "Yeah, why?" I said. "There are so many men here. I don't want you to associate with all these men. You know I don't like to be responsible for you. I don't trust these men," he said.

Castillano recalled, "Well to make my story short, my uncle told me three months afterwards, 'You know I was thinking, you'd better get married or else we should send you back to the Philippines.' 'Why? I did not come here to get married. How do I get married? I do not know anybody.' He said, 'Oh, we'll help pick out a man for you.'"[13] These issues resonated in other communities as well. As Jane Kwong Lee told Judy Yung about her experiences in San Francisco Chinatown in the early 1920s: "At heart I was sorry for myself; I wished I were a boy. If I were a boy, I could have gone out into the community, finding a job somewhere as many newcomers from China had done."[14]

The men, in contrast, had very different options. For virtually all the "old-timers" who emigrated to the United States during this period, asking about their first years on the mainland will bring forth a long litany of work experiences in various locations. Even the fortunate few who were able to attend schools in the United States generally supported themselves through menial labor, unless they were lucky enough to have a government scholarship.

Location also radically shaped people's resources, and here a discussion of Hawai'i helps to throw into relief the experiences of the Filipina/o

American workers on the mainland. Because the Philippines and Hawai'i were U.S. territories in the first decades of the twentieth century, they had similar political and educational systems. The central role of the sugar economy in the Philippines and Hawai'i was another key similarity, and Hawai'i was known among emigrants for its employment opportunities. In addition, Hawai'i sometimes served as a means for reaching the American mainland. Indeed, some Filipina/os who arrived in the United States had already been to Hawai'i. During the 1920s, for example, 15,801 Filipino men and 1,624 Filipina women left from Honolulu for the ports of San Francisco and Los Angeles.[15]

Knowledge of this important migration to Hawai'i also influenced people's sense of possibility. Felix Narte, who left the Philippines in 1924, recalled: "Well, as I said, there are people that went to Hawaii. When they come home it looks like a million dollars so we thought we could go out there too and make the same like that, the way they look when they come home."[16] Zacarias Manangan also remembered the significance of seeing the money that other emigrants sent back to the Philippines: "Those that went to Hawaii, you know, they were sending all that money back home and you know, by doing that why it arouse . . . our feelings to come abroad."[17] These comments suggest how the Hawaiian Sugar Planters' Association (HSPA) actively sought workers, particularly men, to work on plantations on Hawai'i, O'ahu, Maui, and Kaua'i.[18] When Leo Aliwanag was sixteen, he "heard in Cebu" about agents recruiting people to work in the Hawaiian sugar plantations. For every recruited laborer, the agent received ten pesos.[19] Around 120,000 Filipina/os came between the years of 1906 and 1935, primarily through the HSPA, although the association stopped "active" recruiting and paying round-trip passage to Hawai'i after 1926.[20] One of several groups targeted by Hawaiian sugar planters to labor in the fields, Filipino men often sought to earn money quickly and then go back to the Philippines after the expiration of their three-year contracts. A small number of women and nuclear families also emigrated for work.[21]

By and large, Filipina/os worked in some of the hardest and least remunerative segments of the plantation industry. In 1930, 85 percent of Filipina/o laborers were unskilled workers, who were especially vulnerable to changes in the economy. In 1932, when the demand for pineapples dropped in the United States, over six thousand workers lost their jobs. The HSPA redirected these workers to the sugarcane fields and also reduced the numbers of Filipina/os entering Hawai'i.[22]

Despite their similar experiences, Filipina/o workers in Hawai'i had different resources than those on the American mainland and also faced barriers that were particular to their situation. For one thing, the Hawai'i workers could rely on the fact that plantation laborers, particularly other Asian Americans, were the majority population in Hawai'i and thus wielded more political clout. While people might have had more constraints on where they could be in Hawai'i because of the limited choices of work, the very fact that there was less opportunity outside of the plantation may have made them more determined to protest the conditions on the plantations. Furthermore, although Honolulu was also a colonial metropole in a largely agricultural space like Seattle, Honolulu was primarily a center for the U.S. military, and its main value was as a transshipment site in the commercial movement of people and goods to other places. In addition, racial dynamics were very different in Hawai'i, where people of color were the primary part of the population. The Kanaka Maoli, the native peoples of Hawai'i, formed a significant demographic base and the majority of the voters. Also, with their sizable numbers, Asian Americans as a group were able to secure more political gains than in places where they formed only a small part of the population on the U.S. mainland.[23]

In both Hawai'i and other parts of the Filipina/o diaspora, workers also moved *within* industries, such as the Pullman porters documented by Barbara Posadas who had jobs on railways around the country.[24] Railroads offered other kinds of employment, too. Some Filipina/os worked on railroad track construction and maintenance. Felix Narte was employed in 1927 on the Great Northern, changing railroad ties and leveling the ground for twenty-nine cents per hour. He got the job in Seattle through "Japanese employment." Narte labored in a gang of about forty to fifty that traveled to "where they needed us." With the advent of winter, he came home to Seattle after nine or ten months.[25] Teodolo Ranjo worked in a section gang on a railroad, where the crew was assigned tasks such as placing salt on "the switches on the track . . . salt melts the snow or ice . . . so they can operate the switches." In Ranjo's crew, there were "about ten of us, some Hindus plus Filipinos," including "an ex-cop in the Philippines" who was "very good in pistol shooting, target practice."[26]

Antonio Rodrigo's three-year stint as a railroad worker left memories of a vibrant work culture. Working five days a week, the railroad workers traveled by boxcar to where they were needed along the railroad line. Rodrigo shared his boxcar with another Filipino and two Japanese men. In addition to hunting rabbits and fishing, Rodrigo remembered hearing a band that had Filipino, Mexican, and Swedish members.

He also recalled playing baseball with the women in a town, whose men had gone west to find "bigger opportunities."[27]

A great many Filipina/os worked in the U.S. military forces, particularly those who labored on the Pacific. This kind of employment was an essential option for Filipinos, particularly as their status as U.S. nationals enabled them to obtain jobs in the U.S. military.[28] As mentioned earlier, Filipino naval laborers, like their African American counterparts, were usually relegated to galley and mess hall employment, racialized occupations that were often gendered as "women's work" on shore. Nevertheless, navy jobs were a viable employment alternative for Filipinos, and their numbers rose greatly, in part because African Americans had been banned from naval service. Filipinos continued, however, to encounter difficulty in getting promoted, moving into other jobs, and obtaining shore leave.[29] These issues reveal how groups might have faced different forms of treatment because of race, even if discrimination was a relatively common experience.

For those brave enough to work on the seas, the transpacific economy ushered in additional employment opportunities. In 1928, Fred Floresca labored as a cook in a "government steamship" that traveled to Alaska for over half a year. Floresca decided not to stay in the position, as he reported, because of "not being a good sailor." In the course of working, he found many Filipino and Japanese stewards. The Filipino stewards "could hold a job there and stay permanent" until they accumulated twenty years of service and retired.[30]

Another site of employment was in the private maritime sector. In 1930, the number of Filipinos in the U.S. Merchant Marine reached 7,869, although the count usually remained between 5,500 and 5,800 in the years 1925 to 1932. Filipinos faced discrimination here as well. Andrew Furuseth, president of the International Seamen's Union, relied on racial stereotypes when he argued against the employment of Filipinos: "The reputation of the Manila man, as we seamen call the Filipino, is that of being treacherous, swift with the use of the knife, and always in the back." After the Merchant Marine Act of 1936, which required 90 percent of the crews on ships bearing the American flag to be citizens of the United States, many Filipinos were unable to serve, since they were no longer American nationals following the passage of the Tydings-McDuffie Act of 1934.[31] The Filipinos employed on the seas were especially mobile. In 1933, a New York law firm tried to find nine Filipinos who were wanted as witnesses for a case in Seattle concerning the March 1931 death of engineer Robert Curry on the vessel *Sagebrush*. The firm asked the office of the governor general for a "public announcement" as reported by the *Philippines Herald*.[32]

The relationship of migration to labor for Filipina/o workers thus ran the gamut. Overall, many workers stayed in the Philippines or took part in regional migration within the Philippine economy. A portion of the population went to Hawai'i and remained there, while others relocated elsewhere after a period of time. Some joined the U.S. military or worked on the seas, traveling within a single industry. Still others moved to the cities, engaging in urban labor while attending school or deciding to stay there for other reasons such as family ties. The main part of the predominantly male workforce, however, engaged in a regional migration throughout the American West Coast, circulating between Alaska, California, and points in between.

MANAGING WORKERS

When these Filipina/os reached the American West Coast, they found a racially stratified economy. In the latter part of the nineteenth century and the early twentieth century, Asian American populations were larger on the West Coast than elsewhere in the mainland United States. In California in the 1860s, for example, Asian Americans formed over 9 percent of the population, although this percentage would decrease over time, particularly following the enactment of exclusion laws. The visible presence of Asian Americans was tied to transformations in the western economy. For both the northern and southern regions of the United States, expansion to the West became a way for capitalists to increase profits as well as a means for people from these regions to find better opportunities. According to Edna Bonacich, two general forms of capitalism were established in California. The first, dependent capitalism, focused on three businesses—agricultural, mining, and railroads. Connected to the export of raw materials, dependent capitalism was tied to resources from the eastern part of the United States and Europe. The second kind of capitalism, Bonacich writes, "was an indigenous, multifaceted, manufacturing capitalism that grew out of the small-producer class, much as in the northern states," such as the growth of the oil business and the movie industry in the early decades of the twentieth century.[33]

By 1910, 26 percent of the predominantly Chinese American and Japanese American population worked in agriculture, forestry, or animal husbandry. A substantial number, 40.3 percent (compared with the national percentage of 9.9 percent), were in domestic and personal service. Within that group, over 25 percent were laundry operatives and servants.[34] During this same time, the United States was consolidating its interests in the Philippines, developing another significant pool of laborers that would help to build the American economy.

In general, the economic containment of Filipina/os was supported by legal restrictions, similar to those that applied to other Asian American groups at the time. With the justification of racism and imperialism, capitalists could exert greater political and legal control over Asian workers. From the mid–nineteenth century onward, Asian Americans were subject to a number of exclusionary laws, culminating in the Chinese Exclusion Act of 1882, which forbade the immigration of Chinese workers for ten years. This prohibition was extended through subsequent legislation until 1943. Following the pattern of the Chinese, other Asian groups were subject to similar legislation. The 1907 Gentleman's Agreement between the United States and Japan, through which Japan was to regulate the movement of workers, was accompanied by an executive order curtailing the migration of Japanese from Hawai'i to the American mainland. However, because arranged marriages were allowed, the picture bride system, named for the use of photographs and correspondence to set up these matches, enabled men to bring in women for marriages. Exclusion, though, was realized through the Immigration Act of 1924. As Korea was colonized by Japan, Korean migration was also affected by regulations enforced against the Japanese. In addition, after 1905, Koreans were prevented from migrating to the United States by their Japanese rulers. Indian migration was also curtailed in 1917 through an immigration act, also called the "barred zone" law, that restricted immigration primarily from Asia, including India.[35]

Because Filipina/os were American nationals, their migration was not limited in quite the same way, although they did suffer from legal oppression in the form of prohibitions on landownership and antimiscegenation laws; after the passage of the Tydings-McDuffie Act of 1934, they were no longer permitted easy entry as American nationals. In addition, because of the extreme racism of the time against all people of color, Filipina/os shared with other groups the common experience of exploitation and segregation. Perpetually marginalized, they found their options constrained by a plethora of laws that forced them into the least remunerative work available.

Citizenship, for example, was one way in which Filipinos were subjugated. Filipina/os had a unique status compared with other Asian groups because, as residents of a U.S. territory, they were American nationals and thus had open passage to the United States. As colonials, they were exposed to an American educational system and the English language in the Philippines. But, like the Chinese and Japanese before them, Filipina/os found that their legal rights were also severely curtailed. Filipina/os could not be excluded from passage to the United States, but, as nonwhite immigrants, they could be denied American citizenship. In 1925, the *Toyota vs. the U.S.* case before the Supreme Court resulted in a ruling that Filipina/os could not become American citizens unless they had been members of the navy for three years. Seven years later, the Hawes-Cutting Act was passed; it prevented all Filipina/os from becoming citizens and began a quota system that allowed one hundred Filipina/os to enter the country each year. Finally in 1934, the Tydings-McDuffie Act closed immigration from the Philippines.[36]

The settlement of Filipina/os was further inhibited through obstacles to landownership. The Alien Land Law, enacted in California in 1913, prohibited Filipina/os from owning land in that state.[37] In Washington, Filipina/os were also barred from owning land during the 1920s and 1930s. It was not until 1940 that Pio de Cano, a community leader, won a court case that allowed Filipina/os to buy property.[38]

State governments had still other means at their disposal to discourage permanent Filipina/o settlement: the antimiscegenation laws. The California legislature banned marriages of white persons to Filipina/os in 1933 through amendments that included Filipina/os. Washington was one of the major exceptions that allowed for interracial marriages, which accounted for a significant portion of the heterosexual, nuclear families within the Seattle community.[39] Hawai'i was another important context for nuclear family formation.[40]

With few available jobs, Filipina/os were compelled to take whatever pay they could find, particularly after the ravages of the Great Depression. Economic anger and racism translated into systemic violence against Filipina/os, and those who migrated to find work were particularly vulnerable outside of the relative safety of places such as Seattle Chinatown. Zacarias Manangan recalled:

> They see you walking in the street, you know, they called you bad names. And mind you some of the boys cannot take this insults, you know, and they have to fight. That was the beginning of these riots down there. And another thing is, I believe they blame the Filipinos are accepting low wages. . . . We were forced to get these low wages because that time it was Depression then, you know, and in order to live you have to have a little money for the bread.[41]

Racial epithets that dehumanized Filipina/os were common everywhere in the region. In his 1938 dissertation on the canning industry, Lauren Casaday reported that common nomenclature for Filipina/os in the Northwest included *goops, goo-goos,* and *ear-wigs.*[42]

In 1930, Watsonville, California, was the site for one of the most famous anti-Filipina/o incidents when resentment against Filipina/o workers on the part of the local white population exploded. As a population of mostly young males, the Filipina/os were perceived as a threat to the white community because of the attention they paid to local women and the rupture in racial etiquette caused by their showing off through cars, clothes, and the courting of women. These men were considered dangerous, particularly because of the threat of sexuality.[43] The crisis began when Filipina/os rented space to open a club and hired white women from Guadalupe, Santa Barbara County, as dance partners. In response, a mob of vigilantes enforced the racial code of the area through harassment and violence, even aiming bullets into cars containing Filipina/os. Finally, one week after the mob actions began, twenty-two-year-old Fermin Tobera was shot in the heart by a raiding party and killed. Eight people were sentenced as rioters and were minimally punished. One effect of the incident was that Filipina/os left for other areas and kept a low profile in and near Watsonville.[44] Some Filipina/o leaders in California who organized the Filipino Emergency Association requested "leniency" for the eight men, a reflection, perhaps, of the vulnerable political position of Filipina/os.[45] Tobera's body was returned to the Philippines, and February 2 was declared a national mourning day there to remember him.[46] After the incidents at Watsonville, a well-publicized debate about the political status of Filipina/os ensued, including discussions about Filipina/o exclusion and independence.[47]

The Watsonville incident also underscores how the disenfranchisement of Filipina/os was bolstered by the often lukewarm, if not indifferent, response by the police. Filipina/os were well aware of the racialized system of justice. Ray Edralin Corpuz commented on the lack of political options for Filipina/os:

> The caucasians burn and shoot without even telling, it was a big incident [Watsonville]. But what recourse did we have? We didn't have any. We tried to talk to the people in power at that time but it was worse that [sic] talking to a wall. . . . If you go in there, not only in California, I observe this in Chicago too. you [sic] fight with some other groups caucasions, no

questions asked, you go to jail, whether or not the case had been investigated, it's was your fault.[48]

Hence, workers encountered strict limitations and racial hierarchies within the U.S. economy. Furthermore, European immigrant male laborers became part of the labor movement in ways that people of color and women of all backgrounds largely could not. European male immigrants, for example, could gain citizenship and typically worked in advanced industries in which they had greater flexibility and support in labor organization.[49] In contrast, most Filipina/o Americans found work in a select number of industries that were more difficult for unions to organize.

WORKING THE WEST

The majority of Filipina/os who arrived in the United States prior to the Great Depression fit the profile of the most sought-after workers—unmarried young men in the prime of their lives and unencumbered by nuclear families. For example, in the years 1925–1929, California received 24,123 Filipina/os. Of these arrivals, 22,767 were male, and 1,356 were female. Over four-fifths of both men and women were under thirty.[50]

The overwhelming number of Filipina/o immigrants at this time were men engaged in migratory work on the American mainland. Toribio Martin, who landed in Seattle in 1926, was typical of this phenomenon:

> Right away I went to Alaska, worked for the canneries down there. We been getting sixty dollars a month for four months work. And after that we came back to Seattle. That's the kind of life we are use[d] to . . . we follow the season. From Alaska we seek other jobs like agricultural jobs, when you don't find in Seattle. We go to Montana to pick beets and you go to California to pick oranges and after that—why—winter comes, that is the hardest part of our life.[51]

As Martin suggests, movement in the American West (map 4) was determined by the time of the year and the demand for seasonal labor. Workers were thus dependent on the farmers' needs. A bad growing season could wreak havoc on a laborer's plans to earn income; a farmer's ability to find cheaper labor could undercut the salary-earning potential of whole crews of laborers. As Honorato Rapada recalled in 1975, "Even you like to work before, it's hard to look for job. Besides it's too cheap. You got to move like hell before you can get something."[52]

Given their meager wages, the main way that migratory workers could

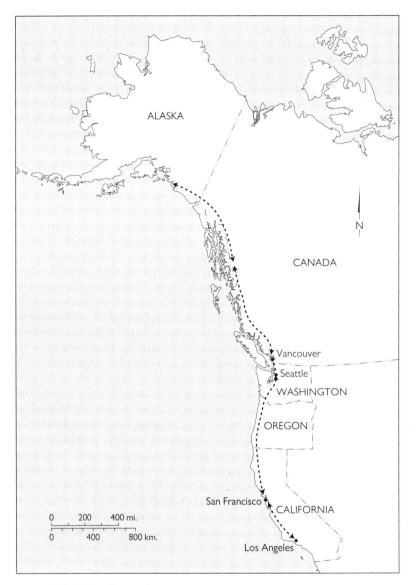

Map 4. The West Coast migratory route.

stay afloat economically was through rapid movement among seasonal jobs, thus reducing to a minimum the times without income. For the most part, Filipina/os were on the move. In the span of a few years, many Filipina/o laborers traveled thousands of miles.

On the one hand, the constant mobility in search of work was dictated by the relegation of Filipina/os to the lowest forms of labor. They not only were engaged in migratory work with low pay and virtually no job security but also were marginalized even within this type of employment. The best migratory jobs still went to white workers rather than Filipina/os or other people of color.

Mobility was also influenced by education. Education radically shaped the community's sense of possibility as a whole, which also changed people's orientation to work as it was seen as a temporary situation until education could be secured. Education also opened up other possibilities, which might have led people to try out different professions as opposed to, for example, settling down on a farm.

It is crucial to note prohibitions to settlement, such as alien land laws or the general racism of many areas of Seattle.[53] Not being able to own homes was an obvious deterrent to settlement. Another was the general difficulty of finding year-round employment and of starting up businesses. While some Filipina/os did own businesses such as restaurants or stores, most did not. The argument that this was so because many came from an agricultural economy and may not have brought entrepreneurial skills with them is somewhat limited. For one thing, Filipina/os typically engaged in dramatically different kinds of labor than they might have in the Philippines, and lack of prior experience was not necessarily a deterrent. Industrialized salmon cannery work in Alaska, for example, was not at all like most agricultural or urban occupations that Filipina/os might have held in the Philippines, and yet they still entered this field.

A major explanation for this pattern might have been the economic context that Filipina/os faced. Filipina/os, many of whom came after the migrations of Chinese Americans and Japanese Americans, entered a segregated community in which ethnic entrepreneurial possibilities were very slim, and limited to a small range of businesses like restaurants and lodging houses. Hence, the cost of raising capital and starting up a business was already very high. This is likely one reason why World War II, which brought the horrific and unjust incarceration of Japanese Americans in concentration camps, also resulted in the movement of other people of color into business spaces that were opened up by the absence of Japanese American community members. In addition, some Filipina/os might

have had relatively easier access to other work because of their familiarity with English and the ability to find jobs outside of the enclave. This
potential to find work elsewhere also might have been a disincentive to
enter commerce, which was extremely competitive.

In any case, one of the few assets that Filipina/os had within the
American workplace was their ability to move quickly from one place
to another. Given their limited options, mobility provided them with
at least a few choices for work. If they did not like a job, they always
had the recourse of leaving. Continual migration offered another major advantage—it was one way for Filipina/os to avoid racial violence.[54]
For example, people on farms could escape to the relative safety of more
urbanized areas. Ben Rinonos recalled, "I didn't suffer anything myself,
but I hear some boys did. In the farms. But for myself, I didn't. We used
to hear about [a] threat . . . then we could go away from it."[55] Thus, familiarity with transportation modes was crucial in the search for work.

The transportation networks that crisscrossed the West Coast, particularly the railroads, were well known to Filipina/o migratory workers.
Toribio Martin told an interviewer that the men would ask yardmen
about train destinations, then surreptitiously climb on board.[56] Sammy
Lopez never "hopped" the trains himself because he was too scared of the
dangerous consequences: "Oh, very, lots of them got killed, some of them
got hurt."[57] One community member, Al Bautista, told a particularly har-
rowing story about riding a freight train in 1931 and being trapped in a
locked car when it was left five miles out of the railroad yard on a side
track. The twenty people on the train panicked, and Al Bautista almost
shot off the lock after seven hours of waiting. Luckily, a railroad worker
happened to pass by and heard their cries for help.[58]

Riding the freight trains was dangerous but cheap, a crucial consideration for those who did not have any money to spare for transportation. Filipina/os who rode trains did not have to worry about the initial
investment or subsequent maintenance costs of owning a car. People also
could save transportation fees, especially if they were not sure about job
prospects at their destinations. Juan Mina explained the rationale for the
freight train rides: "Because they only have a few dollars, they want to
save their dollars for meals so they got a free ride on the freight train.
They even travel from coast to coast and lots of them traveling south or
north. . . . Oh boy, it was a struggle."[59]

Another common way of gaining mobility was to pool money with
other Filipina/os to buy or lease a car, spreading the cost and risk within
a group.[60] Honorato Rapada remembers: "You know Filipinos before,

maybe four or three Filipinos, they buy one car, together, see. To use go all over, look for job. . . . After finish the job you gonna move again."[61]

Workers could travel as a group or take turns using the car.[62] Cars saved vital time for workers who sought better employment options, especially because they needed to move quickly to find seasonal work. This mode of transportation was not without peril, however. Two brothers, Nicholas and Julian Panlo, tragically died when their car was hit by a train. The train engineer said that the brothers did not "heed his warning signals" and tried to "beat him to the crossing."[63] In another accident, a car carrying nine Filipina/os struck another car, killing its driver. Three of the Filipina/os were wounded.[64] Despite these dangers, migration continued to be a dominant feature of the community's experience, as workers sought to make the best of their constrained options.

SOCIAL NETWORKS

In this process of labor migration, one of the primary resources that Filipina/os had was each other. Ray Corpuz, for example, remembered going to Chicago, New York, Seattle, New Orleans, and "all areas in California." In a striking passage that underscores the vulnerability of Filipina/o workers to the vagaries of casual labor, Corpuz reported:

> Well if it's a freight train, we just climb on the train and hopefully we go where we want to go, to look for a better life and sometimes we travel from here to maybe Colorado, lucky we got a dollar . . . hopefully you'll find a "kababayan" a Filipino and talk with them and see if you could find a job. At that time you work for today and forget about tomorrow and also at that time maybe you are a good worker but your smile doesn't satisfy whoever, the boss. Off you go, no questions asked, not until I would say, the outbreak of the war.[65]

Relationships with other Filipina/os often provided the emotional and economic sustenance that enabled Filipinos to move through their work lives. Whether or not an individual decided to use actual or fictive kin ties helped to define the contours of relationships among people. Relationships to other people were key, and if traditional forms of relationships were absent, one could create new ones.

In an interview conducted in 1976, John Mendoza spoke of what it was like to be a young Filipino an ocean away from home: "In the Philippine Island[s], well maybe you don't know it but we Filipinos are a very, very close type families, you know. All the families, even if they get married, they stayed at home. But when I came over here nobody seems to care, you know. They don't even talk to you, they just hate." These comments are striking because they seem to summarize much of the alienation faced by the young Filipina/os. As they indicate, going to the United States was more than just leaving family behind. Filipina/os also lost a sense of themselves as connected family members in an intergenerational setting, although this was more pronounced for men than for women because women typically received more scrutiny. Mendoza discussed the kind of lifestyle that resulted from the absence of family regulation for young men:

> We don't go and steal . . . we just go and pick a fight . . . every day there's always a fight and . . . then that develops in knifing and shooting and everything else. Yes, yes sir, because you don't know, seventeen years old, first time to get away from home nobody tell you, "Don't do this, don't do that." Where as [sic] at home, you know, you better look out, don't do anything wrong because you will be punish by your parents, but over here nobody.

Enjoying the relative freedom of the American culture, these men engaged in behavior that probably would have been censured back home, the fights and the "smoking and stuff like that."[66] As Mendoza's memories indicate, to leave the Philippines was a wrenching experience, despite the excitement of adventure or new opportunity. However, this did not mean that new arrivals to the United States came devoid of ties. Filipina/os found familiar relationships in their new homes and actively made and remade relationships in this new context. These social relationships bound Filipina/os over great distances and were a primary means of maintaining a sense of community and a sense of self.

Emigrants who came to the United States were accustomed to operating within a dense mesh of relationships. Literature about Philippine culture emphasizes its close-knit ties, regulated by well-defined systems of obligations within families and communities. As F. Landa Jocano writes, "It is through kinship that much of the local authority, many rights and obligations, and modes of relationships are expressed, defined, ordered and systematized." Generation and seniority, as well as education and economic wealth, also determined a person's position within the social system.[67]

Kinship was generally considered bilateral—relationships with the mother's and father's side tended to be weighted the same, and a person maintained relationships with both sides. Ties between community members were also strengthened through fictive familial relationships. *Compadrazgo*, or ritual kinship, reinforced kinship ties through sponsors named in times of baptism, confirmation, and marriage. Ties were created between parents and godparents and, by extension, the siblings of *compadres* and *comadres*, thus bonding families closer together. Godparents were selected to help raise children, and children were expected to treat and help godparents as real parents.[68]

According to Jocano, one's social world was defined by kinship, whether actual or ritual. Because kinship was one's primary relationship, giving help to kinspeople had priority over helping others. Withholding help from a kinsperson was considered a move not only against one's own parents but also against one's kinspeople as a whole. Even if a person traveled to a distant destination, it was important to find kin there before becoming members of other groups.[69] Frank Lynch, in his classic essay about social acceptance, writes, "The average Filipino considers it good, right and just that he should go to his relatives in material need, and that he should seek them out as allies in his disagreement with outsiders. Security is sought not by *in*dependence so much as by *inter*dependence." As a result, even if a group may have difficulties with a person's action, it will typically support the person in a conflict with a person from another group. Conflict is then engendered between both groups. This has important implications for the social relations of a community and is partly why, according to Lynch, "smooth interpersonal relations" are highly valued in Philippine society.[70] One community member explained that many organizations functioned within a community ethos that was predicated upon reciprocity. He stated, "Oh and remember . . . this is still Filipino . . . you do a favor for me, I'm forever indebted to you for the rest of my life."[71]

Jocano also identified a number of values that characterized social relations. These are *hiya*, which entailed knowledge of what kinds of behavior were considered appropriate; *utang na loob*, or the system of reciprocal obligations; *pakikisama*, or getting along with other people; *galang*, or respect; and *amor propio*, which dealt with one's sense of self and status.[72]

As these comments indicate, social relations were highly political and formed a central part of community culture. "Family" for the prospective immigrant was thus an expansive concept that included not only immediate relatives or members of the extended family but also townmates and other Filipina/os met while traveling, working, or going to school. Because of the vulnerability of migratory workers, who were largely men, social ties were especially essential for community members far away from their home villages and towns in the Philippines. Through "family," one could potentially receive support in the many sites of the West Coast that were focal points for the Filipina/o American diaspora. The meeting of migratory workers and the stable sector of the community reconfigured relationships, creating new possibilities for social status. How this ideology took shape in the United States, however, was affected by the drastically different environment.

"Home" for this largely migratory population thus seems not so much tied to a particular location as to a group of people. Most migratory workers relied on these social ties to survive, as in Vincent Mendoza's case. In 1938, Mendoza's cousin returned from work in Alaska and was en route to California with "some townmates" who had a "jalopy Ford." Because the cousin wanted to stay with him and Mendoza had "no money saved" (at the time he was funding the education of a brother back home in the Philippines), Mendoza decided to go with his cousin and the other men to California. Mendoza's memories indicate the importance of social ties in the decision-making process of these workers. Mendoza's cousin chose to find work with friends from the same town, and significantly, Mendoza decided to give up the security of his own job in order to be with his cousin, even though he was supporting a brother's education back home. Together they shared the cousin's money and, along with the two townmates, traveled cheaply in a car, making their own food and sleeping in the car to save money.[73] The image of these men traveling in a car on highways en route to California provides us with a sense of the function of work groups in the United States. Lorenzo Pimental also remembered traveling and living with friends to pool resources. As he recalled, "Some of us got a decent job, some don't. Some people are lucky. So we help each other."[74] These relationships between young men were paramount to economic, if not emotional, survival, particularly in the work sites where these men labored: the Alaskan salmon canneries, the Californian agricultural fields, and Washington State industries.

THE ALASKAN CANNERIES

Beginning on the Sacramento River in 1864, salmon canning spread north to the Columbia River, the Puget Sound, British Columbia, and, in 1878, Alaska. Utilizing first Chinese and then Japanese, Mexican, Mexican American, and Filipina/o workers, cannery owners found these people of color communities a cheap and exploitable workforce. Native American and European American populations were also primary sources of labor, with the balance made up of other groups such as African Americans, Puerto Ricans, Hawaiians, and Koreans. Filipina/os first appeared officially in labor statistics in 1918, although they began working in the canneries even earlier. A peak year for Filipino involvement in the canneries was 1930, when Filipina/os constituted almost 30 percent of the 14,135 shore workers.[75] Some Filipina/os also worked as ore sorters, in places such as the Alaska-Juneau Gold Mining Company at Mount Roberts, below Juneau.[76] The majority of Filipina/os who came to Alaska, though, worked in the salmon canneries. Almost all were men, a reflection of general demographic patterns, although there were some women pioneers as well. For example, Socorro Elorde, who came to the United States with her cousin Mateo Ylanan, resided in Ketchikan in the early 1930s.[77]

Because of the distance of canneries from possible employees, male migratory workers were a critical source of labor, drawn largely from major cities such as Vancouver, Seattle, Portland, and San Francisco. As seasonal workers, they could be brought in to can the fish and then released as soon as they were not needed, thus reducing overhead costs. Seattle was a primary place of recruitment, especially for canneries in southeastern Alaska. Felix Narte recalled about finding work in Seattle: "Before you leave to Alaska you have to go ther[e] [to the contractor's office] and ask if you could get a job for that time, so when they said, 'oh yeah, you come with us,' we get ready for that until it's time."[78] Zacarias Manangan also remembered the hiring halls and the tips about possible jobs that Filipinos could obtain through friends.[79] Sacramento, Stockton, Fresno, Los Angeles, and especially San Francisco were some of the other major sites for recruitment of seasonal workers.[80]

The importation of migratory laborers meant fewer jobs for the local population, sometimes resulting in anger and frustration. In one case, when fifty Filipina/os were brought in for work in Ketchikan, twenty-seven white workers were let go. The stated rationale for this policy was the company's desire "to try and protect our investment against professional trouble-makers." When three white women confronted the cannery superintendent for hiring Filipina/os over local white women, the superintendent falsely claimed that the Filipina/os came upon their own initiative, although many Filipina/o interviewees related that they had come as contract labor. Other racial and ethnic divisions also emerged in the canneries. Although historian Lauren Casaday found that people of Filipina/o and Mexican descent related "without great friction" and that African Americans had some affinity with those of Mexican descent, tensions arose between the Japanese and the Filipina/os, Mexicans, and

Chinese. Casaday also reported that Native Americans were positioned low in the social hierarchy.[81]

In the early days of Filipina/o participation in the salmon canneries, the labor contract system was the dominant feature of the industry. Companies could depend on contractors, usually from the same ethnic group, to find and maintain a workforce that could be dispensed with at the end of the season. Because contractors had to be able to recruit workers swiftly and with minimal warning, it was in the contractors' interests to instill some loyalty in their workers, even though contractors' profits depended on exploiting the labor under their control to the maximum extent possible.[82] Although the original contractors were Chinese and Japanese, some Filipina/o contractors emerged, such as Pio De Cano and Pedro Santos.[83] Further changes in the contracting system involved the role of foremen. Casaday reports that from 1925 to 1934 there were shifts in the contracting process, as contractors started to use foremen as employees to hire crew members.[84]

Because of their reliance on ethnic ties to build crews, Filipina/o contractors could offer jobs to fellow townspeople while at the same time leaning upon these ties to command loyalty from their workers. In 1914, Pedro Santos became the first Filipina/o contractor to set up shop, followed by Valeriano Sarasal. Pio De Cano, who began working in the canneries in 1916, initially was a foreman and then secured his first contract in 1927. Later, after Valeriano Sarasal died, De Cano appears to have assumed Sarasal's contracts. Although most of these contractors were male, a few women were involved in the contracting business, such as Pio De Cano's sister, Placida De Cano. After the death of her husband, Bibiana Laigo Castillano also attempted to run his former contracting business.[85]

Sebastian Abella, writing in 1931 after spending five summers in the canneries, reported that cannery jobs were "like a gamble." The season usually ran from May to August, although workers typically were employed for two to four months. Work was dependent on the number of fish. Smaller runs meant less work for the laborers, but if great amounts of fish came in, employees were forced to work "like machines" and received minimal bonuses.[86] Workers would spend the season processing, cleaning, and cooking the salmon, packing the cans into boxes, and then labeling the products for shipping. A company paid the contractor a certain sum per case, with an assurance of a base number of cases.[87] Carlos Toribio remembered that when there was a big catch of fish to process, workers were expected to labor "twenty-four hours straight."[88] As

Trinidad Rojo wrote in a poem about cannery work, laborers dreaded the flush periods: "The fish, let it run low / To give us less to do, Or let the work be through / So home we go."[89]

Conditions in the canneries were severe and coercive. Workers were essentially at the mercy of the bosses. A 1928 contract by Goon Dip and Company for employment at the Pacific American Fisheries in Port Muller, Alaska, underscored the harsh treatment of workers. According to a contract for one worker, the length of the season would be determined by the contractor, until all the fish was canned and ready in cases for delivery. Workers were expected to labor from 6:00 A.M. to 6:00 P.M. The worker would be paid $240 for the season "as butcher machine and other work," with twenty cents per hour overtime. A sum of $2.20 would be paid for labor on Sunday during the fish run. If the employee did not want to work overtime or on Sundays, he or she would be fined fifty cents per hour not worked. If employees decided to "strike, refuse to work, cease work, or demand higher wages," then other labor would be substituted. The employees would lose pay to these workers and have money deducted to pay for their food and board. If problems arose in the operation of the canneries, employers could transfer workers to another cannery or let them go and pay them only for the time in which they worked. The employer provided round-trip transportation for the worker from Alaska, but if the worker did not stay for the whole season, he or she could not get return transport to Seattle, and round-trip transportation costs would be deducted from his or her wages.[90] As this contract revealed, contractors controlled virtually every aspect of the worker's livelihood, in an effort to augment financial returns to the greatest extent possible. A former foreman and subcontractor, Justo M. Jose, even reported the use of guns and clubs by foremen in order to threaten the workers.[91]

In general, contractors worked to separate workers from their wages. Contractors made arrangements with companies and furnished laborers, but they could extract additional money by skimping on food, lodging, supplies, and transportation.[92] For example, contractors could offer advance meal tickets for restaurants in which they had economic interests. Because these restaurants often charged higher prices than other places, the larger food bills would send the worker even further into debt to the contractor. Workers might also be "advised" by contractors to buy higher-priced clothing and other goods at particular businesses, leading to additional profits for the contractors.[93] Inadequate housing was a further means to increase contractors' profits, as contractors would save on the costs of building lodging for their workers. Housing in Alaska, according to one worker, might consist of a bunkhouse with a board for a bed; workers had to provide their own blankets.[94] "A little privacy" could be gained when workers erected their own partitions.[95] Housing was also racially segregated. Before unionization, Filipina/o and white workers had separate living quarters and eating arrangements.[96] Overpriced supplies offered by contractors in Alaska were another source of income, as contractors could monopolize the selling and distribution of goods. Teodolo Ranjo recalls that contractors could extract pay by "selling you all kinds of stuff, you know, soaps and shoes and hats and things like that. By the time you get back you are already in debt, you have to borrow again from them."[97]

If these exploitative conditions left the workers with any money, there were still other ways to appropriate the remainder. Unscrupulous contractors and their foremen had a variety of illicit means of generating income at their disposal.[98] Some sent male prostitutes to Alaska, a cause for alarm among reformers, especially because of the perception of homosexual activities as perverse. These issues typically appear in the historical record as "deviant behavior." Paying for the service of prostitutes resulted in the further dwindling of workers' income.[99] Another way to get money from workers was through gambling. Labor contractors hired professional gamblers, ostensibly employed as "kitchen help," who would keep 10 to 25 percent of their winnings and pad the contractor's wallet with the rest.[100] Some hapless workers lost their money in gambling on the boat even before they returned to Seattle and were left with no money to pay for a taxi to their hotel.[101]

In a frontier situation such as Alaskan cannery work, social relations might also be in more flux than in other sites with greater social surveillance. A striking photograph of ten Filipino men, entitled "Pinoy 'he-men' at a cannery off-day with two workers in grass skirts and another in a dress," in Fred Cordova's *Filipinos: Forgotten Asian Americans*, suggests the fluidity of roles in a culture with such drastically different ethnic, racial, and gender demographics from those in more established settings. The central figure in the photograph is a man posing playfully in a dress, flanked by two bare-chested men in grass skirts. The other seven men are bare-chested as well, with one man ostentatiously clasping his hands in his front to better frame his chest.[102] Susan Johnson's research on the gold rush era suggests the need to consider the range of sexual expression and other personal relationships that might have taken place in these contexts, particularly given the unbalanced gender ratios and the absence of the observation of "back home."[103]

In general, for example, gay and lesbian relationships are seldom discussed in the history of this labor migration, except in relation to the exploitative practice of male prostitution mentioned earlier. Here, the generally negative emphasis on gay relationships by the dominant culture is clear. As one participant stated in a National Industrial Recovery Administration hearing on the Code of Fair Practices and Competition held in San Francisco in 1934:

> To be very frank with you, women are not permitted to go on these ships, but moral perverts are shipped on these ships, by whom, we do not know. Our information is that these perverts are dressed in women's clothes after they get on the ship and prey on the men that are shipped to Alaska. Now, that is a condition that should not be permitted, so far as minors are concerned, and the best way to prevent it is to bar minors from transportation.[104]

A Mr. Morris remarked that this arrangement "is a graft between them and the foreman." He reported, "The system is getting those young fellows to spend their money, buying them candy and tobacco and anything they want, and also from the Alaska Packers' store and the stores that they [sic] foremen has." In revealing imagery, these relationships were characterized in terms of a marriage. One questioner, a Mr. Filippi, asked about "a certain marriage ceremony performed, at least we have been informed of that." Mr. Morris responded, "That is why these fellows, why they go up, and the fellow that looks right to them or spends the most money with them, why, they consider as their husband."[105] More research is needed not only to explore the possible exploitation of these young men but also to investigate how they might have utilized limited economic opportunities, as well as made active choices in the expression of their sexuality. Although this historical document conveys the view of these relationships as a problem, it also can be seen as suggesting that a wide range of social ties existed in the American West.

Filipino workers in Alaska did interact socially with women, particularly Native American women. Mateo Ylanan remembered the relationships of Filipinos to "natives": "Well they come up here in Alaska to work in the Cannery. Of course, all that trips, all that men coming up here every year, every summer, well, they start to become acquainted with the people, the women, then they start getting friends with them."[106] Women from other backgrounds also became part of the Filipina/o American community. For instance, Salvador Del Fierro met his wife, who was of Italian American descent, in Alaska.[107]

A permanent, year-round Filipina/o community was established early. By 1910, a total of 246 Filipina/os were living in Alaska.[108] Cristitoto "Joseph" Llanos, born in 1896 in Cebu, was an early pioneer. After laboring in San Francisco as a domestic worker for the Spreckels family, he eventually moved to Ketchikan and worked as a baker, using skills he had learned while working for the Spreckels. He then met and married Jessie Milton, a Tsimshian Indian originally from Metlakatla, with whom he would have six children.[109]

Upon returning to Seattle, workers back from the cannery season with money in their pockets were lured by the sights and businesses of Chinatown.[110] Gambling, prostitution, and other activities were all pleasures offered by the enclave geared toward the primarily male migratory population. Filipina/os could use their hard-earned dollars to eat, drink, and socialize. But all too soon, it would be time to replenish their quickly disappearing funds by beginning the cycle of migratory work anew. Pete Filiarca explained the seasonal rhythms of the population changes in Seattle: "Yes, well lots of these boys they go to Alaska, then when they come back, lots of them have no money left, because they gamble, and they go to California to work on the farms. And then when it's time to go to Alaska, they come back again. That's why you see so many Filipinos here during the month of May, June and July."[111] Some workers secured agricultural jobs through contractors; others chose to stay in Seattle for the winter using credit extended by contractors, thus guaranteeing crew members for the contractor in the following year.[112] Ben Rinonos recalled, "Some of the boys that don't like to go to California stays in Seattle all winter. I think, no can find job, so what can you do?"[113]

Overall, seasonal work in the Alaskan canneries was characterized by low pay, harsh and dangerous conditions, extortion, and coercive treatment. If workers were lucky, they would eke out enough money for survival until they assumed other seasonal jobs in the West Coast economy. Inevitably, when cannery season approached again, Filipina/os would arrive in Seattle, jockeying for a position as a cannery crew member. But if these positions were coveted, it was less an indication of the desirability of the jobs than of the economic marginalization that made cannery work one of the few viable options for Filipina/os. At the same time, however, the power of these memories suggests not only the perseverance and skill of community members in cannery labor but also the strength of social ties as a resource.

THE SEARCH FOR WORK: THE CALIFORNIA FIELDS

The Filipino men who left cannery work at the end of the season to travel south to California headed for a wide array of agricultural jobs. In California, the development of large-scale land monopolies by growers enabled the industrialization of the agricultural industry.[114] Irrigation was the key to the progress of California's agricultural empire, "the shaping force in the region's history," as argued by Donald Worster.[115] Water made it possible to turn the region's production from extensive crops such as grains to intensive crops that required more manual workers. By 1929, over three-quarters of California's agriculture was directed to the production of fruits, vegetables, and cotton.[116] Cletus Daniel has commented about the Imperial Valley during this period that, "with its large-scale production, absentee corporate ownership, labor-intensive crops, and seasonal reliance on an army of nonwhite migrants, the valley's agriculture represented industrialized farming in its most extreme and unalloyed form."[117] Agricultural monopolies ruled the state. In the hearings held by Senator La Follette's Committee to Investigate the Violations of Free Speech and the Rights of Labor in 1939, Paul Taylor reported that of the 150,000 farms in California, fewer than 3,000 controlled a large share of the agricultural output. In other words, 2.1 percent of these farms were responsible for 28.5 percent of the value of agricultural production in the state and were primary employers for the two hundred thousand migratory workers who came to work the crops.[118]

The richness of California agribusiness was made possible through the labor of underpaid migratory workers. Filipina/os who joined Mexicans in finding work in California followed a way paved by Chinese, Japanese, Italians, Portuguese, Armenians, Asian Indians, and Koreans.[119] Filipina/os were among the last workers to enter the agricultural fields, as restrictive legislation greatly curtailed the previous waves of immigrants. With the specter of diminished numbers of Mexican workers following the Immigration Act of 1924, California agribusiness turned to Filipina/os as a likely source for labor.[120] Through this set of circumstances, California farm labor became a mainstay of the Filipina/o American experience.

Through the Depression, Filipina/o men and women engaged in agricultural labor, especially because their job prospects remained poor in the cities. Although men far outnumbered women, women played a significant role in Filipina/o American culture and economy. Frank Mancao, a contractor and photographer, took one group photograph from

this period, in approximately 1931, that symbolized the central importance of women and children: three women and two children are surrounded by forty-two men. In addition to raising their families and performing the extensive labor required to run a household, women worked
with men in the fields and often prepared food for the workers. Other
labor could include entrepreneurial activities in stores or restaurants, selling "Philippine finger foods," or washing and sewing for other people.[121]

Juan Mina explained the pattern of seasonal work, which was mostly
undertaken by transitory men. He related that jobs were available in California throughout the year, as long as workers would follow the crops.
For example, while there were few jobs in Salinas Valley in central California during the winter months of December through February, Filipina/os
could find work farther south in the Imperial Valley, near Mexico. This
work lasted until late spring, after which the summer brought weather
"hotter than an oven." Then it would be time to migrate north again to
find more work.[122]

Filipina/o laborers were used by farmers for asparagus, lettuce, peas,
tomatoes, citrus fruits, cantaloupes, cotton, and other produce.[123] Working these crops was backbreaking, and returns for the laborers were typically minimal. Garciano Garo remembers making ten cents per hour during wintertime in the Depression, and netting only five cents per day after
paying the daily seventy-five-cent charge for room and board.[124] Toribio
Martin commented, "Those days we work from hand to mouth that's all.
From day in, day out."[125] Furthermore, as agricultural workers, Filipina/os
were highly vulnerable. Changes in growers' decisions about crops, labor surpluses, and bad weather could push Filipina/os across the economic line from bare subsistence to destitution.

As in the canneries, contractors served as mediators between the workers and the growers. Filipina/os labored under the padrone system, in
which workers would move in groups of five to fifty for jobs. They were
usually overseen by a contractor, often a Filipina/o. Under this arrangement, growers were freed from the responsibility of supervising workers and also benefited from the competition among contractors to extract the greatest amount of labor from the workers.[126] Leo Aliwanag
remembered a variety of ways to get jobs. Contractors would meet the
ships to find workers for towns such as Maple Valley and Stockton. Workers could also use subcontractors or, in some cases, dispense with contractors altogether by traveling in groups of two or three to find farm
work, thus resisting contractors' attempts to control their labor.[127] Because there was a surplus of Filipina/o workers, some growers were able

to increase the amount of labor per acre, such as in asparagus, resulting in higher yields. This translated into less money for the workers and more profits for the grower.[128] One worker complained about a contractor's strategy: "Yes, he is putting money in his pocket and he gives us only just barely enough to eat."[129]

Living conditions were difficult. As migratory workers, Filipina/os were constantly exposed to weather that was far more variable than the tropical climate they remembered from the Philippines. In California, for instance, they had "blackfrost," which Vincent Mendoza described as being worse than white frost. In one camp, Mendoza slept "down there in the barrack on the ground," and he recalled being itchy, probably because of fleas. The barracks had only a galvanized roof and a wooden wall, and conditions were so cold that he finally went into Stockton and bought a bed and quilt.[130]

Relations between Filipina/os and other workers were mixed. Ethnic and racial divisions were strong prohibitions to interethnic alliances. A strike in 1928 by the Workers Union of the Imperial Valley (La Union de Trabajadores del Valle Imperial), composed of Mexican and Mexican American agricultural laborers, separated those of Mexican descent from employees of other backgrounds.[131] However, Mexican, Mexican American, and Filipina/o workers together went on strike in the Brawley area of Imperial Valley in 1930, their numbers swelling to some five thousand farmworkers. While the Mexicans, who formed the greater portion of the strikers, could be threatened with deportation, the Filipina/os were nationals and could not be so intimidated. Organizers from the Trade Union Unity League, led by Communists, created a division of the Agricultural Workers Industrial League to bolster the strike. The workers' efforts, however, were crushed by growers and an array of governmental authorities and affected by actions from leaders of the Mexican Mutual Aid Society.[132]

Connections among workers could also be made on a more personal level. Catherine Bilar Autentico recalled her mother having "Mexican 'comadres,'" an indication of the pivotal role of networks among women.[133] Furthermore, there were also marriages between Filipino men and Mexican and Chicana women. In 1939, Tony Siquiz, a thirty-five-year-old Filipino, began courting his future wife, Lily, a twenty-one-year-old Chicana, at a time when interracial marriages were illegal in California. Then, it came time to make the big decision. As Lily Siquiz remembered, "He [Tony] didn't want to wait any longer because he needed to plant his crop." When Tony approached Lily's father to ask for her hand in marriage, Lily's father grew angry and told his daughter that she would be disowned if she married Siquiz. In defiance, the couple drove to New Mexico, where interracial marriages were legal, and said their vows there. When they were interviewed in 1995, fifty-five years later, they were still in love and had eight children, twelve grandchildren, and three great-grandchildren.[134]

In addition to working with other communities, Filipina/os also mobilized on their own. In December 1933, the Filipino Labor Union was organized; it eventually expanded into seven locals and some two thousand members. In Salinas, California, roughly three thousand Filipina/os struck the lettuce fields in August 1934, meeting with heavy resistance. In order to break the strike, Filipina/os were rounded up, one labor camp was destroyed by fire, and seven hundred Filipina/os were run out of the area.[135] Felipe Dumlao remembers the conflict in California from 1933 to 1934 as "the biggest fight in California."[136] Another Filipino was a strikebreaker who worked under armed guard as Filipina/os, Mexicans, Portuguese, and white workers struck outside.[137]

Filipina/o workers in the fields of California were subject to onerous and poorly remunerated working conditions. Even given their limited options, however, they still demonstrated various modes of resistance to their circumscribed position. When conditions became particularly abysmal, the Filipina/os could always move again, hoping to find other work. By forming work groups or circumventing the contracting system, they could gain some power. Organizing in the fields, although it was countered with stiff opposition from the growers, provided another crucial venue of protest. Far from being passive about their circumstances, Filipina/os actively sought ways to improve their means of attaining a livelihood, regularly asserting themselves in a colonial environment that often treated them harshly.

WASHINGTON STATE

Along with Hawai'i, Alaska, and California, Washington also formed a critical site in the American West for Filipina/o Americans. For example, in the central region, the Yakima Valley was another main source of work for Filipina/os. Along with the Wenatchee Valley, the Puget Sound Basin, and the Walla Walla and Spokane Districts, the Yakima Valley was primarily devoted to fruit growing.[138] It was famous for crops such as apples, pears, hops, and asparagus, and agriculture provided a major source of work for migrants.[139] In June, four thousand workers were needed,

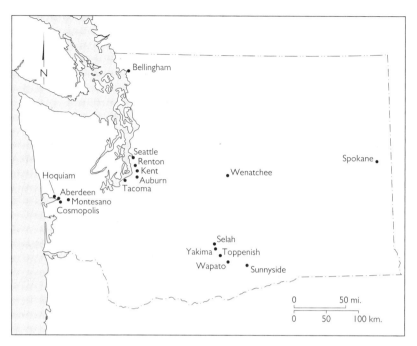

Map 5. Washington State.

but by September, twenty-five thousand would be required, particularly for the apple, peach, and apricot crops. Seventy percent of the jobs lasted for no more than a week. A total of thirty-three thousand resident and migrant workers were needed to harvest hops in September, which, according to Carey McWilliams, was considered "the lowest form of field labor." Almost all the workers who came were white, with the remainder composed of some thousands of Native Americans from British Columbia, Montana, and Idaho and a few hundred Filipina/os.[140] These Filipina/os were frequently recruited from Seattle for this low-wage labor. Honorato Rapada recounted the difficulty of picking hops, "a light flower." If he worked fast, he could make $2.00 or $3.00 a day. A worker who picked a hundred sacks of potatoes netted $2.50. A large box of apples represented five cents in wages.[141]

In addition to offering possibilities for work, Yakima Valley was also a site for regular settlement. During the Depression, farming in the valley offered a few enterprising Filipina/os a base means of subsistence and shelter. Anacleto Corpuz, for example, rented a farm from Native Americans for three years in the early 1930s and raised cantaloupes, tomatoes, watermelons, and onions.[142] Garciano Garo, a farmer in the Yakima Valley, "went broke" in the Depression because he could not sell his crops. Still, while most Filipina/os had to migrate for survival, Garo was able to raise livestock for winter food even though his work bound him to the land. He recalled: "No money, you can live pretty good, you can eat pretty good, you got all your craft and everything but the trouble is you can not [sic] move because you have no money."[143]

Filipina/o efforts to gain access to farming were made in the context of exclusionary discrimination. Alien land laws passed in 1921 and 1923 prevented Japanese immigrants from gaining leases until they were able to lease land in the name of their American-born children. Following the pattern of their Japanese predecessors, Filipina/os gained control of land through arrangements with Native American landowners or white people who had leased land, or alternatively obtained access to leases through their marriages to white or Native American women. Violence was another method used to curtail Filipina/o involvement in agriculture. Whites drove Filipinos from the Toppenish district in the Yakima Indian reservation in November 1927; in Wapato, angry whites also used bombs and arson against Japanese farms that employed Filipina/o workers, as well as farms run by Filipina/os. In response to protests by Native Americans and the Japanese consul in Seattle, the U.S. government arrested the most prominent agitators and sent in investigators. After this incident, the state legislature became the route for blocking Filipina/os by further constricting the alien land laws to include Filipina/os. Eighteen Filipina/os were arrested for allegedly violating the new land laws and eventually given six-month jail terms, although later they were released after court appeals. Although labor contractor Pio de Cano successfully contested the 1937 alien land act revisions in King County Superior Court, the Yakima Valley Filipina/os also needed crucial support from the Yakima Tribal Council, as well as diplomatic pressure from the Philippines, to get the Washington State Supreme Court to overturn the 1937 amendment. As a result of more favorable attitudes toward Filipina/os in World War II because they were allies of the United States, Filipina/os finally gained the right to lease land in 1942.[144]

Farther west of the Yakima Valley, toward the coast, the Aberdeen area provided another locus for Filipina/o settlement, providing alternate employment to the agricultural jobs elsewhere in the state, particularly for a male workforce. Jose Acena accompanied "many boys from Bauang" to Montesano for a month before finding work at Seattle General Hospital.[145] Al Bautista, who caught a ride with a friend to Cosmopolis, remembered competing for a position at the sawmill. Workers would line up, hoping to be chosen for the membership. To "look tough," Bautista rolled up his sleeves, even though it was snowing, and earned a chance to make $2.50 per day working at the mill.[146] Ethnic and racial hierarchies further affected Filipina/os' ability to find employment. Philip Vera Cruz, who worked in Cosmopolis from May to November 1926, reported that many white workers labored in the mills, along with Greeks, Japanese, and Filipina/os. He commented that the most desirable jobs went to the white workers, while among the foreign groups, the Japanese laborers received the choicest assignments.[147]

Filipina/os were characteristically flexible in terms of their employment, especially because of their marginalization in the workforce. Like many other Filipina/os, Mike Castillano relied on a variety of jobs in the area to make his living. If not enough work was available at the sawmill, Castillano found other jobs on the railroad or on a nearby farm. He also worked in a box factory in Cosmopolis, about ten miles from Montesano.[148] Some Filipina/os also became students at area schools, finding nearby employment to support themselves or relying on family members who worked in the locality for financial support.[149]

The reception of Filipina/os by the townspeople in the region varied. Mike Castillano remembered that in Montesano, although "some are good," "most . . . don't like Filipinos . . . they don't like colored guys, if they can help it." When Castillano dated white women, he avoided the downtown area and drove to the beach to court them.[150] Economic resentment also influenced the local residents' response to Filipina/os. Roman Simbe remembered how Montesano residents argued that "there's too many of them [Filipinos] taking jobs away from the people down there." However, when Filipina/os went on strike in 1924 in a sawmill, the owner's nephew negotiated with the workers, earning the Filipina/os "a little bit more respect" from the Montesano townspeople.[151] Philip Vera Cruz also recalled a strike that occurred in 1926 when some Filipina/os were released from their jobs. Others who were still employed also walked off their jobs, not only at sawmills, but also at a box factory and at a planing mill.[152] Nevertheless, during the Depression almost all the Filipina/os had to leave town for other opportunities when they lost their jobs.[153]

For recreation, Filipina/os sometimes went to movies or prize fights in Aberdeen. The primary recreational outlet, however, was the regular trek to the big city—Seattle. Mike Castillano went to Seattle on a weekly basis, pooling money with others to pay for gas for the three-hour ride into Chinatown. He and his companions left on Friday night, rented a room in a King Street hotel for the weekend, and then returned on Sunday afternoon.[154] Felix Narte also attended dance halls in Seattle on Friday nights, purchasing tickets that were exchanged for brief periods of female companionship.[155] Only a few hours away by car, Seattle was an accessible refuge.

Throughout their movement in Washington, violence was a common theme. In 1928, "around forty or fifty" Filipina/os who had been employed in Seattle were prevented from picking apples near Cashmere by a so-called citizen's committee numbering 150. In Toppenish, tensions ran high over an incident involving a white woman, and Filipinos asked to be kept in a jail in Sunnyside, in the Yakima Valley, for safety. Two hundred white workers ran twenty-two Filipino workers out of a Wenatchee camp at roughly the same time. In July, white vigilantes threatened to "hang white ranchers" in the West Wapato district in Washington if they continued to employ Filipinos.[156]

Although the flash point for such violence was often portrayed as the Filipino men's affinity for white women, economic tensions were a primary cause. For example, Jose Acena reported that conflicts in Moxee City, where Filipinos picked hops, occurred because of job competition and because of Filipinos' relationships with white women.[157] Among the most marginalized of workers, Filipina/os felt that they had little choice but to accept the poor wages allotted to them. As a result, white workers condemned Filipina/os for undercutting wages. Toribio Martin, who worked in Selah, Washington, recalled: "Those were the troubled years, you know . . . but growers and farmers they preferred Filipinos because they worked harder, they worked longer hours than the white people."[158] Jose Acena also remembered:

> Well, it was hard to find a job. And lots of the boys, I think, were on the farm. Some of them were even lucky to find a job for ten cents an hour, yeah we have a pretty hard time and at the same time too because of these lack of jobs those white people started to revolt about it. In every place where there were Filipinos on the farm they start to raid them, you know.[159]

This kind of violent enforcement of social codes was endemic, particularly in the rural areas. In May 1930, Filipina/os were targeted by white vigilantes and driven into hiding or forced to leave for other places. Labor competition was at the root of the violence. As the *Manila Bulletin* reported, "In one case white workers, displaced by Filipinos who will work for twenty-five cents an hour instead of the sixty cents an hour formerly received by the whites, aroused Filipino resentment when they issued threats of violence if additional Filipino workers are brought into the Kent district."[160] In January 1931, twelve "American" men broke into a house rented by Filipina/o workers close to Kent, assaulted three of the occupants, and stole their possessions.[161] As Felipe Dumlao complained, "And that damned thing, when we get here in Seattle we go to the country . . . you get your choice, either you want it [jobs in the country] or you get starved."[162]

To focus solely on these migratory male workers, however, would be to overlook other important sectors of the community, including those Filipina/os who settled permanently in Seattle and the surrounding region. In a context where single male migratory workers were the norm, nuclear families such as those in the Yakima Valley often became the center for social activities. John Castillo remembered that some of the Filipino workers from Aberdeen and Cosmopolis who labored in the sawmill were married to white women. These families congregated for ceremonies and events, such as weddings, birthdays, and Rizal Day celebrations.[163]

CONCLUSION

By underscoring the role of migration and labor, this chapter has suggested the importance of region in discerning the experience of Filipina/o Americans on the West Coast. We must understand not only how labor and capital structure the movement of people through an area but also the function of an urban site such as Seattle for Filipina/o migratory workers. These workers had a political understanding of their environment that spanned hundreds of miles over the U.S. mainland and literally thousands of miles across the Pacific to Hawai'i and the Philippines. They integrated themselves in a flow of labor and capital as dictated by West Coast industries, following the transportation networks that connected different sites. Given the difficulties of finding work, the strategies employed by Filipina/o laborers suggest they had an astute understanding of how to use a city to maximize their options for economic survival.

Filipina/o workers were constantly on the move, from the Philippines to labor in the expanded U.S. economy, and particularly within the American West itself. Their sense of place and community was formed not from developing roots in one particular place but from their numerous migrations. This wider conceptualization of the Filipina/o American experience is necessary to combat the "invisibility" of Filipina/os within the city. This movement, however, was gendered, with men tending to have far more freedom than women to be transient. If migratory, women tended to go from city to city, or followed families within rural regions. At the same time, however, men in migratory labor were also in a constrained position because their very mobility reinforced their marginality in an urban setting. Here today, gone tomorrow, they moved through the region looking for their next job. Male laborers canned salmon, harvested hops, repaired railroad tracks, washed dishes in restaurants, or worked as "houseboys" in the households of wealthy white people, crossing the line between urban and agricultural jobs, as well as jobs traditionally considered "men's work" and "women's work." This versatility was both a strength and an indication of their lack of options in a discriminatory job market.[164] When one job was done, they would start again to find new work. For all members of the community, whether migratory or not, the sense of place and community as a whole was greatly influenced by the fact that the dominant pattern of labor was transitory.

This analysis enables us to see that the Filipina/o experience in Seattle, far from constituting a marginalized segment of American culture, in fact represented processes central to American culture, including the growth of the U.S. empire and its impact on the development of the American West. When we refocus our gaze to look beyond the urban limits of Seattle to discern the annual migration between California and Alaska, for example, the transitory nature of the Filipina/o American experience in Seattle suggests the linkages among different states in the American West, as well as to overseas. Filipina/o workers at this time moved as much from industry to industry as they did from site to site and were among the essential group of laborers who participated in the development of the economy of the American West during this period.

In addition, the Filipina/o American experience at this time was predominantly rural and mobile, a reflection of labor opportunities and racial restrictions. Yet these same workers also regularly moved through urban centers, not only Seattle but also other sites such as San Francisco, Los Angeles, and San Diego. Stockton, although surrounded by a rural area, was also a pivotal urban center for Filipina/o Americans.[165] Patricia Limerick suggests that recognizing these kinds of patterns is one way in which there can be valuable dialogue between historians of the American West and scholars of Asian American studies, in our examination of "the relations between the rural West and the urban West."[166] Indeed, in analyses of Filipina/o Americans and other Asian Americans, discussions often center upon looking at how values and attributes of Asian cultures are transplanted and transformed within the context of the United

States, particularly because of the focus on the assimilation of Asian Americans to the American culture. Another valuable area of study, I suggest, would be to consider how agricultural experiences had an impact on city dwellers, and how urban experiences had an impact on those moving within a primarily rural context, particularly because centers of Filipina/o activity, while wide-ranging, tended to develop within confined spaces because of racial segregation. Furthermore, a regional perspective also helps to challenge the necessary but overwhelming focus on urban Chinatown studies, particularly those that document communities in New York and San Francisco.[167] Because they usually are in major urban metropoles and have formed a key interface between "mainstream" populations and Asian American communities, Chinatowns have always held much prominence in American culture, particularly in the representations of the Asian American groups who have resided in them. Understanding Filipina/o Seattle within a regional context enables us to move beyond that model of Asian American community, to more fully understand the function of urban sites not only for those who lived in them throughout the year but also for those who did not, yet still remained a valuable part of Filipina/o Seattle.

CHAPTER 4

Crossings and Connections

In contrast to the dominant characterization of the pre–World War II Filipina/o American community as a "bachelor society" populated by "single" men, a study of Seattle and the area immediately around it suggests a range of different social possibilities.[1] For example, although most long-term relationships between Native Americans and Filipina/os on Bainbridge Island developed after World War II, Mary Rapada and Honorato Rapada were an early couple. They met while both were pickers for Japanese farmers in Bainbridge in 1938, and they married that same year.[2] Bainbridge Island, just a short ferry ride from the Seattle city limits, would become an important part of the extended Filipina/o Seattle community, and the marriages between Filipino Americans and Native American women from the Tlingit, Lummi, Nookta, and other tribes would constitute an important part of the community's formation. As the Rapadas' story suggests, along with places such as Salinas and other sites throughout the American West, communities in the extended Seattle area and the general Pacific Northwest region were critical sites for Filipina/o Americans where they interacted with many different groups. Another Native American community member, who married a Filipino American in the early 1940s, remembered that her grandmother had been coming in the summers for several years to help support her family.[3] The relationships of Filipina/o Americans and Native Americans in the Seattle area are little documented as a whole, yet they demonstrate the complex community formation forged in places around the city. They not only indicate the role of labor in the ongoing migration of peoples in the Pacific Northwest but also underscore the range of possibilities that existed for social interaction.

These kinds of interactions were regularly enacted in a context in which Filipina/o Americans occupied a low status in the Seattle culture. Workers who traveled through the region found that Pacific Northwest culture, like that in other parts of the country, typically relegated Asian American laborers to a position as "sojourners" or "perpetual foreigners." These characterizations both suggested and justified the continued exclusion of Asians from American culture, even though many chose to make permanent homes in the United States. Like other Asian groups, Filipina/os were also considered "indispensable enemies," to use Alexander Saxton's characterization of anti-Chinese sentiment in the late nineteenth century.[4]

This points to another way in which the history of Seattle has been shaped by U.S.-Asia relations. Earlier I mentioned the connections of Seattle's economy to U.S.-Asia trade, as well as the federal government's interest in the Pacific region as a whole. Seattle's history has also been shaped by the valuable labor that Filipina/o Americans and other Asian Americans have contributed to the economy. In addition to these factors, Seattle's history has been further impacted by how the white working-class labor movement consolidated in part against the perceived threat of Asian migration and labor. As Carlos A. Schwantes suggests, the militancy of the region's labor movement stems from "the ideology of disinheritance," as demonstrated by the organization of white workers through the anti-Chinese movement of the late nineteenth century.[5] At the time that Filipina/os entered the Pacific Northwest, Seattle's oldest residents would have been able to remember the "drivings out" and the virulent racism directed against Chinese Americans in the 1880s. These actions and attitudes would have resonance in later decades not only in how people were treated but also in how Asian Americans strategized their place in Seattle.[6]

This chapter focuses on what Seattle and the surrounding areas meant to Filipina/o Americans as a place of crossings and connections, particularly given the harsh racial discrimination that community members faced. My intent is to highlight the complex strategies of Seattle community members whose movements often spanned the United States and the Philippines, as well as diverse sites in the American West, yet who also developed a unique local culture in the Seattle area. How did these strategies shape social interactions, particularly in regard to class, race, and "family"?

DESTINATION: SEATTLE

Seattle was of major importance to Filipina/os as a place to which a migratory worker could always return. Seattle was a big city with a thriving Chinatown, where Filipina/os could find familiar food and a place to sleep, blend in with the crowds on the streets, and find relative safety from the racism and discrimination of more isolated areas, or even other sections of the city where Asian Americans were not common. Chances were good that an arriving Filipina/o could find a *kababayan*, a fellow Filipina/o companion, who spoke the same dialect or other friends and relatives who would help him—and occasionally her—by sharing food and shelter. The sheer concentration of Filipina/os meant there was a greater chance for reunions with friends and family, as Filipina/os passed en route to the restaurants, dance halls, gambling dens, and other entertainments that made the "big city" so popular. Going to Seattle was thus part of the communal experience of being Filipina/o American on the West Coast.

Because employment was so transitory and unstable, the trek to Seattle, as one of the fixed rituals in the constant search for work, came to be a touchstone in the Filipina/o experience. Seattle was vital to Asian Americans as a whole because it had the resources and development of an urban vicinity in a largely rural context. Those Filipina/os who chose not to labor in the area's fields, sawmills, or railroads still had the option of securing jobs as houseboys or finding work in the city's business establishments. Some of them even saved up enough funds to go to school.

Not surprisingly, though, the numbers of Filipina/os in census data appear low, although they rise steadily during the period under study. In Washington State in 1910, only 17 males were counted; in 1920, there were 915 males and 43 females. By 1930, reflecting the peak period of migration, the numbers rose to 3,374 males and 106 females. Seattle in 1930 boasted of 1,563 Filipinos and 51 Filipinas; these numbers decreased slightly by 1940, to 1,213 males and 179 females.[7] But to accept these figures at face value is to miss a prominent reality of migratory workers. These small numbers better represent the stable and permanent population and do not fully reflect the role of the city for the arriving migratory population, or for the Filipina/os in outlying rural areas.[8] Because of the segregated nature of employment, many Filipina/os were located in less desirable jobs on the outskirts of the area. Also, since the population varied depending on the availability of seasonal labor, attempts to count Filipina/os would yield different results throughout the

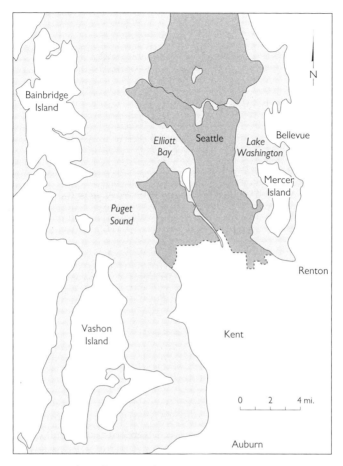

Map 6. Seattle and surrounding area.

year. Thus, historians of the city must use a regional framework like that argued for in the last chapter in order to comprehend the relationship of Filipina/o Americans to Seattle.[9]

Seattle's significance for Filipina/o Americans was in part the result of its integration in the regional search for employment. As a group, Filipina/os made decisions about how and where to work based on an inclusive understanding of the available jobs in a region. A Filipina/o worker moving from California through Seattle en route to Alaska typically encountered an assortment of employment in both farm and city locales. Even those who labored predominantly in agriculture and salmon canneries regularly heard of work in the city. Even if they chose to spend most of

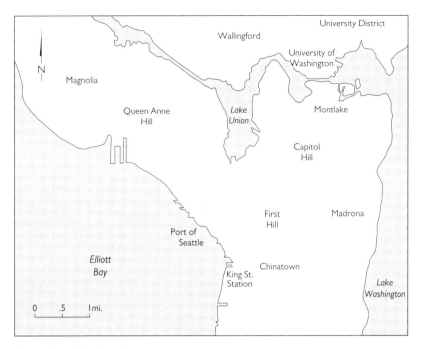

Map 7. Detail of Seattle.

their time in a particular place outside of an urban area, the city was still a primary reference point and a possible refuge if racial tensions and economic discrimination became especially troublesome. Conversely, Filipina/os who stayed predominantly within the city limits could locate work in rural sites if their funds were low, or they could seek work on the farms if they grew tired of the urban environment. In these experiences, urban and rural places would take on different kinds of significance. A rural site might represent possible self-sufficiency if it allowed Filipina/os to grow enough vegetables to support themselves. Decisions to travel to and stay in rural areas could also reflect a personal preference for agricultural labor versus urban work.[10] However, rural labor was generally isolating and physically exhausting, and it increased one's vulnerability to racial harassment and violence because there was not the same safety in numbers as in the city. In contrast, an urban space could mean exciting commercial entertainment, a chance to catch up with old friends, and a release from the drudgery of agricultural work. But it could also translate into increased monitoring and harassment by local city authorities in a smaller physical area, as well as heavy competition for the few available jobs in a segregated economy.

Filipina/os who came to Seattle thus entered a pivotal space in the American West. Seattle was an urban center in a rural region, where travelers could go by highway to the Yakima Valley, by steamer to Alaska, by railroad to Chicago, or even by the President Lines to Asia. In addition to being a transportation hub, Seattle was a principal intermediary in the flow of goods from the Northwest region to other parts of the country and the world. Lumber, grains, fish, livestock, and metalworking ranked among Seattle's important industries following World War I. However, Seattle was not a major manufacturing center.[11] It did not have the same kind of industrial base as cities such as Worcester, Massachusetts, which was well known for its metal and machinery trades.[12] Seattle had nothing resembling New York's flourishing garment industry, or Detroit's motorcar business, or Pittsburgh's steelyards, where people could potentially find work. Thus it did not have a developed infrastructure during this period that could absorb workers on a regular basis. Furthermore, as a relatively new city in the American West, Seattle had an economy that was still very much evolving and was susceptible to sudden downturns and upturns.[13] Instead, in the era before World War II, Seattle was known mainly for its role as a commercial center for port trade and was, as noted by Roger Sale, "primarily a jobbing, wholesaling, and retailing city, heavily into transshipment and all the functions associated with it."[14]

Because of its seasonal industries, Seattle was a stopping point for migrant and casual workers who regularly crossed through its streets. Predominantly male and single, these workers were distinctly different than, as Dana Frank describes, "the other, more rooted world of working-class Seattle men and women laboring in the local-market sector and in small-scale production," which included both skilled and unskilled workers.[15]

In the period before World War II, Filipina/o migratory workers moved through Seattle in the context of a wide variety of transient groups and constituted only a small percentage of the city's stable population. By 1940, 80 percent of the population counted in the census were "native-born white," with 16.2 percent "foreign-born white" and 3.9 percent "non-Caucasian," which could include residents born both in the United States and overseas. The 63,470 foreign-born residents included Canadians (12,666), Swedes (7,670), English and Welsh (6,065), Germans (3,581), and Italians (3,055). There were 2,876 foreign-born Japanese and 830 foreign-born Chinese residents.[16] Despite the relatively small proportion of the city they represented, the Asian American population has always formed a focal point for Seattle culture not only because of the city's interest in Asia and the pivotal importance of Pacific trade and militarization in the development of the economy but also because of the significance of Chinatown as an economic and cultural space. Also, unlike in many other cities, such as Washington, D.C., or Chicago, Asian Americans, not African Americans or other groups, formed the main part of the population of people of color.[17]

Filipina/o Seattle was also characterized by its status as a majority male community, like many Asian American communities at this time, with a deeply gendered culture. However, with its cluster of family households, professional opportunities, and community groups, the city also was a place where women were able to operate relatively freely, although they did not have the same kinds of social mobility as men. Very similar to Mexican women who came to Los Angeles, who have been described by George Sánchez, Filipinas typically came as part of a family unit and remained with family while in the city.[18] A select number of women occupied other spaces that were considered socially acceptable, such as professional environments like health care facilities. Women from other communities were represented, too, because of the high rates of outmarriage for Filipino men.

SEATTLE CHINATOWN

The place where most Filipina/os were concentrated was Seattle Chinatown. Like most major Chinatowns in the United States, such as those in New York and San Francisco, Seattle Chinatown served as both a home and a business area for many of the city's Asian American communities. Like a number of Chinatowns, the one in Seattle was located within walking distance of the port and was a place where people could find resources in relative safety from the hostile discrimination they might face elsewhere. Although some Filipina/os participated in the culture and economy through family businesses, Seattle Chinatown was largely a space for itinerant male laborers.

The part of town occupied by these migratory Filipina/os was in the section designated for people of color, white transients, and other people considered "undesirable" by the dominant population. As sociologist Calvin Schmid notes, "This entire area is represented by heterogeneous racial elements—Filipinos, Chinese, Negroes, Caucasians, and (prior to the evacuation) Japanese. This section is also character-

ized by cheap hotels and rooming houses, restaurants, gambling 'joints,'
night clubs, brothels, and an assortment of retail stores."[19] Near Chinatown were three areas inhabited by predominantly male populations,
identified by Schmid as "slums." The first was the famous Skid Road,
which was 88.3 percent male and characterized by Schmid as a "hobohe-
mia." Another area was Belltown, which also featured "an unstable proletarian white population" and was 64.4 percent male.[20] The final area
included Chinatown and "smaller clusterings of Filipinos, Negroes, and
Japanese" and was 81.1 percent male.

Despite its notorious and seedy reputation in mainstream Seattle, Chinatown served a different function for the Asian Americans and other
groups who inhabited its streets. The heart of the Seattle Pinoy community was in Chinatown, the center for all the Asian groups, especially because of the racial discrimination that existed elsewhere in the city.[21] John
Castillo called it "the Mecca of the Pinoys." Although the area had only
a small Chinese population because of the effectiveness of the virulent
drivings-out campaigns of the late nineteenth century, it did have a
bustling Japanese American community; a predominantly white, male,
transient population; and a small Native American community. African
Americans were also found near Chinatown, in the area of Madison Street
and Twenty-third Avenue, and Jewish, Italian, and Irish residents lived
"up the hill on Jackson, going that way . . . [to] Cherry." By 1930, the
Japanese population in Seattle already numbered 8,448, or 2.3 percent
of the city's total population, concentrated around Yesler Way between
Fifth and Twenty-third Avenues.[22]

Filipina/o Americans entered into this mix, seeking jobs or friends to
sustain them in their search for work along the West Coast. According to
Schmid, the majority of the Filipina/o population was found in the "Jackson Street–Chinatown District." Sixth and King is the area around which
the Filipina/o population revolved to the south of central Chinatown,
with another section of the community "scattered in an area bounded by
Marion Street on the north, Dearborn on the south, 15th on the east, and
the waterfront on the west."[23] As Marco Aquino wrote in his column
"Little Manila" in the *Philippine Advocate,* "Our 'Little Manila' really
centers on King street, Maynard, Jac[k]son and Sixth avenue."[24]

Racism enforced the multicultural makeup of the area. Most Asian
Americans, Native Americans, and the majority of African Americans
from the Central District lived on lower Jackson Street, or Southside,
along with transients, people without homes, vice workers, and work-

ing-class and poor European Americans.[25] Jackson Street in 1935 was almost 70 percent Asian American, nearly a quarter African American, and less than 10 percent white.[26]

Among Asian Americans, Chinese Americans and especially Japanese Americans tended to have more economic success in the segregated economy, particularly in small, entrepreneurial businesses such as restaurants or hotels.[27] Monica Sone's family, for example, owned a hotel in downtown Seattle.[28] While competition was typically fierce, sometimes people helped each other across ethnic lines. Fred Floresca remembered being one of only two Filipina/os with jobs among a group of townmates. He reported, "We took care of them [the townmates] until they are able to get a job." Their friends would come in the evening and cook meals, use bed rolls on the floor, and, the next day, put away their bed rolls in the closet. They would leave in the morning before the Japanese landlord discovered the number of occupants in the apartment. Floresca was not sure whether his landlord was aware of the arrangement, but there seemed to be a tacit agreement. As he recalled, "We were very good friends and . . . she found out that many of the Japanese [were] in the same boat so she allow us since we di[d]n't bother her at all."[29]

A handful of Filipina/os also owned small businesses that served the needs of migratory male workers in Seattle Chinatown. In its January 30, 1930, issue, the *Filipino Forum* featured an advertisement for "Mrs. Nator's Pool Halls and Employment Agency" on, respectively, 516 Jackson Street and 662 Jackson Street, which probably were run by Mrs. Nator herself.[30] Other work could be found in these establishments as well. In 1931 the *Philippine Review* carried an advertisement for the Manila Restaurant, which featured "Filipino Waitresses and Cooks."[31]

At the same time, those who extended help could also be on the deficit side of a relationship. Workers could take advantage of their transience to avoid paying their debts. Felipe Dumlao explained that a Filipina/o restaurateur might offer meals on credit to a worker, who promised to pay after the Alaska season. Instead, after the season was over, the worker might go directly to California to avoid his bills. The following year, he would go to a different restaurant to eat meals on credit and claim to have no money available to pay the first restaurateur.[32]

African Americans numbered roughly 1 percent of the city's total population, with 3,303 people enumerated in 1930 and 3,789 people counted in 1940. This community revolved around Madison and Jackson Streets, with some homeowners in the Madison community who gained access to homes through jobs as cooks or stewards in the Pacific shipping industry. Some African Americans also lived in the Twenty-sixth Avenue community and the Cherry Street community. Most significant to this discussion, however, is the African American presence in the Jackson Street area called "Cross-town," which seemed to overlap with China-town. Before the Japanese evacuation, the Cross-town area contained 1,168 residents: 275 African American, 96 white, and the rest Chinese, Filipina/os, Japanese, and members of other groups. As suggested by its name, Cross-town was an area of heavy traffic. Schmid describes it as "an area in transition, which surrounds the central business and bright-light area of the city." It was also considered a less desirable part of the city, with inferior housing.[33]

The culture and economy that Filipina/os found were especially com-pact because of racial segregation. Although there was a continuous flow of workers through Seattle, the physical space that they moved through in Chinatown spanned only a few blocks. The density of Filipina/o work-ers increased notably at certain points of the year, particularly before and after the summer cannery season. These were the prime months for Chi-natown, and the economy was very busy. This had a major impact on the development of the community and highlighted the importance of Seattle as a space where one could find word of people and jobs or, at the very least, a bowl of rice and a place to sleep. Seattle was a stable nexus for Filipina/o workers, even if the faces of the workers changed.

Filipina/os found relative safety from discrimination in Chinatown. Mariano Angeles recalled that Filipina/os and other Asians could not go to the main part of a theater in Seattle but were relegated to the bal-cony.[34] Al Bautista remembered two downtown movie theaters in which Filipina/os were made to sit in the balconies instead of in the more de-sirable main seating areas.[35] But even in Chinatown, harassment was per-vasive, particularly for the men who congregated in public places. When Filipina/os socialized in the streets of Chinatown like a "town fiesta," policemen regularly broke up the crowd. Felipe Dumlao recalled, "You could even see Filipinos beaten by policemen over there in the [street] corner, kick them out why [while] they are bunching together and all that kind."[36] In one case, Mariano Marapoa, who was staying in the Free-dom Hotel, was shot to death by two Seattle police officers in Marapoa's room. The policemen claimed self-defense and were "exonerated," even though Marapoa was only holding scissors at the time he died.[37] Felix Narte described the harassment of Filipina/os: "They saw a Filipino there, they call him 'Oh you monkey,' like that see."[38] Male Filipinos who pos-sessed the temerity to be seen publicly with white women were quickly censured by city authorities. Felipe Dumlao remembered that "when you date up a [white] girl—they pick you up[,] put you in jail." Socializing with Mexican American or Native American women did not get Filipinos into the same kind of trouble.[39]

In his 1931 study, Bruno Lasker reported an incident in which eight Filipinos were arrested by a policeman one night at a street corner, allegedly for "accosting women." The charges were dropped by the magistrate after it became apparent that the policeman had no witnesses, and the Filipinos claimed that they had nowhere else to gather after work.[40] Violence could also erupt in the streets. In 1926, fighting between whites and Filipina/os during a New Year's celebration led to stabbings and beatings; in 1927, another street fight in Seattle involved two hundred participants.[41]

As discussed earlier, the part of town that Filipina/os frequented was founded upon an economy geared toward transient populations of whites and people of color. Chinatown had its own particular culture of dance halls, restaurants, gambling places, barber shops, pool halls, and hotels, all set up to serve passing laborers, to which new arrivals were quickly introduced. Local merchants were well aware of the buying power of the Filipina/o clientele, as reflected in a letter sent by merchant Charles Drennan of the Western Leather Works to the *Cosmopolitan Courier* in 1938: "The swarthy little lads from the Philippines are model customers. They are friendly, polite and good in every way. In general, they elicit the best in service, quality and price, and their patronage is appreciated and prized by Seattle retail merchants."[42]

Neighborhood restaurants offered cheap meals for the male workforce coming through and offered a chance to get some "home cooking." One writer for the *Cosmopolitan Courier,* pointing out the predominance of new eating places in Chinatown, noted: "There is a feeling of homesickness creeping in my conscious mind as I stroll along my favorite rendezvous (King & Sixth) and welcome the balmy breeze of spring made pungent by the stench of frying garlic and the classic 'adobo' wafting its unique and tantalizing aroma from cafes crowded by brown faces."[43]

Eddie Acena recalled that a full meal in a Japanese restaurant, including dessert and salad, might cost twenty-five cents.[44] Five cents might purchase some coffee and a doughnut.[45] If Filipina/os did not have money to pay for food in the Asian or "American"-style restaurants in the section frequented by Filipina/os, there were other options. Some contractors offered credit in restaurants, and workers paid off their tabs by laboring in designated canneries.[46]

Communal living was the rule, reinforced by social mores and economic exigencies. Hotels in the area were managed by mostly Japanese and a few Chinese immigrants, while only a handful of Filipina/os had businesses. Toribio Madayag recalled that Filipina/os could live at a hotel for one dollar a week, which also paid for a weekly change of sheets.[47] When times were especially tough, some Filipinos had to resort to asking other Filipinos for money on the street. Once, a few Filipinos asked Vincent Mendoza for fifty cents to buy rice because they had gone without food for a few days. Because Mendoza knew one person in the group, he gave them money for food and one night's rent. Since the room was leased to only one person, the Filipinos left after eating their meal and returned at night to bed down on the floor.[48]

If someone knew other people, it might be possible to scrape together a meal by sharing coffee and rice and cooking in hotel rooms.[49] Some merchants also gave away food. If a Filipina/o knew someone who worked on a nearby farm, it was possible to get free vegetables.[50] Once one worker was so hungry that he went into a Japanese store and, while the employees were having a meal in the rear, surreptitiously hoisted a bag of rice on his back. He then crept along the side of the store's interior with the heavy bag and dashed to the safety of his hotel.[51] Other enterprising Filipina/os fished off the docks of Seattle's port. While staying in Chinatown, Toribio Madayag used to catch shiners for food.[52] Some Filipina/os stood in breadlines or went to soup kitchens to obtain food.[53]

Toribio Martin explained that in lieu of other recreation, Filipina/os congregated at gambling houses, dance halls, and pool halls.[54] Ray Corpuz commented, "We are young so we go to Chinatown because there are a lot of . . . things going on there. Taxi dances, prostitution, whatever, they are there."[55] Reflecting the instability of economic life, gambling was a preoccupation for Chinatown residents. John Castillo reported that many Filipina/os were "habitual gamblers." Students went to Alaska and saved their earnings for school, but most people were "naturally gamb[l]ers," particularly because they had no other social alternatives. They gambled in Chinese establishments or "in places where Pinoys meet."[56] Games such as "Sicoy-Sicoy," "Py-Kio," "Ong-gao," poker, "High-Low," "Chuck-Loock," and the lottery were common. To attract patrons, these businesses offered free meals.[57] In 1934, the *Philippine American Chronicle* complained about Chinese gambling places that there were two thousand Filipina/os, "residents of Seattle," who lost 65 percent of their $200,000 to $400,000 earnings in gambling places.[58]

Pool halls and taxi dance halls provided another way to pass the time.[59]

Jose Acena commented, "Gambling and girls. That's it." Acena explained that fights would break out because "they would fight for a girl or they would fight for the money they lost, see."[60] Trinidad Rojo reported that the majority (81) of 135 arrests of Filipina/os "took place in or near gambling joints, dance halls, and poolrooms in Chinatown," mostly on King Street.[61] Boxing was another featured activity in the community at this time, and fighters such as Pancho Villa and Speedy Dado had eager followings among Filipina/os before World War II.[62] Marino Guiang's story illustrates the attractions of the ring, as well as the context in which boxing became so important as both a leisure activity and a form of labor. Guiang's uncle arrived in 1918 and eventually earned a doctoral degree at the University of Washington. But Guiang arrived during the Depression and had a difficult time trying to work his way through Franklin High School. As he recalled, "You couldn't even find a school boy's work at that time, see." While still a high school student, Guiang began attending boxing shows at the Austin and Bishop Gymnasium at Ninth and Olive Streets; eventually he entered the ring himself.[63]

Thus, the Chinatown economy was very geared to migratory workers. Those Filipina/os fortunate enough have businesses regularly participated in the migratory worker economy, from contracting laborers to setting up small businesses that served migratory workers. These workers then not only represented the investments of contractors but also were potential customers for small business owners. Because of the racial segregation of the Seattle economy, the interdependence of Filipina/o community members across class was especially pronounced.

COMMUNITY MEMBERS

There were a variety of choices for Filipino men who wanted to stay in the city, and relatively fewer for women. Service work, household labor, and some white-collar work were a few of the avenues of employment open to Filipina/os. Pete Filiarca, who worked at Seattle General Hospital, reported that Filipinos found employment as orderlies and maintenance workers in hospitals and hotels.[64] In 1938, Lorenzo Pimental found a job as a delivery boy in a drugstore, then moved on to other employment in a hotel and a restaurant.[65] Fred Floresca began working as a dishwasher at the Frye Hotel on the second day after he arrived in 1927. He got his job through someone he had known in the Philippines, who "was more or less the boy in charge of the Filipinos in the hotel." He began as a dishwasher, then became a helper to the pantry man and eventually worked his way up through the ranks to become a pantry man. He then prepared himself to be a baker by coming in at three or four o'clock in the morning to learn from the baker until it was time to begin his paid shift as a pantry man around ten o'clock.[66]

Domestic work was another type of employment open to Filipina/os. In his housekeeping duties, Vincent Mendoza learned how to clean, dust, and scrub, as well as to do some plumbing and electrical work.[67] Sinforoso Ordona worked as a houseboy in Seattle, even finding out how to make meringue pie. He considered himself "lucky" to get twenty-five dollars a month during the Depression, as well as free lodging, and still went to do cannery work in Alaska. Other less fortunate Filipina/os earned only ten to fifteen dollars a month. In 1932, Ordona returned to the Philippines to get married and then came back to Seattle. With the help of his employers, he was able to have his wife come in 1937, and she joined him in his job and helped with the housework.[68]

Other Filipina/os, usually men, took jobs as service workers in the city. Here the pattern of hiring people of color for the most menial and lowest-paid work continued. Carlos Toribio spoke of the difficulties of economic competition against white people, as well as Chinese and Japanese immigrants.[69] Although seasonal jobs in Alaska might offer relatively good wages, even higher-status hotel and restaurant work paid a mere twenty-five dollars per month.[70] Filipina/os competed against African American and European immigrant women workers and other Asian male laborers for these positions—devalued jobs that in other cities were dominated by African American women.[71]

Another sector of the population consisted of Filipina/os who remained in the city because they could not find other work. These men were among the most destitute Filipina/os, and they included the elderly and those unable to compete for jobs on the farms or in the city. They lived in Hooverville, which ran from Pier 54 to Pier 61. Belen Braganza, who arrived in Seattle in 1930, remembered her first impressions of Hooverville along the waterfront: "Those are all lean-tos and shacks and terrible things because it was Depression time."[72] The Filipina/os there built homes out of wood and discarded materials, as Zacarias Manangan remembered, "throw-away lumber on the oceans." Manangan recalled that the men tried to live near the ocean so that they could set up fishing lines close to their homes. If a guest entered their homes, Manangan reported, "all you could smell was fish."[73] Felipe Dumlao's memories indicate the resourcefulness and caring of these communities, as well as the sharing of survival strategies. For example, he was also taught by the "old men" to catch fish, and on occasion would return to his hotel with a "bucket full of fish."[74]

Although their choices were limited, these Filipina/os still exercised options about their political opportunities. Jesse Jackson, known as the "'Mayor' of Hooverville," remembered that in 1932 two Filipina/os served on "a board of commissioners" organized by Hooverville residents, along with two whites and two African Americans.[75] Six years later, more than one hundred Filipina/os lived in Hooverville. However, the Hooverville community was short-lived.[76] During World War II, the squatters' homes were destroyed by bulldozers to make way for a new dock.[77]

As in many other cities, some Filipina/o residents of Seattle had more economic resources, such as the owners of small businesses and the contractors who recruited workers in Seattle.[78] Some people also received specialized training and were able to command professional positions. The full-time students at schools such as Broadway High School and the University of Washington formed another segment of the community. Many lived not in Chinatown but in more residential areas, often closer to the school they attended. Or, because of the prevalence of domestic jobs, some were spread out in residential areas, depending on the kind of work that they could find.

Women who ran households were faced with tremendous responsibility, typically assuming the primary role in raising families and often taking on outside jobs as well. Here, it is important to highlight the crucial role of women's labor and the importance of work within the household as a contribution to the family, even though it was typically unpaid. Bibiana Laigo Castillano's narrative offers us insight into women's responsibilities. After her first husband, Valeriano Laigo, was killed in the 1930s, Castillano tried to run his businesses (he had been a cannery contractor and had also owned a restaurant). She finally gave them up in 1938 because of the difficulty of trying to maintain them and take care of her children. As she recalled:

> I got to quit those jobs, I get up at 6 in the morning to run those things and then I work through, then I have to bring my children with me over there, keep them apart in the next room in the back. Come home at 8 in the evening, wash the clothes, iron the clothes. I go to bed at 2 in the morning at night, every night. Fixing the papers, fixing the budget, and everything, so the time I go to sleep is 2 o'clock. Then I get up 5, 4 in

the morning because I have to prepare the children, I have to prepare the food, and everything. We had help, a young girl, a 16 year old girl, who used to take care of them in the house, while I go and work.[79]

The burden of household care was considerable, even with help from outside workers, and presumably from other children in the family as well. Although they are often overlooked in documentation about Seattle, women like Bibiana Laigo Castillano were instrumental in the formation of the city's culture.

Urban jobs were not the only choice in the Seattle area, again underscoring the link between rural and urban options. Filipina/os found agricultural work near Seattle because farmers in the region relied on a wide range of laborers to harvest the crops quickly. Filipina/os who picked strawberries, for example, joined a workforce that included local community members, as well as others who followed the fruit harvesting, white families that were traveling from other regions in the country or in the state, and Native Americans from British Columbia, Vancouver Island, or local reservations.[80]

In the immediate realm of Seattle, short-term work might be available on truck farms or in vegetable canning businesses in Kent, Bellevue, Auburn, Renton, Puyallup, and Sumner both before and after the Alaska season. King County, around Seattle, was also a major truck farm area. Before World War II, Japanese immigrants were the major workforce in this business, with other labor supplied by Mexicans, Mexican Americans, and Filipina/os.[81]

For some Filipina/os, jobs within the small community of Bainbridge Island provided another option for employment. In 1927, when Japanese farmers from Bainbridge Island advertised for workers in Seattle newspapers, three Filipina/os arrived to work on the strawberry crops, heralding the arrival of a regular stream of Filipina/o workers. Filipina/os labored alongside Native Americans for these Japanese farmers.[82] Sylvestre Tangalan, for example, remembered picking strawberries and loganberries before going up to Alaska.[83]

Work was hard in the berry fields. During the Depression, wages dropped to ten cents an hour, so low that Felix Narte quit after three hours.[84] And, as in other parts of the region, Filipina/o workers were met with harassment from whites. At one point, when a mob persisted in throwing rocks at a Filipina/o bunkhouse over many nights, Filipino workers armed themselves with a gun.[85] But there were also more positive memories. Toribio Madayag recalled digging clams at Fletcher's Bay;

Honorato Rapada remembered attending dances at Bainbridge Island during the strawberry season.[86]

"FAMILY" AND THE CITY

In Seattle, as well as throughout the region, the labor patterns of Filipina/o Americans had a great impact on social relations. Patron-client relations were essential to the majority of the Filipina/o population and infused community ties as a whole, a reflection of the economic livelihood and segregation of the community. As a result, the crucial function of Seattle in the wider context of Filipina/o America derived from its proximity to the Alaskan cannery industry. By and large, community leaders earned their positions through their work as contractors for the canneries. By wielding the power to distribute jobs, these contractors were able to amass both economic and social capital. Their leadership was premised on their ability to grant favors in a culture founded upon reciprocity. Because of the seasonal nature of cannery work, it was in both the contractor's and the worker's interest to develop a long-term relationship as a hedge against the vagaries of cannery hiring.

In the capitalist setting of cannery work, relations were typically invested with familial significance and often gained their resonance from economic terms.[87] Almost everyone who came to the United States before World War II was male and under thirty, since the global economy privileged certain kinds of social demographics among Filipina/o laborers. In turn, these demographics influenced the constellation of familial relations available in the United States. There were many exceptions to this rule, of course, particularly because of the central significance of women in the community. However, for migratory male laborers, the dominant relationships tended to be "brothers" and "uncles." By "brothers" I am referring to the close ties often found among young male laborers.[88] By "uncles" I mean not only the many actual uncles who, having previously traveled to the United States as single males, supported the passage of younger relatives, but also the "uncle" relationship caused by fictive ties—because an "uncle" came from the same town or province, or simply because he was older and more powerful.[89] If a young man was sent abroad and became a family representative overseas, he could become a magnet not only for other male siblings but also for the children of these siblings. Because of family rank, he would have responsibilities toward these nephews (and sometimes nieces) and required obligations from them in turn.

Even as these relationships in the Philippines evolved, patron-client relations also took on different forms in Seattle, particularly because of the nature of the West Coast economy. Entrepreneurs such as Pio De Cano and Valeriano Sarusal formed the ranks of the Filipina/os who owned contracting and other related businesses.[90] They were among the most influential members of the Filipina/o American community and profited from managing the available labor force of migratory workers. The ideology of the "uncle-nephew" relationship also informed patron-client relations, with older men typically employing younger men. Because they relied on ethnic ties to build crews, Filipina/o contractors could offer jobs to fellow townspeople, while at the same time manipulating these ties to command loyalty from their workers. To maintain his foremen's allegiance and prevent possible rivalry, for example, Pio De Cano relied on ethnic loyalties to control his workers. De Cano recruited foremen from his former home in Santa Maria, Ilocos Sur; his brother Herman De Cano was a foreman; and De Cano even directly managed workers at one of his larger contracted companies. De Cano also lent transportation money to Filipina/os from his province so that they could come to the United States and helped them with room and board until they got on their feet. At the same time, De Cano gained great wealth, thus consolidating his class position.[91]

Even if people brought a similar understanding of these social relations to the United States, the realization of these interests was quite different in the United States than in the Philippines. Because of the American capitalist economy's emphasis on recruiting young male laborers, gender and age demographics were highly skewed in Filipina/o Seattle, as noted previously. The expected returns were more short-term. Even if these workers made the decision to stay in the United States, they were highly transient. These young male workers were valued as laborers because of their mobility—they could follow the crops or work in canneries because they maintained a migratory lifestyle. Hence, although patrons could make investments in these workers' labor by recruiting them to come to the United States, the ties of loyalty were stretched very thin. A young worker who was very mobile had less chance to realize the benefits of patronage, especially if he (or rarely she) was seeking quick returns.

Charles Tilly writes that we should think of migration not in terms of the individuals or households involved but as "transplanted networks" that helped people gain information and support in their move to another place. In turn, the newly settled immigrants helped others, thus enabling the network to grow.[92] These kinds of bonds drew Filipina/o community members together within a hostile American environment. As one Manila paper reported about Filipino workers in the United States, "A good majority of them are without means of visible support were it not for the natural bent of our more fortunate boys to share their providences to those who are without roof or shirt."[93] But familial ties did not just confer advantages; sometimes they provided a means for enforcing limits or restrictions. Receiving the benefits of family relationships required the recipient to give in return. In addition, instead of always drawing community members closer, these ties also could reinforce factionalism, since any particular member might have several affiliations.

Because the Filipina/o community in the period before World War II was predominantly male, this also affected relationships between men and women. Census information from 1930 reveals a male-female ratio of 15:1 in Washington State; out of a total of 3,450 Filipina/os, roughly 3,200 were men. Since the Filipina/o population in the United States was skewed to young, single men, many of them did not have the opportunity to marry within the Filipina/o community. Sammy Lopez reported, "Very few [women] before the war, so few Filipina[s] during that time. Very hard to come with the women before."[94] As Belen Braganza noted, "Most of the men that came here, you know, they didn't have their family . . . you could count women on your two hands."[95]

Men seeking female companionship had other options in Seattle. For example, Felipe Dumlao spoke of white women who would "come to the Filipino side" to visit dance halls, pool rooms, and restaurants, as well as Washington Hall, a local meeting hall frequented by Filipina/os.[96] Dumlao remembered that the women might be "young girls" attending college who were earning extra money by dancing with patrons.[97] But Al Bautista also remembered being fleeced for his money as a new arrival by a young woman at a dance hall who told him a pitiful story and won his sympathy.[98]

The precarious nature of both social and economic opportunities made it especially difficult for Filipina/o Americans to sustain long-term partnerships. In part because of their rarity, nuclear families often served as social centers for the Filipina/o American community, although for some individuals other relationships were at least as important both in the United States and in the Philippines. Family ties stretched across the Pacific Ocean, and Filipina/o workers in the United States were often vital parts of family networks back in the Philippines. While male-male ties were *the* pivotal form of social relationships in the United States, the travel of so many men (and some women) to the United States also distorted the gender balance in home communities in the Philippines, leaving women in the majority there and leading to the existence of many unmarried women and widows. Stephen Griffiths has noted that one option for these women was to keep house with another woman.[99] On a similar note, there is a need to record expressions of sexuality in the pre–World War II period, beyond the preoccupation of the affinity of Filipino men for white women. In particular, we know very little of gay, lesbian, or bisexual relationships.[100]

In general, heterosexual nuclear families were more the exception than the rule. The existence of these families tended to be an indication of privilege rather than the expected lot of most heterosexual men. Most Filipino workers simply could not afford to get married. Zacarias Manangan recalled:

> So we were allowed to get our families if we would want to but the problem is some of us hesitated to get them because of the condition of living, you know. We don't earn enough money to support them and we have to support them so we thought . . . it would be better for us to be alone and if we have some money left . . . what we have to do is send [it] back home.[101]

Antimiscegenation laws discouraged intermarriage in many cities. In California, for example, legislative bills passed in 1933 prohibited Filipino-white marriages. However, Filipina/os were able to engage in interracial marriages in Washington State, which had a great impact on the formation of heterosexual nuclear families in Seattle.[102]

Reflecting the skewed demographics in the community, Filipina women who desired marriage were heavily courted. John Castillo recalled meeting only two Filipinas at the University of Washington.[103] Although Filipino men often engaged in relationships with non-Filipinas, Filipina women suffered censure if they engaged in relationships with men from outside the community. Belen Braganza remembered: "I did date some American men too. Only I get in trouble because the Filipino want to beat them up you know. . . . I dated an American fellow once and . . . he came from Bremerton and the Filipinos gang up on him and he ended up lame. Another time I dated another fellow and he was from Seattle and one of the boys wanted to stab him."[104] Despite such reactions to Filipinas' dating white men, many Filipino men married or had relationships with outsiders to the community.

Heterosexual nuclear families were typically not transient, especially because Filipino male heads of households tended to find more stable jobs. Most of the heterosexual nuclear families in Seattle in the 1930s lived either near Chinatown or on First Hill.[105] Those who had more money were expected to share with other family and community members. Salvador Del Fierro remembered how many Filipinos lived with him and his wife in both Ketchikan and Seattle: "When we move to Seattle we had men, by golly, underneath our beds, in the toilets, all over the place."[106] Del Fierro's wife, Elizabeth, an Italian American, protested against the additional responsibility. As Del Fierro reported, "She said, 'Honey, how come! I didn't marry all those Filipinos.' Well you can't turn them down. They were your friends and they were up against it. I was working. I was fortunate enough to have a job so we keep the roof over their heads."[107]

"Family" was also contested terrain and the site for class, ethnic, racial, and other social hierarchies. Indeed, the antimiscegenation laws can be read as an attempt not only to enforce control of social boundaries but also to discourage the permanent settlement of Asian immigrants. Racial hierarchies in marriages shaped community formation in a critical way. Toribio Martin reports that if Filipino men were married to white women, "they remained incognito." But marrying a non-Filipino person of color, such as an Indian or black, was "less dangerous" than marrying a white person.[108] When Salvador Del Fierro married in 1925, his wife's father, who was Italian, disapproved of the match. The couple moved to Seattle, and Salvador Del Fierro worked at the Olympic Hotel for a year, but he was not satisfied with the situation. The Del Fierros decided to go back to Elizabeth's hometown and finally were accepted by Elizabeth's father.[109]

These interracial couples suffered the censure of the communities in which they lived. Hazel Simbe recalled the discrimination she faced from her neighbors: "I never paid attention to them [neighbors] because they wouldn't speak to me. They said all kind of rude things you know to my mother, I realize now that she suffered a lot on account of me too . . . really on account of us because they were so rude, just rude."[110] Relationships between Filipino men and Native American women are less well documented in the Pacific Northwest except for the Alaskan case, but they also were important in the area. Some of the main tribes that women represented included the Tlingit, Tsimshian, Yakima, and Haida, as well as Nootka and Lummi.[111] In her study of the Filipina/o community in Alaska, Thelma Buchholdt presents several examples of Filipina/o–Native American marriages, such as that of Casimiro "Roy" Aceveda

Sr., who married his wife, Gladys Friday, a Tlingit Indian, in 1941.[112] In general, the evidence suggests that Filipino men met Native American women through the course of work in Alaskan canneries, in the fields of central Washington, or elsewhere in the region. They labored side by side, processing salmon or picking fruit, and met and mingled. Like the other heterosexual nuclear families, these families often served as a focus for the Filipina/o community and provided a rare counterpoint to the experience of the largely male migratory workforce.

Not surprisingly, when one considers the difficulties of economic survival and the multitude of social pressures that the Filipina/o American community faced at the time, many family units were under regular stress. Although I found only one case in which domestic violence was explicitly discussed, given the general uncertainty and violence of the times, such as the anti-Filipina/o race riots in Washington State, one can speculate that domestic violence might have been more widespread than is commonly indicated. Documenting these issues is an important part of more fully measuring the hardships that the Filipina/o American community faced at this time, both within and without the household.

CONCLUSION

Although sharing commonalities with other Filipina/o American communities, the community that developed in Seattle took on unique resonance. In contrast to the common portrayal of Asian immigrant communities as insular and bounded, Filipina/os in Seattle used their urban community as a base from which to explore options in the city and the region, and in particular to locate work in Alaskan salmon canneries.

Furthermore, because Filipina/os found a range of opportunities in Seattle, particularly as a result of receiving an American education, there was a diversity in class experience, with both the working class and those with more resources inhabiting a similar space in the city. Reflecting this class differentiation, community members took advantage of the urban environment in different ways. While the passing worker might value Seattle for the variety of hotels available in Seattle Chinatown, others in the city might remain in this environment because of the opportunity it offered for jobs in the service sector as well as for small business entrepreneurs. In addition, there were the privileged few who were able to practice their professional occupations, although typically only within their ethnic communities. In part because of the city's less developed industrial base, Seattle's importance also resulted from its place as an urban center for rural areas, both in the surrounding area and in the American West as a whole. Once again, region was an important factor in the development of Filipina/o Seattle, and the formation of the city must always be considered in a wider context.

Racial demographics were another prominent reason for the uniqueness of the Seattle experience. The Filipina/o experience in Seattle contrasted greatly with that of communities in California, which have commanded the dominant share of attention within Asian American studies historiography. For example, unlike their fellow community members in California, Filipina/os in Seattle did not regularly operate in a primarily Mexican American context. In the regional experience of the Pacific Northwest, the dominant groups of color during this period tended to be Native Americans and Asian Americans. Stories like those told by the Rapadas, whose tale opens this chapter, highlight the interaction between Native Americans and Filipina/o Americans and were far more common in the Pacific Northwest than in California. Some of the material presented in this chapter also contrasts sharply with the common characterization of Filipina/o community life of the pre–World War II era, especially as popularized in American culture by Carlos Bulosan's famous work, *America Is in the Heart*. People often refer to the "bachelor society" of Filipina/o America at this time. Although this notion provides rich insight into the predominantly male community in places such as Seattle, it downplays the multiplicity of familial relations that connected members of the Filipina/o American community across space and time, particularly those involving women.

Figure 1. Salvador Caballero in Seattle, ca. 1920s.
Photograph from the Salvador Caballero Collection
and courtesy of the Filipino American National Historical
Society.

Figure 2. Mary Estigoy and daughter Dolores, Seattle, ca. 1930s. Women played a central role in the formation of pre–World War II Filipina/o Seattle on both sides of the Pacific Ocean. Photograph courtesy of the Filipino American National Historical Society.

Figure 3. Bauangenian Club, Seattle, ca. 1934–1935. Organizations based on ethnic and regional loyalties were a prominent part of community life, such as this one for Filipina/os from Bauang, La Union. Although the majority of the people in the photograph are probably of Filipina/o descent, a number of the women appear to be European American. Photograph courtesy of the Filipino American National Historical Society.

Figure 4. Paterno Hamoy and unidentified companion, ca. late 1920s. Migratory labor in the American West was a common form of employment for men in the Filipina/o American community. These men are standing in front of a lodging house that catered to these workers. Photograph courtesy of the Filipino American National Historical Society.

Figure 5. Filipino laborers in Alaska, ca. 1920s–1930s. This group photograph demonstrates the close ties that many of these workers had with one another, as well as the gendered nature of many forms of employment open to Filipina/o Americans at the time. Note the formal clothing of these laborers. Photograph by Phil Bracero and courtesy of the Filipino American National Historical Society.

Figure 6. "Casing the Salmon," Larsen Bay, Alaska, 1938. Photograph by Salvador Caballero, Salvador Caballero Collection, and courtesy of the Filipino American National Historical Society.

Figure 7. Agricultural workers, ca. 1930s. Farm labor was a mainstay of the Filipina/o American experience throughout the American West in the pre–World War II era. Photograph courtesy of the Filipino American National Historical Society.

Figure 8. Employees of the Rainier Club, ca. 1940–1941. Mike Castillano is at the far right of the picture. Many Filipina/os found labor opportunities within Seattle at area businesses. Photograph courtesy of the Filipino American National Historical Society.

Figure 9. The Ordona family, ca. 1940. Although most of the community at the time was composed of young men, there were also some nuclear families in Filipina/o Seattle. Photograph courtesy of the Filipino American National Historical Society.

Figure 10. Inscription on photograph reads, "Memorial Services for Brothers V. Duyungan and A. Simon, December 7, 1936." It is signed by Antonio Rodrigo, the secretary for the Cannery Workers' and Farm Laborers' Union at this time. In 1936, union officials Virgil Duyungan and Aurelio Simon were slain during a period of fierce contestation over unionization in the Alaskan salmon canning industry. Photograph from the Antonio Rodrigo Collection, and courtesy of the Filipino American National Historical Society.

PART THREE

Power and Choice

CHAPTER 5

Resistance, Return, and Organization

In the 1920s and 1930s, Filipina/o Americans had an expanded sense of their place and space within the Filipina/o diaspora, and they made their decisions according to these options. Unlike most Chinese Americans and Japanese Americans, they were able to travel relatively freely between Asia and the United States at a time when the United States' interests in the Pacific region increased the possibility of their travel, education, and employment, despite the hardships of the Great Depression. This mobility in the pre–World War II era is demonstrated by the choices made by Josefa Barrazona.

Like many of her generation, Josefa Barrazona was a community leader on both sides of the Pacific Ocean. In the Philippines, she endured the loss of her husband and four children before coming to Seattle in 1921 to attend the Northwest Training School, a religious college. She then returned to the Philippines, where she was a leader in the Filipina/o Methodist community, and eventually won an election to become a councilperson in a town in the province of Nueva Ecija. Later, after World War II, she came back to Seattle and spent the next several years continuing her career at the YMCA. In a *Seattle Times* article profiling her life on the occasion of her reaching one hundred years of age, Barrazona is quoted as saying, "I have passed through hardships, happiness, sorrow, and everything in the life of man. . . . I thank God that he has given me this life and that I am still living this life."[1]

The history of early professional pioneers such as Josefa Barrazona who operated within the transpacific economy has generally received limited attention in U.S. culture. However, these individuals' experiences reveal that transnationalism has been a regular feature for Asian Americans and that these processes were well under way prior to World War II. They also suggest, once again, that viewing Filipina/o American community formation solely in terms of the incorporation and assimilation of Filipina/os into American culture makes it likely that one would miss or oversimplify vital dimensions of the community's experience.

COLONIAL TALES

In contrast to the contributions of community pioneers such as Josefa Barrazona, the case of Marcelino Julian was front-page news in Seattle during the pre–World War II era. His story starts in the Philippines and also illustrates the workings of the American empire. Before emigrating to the United States in 1929, Marcelino Julian was a soldier and for three years served in the Philippine Constabulary, the American colonial military force in the Philippines. Like many young Filipino men of his generation, Julian decided to journey to the United States. After arriving in 1929, he found employment as a migratory worker and, as he reported, "followed the vegetable harvests from south to north along the Pacific Coast."[2]

On the night of November 23, 1932, Julian was robbed in Seattle by two African Americans, who took his $200 and beat him. Misfortune followed upon misfortune. The next morning, Julian visited a sick cousin at Harborview Hotel and later returned to his room to find another $100 stolen. After accusing Tito Guatlo of stealing the money, Julian stabbed him, and then Guatlo's nephew Cristolo Bayaoa.[3] Julian then went to a grocery to buy an orange with his remaining fifteen cents. As he recalled, "I remember I went into a grocery store at 424 6th Avenue South, and when a man there called me a 'monkey Filipino,' I stabbed at him."[4] According to Julian, the grocer said, "You ——— Filipino, you'd better go back to your own country."[5]

At this point, as Julian later recounted, his mind went blank. According to witnesses, he ran through the area of Sixth Avenue and King Street, knifing those people who were unfortunate enough to be in his way. The final count was six dead and thirteen wounded. Four Filipinos and two white men were killed, and three white men, two African American men, six Japanese men, one Japanese woman, and one Filipino were wounded. Julian was taken to jail and charged with first-degree murder.[6]

From the start, the Seattle newspapers used racialized imagery to explain the case, portraying Julian in subhuman terms. The day after the murders, the headlines of the *Seattle Post-Intelligencer* blared: "6 Killed, 12 Wounded as Crazed Filipino Runs Amuck with Knife in South End." It also reported: "'It was a mad dog chase,' officers who swarmed in scores through the death-haunted streets said. 'It was like chasing a wild beast. There was nothing human about it. The mob—ourselves—and ahead of us, that calm, trotting figure, dealing out death and shrieking unintelligible words each time he struck.'"

The newspaper described the final stabbing in lurid fashion, portraying Julian as a crazed figure: "Uttering a wild, maniacal shriek [Julian] sank his knife into the aged man and cowered over his body in a dark corner." For its readers' interest, the *Post-Intelligencer* published a grisly map marking where the stabbings occurred in Chinatown and a photograph of the seven-inch murder weapon.[7]

On the day after the murders, the *Seattle Post-Intelligencer* sought to explain the incident through cultural grounds. Quoting from the *Encyclopaedia Britannica,* the article reported that "running amok" was "the native term for the homicidal mania which attacks Malaya." It ended by saying that this problem was becoming less common because Filipino emigration to the mainland United States was decreasing.[8] The following year, in April 1933, Julian was convicted of first-degree murder and sentenced to life in the Walla Walla penitentiary.[9]

This terrible and tragic tale, in which people were killed and others wounded, stands at the juncture of several narratives that come together in the border city of Seattle. My purpose here is to concentrate less on the crime than on its impact upon the Filipina/o American community. Although Julian's killing spree was clearly horrific and unpardonable, here I focus on how his actions were understood and interpreted by both the mainstream press and his fellow Filipina/o community members. These kinds of newspaper accounts suggested that all Filipina/os had the potential to "run amok" and thus posed a danger. The overriding characterization of Julian as an unassimilable "savage" helps to demarcate several boundaries: "American" versus "alien," "white" versus "colored," "human" versus "animal."[10] Filipinas and Filipinos in Seattle, no matter what their relative standing in the community, encountered an American mainstream society based on ideologies about race that largely excluded them and other people of color. Attempts to exclude Filipina/os, like barriers erected against Chinese, Japanese, Asian Indian, and other Asian workers, were part of a long legacy of exclusion of Asian immigrants.[11]

The narrative also had important meanings for community members. Over the years, Julian's example became absorbed in the communal memory of Filipina/os, partly because of its extreme nature and partly because of its resonance for other community members. Unlike the characterization of the event by the Seattle newspapers as an example of the inherent animalistic nature of Filipina/os, the remembered story illustrates their social and economic vulnerability. Filipinos understood only too well the discrimination and racism directed against them and how the actions of one community member implicated others. Community member Jose Acena recounted a version of Julian's story some decades later, telling an interviewer that the man who ran amuck came from Pangasinan, was living in Chinatown, and "lost all the money that he made from Alaska."[12]

Several years after this incident, in his fictionalized autobiography *America Is in the Heart*, Carlos Bulosan presents what was likely a variation of Julian's story. Bulosan's narrator goes to a Chinese gambling house in Seattle and sees "a Filipino farm worker, an elderly man," who gambles away all his money. The man leaves the gambling house, returns with a gun, and fires at the Chinese dealers, a possible indication of Filipina/o resentment against Chinese and Japanese entrepreneurs in Seattle Chinatown. In the streets, the narrator finds that the Filipino "had gone completely crazy" and was stabbing people in the streets, killing eight and injuring sixteen.[13]

We do not know what Julian had hoped to do with the money he lost, which led to his murderous rampage through Chinatown. Perhaps he was planning to return to the Philippines. Or, as community member Carlos Toribio commented, he might have wanted to use the money to start his own business and gain economic self-sufficiency, one of the few options that Asian Americans could aspire to in a racially segregated city economy.[14] In that way, Julian would have been able to cross the line from being a migratory worker to becoming a small-business entrepreneur. The precariousness of that line of division underscores the vulnerability of the Filipina/o community as a whole.

RIGHTS AND RESISTANCE

In contrast to this image of the "crazed Filipino," which dominated Seattle papers as a result of Julian's crime, other ongoing campaigns by Filipina/os who sought to gain more rights for community members tended to get less media attention. One approach was to actively protest issues they considered unjust, such as the campaigns around attempted exclusion and repatriation in the 1930s. Another way, particularly for workers who were dissatisfied with their labor situation, was to migrate and find alternate means of employment, or actually to join together for strikes or other labor agitation. An additional option was to articulate these issues on a community level through the voice of community newspapers. Others formed organizations, such as the nurses group in which Paula Nonacido participated, using student groups as bases to voice a response to different issues.

These challenges to the system can be construed in the same context as challenges made by many communities of color. The protests over exclusion laws, alien land laws, or segregation in education by other Asian American groups were also important to Filipina/o Americans. Mexican Americans also shared a parallel political space with Filipina/o Americans, particularly in terms of shared labor organization and the exclusionary legislation of the 1935 repatriation act.[15]

At the same time, Filipina/os differed greatly from many of these other groups, primarily because they were American colonials who had free passage to the United States before 1934. And, unlike other immigrants who might not have had prior exposure to the English language through American or British imperialism, first-generation Filipina/o immigrants often had English-language skills. They also tended to be far more oriented toward the American educational system, in part because it was a continuation of education they might have received in the Philippines. Furthermore, their status as American nationals put them in a different relationship both to the American government and to the Philippine government than that of groups that were not part of the American colonial empire. Despite this political relationship, they tended to use unionization as a dominant site for protest, as opposed to requesting extensive government intervention from colonial authorities. While Filipina/os had significant interaction with the legal system, for example, they did not employ the legal system as actively as did, say, the Punjabi workers in California, who not only brought a tradition of litigation with them to the United States but also vigorously pursued this tradition in their settlement in the Imperial Valley.[16]

Place also mattered. In Hawai'i, political strategies took on other forms because of contrasting demographics in which Asian Americans were in the majority, and also because of the nature of the sugar plantation economy. Despite the severe oppression of the working class, Filipina/os in Hawai'i had a different base of support than on the American mainland, if only because the population was more stable as a whole and thus easier to organize as a group. On the U.S. mainland, organizing was made more difficult because workers moved so quickly from site to site. By contrast, in Hawai'i, people usually were relatively stationary because of the nature of plantation labor, and they forged common—if typically contested and factionalized—links with people from other groups.[17]

The kinds of resistance and struggles promoted in the public sphere were overwhelmingly male, as exemplified by the union movement. This can be explained in part by demographics, once again, which favored men, as well as by the heavy family responsibilities typically assigned to women in this period. At the same time, though, women were often constrained in the kinds of leadership positions they could hold in which they would be supported by the general community, although there were some notable exceptions.

STRUGGLES IN SEATTLE

In 1911, M. F. Bolima, who had been in the United States for five years, spoke of the treatment of Filipina/os in Seattle to the *Seattle Times*. In a rare published account, which was later reprinted in the *Washington Post* and gained the notice of the Bureau of Insular Affairs, Bolima articulated the hardships faced by Filipina/os in Seattle during the early years of the twentieth century. He reported, "We were led to believe that this civilized land stood for liberty and freedom from tyrrany [sic] and oppression, but we are not even left alone to pursue happiness in our own way, being made the butt of coarse language, and coarser treatment almost daily." He continued, referring to a local controversy about the poor treatment of Filipino workers by officers on the American transports *Burnside* and *Dix:*

> "They are men, not dogs, and deserve to be treated as men, but their treatment from the petty offices up is such as these officers would not give a dog. . . ." The Filipinos have no grudge against Uncle Sam. They have been doing and will continue to do faithfully everything that is required of them, and they do not believe that the Federal authorities give the officers on the Dix and Burnside permission to make tyrannical oppressors of themselves and to rough-handle the Filipinos and hurl vile epithets at them constantly.[18]

As an American colonial, Bolima was both protesting the treatment of Filipina/os by Americans and stressing that, as "good" nationals, they were entitled to fair treatment. Filipina/os had kept their part of the colonial bargain, and they expected Americans to do the same.

Since they were American colonials, there were government channels set up to address their concerns. Officially, Filipina/os in the United States were under the auspices of the Bureau of Insular Affairs, a United States government agency based in Washington, D.C., which oversaw the United States' territories and possessions. Philippine officials were also placed in the United States government, with resident commissioners from the Philippines located in the House of Representatives.[19]

American private citizens also attempted to intervene on behalf of Filipina/os. In 1917, Charles M. Baxter, a lawyer, began working on behalf of Filipina/os in Seattle who were being exploited by contractors. Baxter lobbied for years to get a commissioner appointed to Seattle, even collecting petitions from Filipina/os in Seattle and Bremerton supporting himself for that position.[20] Filipina/os themselves, as demonstrated by M. F. Bolima, were active instigators in protesting their situation and seeking remedy. The records of the Bureau of Insular Affairs contain numerous letters and petitions for intervention by the American government to improve the situation of Filipina/o laborers. As early as 1921, Filipina/os in Seattle campaigned for an employment agency and asked the Philippine government to grant aid to "one hundred homeless Filipinos," "very few" of whom wanted to go back to the Philippines or find work in Hawai'i. Eventually, despite their efforts to get a Seattle agency, authorities decided to concentrate their resources in California, and $1,500 was allocated to start a program in San Francisco.[21]

With the onset of the Great Depression, the position of Filipina/o laborers became more dire. In 1930, concern over Filipina/o workers in the United States led to the passage of House bill number 3208, calling for commissioners to look into the situation of Filipina/o workers overseas. This would allow the Philippine government to officially investigate reports of the plight of Filipina/os in the United States and American territories.[22] Some political leaders went directly to the United States to advocate for Filipina/os, in the process gaining themselves political visibility. In September 1930, Vicente Villamin, "lawyer, economist and legislative agent," toured the West Coast, stopping in Filipino labor camps in California clad in overalls, and visiting local chambers of commerce. Villamin suggested various solutions to ease tensions, including having "growers and bankers in California arrange a saving system for Filipinos," further opportunities for organized religion, and recruiting workers for Hawai'i from the abundant labor pool in California.[23] The following month, Villamin spoke in Yakima against further migration of Filipinos to the United States.[24] In his quest to aid workers, Villamin was joined by Juan Sumulong, another political leader, who came to California in 1930 to try to remedy the Filipina/o labor situation and to organize meetings between Filipina/os and "California state officials."[25]

Filipina/o workers also actively made their position known to government officials, particularly in Hawai'i. Given the greater percentage of Filipina/o workers in Hawai'i vis-à-vis the general population, this increased activism was not surprising. In 1932, three hundred out-of-work Filipinos protested in Honolulu, asking Cayetano Ligot, Filipino labor commissioner, for work, economic aid, and passage to the Philippines.[26] Less than two weeks later, over four hundred out-of-work Filipina/os again demonstrated, asking for work or free passage back to the Philippines.[27] In October 1933, the Filipino Labor Union also cabled the Philippine legislature to ask for repatriation of unemployed Filipina/os in Hawai'i.[28]

But no matter what their location, Filipina/os received limited economic aid from the Philippine government during their plight. For example, President Manuel Quezon told protesting laborers in Hawai'i that although an "office of inspector-general of labor" had been organized, the Philippine government generally was not able to help out-of-work Filipina/os in Hawai'i.[29] Other voices in the Philippines were also unsympathetic. One editorial in the *Philippines Herald* argued vehemently against funding the return home of workers who left for Hawai'i, claiming, "They went there at their own risk and to bring them back here at our public expense were *[sic]* not only to encourage irresponsibility, but to penalize the government for the acts of its subjects which are clearly in contravention of its established policies."[30] Governor-General Davis commented in 1930 that rather than trying to keep Filipina/os from going to the United States, it would be better to provide workers with the opportunity "to stay here and develop their own country."[31] In contrast, Gilbert González has noted how the Mexican consul had an instrumental role in strikes of Mexican workers in the United States and charts the consul's significant involvement in four major California strikes in the early 1930s. In one strike in Los Angeles County in 1933, for example, the Los Angeles consul was instructed by the Mexican government to remove communist leaders from the organization of the strike.[32]

Given the turmoil over the relationship of the United States and the Philippines during this period, this indecisiveness on the part of the Philippine government is not surprising. Clearly, it had enough problems at home. For example, in 1930 and again in 1932, the Philippine Bureau of Labor estimated that the country had forty thousand unemployed agricultural workers.[33] With massive unrest among workers in the Philippines, the government had few resources to assist the relatively privileged laborers who had made their way across the Pacific Ocean. Characteristically, though, the U.S. government did keep close records of labor activism not only in Hawai'i and the mainland United States but also in the Philippines itself, particularly through the Bureau of Insular Affairs.[34]

In the Philippines, workers responded to their oppression in varied ways. In the face of difficult circumstances, some chose to move. In 1932, the Bureau of Labor relocated eight hundred families to Mindanao. The following year brought dismal reports. Workers in early 1933 told of a difficult life in Mindanao, where locusts ruined their crops and families were forced to subsist on "tubers and root crops."[35] Other Philippine workers chose active protest. As one article reported, laborers located in Nueva Ecija might even take the lives of or hold for ransom carabaos belonging to landlords. Fellow workers could be signaled by red flags to avoid certain landlords. These kinds of protests demonstrate the hardship of the times, as well as the methods of resistance available to workers.[36]

This kind of class-based protest was increasingly widespread. In the daylong rebellion in Tayug in 1931, the workers burned the Constabulary barracks and houses of the elite, as well as tax and land records.[37] Although many such uprisings were of short duration, they were characteristic of worker rebellions in the late 1920s and 1930s. One strike in Bulacan, Pampanga, and Nueva Ecija involved 30,000 rice and sugar workers; other laborers protested in railroads, cigar factories, and other urban sites from 1925 until the close of the 1930s. From August to October 1934, an estimated 11,500 tobacco laborers participated in a cigarmakers' strike, virtually closing nineteen related establishments.[38] One of the most notable events of social unrest was the Sakdal movement, headed by Benigno Ramos, a former beneficiary of Quezon. Ramos began a Tagalog weekly called the *Sakdal* that fervently denounced the American administration and organized its readers into a movement. In 1934, the Sakdalistas sponsored electoral candidates whose platforms included condemnations of colonial education and imperialism and calls for full independence. Nevertheless, Sakdalistas were targeted for arrest and harassment when they protested against the plebiscite for the Commonwealth Constitution. The revolt began in Bulacan with 150 protesters, spreading to 68,000 workers. The Constabulary hastily clamped down on this unrest, and at the end, 57 were dead, with hundreds more injured or imprisoned.[39]

Other class-based organizations, such as the National Confederation of Tenants, were active in the Philippines during this period.[40] Further working-class organization in central Luzon led to the establishment of the Socialist Party in 1929.[41] By the late 1920s, labor leaders in the Philippines had also made contacts with the Communist movement abroad. The Congreso Obrero de Filipinas (Proletariat), or the Katipunan ng mga Anak-Pawis ng Pilipinas, was formed, with the Communist Party of the Philippines (CPP) gaining official status in November 1930. In January 1931, when a CPP Central Committee member died in a car accident en route to prison, more than 10,000 protesters were estimated to have demonstrated, bearing red flags and signs denouncing imperialism. Although the colonial government soon bore down upon the CPP, Communists such as Patricio Dionisio had an impact on the workers' movement. In 1930 Dionisio formed the Tangulan, a secret society calling for independence through armed force, which grew until it had 40,000 supporters. However, a planned uprising by this group on Christmas Eve 1931 was quelled by Constabulary soldiers.[42]

RETURNING HOME: EXCLUSION

During this time of increasing political dissension in the Philippines, debate continued there and within the United States about continued colonization. In the 1930s, the impetus for independence came from a combination of forces, including a Filipina/o independence movement, the desire of organized labor to curtail competition from Asian workers, and American agricultural interests, which feared competition from Philippine sources. The Smoot-Hawley Tariff of 1929 was followed by the Hare-Hawes-Cutting Bill, under which ten years were allotted for free trade, the placing of quotas on Philippine exports, immigration quotas of fifty Filipina/os per year to the United States, and "special American rights" in the former colony. Despite President Hoover's veto, Congress passed the bill, particularly because the Great Depression left farm interests in the United States in an untenable position, and Asian exclusion was an easy issue around which to rally. In 1934, when the Tydings-McDuffie Act was passed, the Philippines was promised independence after ten years of commonwealth status. The ten-year transition period maintained American control within the islands until the recognition of sovereignty on July 4, 1946.[43]

Before the close of easy passage to the United States with the onset of the Tydings-McDuffie Act, political leaders continued to debate the fate of Filipina/o laborers in the United States. One solution was to try to bring workers back to Asia. In the Philippines, Hermenegildo Cruz, the director of labor, suggested two plans: that the Philippine government work with the U.S. federal government to bring impoverished Filipina/os home on navy and army transports, and that the legislature set aside money for the repatriation of Filipina/os.[44]

Laborers began to make their way home, particularly because options in the Philippines seemed to offer relative hope. A Philippine newspaper article in 1932 announced that Claro Tagaragan, from Menlo Park, California, and about thirty others informed the Bureau of Labor that they were interested in the funds offered for transportation of people from anywhere in the Philippines to Mindanao.[45] Others returned because their overseas stint had ended. Three hundred workers came back from Hawai'i to the Philippines in July 1933. The article indicated that around 70 percent of these workers were from the Ilocos region.[46]

Stephen Griffiths's study of the Ilocos Norte village, based on research conducted in the 1970s, offers an indication of emigrant patterns and the rates of return to the home region. Griffiths found that 75 percent of the men sixty years old or older in this particular locale had worked in California and Hawai'i. Over 50 percent of these men had come back home prior to World War II, when their three-year terms were finished. Eleven of the men eventually came back at "retirement age," to marry and raise families. A significant one-third of the women who were sixty years old or older had never been married. Although there probably was local differentiation in rates of migration, Griffiths's community profile offers a sense of the long-term migratory movements within the Filipina/o community. His analysis is also useful because it is extremely likely that many of the workers who labored in California made their way through Seattle at some point in order to work in the Alaskan canneries.[47]

Others decided to return to the Philippines because they were needed at home. Paula Nonacido, whose story was recounted earlier, came back to the Philippines in 1939 because of the outbreak of World War II and her concern for her mother, and was granted "a position as matron for the home for Women and Children."[48] Even if people did not return themselves, many had family members who traveled home to the Philippines, further consolidating the back-and-forth ties of extended Filipina/o community. Felipe Dumlao's brother went to Hawai'i and later came back to the Philippines.[49] One of Jose Acena's brothers traveled overseas for just two years and then returned. Jose Acena explained, "So those that went home, you know, took a chance anyway, to go home and get a good job, they find employment in the islands. Those that stayed here stayed here until things became better."[50]

Filipina/os also returned home because of family ties, particularly because they wanted to see parents or other cherished relatives. However, that did not necessarily mean they were planning to stay in the Philippines. In 1930, the Laigo family journeyed back to the Philippines. Bibiana Laigo Castillano remembered, "My mother said, 'Before I die, I want to see at least one of your children so that I have something to remember your family. And besides, we also want to see the man that you married.'" Castillano's fifth child was born in the Philippines, and when the baby was six months old, the family returned to Seattle. Through connections ("a friend who was a real estate man"), the Laigos were able to purchase a house, an unusual event at the time because of the transience of most community members.[51]

Some Filipina/os were forced by American authorities to go home to the Philippines. One article published in the *Philippines Herald* in 1932 reported that two women and one man from Seattle returned to the Philippines after being deported by Seattle immigration officials on the S.S. *President Cleveland*. The article commented that they "had gone insane due to mental preoccupation [sic] over lack of subsistence while in a foreign land."[52] In January 1933, seventy Filipinos who were "public charges of the state of California" were shipped home to a hospital in San Felipe Neri.[53] Not all the Filipina/os who took advantage of this offer might have been really sick. Two Filipinos who were shipped from King County, Washington, in 1933 by American immigration officials were suspected by Philippine officials of having feigned mental illness to get a free ride home.[54]

In January 1935, Francisco A. Delegado, the Philippines resident commissioner, wrote Brigadier General Creed F. Cox concerning the problems of the Filipina/o population in the United States: "Again, that communities of Filipinos have been shipped back to the Philippine Islands in order to avoid giving them relief or public works jobs, and that not a few are being sent to forced labor camps for identical reasons." Delgado continued regarding disputes over Filipina/o workers, "The most recent unfairness in the situation [is] now existing in Seattle, where longshoremen obstinately refuse to unload cargo from ships employing Filipinos in their crews, in an endeavor to have them ousted."[55]

With the rise of this kind of sentiment, campaigns to exclude Filipina/os continued. Some Filipina/os in California tried to argue for voluntary repatriation in 1931 to ward off exclusion, but the repatriation bill was finally passed in 1935. Filipina/os were able to return to the Philippine Islands through a federal program, but they lost the privilege of being able to reenter the United States unless they were part of the specified annual quota of fifty people. However, just 2,190 Filipina/os out of the roughly 45,000 who were eligible took advantage of this offer. The Great Depression and the Tydings-McDuffie Act of 1934 had already greatly decreased the number of Filipina/os coming into the country.[56] Emory Bogardus noted that some chose not to take advantage of the 1935 legislation because of an upturn in the economy or because they wanted to retain the option of returning to the Philippines. Paying one's own expenses was preferable to the shame of coming home at government expense or being faced with the ignominy of not being able to go back to the United States. Community sentiment also recognized the plan as a form of exclusion.[57]

Whereas only a small percentage of Filipina/os used the repatriation bill to go home, this exclusionary legislation had a large impact on Mexican immigrants and their American-born children. Between 1929 and 1932, over 365,000 people from these groups journeyed to Mexico. Camille Guerin-Gonzales notes that many of those targeted for repatriation to Mexico were American citizens or legal residents. As she argues, "U.S. authorities, though, did not simply 'return' Mexicans to their home country, but sent many American citizens into exile in a foreign country."[58] While discussions of repatriation should properly concentrate on what was happening in the Mexican American community because of the virulence of repatriation there, and while Filipina/o Americans were affected on a far smaller scale, the fact that repatriation legislation was enacted against Filipina/o Americans is an indication of the extreme racism of the times. Only seven years later, Japanese Americans, including both immigrants and American-born children, would be targeted for forcible removal either to concentration camps in remote parts of the American West or to Japan.[59]

As shown by the numbers, most Filipina/os already in the United States did not wish to return to the Philippines, and so the repatriation program was a failure in terms of its exclusionary purposes. For example, Toribio Martin was nearly deported in 1935, when he woke up in a guarded hospital room after blacking out. Among his fellow deportees in custody were Filipina/os who had been houseboys in the red light district. Martin was lucky: both the president of the Bush Bank and the president of the Hop Growers Association vouched for him in Oregon, and he was released for work. He rode a freight car to Oregon to his former job and remained there for fifteen years.[60] Juan Mina also stayed in the United States despite the lure of a free ticket home because he did not want to return to the Philippines "bare-handed."[61] After her husband's death, Bibiana Laigo Castillano was offered $5,000 by her lawyer to return to the Philippines. She did not take the money, for, as she recalled, "Why should I go to the Philippines? I have no one to look for. They are all gone. So I better stay here." It took two years for Castillano to make her decision to stay in the United States with her young children, and then she finally buried her husband in the United States.[62]

THE RETURN OF THE REPATRIATES

The Filipina/os who returned to the Philippines did not necessarily come back to the life of luxury they might have dreamed about during their years of struggle and hard work in the United States. Benicio Catapusan reported that Filipina/os without education might face resistance from their home communities in their efforts to offer "American ways." As Catapusan writes regarding their reception: "Their 'superior air' and 'American ways,' and their hyperaggressiveness appear irritating to most villagers and are oftentimes the subject of gross criticism, which in turn creates a low estimate of all the Filipino repatriates from America. They sometimes appear independent, self-conscious, and indifferent, which is oftentimes regarded as 'high-hatting' their fellow citizens. Such airs are oftentimes overestimated."[63]

Some workers brought home technological and cultural knowledge from the United States. Those who returned with capital were able to purchase land, and some became small entrepreneurs. Catapusan listed restaurants, stores, real estate, irrigation, "animal husbandry," poultry businesses, and dairy and ice businesses as the areas in which returnees established themselves.[64] Their reception, though, was uneven, similar to that of members of other communities who also went "home." For example, George Sánchez notes regarding Mexican Americans who went to Mexico that "the most skilled and the most Americanized repatriates—the very people the Mexican government hoped would bring progress to their villages—became the most discontented."[65]

Some Filipina/os consisted of a "minority group" characterized by "deported criminals and problem cases." Catapusan found that "it appears that although some of them hold adverse attitudes toward the United

States they have become devoted workers in their own community."
While some might have attempted "to introduce modern racketeering"
at home, these repatriates apparently faced resistance from their communities. Catapusan reported that they were perceived as bringing home
undesirable traits from United States culture. Although their activities
engendered much discussion by others, they were nevertheless welcomed if they demonstrated a desire to become part of the community
again.[66]

In contrast to the looser standards present in the United States, returnees
to a rural region often came home to strict community surveillance. As
Catapusan noted, "This is the kind of social control in the Islands' rural communities, where conformity to the group is the rule rather than
the exception."[67]

Other Filipina/os likely returned with an interest in labor activism.
George Sánchez has found that some Mexican repatriates agitated for
greater gains and for the government to implement its land reform policy when they came back from the United States, because of factors such
as having had higher wages, experience with unions, exposure to other
kinds of religious practices, and greater literacy.[68] Similarly, although it
has been less documented, the movement of workers between Hawai'i,
the American mainland, and the Philippines likely had some impact on
what was happening in the Philippines. In 1929, Pedro Calosa, let go in
Hawai'i for organizing workers, returned to Pangasinan and organized
a major political uprising in the Philippines. Participants attacked Tayug,
a town in the Pangasinan province, in 1931. The controversial labor
leader Pablo Manlapit, in another example, first came to Honolulu in
1910; he went to Los Angeles in 1927 after being convicted in a trial,
which he perceived as harassment because of his organizing activities.
Manlapit lived in California from 1927 to 1932 and then returned to
Hawai'i in that year. In 1934, he was again convicted for requiring too
much payment in helping an army veteran to secure money from the U.S.
Veterans' Bureau and went back to the Philippines.[69]

Regardless of who was able to come, political and economic relations
in home communities were profoundly affected by the travel of so many
workers to the United States. With the influx of overseas money from
successful emigrants, some former tenants could buy property. At the
same time, American colonization brought new educational and political opportunities, motivating landlords to sell property to generate
funds.[70] Many onetime sojourners ended up staying in the United States,
biding their time until the economy improved. As their stakes in settle-

ment in the United States increased, they continued to utilize community organizations to develop resources and opportunities.

ORGANIZATION IN A COLONIAL ENVIRONMENT

Whether directly invoked or not, the experience of colonialism undergirds the entire experience of being Filipina or Filipino in Seattle. Historian C. L. R. James's comments about the role of cricket in Trinidad when he was growing up provides insight into this phenomenon. James was an avid fan, whose enthusiasm for cricket would become a lifelong passion. He remarks about the function of this colonial game in his home community:

> I haven't the slightest doubt that the clash of race, caste and class did not retard but stimulated West Indian cricket. I am equally certain that in those years social and political passions, denied normal outlets, expressed themselves so fiercely in cricket (and other games) precisely because they were games. . . . Thus the cricket field was a stage on which selected individuals played representative roles which were charged with social significance.[71]

In the same way, mutual aid provided the social and political state in which Filipina/os could realize their ambitions. Because community life was premised upon exclusion from mainstream American culture, these organizations provided essential help as well as status. Participation in social organizations provided alternative "families," with memberships that typically stretched up and down the West Coast and across the Pacific Ocean to the Philippines. These organizations were particularly important in a context of regular political disenfranchisement. In contrast to the barriers and oppression Filipina/os regularly faced in mainstream society, the organizations provided a space in which they could regain some status. As one community leader commented:

> In the '20s and '30s, these men, bright men, were called boys by their bosses. "Boys, do this, do that," you know. They would refer to their crew as "my Filipino boys." . . . That's six days out of a week which gets to be pretty dehumanizing. The seventh day of the week . . . they were masters of their own destiny, because they could become presidents, they could become vice-presidents.[72]

There were several kinds of community organizations, and Filipina and Filipino Americans typically held multiple memberships in various groups, creating intricate networks of loyalties. John Mendoza recalled about the communal ethos at that time: "I think they seem to take care of the Filipinos in here because somebody takes care of them. . . . They took it among themselves to do it. That was very, very nice."[73] Many of these organizations were centered around the experience of migration, offered concrete economic assistance for arriving Filipina/os, and were based on ethnic ties.[74] They thus provided crucial help for Filipina/os far away from their home villages. One of the most important functions of the fraternal lodges, for example, was to ensure that members were buried properly and that their funerals were attended by other lodge members.[75] This significant role of many immigrant organizations at the time, such as in the Chinese American community, is a telling indication of the persistence and centrality of ethnic loyalties, and of their absolute necessity given the fact that the communities of origin were literally an ocean away for most immigrant workers. At the same time, however, the historical evidence suggests that the focus on ethnic and regional identity sometimes divided the Filipina/o community, particularly in labor struggles, and inhibited the forging of class consciousness in many parts of the expanded American community. In the 1924 strike in Hawai'i, for instance, Ilocana/o laborers were brought in as strikebreakers to counter the militancy of Visayans, which further exacerbated tensions.[76] Similar ethnic divisions would also inform community life in Seattle.

Religion was also a prominent component of Filipina/o American community life, as illustrated by the experiences of Josefa Barrazona, mentioned earlier. Barrazona first learned about the Methodist religion from missionaries living in her community in the Philippines. The small Methodist community had to meet discreetly because, as Barrazona said in an interview, "People who found out would throw rocks at the building." A graduate of a Methodist Bible school in the Philippines, Barrazona later became "the first Filipino dean" of Hugh Wilson Hall, a residence for Methodist girls. Later, after being widowed, she came to the United States to learn to be a deaconess. In Seattle, she met her second husband, an evangelist.[77]

There were several important spaces for religious worship in Filipina/o Seattle. The Maryknoll church, where a number of community members worshiped, was organized in Seattle in 1920, after Maryknoll sisters came to the city to begin a convent and school. The school was shut down in 1942 because of the Japanese American internment. During that era, both Japanese American and Filipina/o American Catholics transferred to Our Lady Queen of Martyrs. After this church closed in 1953, many of these Filipina/os started regularly worshiping at the Immaculate, which was a shorter distance from where the community as a whole resided.[78]

Another important organization was the Filipino Catholic Club, a key communal group with which the Filipino Holy Names Society and the Filipino St. Vincent de Paul group were also associated.[79] These networks offered both spiritual and material help to community members, particularly in the context of the migration experience. For instance, Eddie Acena, from Ilocos Norte, came to Seattle for school because four of his cousins were studying at the University of Washington and St. Martin's College in Olympia. When he arrived, he was able to go straight to the Filipino Catholic Club on Eleventh Avenue and Terrace.[80]

Belen Braganza participated in activities at Maryknoll Church, Blessed Sacrament Church, and another cathedral. She recalled that after her marriage, she would "go to Cathedral early in the morning and then go to Maryknoll at the ten o'clock Mass." Braganza also remembered that the Methodists "were really active."[81] John Castillo's memories resemble Braganza's observations. Castillo reported of the Filipino Christian Fellowship Association of the First Methodist Church: "Every Sunday they hold a sort of a social gathering, a program. And that's where we get all acquainted and that's where we air the problems that we have. And that's where we get counsel. You know, constructive counsel, so that we shall not, you know, despair. You see, and keep on fighting to get what we wanted."[82]

The Filipino Federation of America was also a major Filipino organization, particularly in Hawai'i and California. Its members believed that Hilario Camino Moncado was divine, that he "was God and the Filipino 'brown Christ.'"[83] However, the federation did not have a strong following in Seattle, probably because of the deep-rooted Catholicism in the community.[84]

Fraternal lodges were crucial social organizations, particularly given the harsh treatment of Filipina/os outside of the closed community organizations. John Mendoza remembered an early lodge that "was composed of those old timers, like, real old timers, older than me." It was associated with the Prince Hall, an African American lodge that had formed a separate group because of racial segregation that prevented their membership in the white Masonic organizations.[85] In later years, three of the most prominent lodges were the Dimas Alang, the Legionnarios del Trabajo, and the Gran Oriente Filipino. The lodges were not officially Masonic but were "Masonic in nature," and some dated back to "the anti-clerical feeling during the Philippine Revolution."[86] Mendoza commented: "We banded together to help one another. To promote better understanding of the American people after we came over here and to promise business and things like that. But we mostly, we tried to improve our lot. We tried to fight for our rights. I tell you we were really respect[ed]."[87]

John Castillo reported about membership in a fraternal lodge in 1936:

> I've been very much interested in the Filipinos. I thought, perhaps, by being connected with some of these fraternal organizations, I'd be more in a position to help, you know, in the social and civic activities of the Pinoys here. . . . [For the Masonic programs, the] cream of the American Public are invited as usually guests of honor. And being a guest in any of these occasions, they learn more about the history of the Filipino and the history of the fraternity. The part they played in the development of the community for example, or the contributions that matter.[88]

Nevertheless, Filipinos faced discrimination even in the fraternal lodges. The Catholic-based Knights of Columbus chapter in Seattle was racially segregated, and Filipinos had to join a chapter in Chehalis, a hundred miles away from the city. Hence, they formed the Filipino Columbian Club, which represented Filipino members from various councils.[89] Other organizations were centered around social activities or recreational sports. Pete Filiarca reported that there was a Filipino tennis club, which practiced at Broadway and Volunteer Park and held tournaments and banquets.[90]

Although most of the leaders in community organizations in this period were male, some women also had prominent roles, although typically within a space designated for women. Perhaps the most important of these groups was the Filipino Women's Club, essentially a social club whose members were predominantly married women. One of its main functions was to hold dances. According to Belen Braganza, the Filipino Women's Club was begun in 1932, with a membership of under a dozen women. Women in this group maintained social obligations despite heavy responsibilities in their households. Braganza reported, "[Bibiana Laigo Castillano] was here but . . . but she was never able to go to the meetings, you know why, one kid after the other, (laughs) but anytime we needed her she's willing to help." Because the women's club was established before the Filipino Community Club, which after World War II would become a dominant organization in the community, according to Braganza, "it [the Filipino Women's Club] was actually the one that started them [the Filipino Community Club] going."[91]

NATION AND COLONIALISM

With such a far-flung Philippine community, Filipina/os devised many strategies to retain and to forge a Filipina/o identity, which was usually centered around male nationalism. Teodolo Ranjo, who joined the Dimas Alang in 1941, reported that these organizations were a substitute for going home because passage to the Philippines was so expensive: "Yeah, all the different fraternities here, Dimas Alang, Tyee and all that, you know, I think we were really lonesome. We dream about our Philippines."[92] Community organizations maintained the diaspora not only by giving support to Filipina/os far away from home but also by promoting a cohesive Filipina/o identity across the Pacific Ocean.

This strategy was similar to efforts within comparable communities. Renqiu Yu, for example, has discussed the importance of nationalist organizing among laundry workers in the Chinese Hand Laundry Alliance in New York.[93] In her autobiography, Mary Paik Lee recounts the political support that Korean American communities gave to the nationalist effort in Korea, and in fact opens her book with a discussion of the occupation of Korea by Japan following the Russo-Japanese War.[94] Karen Leonard has shown the central role of such groups within the Punjabi community, which also had a range of organizations typically informed by religious lines or by reference to the region from which participants came. For example, Punjabis in Stockton organized a Sikh group called the Pacific Coast Khalsa Diwan Society, which had the important task of ensuring that Sikhs were properly cremated after death, in keeping with religious beliefs. Another group, formed in Sacramento, was the Moslem Association of America, which, among other responsibilities, maintained an area in Sacramento City Cemetery for the burial of Punjabi Moslems from northern and central California.[95]

Because of their relatively greater access to capital and education, Filipina/os in the United States were particularly valuable members of the overseas communities. Several organizations promoted nationalism, such as the Balagtas Society, which was inaugurated to promote the Tagalog language.[96] When the Philippines gained "independence" and commonwealth status in 1935, elaborate celebrations lasting for two days were held in the Filipina/o community to herald the new era.[97]

Fraternal organizations were primary outlets for nationalist sentiment. Teodolo Ranjo, who joined the Dimas Alang in 1941, reported of the group, "It was a civic organization, mainly fostering the idea of the dreams of the 'Katipuneros,' . . . our forefathers who fought for our independence." The Dimas Alang was initiated by Andres Bonifacio as part of the resistance movement against Spain. The organization moved overseas "around 1922" and began branches in Hawai'i and the mainland United States. In 1923, Filipina/os organized a branch in Seattle.[98]

Newspapers provide valuable insight into how, on a communal level, a national consciousness was both forged and contested. Newspapers regularly featured news from "home" in the Philippines, along with Tagalog-language columns. Front-page articles avidly followed developments concerning the relationship between the United States and the Philippines, helping to mold public opinion in the Seattle Filipina/o community.[99] As an illustration, laudatory front-page articles in the *Philippine Advocate* in September 1935 about Manuel Quezon's election to the presidency left little doubt as to whom the *Advocate* supported.[100] Reports from Filipina/os in different sites of the Philippine diaspora further encouraged the spread of nationalism and kept communities in touch with each other.[101] These channels of communication were essential because of the dispersal of Filipina/os on both sides of the Pacific Ocean.

Community newspapers reveal the range of opinions that might have characterized debates within Filipina/o Seattle. For example, in 1928 an article in Seattle's *Philippine-American Review* about Filipino nationalist leader Artemio Ricarte reported that he advocated "immediate independence." The article remarked, "Says he fought for it, the American government solemnly promised to the people of the Islands their freedom if a stable government can be established therein. Nowadays the government of the Philippines is stable, and therefore now is the time to make the Filipinos free."[102]

During the debate over independence, one paper featured a mention of a group's attempt to restore Spanish influence over the Philippines. The *Philippine American Chronicle* reported in 1934 that a "Hispano-Philippine Society" was formed in Madrid "so that bonds of union and friendship between Spain and the Philippines could be renewed and strengthened."[103] More immediate than this example of wishful thinking was the threat of Japanese occupation. One person, a law professor at the Philippine University, was quoted in another article as saying, "If it is to be that fate of the Philippines forever to be under the control of a foreign power, the Philippines, I am sure, would rather see their country under the sovereignty of an Oriental nation than owe allegiance to a western power."[104]

Clearly, the colonial relationship might have constrained the public display of some community sentiment in Filipina/o Seattle. In contrast, the Punjabi community in California had the Ghadar Party organized in California in 1913; the party protested British colonialism, taking some of its moral authority from the revolution of the United States against the British.[105] The struggle of Korean immigrants in the United States against Japanese occupation also provided a central focus for the Korean community in Hawaiʻi and the mainland United States, and funds for the resistance movement were regularly raised in these communities.[106]

In protesting colonialism, though, Filipina/os in the United States were addressing resistance in the land of the colonizer, and this likely shaped the response in some sectors, particularly among those who were more privileged. One of the most interesting examples of this "careful" nationalism was the annual stories about the nationwide celebration of Rizal Day in Filipina/o communities throughout the United States.[107] Jose Rizal was a doctor and writer who was executed by the Spanish administration for his works promoting Filipina/o nationalism and independence.[108] One writer described him as the "great martyr and true saviour of our beloved Philippines."[109] Because Rizal was a hero against Spanish imperialists, Rizal Day was a "safe" holiday around which to rally for American colonials. Filipina/os could debate nationhood and patriotism, but in a context that was not necessarily anti-American. Nor were these nationalist celebrations anticapitalist. Like the popularity contests discussed in the next chapter, they usually showcased community leaders, typically business leaders.[110] Roland L. Guyotte and Barbara M. Posadas, who explore the meanings and contested nature of Rizal Day, also point out how the event became a site of factionalism. They note that in Chicago in 1932, Rizal Day was marked by at least three programs. Two of these were a product of divisions over how many representatives of sponsoring groups would be able to sit at the speaker's table.[111]

As the Rizal Day memorials suggest, the manner by which Filipina/os constructed their national identities as "Filipina/os" was heavily determined by the colonial relationship to the United States. Filipina/os were well aware that legal and economic barriers to their inclusion in American culture were selectively built or dismantled depending on American political prerogatives.

Just as the Rizal Day celebrations tended to promote those with more class resources, the newspapers often showcased the viewpoints of the community's elite, tending to privilege the class viewpoints of the Filipina/o intelligentsia who were contributors to the publications and who likely had decided to stay in the United States. In response to the unrest in the

Philippines in the mid-1930s, even pro-labor newspapers hastened to prove the loyalty of Filipina/os. In 1934 a front-page article in the union-oriented *Philippine-American Chronicle* about the Sakdal rebellion declared in its headline, "No Communists in the Philippines." The article called for a liberal solution to popular discontent by asking the Philippine government to ameliorate the situation:

> Surely, the Philippine government is well informed; when slavery of workers is not tolerated, there is no fear of the Philippine Islands of becoming a fertile soil for communistic principles.
> Wages as low as fifty cents a day without board or lodging and fourteen hours will surely aggravate the situation. We hope, therefore, that the Philippine authorities will take action and perhaps legislation for shorter hours and higher wages which will end the so-called communistic rebellion.[112]

On its editorial page, the contractor-oriented *Philippine Advocate* also hastened to minimize what it called the Sakdalista uprising, arguing, "It would not do the least damage, either to the political prestige of the Philippines or to the intellectual capacity of the Filipino people, to dismiss the Sakdalista incident as a minor and almost insignificant event that has popped up only as a political demonstration of a minor party among fourteen million Filipinos."[113] In another editorial directly below the first one, the newspaper's editors seemed to try to minimize the implications of the unrest with an announcement about a new trade organization called the Philippine-American Society, whose chief aim was "the promotion of goodwill between the Philippines and the United States through a closer and more harmonious trade relationship."[114]

The complicated nature of community opinion as expressed in Filipina/o newspapers is also evidenced in the same issue of the *Philippine Advocate* by Trinidad Rojo, a University of Washington graduate. Rojo criticized American colonial control of the Philippines and argued that the central cause of the unrest was the "unfair provisions" of the independence legislation, which he labeled an ingenious creation of self-love. Simultaneously, Rojo also downplayed the Sakdal uprising, stating, "In duration, extent and cost, the longshoremen's strike in America last spring was more menacing to order and business than the Sakdalista trouble."[115] Rojo's claim is intriguing, particularly given the massive upheaval in the Philippines at the time. His words emphasize the need for Filipina/os to justify their inclusion in American society, especially because of the general hostility directed against Filipina/os during the economically difficult times of the 1930s. As he later emerged as president of the Seattle cannery workers' union, Rojo's commentary underscores the complexity of class identity in Filipina/o Seattle. These reactions to the Sakdal rebellion suggest the importance of placing Filipina/o American history not only in the context of developments in both the United States and the Philippines but also within the regional politics of the American West and the local framework of Seattle.

POSSIBILITIES

Filipina/o leftists in Seattle in general were infrequently discussed in the oral history interviews. There are multiple reasons for this silence. One, perhaps, was the federal government's monitoring of leftist Filipina/o activity on both sides of the Pacific Ocean, and the awareness of possible harassment that might ensue following public discussion of leftist politics. For example, information from the records of the Bureau of Insular Affairs in the 1930s reveals that in at least one instance, the United States watched Communist representatives who were on ships that went to the Philippines.[116] Later, in the red scare of the 1950s, some leftist Filipina/o workers would be prosecuted by the United States government, which resulted in arrests and deportation hearings. The cost of this kind of political oppression was steep, both in terms of the community's orientation to the union movement and in terms of the personal cost to the individuals involved.[117] This hardship was faced within other communities as well. For example, Renqiu Yu has written about the harassment of Tan Yumin, who managed the Wah Kiu Wet-Wash Factory in New York and eventually committed suicide by jumping off the Brooklyn Bridge in the 1950s.[118] Just a few decades later, in the 1970s and 1980s, the anti–martial law movement would split the Seattle Filipina/o community, particularly because of the outcry over the murders of union activists Silme Domingo and Gene Viernes.[119] President Ferdinand Marcos was Ilocano, and because of the strength of the Ilocana/o community in Seattle, this would also create divisions in the community because of ethnic loyalties. All these issues likely framed how people would discuss political movements from earlier eras.

The historical evidence, however, suggests important, if little-discussed, activity within the Filipina/o community in the United States. According to Chris Friday, one important site for leftist activities was the Fishermen and Cannery Workers' Industrial Union (FCWIU), organized by the Trade Union Unity League to combat the influence of the Cannery

Workers and Farm Laborers Union (CWFLU) prior to 1936. However, when the Comintern organized a united front in 1935, the FCWIU was disbanded.[120] In addition, there are some clues about leftist activity in the available documents. One photograph housed in an album in the Demonstration Project for Asian Americans collection bears the following caption: "1938 Labor School in the 84 Union St. under the waterfront section of the Communist Party intigrating [sic] the Union." The photograph is particularly striking because part of it is torn off, possibly because it was edited. In a later interview, a community member did indicate that Communists tried to recruit Filipina/o workers in 1938 and 1939. He recalled one Communist organizer named Rupert, "who invited lots of Filipinos . . . to attend their meeting."[121] This kind of evidence, however, remains sketchy. Certainly, Seattle was an important site for Communist activity, as exemplified by the testimony given in 1948 concerning "Un-American Activities in Washington State," and there is much to uncover regarding these kinds of political processes.[122]

To place the leftist tradition of Seattle in perspective, it is useful to compare the activism there with other leftist work that was going on in New York City, such as that of the International Labor Defense (ILD). Michael Denning explains that the ILD, organized in 1925, "combined legal action with a mass protest campaign, building popular support for jailed unionists, political prisoners, immigrant radicals facing deportation, and black defendants facing racist trials." Denning views the ILD, developed by the Communist Party, as the first Popular Front organization. It was involved in several of the major legal cases of the time, including the Sacco and Vanzetti case, the Scottsboro Nine case, and the Sleepy Lagoon case.[123] New York, according to Denning, was the main location for Communist Party activity and had a constellation of other leftist groups as well.[124]

Through the ILD, Filipina/o activists participated in campaigns to advocate for Filipina/o causes both in the Philippines and in the United States. For example, about a dozen Communists came to the Office of the Secretary of War on March 5, 1934, to advocate for the release of a Filipina/o leader named Evangelista and other people who were incarcerated in the Philippines because of suspected sedition. One Filipino leader "stated that the imprisonment of Evangelista and other Communistic leaders was a violation of the Organic Act and of the principles of freedom of speech and that it was instigated by the fact that they advocated immediate independence." Another speaker from the ILD, characterized by the memo as "tall, dark and offensive," was reported to have commented "that the revolutionary struggle for real independence of Philippine workers was connected with a similar struggle in the United States for the complete independence of the workers."[125]

These political activists made explicit linkages between the American and Philippine situations. Two hundred workers in South Brooklyn sent a letter to Franklin D. Roosevelt through the Filipino Anti-Imperialist League of New York, protesting police violence against striking cigar-makers in the Philippines. Four of the strikers had died, and nineteen were wounded at the time of the resolution. The letter read, in part, "We pledge ourselves to organize the workers in America, particularly the Filipino workers and those connected with the cigar industry, to arouse a mighty wave of protest against Murphy's murderous deeds." The letter ends with a call for Philippine independence and is signed by a B. Schor, secretary for the Filipino Anti-Imperialist League of New York.[126]

In developing their political authority, these Filipina/os also relied on a range of other supporters for their causes, including the Mexican Mutualist Workmen's Association in New York City, the United Front Supporters, "a mass organization of professionals, intellectuals, and white collar workers," and the Asociacion Anti-Imperialista Puertorriqueña from Brooklyn, New York.[127] The political labor of Filipina/os working within the ILD thus puts into context the efforts of Filipina/os involved in the CWFLU in the Pacific Northwest, particularly in discussions regarding nationalism and the role of the United States in the Philippines. Analysis of the New York campaign highlights how closely linked the Seattle union was to the business leaders in the community, as exemplified by Virgil Duyungan, and to other organizations in the Filipina/o American community. Given the more established nature of the Filipina/o community in Seattle, it is not surprising that the union became a pivotal site for social status and political control within the framework of the Filipina/o American community.

CONCLUSION

One of my themes in this book has been the problematic nature of the assimilationist model that so dominates American history. According to this model, as immigrants come to this country, they gradually dispense with those traits that marked them as "Old World" community members despite hardships and barriers, and become transformed as "Americans" in the context of the United States. This chapter once again underscores the difficulty of applying this to the Filipina/o American case, particularly because Filipina/o Americans arrived as American nationals and did not enter this country as "immigrants" in the same sense as other groups. De-emphasizing the colonial framework that brought these people to Hawai'i and the American mainland, I would argue, does a disservice to their experience, particularly because they regularly encountered so much resistance to their permanent residence in the United States. Furthermore, the assimilationist model tends to characterize the path to the United States as being unidirectional, when in fact Filipina/os moved back and forth between United States and Philippine contexts as needed.

As this chapter has detailed, Filipina/o workers responded in a variety of ways to their marginalized position in the American culture. In addition to active protest to the American and Philippine governments, they also made choices regarding whether to remain in the United States or to return to the Philippines. The fluidity of their movement is an indication not only of the continued growth of the transpacific society that connected the United States and the Philippines but also of growing movements to exclude Filipina/os, particularly because of the hardships of the Great Depression. The travel back and forth of Filipina/os both shows the ties of colonial metropole and colony and reveals that although some people were deported to the Philippines, others actively opted to make their livelihoods "back home."

For those Filipina/os who stayed, one of the fundamental ways they chose to improve their lot in the United States was by pooling resources with other Filipina/os through mutual aid organizations. In a harsh, discriminatory environment, community organizations offered crucial respite. These groups provided essential support for men and women far away from home and also created cherished opportunities for social status within the Filipino community. Furthermore, in an existence dominated by constant mobility, mutual aid organizations offered an opportunity for some social stability.

At the same time, however, it is important to recognize how political hierarchies profoundly organized these kinds of social and political status, whether because of gender, ethnicity, or race. The fact that Rizal Days, for example, became such a focal point for community attention is also an indication of the contested nature of colonial politics, since Rizal was a political martyr in the cause against Spain and not the United States.

Class also was a primary determinant of who emerged as the spokespeople of the community. The organizations as a group, even the

CWFLU, which advocated primarily for the position of migratory male workers, were often dominated by leaders who had more economic privilege and connections. These issues of class were further complicated by the fact that so many Filipina/os had aspirations of, if not access to, a university education, a result of the Philippines' position as an American colony.

CHAPTER 6

Insiders and Outsiders

Margaret Duyungan Mislang, the wife of Virgil Duyungan (who was the first president of the Cannery Workers' and Farm Laborers' Union in Seattle), offers one story of the union's founding in the 1930s. According to Mislang, she and her sister learned from a German baker about new opportunities for unionization. As she recalled, "He told me that [the] Chamber of Commerce was starting, you know, for the businesses [*sic*] people now to take in and start a union." Mislang related, "So I went home and I talked to my husband about it and he thought it sounded interesting from what the baker said so he went down and he started a union . . . and those seven of them together and they formed it."[1] According to this telling, the formation of the union thus emerged from business interests in the community and not from the working-class base that others suggest, which possibly sheds light on Duyungan's later conflicted behavior as a union leader.

Analysis of the Cannery Workers' and Farm Laborers' Union (CWFLU) has always been pivotal to studies of Filipina/o Seattle, from Carlos Bulosan's description of the unionization movement to Chris Friday's analysis of organizing in the canned salmon industry. In this chapter, I will examine this union activity in the broader framework of political developments in Filipina/o Seattle and what was at stake in the different campaigns and contests that unfolded in the community's political arenas.

The focus of previous historiography on the union movement is not surprising for two reasons. First, it is in keeping with the progressive orientation of many who are interested in Filipina/o American history. In the search to reclaim history and to chart Filipina/o American resistance to the barriers enforced by American mainstream culture, unions form a logical place to see this kind of political activism. Furthermore, unions were a major site for Filipina/o Americans not only to connect with other groups of color but also to interact with the European American population, whether in confrontation or in alliance. In a sense, just as Chinatowns and Japantowns were a primary interface between the Chinese American and Japanese American communities and the European American community on an economic level, unionization performed a similar function for Filipina/o Americans, especially because they did not own small businesses to the extent that Chinese Americans and Japanese Americans did. In a society that imposed tight restrictions on Filipina/o Americans and other people of color, unions were one site that provided relatively more access to power.

Although unions form a valuable and integral part of community life, the focus on unionization has limited our understanding of this period in several ways. To begin, because much union activity was dominated by men, women typically appear only as peripheral players or in a support capacity. As a result, women's history is often downplayed, and the full significance of their contributions may be overlooked. Furthermore, even though the union culture was primarily male, women also had roles within the union activity, and their identities were also defined by unionization, although perhaps quite differently than for men. These issues are reminders of the importance of analyzing both private and public spaces in our considerations of community politics.

Second, unions were part of a range of possible organizational activity for the Filipina/o American community, and most members who participated in unions tended to see them as only one of the many sites where they "belonged." Being a "union man" did not exclude having close ties with other people in different settings, such as regional ties that were promoted across class. Thus, despite the claims to brotherhood and the various coalitions created during the course of organizing, union activity could also be a site for intense rivalry and political negotiation. Hence, it is an important site for discerning not only how class consciousness was organized but also how community members further addressed race, ethnicity, and gender.

"UNION MEN"

When Filipina/o Americans joined the union movement in the 1930s, they did so during a period of unprecedented labor mobilization. Following the National Industrial Recovery Act (1933) and the wave of general strikes in 1934, laborers swelled the ranks of the American Federation of Labor (AFL) and the Trade Union Unity Leagues. Their increased militancy swept the country, and the AFL was openly challenged by the growing dissatisfaction of the rank and file. John L. Lewis, a leader in the United Mine Workers, played a significant role in this labor organizing by advocating organizing laborers around the workplace rather than by craft. Lewis, joined by David Dubinsky of the International Ladies' Garment Workers' Union (ILGWU) and Sidney Hillman of the Amalgamated Clothing Workers, first organized the Congress of Industrial Organizations (CIO) as a dissident movement within the AFL. Later, after the AFL pushed the CIO out of its movement in 1935, the CIO in short order emerged to represent a group of industrial unions, quickly gaining in strength over the AFL. The CIO would include the United Mine Workers, led by Lewis, and, by the next decade, the United Electrical Workers, the United Auto Workers, and the United Steel Workers.[2]

The CIO organized across race and ethnicity, as well as gender, hence becoming a major site of organization for Filipina/o Americans and other previously marginalized groups. As James Green writes, "The CIO unions did not dissolve ethnic and racial group consciousness or end cultural antagonism, but they did give a highly divided work force a basis for cooperation on issues of common concern."[3] Support across race brought many new workers of color into the CIO movement and provided another area for the working class.[4]

In 1935, the National Labor Relations Act (NLRA) became law, providing new protections for industrial workers, including collective bargaining, free speech, and provisions for elections, protests for unfair labor practices, and grievances.[5] Overall, however, powerful farm interests would effectively keep agricultural workers from profiting from the NLRA's provisions.[6] Agricultural laborers could thus be denied access to coverage from legislation regarding such pivotal matters as social security and unemployment insurance. As Devra Weber argues, "By this omission, the government institutionalized farm workers' separation from industrial workers and reinforced their economic and political powerlessness in relation to the agricultural industry."[7] Nevertheless, new options continued to open up for Filipina/o Americans. For example, Carlos Bulosan also worked with the Popular Front, a group of social movements that emerged from the increased militancy of the Depression era and an internationalist vision of combating antifascism and participating in other political struggles abroad.[8]

For the Filipina/o American community, these events would radically shape possibilities for local struggle, particularly for cannery workers. Labor militancy, however, was not new to Filipina/o workers, and knowledge of labor struggles in the United States and the Philippines formed part of the general consciousness of many community members. Because most of these people worked as unskilled laborers, the same sets of people moved among various work sites, thus promoting a common consciousness about the need for unionization.[9] For example, there was migration to the mainland United States of workers who had experienced union struggle and collective action in Hawai'i, further promoting the possibilities for a shared knowledge of struggle.[10]

Asian Americans took part in labor activity throughout these various sites. In Hawai'i, for example, several Filipina/os were involved in labor organizations, such as the Filipino Labor Union, begun in 1919, and Vibora Luviminda, established in 1933. Filipina/o workers participated in many significant protests in the 1920s and 1930s, including important strikes in 1920 and 1924.[11] In 1920, a total of eighty-three hundred Japanese and Filipina/o plantation workers went on strike. Even when Filipina/o labor leader Pablo Manlapit, in a controversial move, called for an early end to the strike, many Filipina/o workers remained out with their fellow Japanese laborers.[12] Another major strike in 1924 on the islands of O'ahu, Hawai'i, and Kaua'i brought tragedy, resulting in the deaths of sixteen strikers and four policemen, along with others wounded.[13] This labor agitation continued into the 1930s. In June 1933, for example, some fifteen hundred Filipina/os walked out of three plantations when three workers were let go from the Waialua plantation. Later that month, three hundred laborers left the Waimanalo sugar plantation.[14] Filipino men were also brought in by the management as strikebreakers, in keeping with the planters' "divide-and-rule tactics," which pitted groups against each other.[15] In Maui, fifteen hundred Filipina/o workers struck at Pu'u-nēnē in 1937.[16]

Those workers who traveled to California also found widespread labor mobilization—Filipina/o laborers were involved in over twenty struggles from 1930 to 1936. Filipina/o farmworkers used these unions not only to gain a voice in establishing better work conditions but also in response to the regular violence and exploitation they faced.[17] In December 1933, for example, working with the Communist-organized Cannery and Agricultural Workers' Industrial League, Mexican and Filipina/o labor unions organized several protests. In January 1934, some three to five thousand farm laborers left lettuce fields in the Imperial Valley. In Salinas, California, roughly three thousand Filipina/os struck lettuce fields in 1934, meeting with heavy resistance. Violence and intimidation were common, and in early September 1934, hundreds of Filipina/o workers were forced out of the Pajaro Valley.[18] This struggle and others, however, maintained the drive for labor organization not only in California but also in other sites such as Seattle.

LOCAL 18257

The decision to base Local 18257 in Seattle reflected a structural recognition of what workers already knew about the importance of this regional center. The founding of the union represented an attempt by workers to mark permanent turf and ensure some kind of security in their marginalized, regional employment. Seattle's location undoubtedly influenced the decision to place Local 18257 there, for the city was the pivotal place from which workers left and to which they returned during the cannery season.[19]

Both cannery and agricultural workers were included in Local 18257, particularly laborers from Alaskan canneries and White River Valley farms.[20] The union fits David Montgomery's description of the kinds of ethnically based organizing accomplished by laborers to deal with low salaries, harsh supervision, and a lack of control over hiring and workplace conditions.[21] In the winter of 1932, a "secret caucus" began planning a union and took to the streets of Seattle Chinatown to enlist workers in their cause.[22] Ponce Torres remembered: "Yes, because that [King Street] was the only place where we can gather . . . lots of workers easily because during those times you may notice that there would be . . . fifteen to twenty thousand people in King Street around four blocks from Sixth Avenue to Eighth Avenue and you could see [an] ocean of Filipino workers."[23]

On the corner of King Street and Sixth Avenue, organizers addressed listeners in English and Filipino dialects, "explaining to them that if they have a labor union they will be better off than to live with this contracting system."[24] On June 1, 1933, seven Filipino men were elected as organizers for Local 18257 of the CWFLU, affiliated with the AFL.[25] One leader had returned to Seattle after working on the railroads in Montana to find that times were still difficult for Filipina/os. As he remembered, "They are kicking Filipinos in the street and all that." Still, Seattle was a good site to begin planning for a union because "we meet every day, either on the street, or in the cafeteria or restaurant." The organizer recalled:

> Well, we have to figure out something that could be done. Either go to the cannery again, or do something else. And it so happen that these three guys and myself [have] been talking in . . . a café. I said, "You know, why don't we organize all these Filipinos in here in the union." They said, "How can we do that, organizing. We're just a bunch of sheep that they sweep from one way to another."[26]

At the time, the AFL, which had been a central movement in the labor force since the last decade of the nineteenth century, was focused on skilled white workers. Not surprisingly, the local labor movement in Seattle largely excluded Filipina/o workers. In the 1920s, the Seattle AFL had organized around white workers, and it generally regarded African American and Asian American workers as a threat to their position. While the Central Labor Council in Seattle first reported positively about conferring with Filipina/o American cannery workers in 1925, anti-Asian sentiment inevitably won out. By the latter part of the decade, the familiar tirade against Filipina/o Americans as being a source of unfair economic competition, as well as being disease-ridden and socially immoral, was adopted by white officials in the labor movement.[27] When Local 18257 formed in the early 1930s, it was not recognized by the "prejudicial and reactionary" Seattle Central Labor Council, as one disgruntled Filipina/o union official later wrote.[28]

Notably, all the original founders of the CWFLU were Filipino men, which suggests not only that class mobilization in the union was reinforced by ethnic ties and gender privilege but also that the union provided an alternative political base for these workers. For Filipina/os, unionization was an important route to power in the salmon canning industry, since contracting was primarily dominated by Chinese American and Japanese American businessmen, with only a few Filipina/os involved. Filipina/o laborers had difficulty gaining authority within this system. A turning point for the Filipina/o workers came in 1934, when the National Recovery Administration (NRA) implemented the Code of Fair Competition for the Canned Salmon Industry, formally ending the contract system by law, if not in practice. The following year, the National Labor Relations Board acknowledged the CWFLU.[29]

Although most historical records indicate that the union was begun through all-male activity, other information suggests that this was not necessarily the case. Margaret Duyungan Mislang, who stated that she was involved in the union, recalled, "I used to help them in the union. I listened, I was very interested in it. I'd go down and I'd help them write the Constitution."[30] Given the intensive labor required to begin a union, this account of her participation seems quite plausible, and it certainly disputes the all-male history that is typically presented. On another level, because she and Duyungan had several children, her labor in taking care of the children likely made it possible for her husband to devote time to the formation of the union. Similarly, the wife of vice president Aurelio Simon, Matilde Simon, probably had heavy family responsibilities as well. Like the Chinese American women who organized in San Francisco in the late 1930s, women who participated in the Filipina/o American labor movement faced an uphill battle, despite their vital participation in the effort for fair wages.[31]

LABOR MOBILIZATION AROUND SEATTLE

Although the organization of cannery workers in Seattle is far better documented than the efforts of agricultural laborers to improve working conditions, farm laborers also engaged in work stoppages and strikes. Early organization included the Filipino Laborers' Association in Seattle and the Philippine Commerce and Labor Council of America, which was established in 1931 by community business interests.[32]

Laborers continued their organizing efforts in the region around Seattle. Antonio Manzano remembered the 1930s as "the time when we organize the unorganized"—the workers on the farm. In their first strike, agricultural laborers, who were receiving just one dollar per day for working long hours, stopped their jobs in protest, and the "big Seattle farmers" called the police. Manzano's brother was jailed for two days as an alleged Communist for striking, as were other leaders in the union. The agricultural organizers then met with the cannery workers' organizers and offered to join their efforts.[33]

Other actions took place in sites such as Monroe, Washington, in Snohomish County, as well as in the Yakima Valley in the early 1930s.[34] These organizing efforts became part of the communal experience of Filipina/o Americans in the region. Zacarias Manangan, for example, remembered being involved in strikes for higher pay in Kent, Renton, Auburn, Sumner, and Puyallup, "as far down as to . . . this side of Tacoma," in the

1930s. To address discontent among workers, some businesses, such as the Desmond Brothers and Lucky Lady, increased wages. Manangan also recalled farmers who constructed better bunkhouses and bathing facilities to appease the workers.[35]

The gains made in the agricultural fields might seem secondary compared with those in the canneries, but it is important to measure the success of farm laborers against the tremendous odds they traditionally faced. Sucheng Chan notes the relative difficulty of organizing farm labor and other seasonal labor versus the industrial workers in the East and Midwest.[36] In later years, powerful farm interests would effectively keep agricultural workers from profiting from the NLRA, so critical in the protection of the rights of industrial workers.[37] Still, Filipina/os were involved in labor agitation, including a strike by the Shafter United Cannery, Agricultural, Packing and Allied Workers of America (UCAPAWA) local in California's San Joaquin Valley in 1938.[38] Although the organization of farmworkers has been overshadowed by discussions of unionization in the Alaskan canneries, one can speculate that increased militancy on the farms contributed to a stronger drive for organization in Seattle and elsewhere.

LEADERS AND FOLLOWERS

Unionization, however, was just one site for the achievement of status in the community. As indicated by the case of Virgil Duyungan, examining the routes to political power leads us not just to union leaders but also to people with business ties. A survey of publications reveals that the same names appear as both political figures and community benefactors. By and large, the contractors' names dominate, as when the Philippine Commerce and Labor Union of America was organized in 1928 by Filipino businesspeople and other community leaders.[39] These "uncles" were central to the social life of the community. For instance, Pio De Cano gained authority in Seattle not just from directing the economic livelihood of other Filipinos but also from the loyalties and tributes he demanded from these workers. Public events organized by contractors showcased these demonstrations of power. In contrast, single male workers, who typically just passed through Seattle on their way to other employment, were often more peripheral to communal social events in the city. Nevertheless, community leaders like De Cano often expected them to participate in these occasions.

The efforts of University of Washington students to gain a clubhouse

offer an illuminating window onto the complexity of community politics. In some respects, students also held a devalued position in the community, like the single men who engaged in common labor. They, too,
tended to be young, single males (there were some women as well) who
subsisted on very low incomes and often were dependent on others. The
male students in particular could easily slip into the status of migratory
workers. However, as students, both men and women were affiliated with
prestigious educational institutions and could be seen as embodying the
promise of colonial education. As members of a privileged elite, especially if they came from a higher class background in the Philippines and
benefited from male privilege, they might have had expectations of higher
status within the Filipina/o American community. When contractors gave
financial aid to students, it is possible that the contractors might have
genuinely supported the students' educational aims. On the other hand,
donating finances to students also could have stemmed from a political
desire to gain prestige within the community and to have these future
leaders indebted to the contractors. In a communal culture founded upon
reciprocity, every gift had a price.

Moreover, even if the contractors themselves were unable to achieve
an education, they still asserted their authority by displaying their financial power. For example, in 1928 Pio De Cano gave a fifty-dollar scholarship prize for a Filipina/o student, and in 1934 he again donated prizes
of one hundred dollars to Filipina/o students. These gifts, the contractor-dominated *Philippine Advocate* suggested, were an indication of De
Cano's "social and cultural leadership."[40] In return, it appears that students lobbied for contractor support. In 1928, for instance, some University of Washington students requested special preference for employment from canners in the region.[41]

The campaign for the University of Washington student clubhouse
brings all these issues to the fore. Funds for a clubhouse were first gathered in 1927 or 1928 by Filipino contractors who collected a few dollars from each worker every time he or possibly she went to Alaska.[42]
Whether or not the workers wanted to make a contribution, they were
required to do so as a presumed condition of their employment. Although
a site for the clubhouse was chosen in the fall of 1928, the initial housing deal folded, possibly as a result of racial prejudice.[43]

The social dynamics of the campaign reveal the hierarchical arrangement of community sectors. This required "donation" was in keeping
with a communal ethos, since the money allegedly would benefit the community as a whole. But the costs of the campaign and the benefits de-

rived from the "community" project were levied unequally. The benefits
accrued to the contractors, in terms of the social prestige they could wield,
as well as to the students who would use the facility, but less to the workers. One editorial in the *Filipino Forum* noted sourly in 1928 about a
lack of reciprocity on the part of the students: "All the movements in the
Filipino community have seen no attendance from the university boys'
group. . . . Deeds should be louder than words."[44]

The use of the University of Washington student clubhouse campaign
as a means for prestige is further underscored by the factionalism and
dissension exhibited by the clubhouse's board of trustees. By the following spring, the clubhouse campaign was charged with mismanagement,
and some board members resigned.[45] In a long editorial about the campaign's problems, Victorio Velasco complained that there was no public accountability for the clubhouse funds.[46] A total of $6,000 or $7,000
was eventually collected, although several thousand dollars of this dis-
appeared.[47] In 1934 the pro-labor *Philippine-American Chronicle*
grumbled about the class dynamics of the campaign and the different
interests of workers and students. While members of Philippine Seattle
had much in common, in some ways the divide between groups was pronounced. The editorial continued with the pointed remark, "What keeps
the boys in Chinatown wondering is why do they still have to go around
the back doors of fraternity and sorority houses to look for their University friends?"[48]

POPULARITY CONTESTS

Despite these complaints, the function of cannery workers as "contributors" and "audience" was well established, especially as demonstrated
by popularity contests, also known as queen contests. These events were
a time-honored tradition from the Philippines in which different community factions competed for power by sponsoring a candidate, typically
a young, single woman, in a public contest. Factions would lobby for
their candidate by purchasing votes, and the winner was the contestant
whose faction purchased the most votes in an allotted time. The drama
of the program did not rest only on the merits of the contestants, then,
but also on the economic power displayed by various factions. Queens
were usually crowned in conjunction with a community program such
as a celebration commemorating Rizal Day.[49]

In newspaper coverage of these events, the supporters were regularly
named, for the crowning of the queen was only the highlight for the real

community drama—how various community factions succeeded in marshaling support. For example, the *Philippine Seattle Colonist* reported in detail on the crowning of Neny Encarnacion as Miss Philippines for Rizal Day in 1926. Through a four-way contest among Encarnacion, Flora Sueco, Virginia Nicol, and Angela Salvacion, a sum of $1,360.80 was raised at the cost of one cent per vote. Neny Encarnacion's camp was led by Joe de Guzman, along with Vincent Agot, Pio De Cano, the "U.S.S. DELWOOD Filipinos," who were likely Filipina/os associated with that vessel, supporters from the Japanese business community, and "many others." Flora Sueco's campaign was headed by Valeriano Sarusal and included a representative from the Dimas Alang and Filipina/os from Cosmopolis; Angela Salvacion's campaign was run by Mariano Milanio and Filipina/os from Montesano and Seattle; and Virginia Nicol's campaign, organized by David P. de Tagle, also featured contributors from Bremerton, Moscow (Idaho), Redlands, and more locally from the University of Washington Filipino Club.[50]

Ten years later, another popularity contest in the regular series of queen contests demonstrated the prevalent economic dynamics. In May 1936, the pro-contractor *Philippine Advocate* announced a popularity contest for its Winter Frolic. As the article noted, "Cannery agents, foremen, and other Filipino business men in Seattle are all loud in their approval of this contest, which, they think, will bring back into our community a lively interest and alertness in community welfare." Beginning with the introduction of candidates at the *Advocate*'s spring goodwill dance on May 10, the campaign was to be organized around the rhythms of the summer cannery season. On the same page, the newspaper ran a group picture of fourteen foremen, eleven of whom were affiliated with De Cano and Company, who stated their "enthusiastic endorsement" of the contest. This photograph likely carried suggestive meanings for anyone seeking to gain employment with Pio De Cano's business.[51] The rules of the popularity contest stipulated that votes were made in cash or by subscription to the *Philippine Advocate*. Each vote cost one cent, and an annual subscription to the *Philippine Advocate*, costing one dollar, would be the equivalent of fifty votes. A candidate received 20 percent of votes she submitted herself and 15 percent of the other votes turned in for her.[52]

As in other events, the contest was less about the respective merits of the candidates than the relative power of their supporters and the "community solidarity" that ensued. The leading candidate in 1936 was Rita Composano, "known as the 'darling' of the cannery foremen," who, it was hinted, had the support of Burgos Lodge Number 10 of the Dimas Alang, Pio de Cano's lodge. Kathleen Darrah, "one of the popular girls at the Rizal Hall," had writing and piano-playing skills and was also "a lover of outdoor sports." She reportedly was backed by the "ranks and file of the South End district," and there was some interest in her campaign by "a cannery foreman now at Alaska, the uptown employees and the combined tonsorial artist[s]." Lorena Campo, "the 'dark horse' of the popularity contest," was "decidedly popular with the younger set and very much in demand in all social activities being a cute little dancer." Peggy Nelos, a staff member of the labor-oriented *Philippine American Tribune*, was a "talented toe dancer."[53] Among the remaining candidates was Betty Woods, a student at Wapato Senior High School who was the secretary of the Filipino Women's Club and was backed by the Yakima Valley Filipino Club and Women's Club, and Angelica Floresca, a student at Broadway High School. Floresca also played the piano, sang, was a social and civic worker, and acted as secretary of the Naguilian Club. She was supported by four important clubs in Seattle—the Santa Maria Association, the Naguilian Club, the Bauangenian Club, and the Filipino University Club—and was also backed by some "well known" contractors, including Pedro Mendoza, a secretary to De Cano and Company.[54]

In September, to mark the return of the cannery workers to Seattle, a "swell party and dance" was planned at Washington Hall, featuring the contestants and a Filipino jazz group. Finally, the culminating ceremony was held at Washington Hall on October 30, with a dance and a box social, a common fund-raising practice at community programs.[55] When the votes were tabulated, Angelica Floresca emerged as the winner in a last-minute drama, with 10,815 votes.[56]

Organized at the beginning of the summer to coincide with the cannery workers' departure for Alaska and culminating in events that happened as the workers returned home, the event capitalized on the availability of both audience and funding. Generally, the workers would have the most available disposable money after they were paid in the canneries. In supporting candidates, they not only were giving money for a communal event but also were displaying their allegiance to a particular faction and investing money that they likely hoped would ensure jobs at the same cannery the next year. Yet, although migratory workers were expected to participate by "casting votes," that is, giving money, presumably they would not directly gain prestige from this event. Nor would they necessarily expect to be considered in the same social circles as these women, since the workers occupied a relatively low position in the community's social hierarchy. Typically, too, they were mobile, about to leave for their next job, which also marginalized their presence. At the same time, they were vital to the contest as potential "voters" and as audience members. Part of the prestige of the event derived from its public nature. Without onlookers, the popularity contest could not have had the same impact as a spectacle.

In keeping with the emphasis on social prestige, the composition of the candidates also made a statement about gender. In a largely migratory male worker context, the young women candidates were idealized, and descriptions of them highlight conventional values about femininity. In addition, male community workers could assert their identities as men in the heterosexual context of these contests. One suspects, too, that for the women, the responsibility of being a contestant and being subjected to such intense public scrutiny might also have been a serious obligation, if not a burden.[57]

Furthermore, the contest implicitly commented on the community's racial hierarchies. In the Seattle-based *Advocate* contest, the top three contenders were all Filipinas, presumably because the business and political factions within the community generated the most funds. In this contest, other contestants, who were probably white, dropped out, although Betty Woods resurfaced as a top contender in the Yakima Valley contest.[58] Filipina candidates were rare, not only because the ratio among Filipina/os was so overwhelmingly male to female but also because the contestants had to be single women in a society where female partners were eagerly sought. But no Japanese American women were represented, a reflection of limited Japanese-Filipina/o interaction on a social basis, particularly because of a lack of Japanese American outmarriage. In addition, despite the many relationships involving Native American women and Filipino men, I did not find in the course of my research any Native American women who represented political and economic groups in Seattle in these contests. This was a possible reflection of the prevalent racism against Native Americans as well as prejudiced standards of beauty.

Both the campaign for the student clubhouse at the University of Washington and the *Philippine Advocate* popularity contest of 1936 were sites for the public display of power by community factions. Clearly, the contractors led by Pio De Cano played a prominent role in the battle for prestige, as ostensibly "community" events provided situations in which businesspeople could flaunt their relative might—all for the general good. In both cases, migratory workers played an important role in supporting these events. But typically these workers were passive players whose

contributions were "encouraged" by contractors and who remained secondary players in this community drama.

In the *Philippine Advocate* contest of 1936, the final crowning of the
queen was to be held in conjunction with the celebration of the beginning of the Philippine Commonwealth anniversary in mid-November.
Not surprisingly, contractor and community leader Pio De Cano was the
chair for this event. In a revealing list, Pio De Cano, who was also grand
master of the Burgos Lodge of the Cabelleros de Dimas Alang, decided
on different contributions for local organizations, suggesting these
groups' relative power in the community. If the amount of money
reflected both the prestige and the responsibilities of the intended donor,
at least according to Pio De Cano, then his own company ranked at the
top, along with the manager of the Rizal Club and the CWFLU.[59]

The surprise in this list is that De Cano listed the CWFLU along with
his contracting company and the manager of the Rizal Club, given that
the union's aims would seem to be at odds with De Cano's vision of "community." The rationale for this ranking could be explained in several ways.
Perhaps De Cano was fitting the union into his scheme of community by
requiring this hefty donation. If it was named one of the major community organizations, the union could be expected to be obligated to the
majority communal ethos, in which De Cano was the primary patron of
Filipina/o Seattle. Another explanation might lie in how the union was
positioning itself within the array of community organizations in Filipina/o
Seattle, in recognition that community members typically had multiple
and crosscutting organizational memberships. Furthermore, the nucleus
of community leaders was relatively small, and these leaders often shared
responsibilities in similar community projects. In any case, this ranking
demonstrates the union's growth in power from its beginnings in the early
part of the decade, as well as its connections to other organizations.

GROWTH OF THE UNION

One of the main reasons the union fit in so well with other community
organizations was that, similar to other regional or fraternal groups, it
functioned as a mutual aid organization to provide economic and political support for its members. Second, at least in its initial phases, the union
remained sensitive to the attitudes of other community sectors. Unionists were well aware of the tight ethnic and familial ties that cut across
class between contractors and workers. As union leader Ponce Torres
told an interviewer concerning the early days of the union:

And that was where we come in as organizer[s] of the union, to make them realize that we are but [one] laboring family that would belong to one class, that we [are] brothers, rather than to be Vis[a]yans or Ilocano or Tagalog or Pangasinan or any sectionalistic feeling. . . . And it took us four years in the making to make these people believe that we have but one goal, we have but one struggle to better our working conditions and to better up ourselves and to discipline ourselves so that we will be . . . recognized people in the society.[60]

Torres called the formation of this class identity "the hardest part for us to do, to make ourselves understand that we are one Filipino race."[61]

Ethnic divisions were a big challenge in this regard. Jack Masson and Donald Guimary suggest that factionalism among the Visayans, Ilocana/os, and Tagalogs also contributed to divisions within the union, and that most of the local's members in the later part of the 1930s were Ilocana/o.[62] Another issue was the complexity of social networks. Because of the intricate familial and organizational connections among Filipino contractors and workers, developing a class-based identity always required delicate maneuvering. Teodolo Ranjo commented on the bonds among Filipina/os that influenced people's responses to the labor movement: "Oh, yeah, we had a lot of strikes, we had confrontations with, even some Filipinos against Filipinos. I hate to tell, those who favor contractors, those who have Uncles . . . [who are] contractors, townmates [who are] contractors like Pio De Cano [who] was [a] contractor."[63]

By going up against the contractors, the unionists were combating the most powerful sector in the community, as well as business leaders in the Chinese American and Japanese American communities. One union leader responded to people who doubted that Filipina/os could be organized because of the foremen and contractors: "I said, 'Do not fool yourself. Some of the guys don't like to be under the thumb of those people that 'you do this or else.' You are no longer free if they do that to you. 'You do what I tell you or else, or you cannot go to the cannery.'" The organizer mentioned Pio De Cano as one example: "He sees most of his people from his hometown coming here and let[s] them work in his contracting cannery. So, they come. They come. But during those time[s], they think that this is just as rosy as they think [it can be]. But that's the word, you do or you don't. Do this or else. In other words, he got them by the . . . collar." Thus, as the union leader recalled regarding early confrontations with the contractors, "We did not make any drastic action. They don't know that we were trying to cut their own livelihood, see, they don't know that." Instead, the unionists tried to circumvent the contractors by talking directly to the companies.[64] As another indication of this cautious policy, at the inception of the union, the constitution of the local dictated that first foremen, second foremen, bookkeepers, and cooks could be eligible for membership, although contractors and labor agents involved in labor racketeering were not. However, the CWFLU's drive to recruit foremen was unsuccessful.[65]

Virgil Duyungan's record as a union leader was, one could suggest, not always in keeping with his union rhetoric. During the waterfront strike in Seattle in May 1934, Duyungan worked with other strike leaders to ensure that cannery workers had to show proof of belonging to the CWFLU. According to historian Lauren Casaday, to get initiation fees, Duyungan collected money from laborers or had companies and contractors deduct money from each person's wages, although Casaday was unable to get any "company representative" to verify this practice. Duyungan did secure a wage increase for workers, with "promises of 'improved conditions' of the sort contemplated in the proposed standard NRA wage agreement for the industry." But when the workers came back from the canning season, according to Casaday, they found out that the money they had paid did not ensure membership in the union, "but had been merely a 'guarantee' that they could pass the marine picket line in safety.... The returning workers noticed, too, that Duyungan and other union officials had acquired new automobiles during the summer and that the former had purchased in his own name a combination cafe and pool room on one of Chinatown's popular corners."[66]

To complicate matters even further, union president Virgil Duyungan had an established relationship with leading contractor Pio De Cano. In a 1935 trial in which Pio De Cano and Placida De Cano accused Duyungan of misappropriating funds, Duyungan claimed he had borrowed money from De Cano in order to pay his landlord. He also was paid by De Cano for taking 350 workers across picket lines during a longshoremen's strike in 1934. In any case, the larceny charges were finally dismissed.[67] Duyungan's testimony during his trial demonstrates his attitudes toward union solidarity and his affinity for Filipino community leaders such as De Cano. On the one hand, he remarked that he had been friends with De Cano for several years; on the other, he voiced staunch support for the union:

> I think also that since the canning season is through for the present, and that the Code for the salmon industry is outlawed, the packers as well as their labor contractors are working hard to smash the Cannery Workers Union so that they can control labor again for the next season, a contract

system which has enslaved the Filipinos in this city for the last fifteen years.[68]

Once again, Duyungan's defense of his actions exposes the importance of personal relations even among allegedly rival organizations.[69]

At the same time, the union offered a means by which Filipina/os could challenge social hierarchies. The Filipina/os may have formed a dominant part of the workforce, but Filipina/o contractors did not have as much power as Chinese, Japanese, or European American cannery interests.[70] Thus, in its campaign against contractors, the union decided to focus on Japanese and Chinese contractors, but not Filipino contractors, even corresponding privately with Pio De Cano about the need to work together. A meeting of the union's leaders with Filipino foremen and contractors in March 1934 resulted in contractors agreeing to hire union workers, with De Cano sending eleven union workers to Alaska two months later. Even so, Virgil Duyungan and Cornelio Mislang, in correspondence to the NRA, complained about contractors from all three ethnic groups.[71]

In public, however, Duyungan was less likely to target Filipina/o contractors. At the NRA hearings on Codes of Fair Practice and Competition held in San Francisco in 1934, he condemned Chinese and Japanese but not Filipina/o contractors. Duyungan constructed his testimony to argue for the privileging of Filipina/o interests over Japanese American and Chinese American concerns. Invoking terminology that portrayed Filipina/os in a dependent role, Duyungan implored the committee to help them: "The Filipinos like myself are born under the American flag, the Stars and Stripes. During the World War our government there provided some 300,000 strong to fight for the cause of Uncle Sam. . . . Under the American flag we are supposed to have your protection. You are supposed to be our godfather, our benefactor."[72] He also spoke of differences with the Japanese and Chinese communities: "The Japanese people, they have their own counsels in this country. The Chinese, they have their own counsels in this country. . . . The Filipino people do not have anybody to represent them in this country. So when we come to this country fatherless, motherless, and without friends, we are being prejudiced by our American neighbors."[73]

Duyungan went on to complain that while money to Japanese contractors went back to Japan for groceries to be shipped to Seattle, and Japan did not buy salmon from "us" but shipped five thousand cases to the United States, the Philippines in 1933 bought $180,000 worth of salmon.[74] In response, Clarence Arai of the Japanese Cannery Workers Association reminded the committee that there were Filipino contractors in addition to Japanese and Chinese contractors.[75] Duyungan seemed to omit mention of Filipino contractors, even as he emphasized the Philippines' colonial bond with the United States. The following year, in a list that historian Lauren Casaday procured from Duyungan himself, three of the enumerated contractors were Chinese, four were Japanese, and four were Filipino.[76]

Union membership was another arena fraught with intense ethnic hierarchies. According to historian Chris Friday, the local voted in early 1935 to give Filipina/os in Seattle privileged employment over other ethnic groups.[77] Later, the local realized the need to organize among Chinese American and Japanese American workers to bolster its political support.[78] In addition, the local gained some African American workers in 1935 and white members in 1935 and 1936, some of whom were clearly leftist in orientation.[79]

This expansion of the union's ethnic base was essential in the face of challenges by other organizations, particularly those based on ethnic alignments. Characteristic of the always burgeoning field of community organizations, the field of competing labor organizations expanded as the CWFLU gained in strength. Before the hearings of 1934, Pio de Cano had already created a rival Filipino Cannery Workers Association, and Clarence Arai had initiated the Japanese Cannery Workers Association.[80] In 1935, the contractor-influenced Filipino Labor Protective Association (FLPA) was begun, headed by John Ayamo, formerly a lawyer for the CWFLU.[81] The pro-labor *Philippine-American Chronicle* noted that the makeup of the FLPA was "mostly businessmen and labor agents," including a lawyer as president, and that Leo Roduta, who had recently brought suit against Virgil Duyungan, was part of the group.[82] Ponce Torres spoke out strongly against the FLPA: "The operators remember are backed up with powerful dollar[s], million[s] of dollars. . . . if they want to bribe somebody to kill or to make proporganda [sic] and things like that in order to destroy the union they were able to because they have that power behind them."[83] Torres claimed that the FLPA was a "bribe system": "They want to make money and try to fool the other common workers in order to destroy this . . . genuine membership."[84]

Competition among the groups involved in labor organization was fierce. The CWFLU, the Japanese Cannery Workers Association, and the Filipino Cannery Workers Association, according to historian Chris Friday, all aimed to position themselves as "specialized recruiters and distributors of labor for their ethnic constituents." The Fishermen and Cannery Workers' Industrial Union also organized leftist Filipina/os, although it was later disbanded in the mid-1930s.[85] Furthermore, another Filipino, S. M. Estepa of the Filipino Alaska Canneries Workers Association, tried to gain power through his nonunionized organization.[86]

The primary battle over control was between the CWFLU and the FLPA, as reflected by their rival newspapers. In response to the CWFLU's *Philippine-American Chronicle*, the FLPA began the *Philippine Advocate*. With so much dissension, Harry Lundeberg, the Maritime Federation's president, brought the CWFLU and the FLPA together to investigate both organizations and ended up condemning both groups. Lundeberg called Ayamo's group a "fink" organization and Duyungan a "labor faker." He further noted that both sides were using cannery laborers, and that Duyungan could not expect the maritime unions to help him until he cleared his record.[87]

Still, the CWFLU gained in strength. In February 1936, the union stated that it had about 1,700 members, with 1,100 Filipinos and 575 "Americans." These numbers expanded rapidly throughout the season.[88] At the same time that the contractors were running the *Philippine Advocate* popularity contest in 1936, the laborers were organizing on their own. Just before the season began that year, the workers staged a "big demonstration along the waterfront where . . . steamships are ready to bring those boys to [the] cannery." According to Ponce Torres, "from ten to fifteen thousand Filipinos" struck, and because of the imminence of the season's opening, companies were forced to sign a contract improving working conditions. Ponce Torres remembered: "By giving us, raising us good wages, better conditions . . . we all come to agreement that there was no speed up, there was no cheating in the overtime and also the food should be improved and . . . it was all improved during that season."[89]

By the last month of 1936, however, conditions would look drastically different. One community member recounted that as the union prepared to "give them a little bit more pressure," tragedy struck. President Virgil Duyungan and Secretary Aurelio Simon were murdered in a meeting in Chinatown, supposedly by the nephew of a contractor. The events surrounding the murder are unclear. Before Duyungan died, he allegedly shot the assailant, who died as well.[90] The community member who was the union's treasurer at the time believed that this was not the full story, that "somebody professional" killed the men.[91] Teodolo Ranjo concurred,

saying, "I don't think they tried very hard to locate the murder[er]. . . .
authorities just cross it off."[92]

The union leaders' memorial provided another occasion for a public
spectacle, as mourners paraded through the streets of Seattle. By calling
upon other representatives of organized labor, the union organizers were
able to display the widespread nature of union support. Ponce Torres remembered asking union people from around the country to attend the
funeral "so that almost . . . every local union who are sister union to our
affiliations were all represented." He recalled twenty thousand mourners paying their respects, making up "the biggest . . . funeral parade ever
seen here in [the] City of Seattle."[93]

The murders galvanized the membership. Whatever bad press had appeared surrounding Duyungan died down as he and Simon became union
martyrs. As one Filipino unionist said, "We know now that we have to
get rid of those people out of the company. It's time because we cannot
allow such things to happen to our officials and our members."[94] The
following month, however, the union was faced with a new problem.
The AFL tried to divide the union along ethnic lines and organized what
the CWFLU deemed a "puppet union."[95] Conrad Espe reported in a meeting of the executive board that the union had not "been in good standing
with the American Federation of Labor since 1933, and the union was
considered 'too democratic.'" The AFL proposed to charter a Japanese
local, which would be administered, along with Local 18257, by a council of AFL officials.[96] Meanwhile, despite the earlier controversy, Local
18257 continued to receive support from organizations such as the Maritime Federation.[97] By February 1937, it was already working with the
Alaska Cannery Workers Union (ACWU) in San Francisco.[98]

In mid-February 1937, the CWFLU started meeting with the cannery
industry to develop that year's contract. Despite opposition from rival
interests, including a competing AFL local, the union finally achieved a
closed shop on April 28. It negotiated a contract granting wages that
were 35 to 40 percent higher than those of the previous year, banning
labor contractors, and making the CWFLU the exclusive representative
of cannery workers in southeast and central Alaska.[99]

The organization of the CIO further promoted industrial unions on
the West Coast. When Conrad Espe returned from a national conference
in Denver for cannery and field laborers that gave birth to the UCAPAWA,
he encouraged the CWFLU to change its affiliation.[100] The acrimony between the CWFLU and the AFL continued to drag on until that fall, when
the matter was brought to court. According to union records, accusations

levied against the CWFLU included claims that it was an "irresponsible organization" whose members were a "bunch of conflicting cliques." The CWFLU emergency committee voted to withdraw from the AFL and to put affiliation with the UCAPAWA, CIO before its membership.[101]

Although Filipinos dominated CWFLU membership rolls, Chinese American and Japanese American support was also critical, particularly because the AFL organized around the always easily divisible ethnic lines. In a heavily disputed vote, the CIO won in May 1938 with 1,560 votes, with the AFL close behind with 1,307.[102] The development of the CWFLU is essential to chronicle because its emergence signified a new base for Filipina/o laborers specifically organized around their working-class identities. In his discussion of the CIO movement, James Green notes that African American workers turned away from middle-class leaders in the community who were against unions, thus reshaping class alliances. A similar development occurred in the Filipina/o American community as well.[103] Ponce Torres remembered how the union "eliminated completely the power of the contractors." He recalled, "Not even one of those big people, contractors or anybody connected with the company could ever make any recommendation or could even be seen in the dispatching hall."[104] Thus, the union challenged relationships between contractors and workers, as well as the balance of power regulated by family and ethnic ties, and the patronage hierarchies that structured Filipina/o Seattle.

POLITICAL VOICES

During this same period, the CWFLU struggled to develop a policy for agricultural labor. Despite its stated objective of assisting members both in the canneries and in the fields, agricultural workers remained much more difficult to organize. Once laborers left Alaska or Seattle, they were hard to find. Highly mobile and earning marginal wages, agricultural workers quickly dispersed to other sites. Furthermore, the agricultural industry tended to be more resistant to organization as a whole. Even if the very same laborers moved from Alaskan canneries to agricultural labor farther south, as farmworkers they had far fewer options. They were also especially vulnerable to physical harassment, which is one reason a farm division was so essential for the union.[105]

In March 1937, Ponce Torres of the Farm Policy Committee of the CWFLU reported that there were five to six hundred workers in the Seattle/Tacoma area, and that "conditions on these workers as regards to wages, hours, working conditions, and sleeping quarters are intolerable." Auburn workers earned twenty-five to thirty cents an hour, while wages in Kent were as low as twenty-five cents an hour. The majority of these laborers were union members.[106]

Violence continued in rural locales, at times instigated by political officials. Isolated farm laborers did not have the relative protection of public scrutiny found in the cities. Ponce Torres, then secretary of Local 18257 and chairman of the Farm Organizational Committee, wrote a letter to a political official in Kent, Washington, vigorously protesting the harassment of Filipina/o strikers in Kent:

> We have fully understood that you have mobilized a big force of Vigilantes and that you are directing and commanding it with the full idea to terrorize all the farm laborers in the White River Valley. We further noted that you and your Vigilantes are in full accord to drive all those strikers out of the Valley should they refuse to work under those deplorable conditions and the slavery system which the employers are practicing for years upon them.

Referring to the support available for their efforts from organized labor, Torres continued, "I want further to refresh your mind that we are now living in this age of organized-labor-society."[107]

Farm organizers were well aware that agricultural workers were receiving less attention from the union than were cannery laborers. In April 1937, Torres advocated "that [farm] workers be given as much attention as the Alaska Workers, since our Union has jurisdiction of the Farm Workers too."[108] A farm division of the CWFLU was finally voted in during January 1938.[109]

In addition to the difficulty of organizing in the fields, the union continued to face a challenge in building class identity in the face of divisive ethnic politics. Contrary to the stated attempt to unite cannery workers across groups, ethnic barriers remained.[110] For example, during a preelection rally in May 1938, Filipina/o community organizations made a roster which listed community groups that backed the union. Most tellingly, the majority of the groups represented Filipina/o regional and ethnic organizations, including the Narvacan Club, the Bauangenian Club, the Pangasinan Association of the Pacific Northwest, the Vigan Club, the Santa Maria Association, and the Laoaginian Club, indicating, once again, how fundamentally identity in Seattle was organized along regional lines.[111]

An illustration of how ethnic loyalty operated in the union is found in the records of a 1941 hearing concerning the dismissal of the second fore-man of the Union Bay cannery, Lucas Corpuz. Corpuz testified that in 1937, when he was a student at the University of Idaho, Felix Narte or-ganized a petition to place Corpuz as second foreman. According to Cor-puz, the arrangement specified that after Corpuz returned to the Philip-pines, Narte was to assume the position. Corpuz objected to Narte's claim of the job. As he reported, "When he tries to get it this year, he's break-ing a promise." Dyke Daisho Miyagawa, the timekeeper at Union Bay, reported "that the whole question arises because of rivalry between kins-men and town-mates in the cannery; that the existence of job politics can-not be denied." As Miyagawa explained, "It seems that the majority of the Filipino boys in the crew are behind Corpuz, possibly because Cor-puz has more relatives among them." Corpuz and Narte eventually worked out their differences, and the union's executive council voted that the petition for Corpuz "be dismissed because of its dual nature."[112]

As the union gained strength, it also developed a wider political base. Like other Filipina/o communities in the mainland United States and Hawai'i, laborers maintained an interest in affairs in the Philippines, as seen in their reception of Francisco Varona. Varona was a representative from the Philippine government who came to the United States in March 1938 at the behest of the National Economic Council of the Philippine Islands to investigate the social and economic status of Filipina/os in the United States. A former president of the Filipino Labor Congress back in Manila, Varona was granted honorary membership in the CWFLU.[113] His visit was controversial, as some members of the board reported "that Varona has been engaged by certain group to slander the CIO as evi-denced from the dispatches in California papers." The local's leaders found out that the Filipino Agricultural Laborers' Association had be-come affiliated with the AFL, allegedly at the instigation of Francisco Varona. Navea reported from a Los Angeles visit that Varona had en-couraged the culinary laborers to join the AFL and that "in Sacramento, the feeling of the workers were unanimously against Varrona [sic] and against affiliation with the AFL."[114] In his comments to the audience, Varona also answered questions about the political and economic situ-ation in the Philippines.[115]

Other evidence indicates that union members used their power as or-ganized labor in the United States to lend support to workers back home. For example, the union passed a resolution in 1940 supporting the strike of the Filipino Seamen and Dockers' Union against the Manila Steamship

Company, sending copies to the U.S. high commissioner at Manila, the Filipino resident commissioner in Washington, D.C., President Manuel Quezon, and the secretary of labor of the Philippines.[116]

The union also advocated for Filipina/os in Washington State. For example, in 1937 C. O. Abella, the union president, sent a resolution to Clarence Martin, governor of Washington, petitioning against House bill number 633, which was intended to bar landownership and leasing arrangements for Filipina/os in Washington State. This resolution had support from the Maritime Federation of the Pacific, District Council Number 1, and the CWFLU in Portland.[117]

Increasingly, the union emerged as a site for university-trained leaders in the community, as demonstrated during the campaign to affiliate with the CIO. In 1939, for example, Trinidad Rojo was even elected president.[118] Not all the "college boys" joined the side of the union. For example, Victorio Velasco served as the editor of the *Philippine Advocate*, the contractor-dominated paper. However, the role of the university-trained Filipina/os within the union indicates again that the union was also an alternate base for power within the community and a public arena for men of diverse class orientations and interests. The affiliation of the community intelligentsia not only with the contractors but also with the workers revealed how the political climate had changed. This is not to say that contractors did not retain power within the community. In 1940, Pio De Cano secured a ruling by the King County Superior Court that deemed unconstitutional the 1937 amended alien act, which classified Filipina/os as "aliens," demonstrating his authority within Filipina/o Seattle.[119] But in a community where social relations were heavily dependent on the economic sphere, the increased power of male workers also influenced community dynamics as a whole.

GENDER, RACE, AND PRIVILEGE

The political role of the CWFLU can be measured not only by how it addressed people central to its organizing effort, such as the male migratory workers and business leaders, but also by its relationship to other groups, namely women. Not everyone benefited from the progress in organizing in the same way. While it is important to recognize the important strengths of the union, it is crucial not to overvalorize its efforts. To explore some of these issues, I will present the stories of three women: Bibiana Laigo Castillano, Matilde Simon, and Margaret Duyungan Mislang.

Bibiana Laigo Castillano, as mentioned earlier, met her first husband, Valeriano Laigo, through her uncle. Valeriano Laigo, a cannery contractor who had come to the United States in 1916, was prominent within Filipina/o Seattle because of his class position. Without Castillano's knowledge, he had already sent a letter to her parents, asking for her hand in marriage. After her parents corresponded in return, the couple married in 1928. Soon, Castillano and Laigo had four children.[120]

Tragically, however, her husband was murdered in 1936 in a dispute over a gold mine in Oregon, and she was left to raise their children by herself.[121] In an interview with her grandson, Castillano recalled about that period of her life: "I had a hard time. When I had money, everyone seemed to be my friends and relatives. When your grandfather died, you know, when you're poor, nobody comes around. And so that's how I started to struggle by myself."[122] Although she was expecting another child at the time, Castillano decided to run her husband's cannery and restaurant to support herself and her children. She had some familiarity with the canneries "by observation." Castillano handled the various aspects of the business by negotiating with the owners, bidding for contracts, sending workers to Alaska, and buying supplies. She remembered how she had to struggle against the union in order to support her family:

> The union didn't like me because the contractors were already abolished. "Why are you running it and the contractors are already gone." I said, "It is not my fault that I am still running. And it is not my fault that my husband died, but my children have to eat and so do I. This is the only kind of job I know I can do for the present in my present condition."[123]

Because Castillano's crew included nonunion members, she was boycotted and threatened. But Castillano's former husband had known the secretary of the fisheries from his cannery days, and he was able to offer her police protection when Castillano would send male workers up to Alaska.[124] She recalled, "Two policemen carrying machine guns would always guard me. Side by side, because you know this union with those big clubs in their hands, they block the gate to the boat."[125]

Finally, because of her struggles, Castillano's health was at risk, and her weight had dropped to eighty-eight pounds. She had to quit running the cannery in 1938, although she had few alternatives.[126] A priest who knew her said, "You'd better get married because you are so young. When you can never tell what may happen. If you are living by yourselves."[127] Castillano commented about the pressure she faced: "The old men again. They are the ones who ask me would I marry him [Mike Castillano].

'If you don't marry him, we don't talk to you anymore. Well, he's the only man that we could pick for you.'"[128]

Castillano's story indicates how gender interacted with class to structure people's positions in Filipina/o Seattle during this era. The contrast in her experiences before and after her husband's death illustrates both how a woman's position was often tied to that of her husband and the apparent requirement for women to be married. The lack of assistance following her husband's death, despite the fact that he had granted much help to other people during his lifetime, illustrates the difficult position of women who were trying to establish a livelihood and suggests the male-centric nature of authority. After her husband's death, men in the Filipina/o community applied pressure on her to marry again.

What is particularly interesting about Castillano's story, though, for the purpose of my discussion, is that Castillano actually struggled against organized labor as a contractor. She was able to get help from the police to ensure that her crews could leave Seattle, a startling feat in itself given the police's tendency to respond differently to the migratory male workers in Chinatown. These issues illustrate the role of political connections and class. Although, on the one hand, Castillano might be judged for crossing union lines, on the other hand, she had little recourse to other kinds of livelihood, given that she had four children and received little support from other sectors of the community. Furthermore, women were by and large excluded from the union movement as a whole. In fact, I found little evidence that any woman from the Filipina/o community publicly participated in the unionization effort. Inclusion in the union for some sectors of the community, namely, the migratory male workers, did not preclude continued exclusion for others, namely, the women, regardless of their background.

Margaret Duyungan Mislang and Matilde Simon, the widows of slain labor leaders Virgil Duyungan and Aurelio Simon, offer another way to enter into the history of the CWFLU. In the late 1930s, both of these women took the union to the Superior Court of Washington State to get monies from the Duyungan-Simon Memorial Fund organized by the union. Matilde Simon's case began in 1937, when the CWFLU and five of its officers were summoned to court.[129] According to Simon's complaint, she had lost her husband, Aurelio Simon, on December 2, 1936, when he was killed in a union-related tragedy. With three young children and "no property, money or means of support," Simon was suing the union for support for herself and her children, all of whom were under six years of age. After the deaths of Duyungan and Simon, a memorial fund was organized by the union, and so far Matilde Simon had received only $325.00 from it. However, Simon's side contended that, in 1936 and 1937, not only did each union member donate a dollar for the fund, but other unions also made contributions, including workers in California and Oregon, and speculated that the fund contained about $7,000.[130] Simon's side argued that Matilde Simon thought she and her children were entitled to more money, and they wanted the court to intercede on their behalf. Juan Ayamo, a prominent community leader and a lawyer, and also a founder of the rival FLPA, was appointed as guardian ad litem for the children.[131] On March 12, 1938, the case was settled, with Simon winning $800 from the union.[132]

Margaret Duyungan went to court later that year to get funds from the union. She sought funds for herself and her seven children, all twelve years of age or under at the time of the trial. Duyungan claimed that she received $1,175.70 from the union, which included transport for herself, her children, and the body of her husband to the Philippines.[133]

In her testimony in court, Duyungan offered the following: "We took it for granted that they were going to help me, because according to the constitution they shall help the widows, and it was their right." Duyungan reported, "That time the union was a little hard up and they said of course the men would all give money and I did not need to worry as they would raise money."[134] According to her trial transcript, Duyungan claimed that records showing $14,000 in contributions raised for the family were gone. The issues were apparently hotly contested, and Duyungan recalled the atmosphere of the time. Her oral history transcript is a bit unclear here, but she said, "They took a gun at me. Right in the courthouse."[135] Whatever coercion might have transpired, in July 1939 it was finally decided that the union, I. R. Cabatit, and Antonio Rodrigo would have to pay $1,768.06 to Duyungan and her children, along with her "costs and disbursements herein" and a typewriter that was purchased with monies from the memorial fund.[136]

These superior court cases are significant on several levels. First, they underscore both the expectations and the limits of union aid to families of the deceased leaders. They not only indicate the problems in union funding at the time but also show the expectations of the widows that they were supposed to get funds, particularly when monies were solicited from a variety of sources. On another level, they show that the women felt bound to recover more of those funds and that little economic support was available for them and their children. One could argue that other options were available. For example, the union could have provided employment to the women or assisted them in meeting their considerable child care responsibilities. In the 1920 strike in Hawai'i organized by Japanese and Filipina/o workers, the Federation of Japanese Labor in Hawai'i included eight weeks of paid maternity leave as one of its demands, a reflection of the numbers of immigrant women employed in the fields.[137] Because of the high level of Filipina/o participation in this strike, this issue probably could have become part of the extended communal knowledge of Filipina/o Americans. Also, around the same period as the Simon and Duyungan court cases, similar issues were articulated by other constituencies. Vicki Ruiz has documented, for example, how Mexican and Mexican American women engaged in California cannery work at the end of the 1930s and through the 1940s demanded benefits such as day care and maternity leave through the UCAPAWA.[138] While the Seattle union was primarily male in composition, the fact that union activity elsewhere in the American West included these kinds of campaigns indicates the array of possible solutions.

Lizabeth Cohen has pointed out in her study of pre–World War II Chicago how, as in the Seattle case, the "family orientation" of the CIO inhibited the participation of women as leaders. As Cohen notes, "Consequently, by reinforcing the patriarchal family, the CIO did not encourage workers to challenge traditional gender relationships as much as ethnic and racial ones." Although the Seattle Filipina/o community had many fewer women, Cohen's study highlights how challenges to gender restrictions were not a high priority for the union.[139]

But this was also a community in which the overall position of women was linked to the position of men, where even an independent spirit such as Bibiana Laigo Castillano was told by community elders that she needed to be married. Many women were able to pursue professional opportunities, such as Paula Nonacido, a nurse who held respect within the community, but they tended to be the exception rather than the rule.

Furthermore, it is important to note how power within the community was also structured by race and site. Although many of the marriages between Filipino men and Native American women took place in more rural areas around Seattle or in Alaska, the role of Native American women in Filipina/o Seattle is little discussed outside of areas such as Bainbridge Island. There is also a general lack of discussion about Filipina/o American and African American or Mexican American relationships, except for the case of the Jenkins family.

In contrast, in Alaska, where marriages between Filipinos and Native

Americans were fundamental to the community, there was clearly more integration of Native American women within the Filipina/o American community itself. Thelma Buchholdt's study of Filipina/o Alaska is notable for its description not only of Native American women who adapted to Filipina/o American culture, taking pivotal roles in community organizations, but also of the ways that Filipino men integrated themselves in their Native American partners' culture. Although events such as Rizal Days and other Filipina/o American cultural practices took place in sites such as Juneau, Filipina/os in Alaska also adapted themselves to the local culture.[140] For example, Ricardo "Dick" Lopez, originally from Cebu, traveled to Alaska for a cannery job at the beginning of the 1930s after laboring in San Francisco. In 1938, he was married to Anecia Iyuptula, an Aleut and Yup'ik Eskimo, with whom he would eventually have ten children. Their marriage came about when Iyuptula's father, Yako Iyuptula, who was dying, asked Lopez about marrying his daughter. After marrying, they would stay in the winter in a cabin next to the home of Anecia Iyuptula's mother. In the spring and summer, they stayed in Ekuk, where Dick worked as a fisherman for a cannery and Anecia fished to obtain food for the family and extra fish for their dogs. Their daughter Lisa relates how her father learned about the local culture. He learned how to trap animals for the family income, as well as to handle dogs for a dog team. Lopez sold wolverine, mink, fox, and beaver furs and also obtained ducks, geese, porcupine, ptarmigan, and moose as food for the family, cooking adobo with whatever meat was available, including beaver and moose.[141] In another example, Marcelo Quinto Sr., who first came to labor in a Juneau gold mine and also in the canneries, entered into marriage with a Tlingit Indian, Bessie Jackson from Haines, in 1940. Quinto's grandson Ricardo Worl notes that in Tlingit culture sisters were expected to share responsibilities for raising each other's children; thus Quinto also had duties in raising his sister-in-law's children.[142] Hence, in contrast to more stereotypical descriptions of Native American women, these women were seen as central members of the expanded Filipina/o Native American community in Alaska.[143] In Filipina/o Seattle, with its urban atmosphere and the relatively greater numbers of Filipinas and white women, the social dynamics were quite different than those in Alaska. Thus, in assessing the history of Filipina/o Seattle, we need to place these issues in the context of Filipina/o communities elsewhere in the diaspora in order to gain a greater sense of what relationships and events might have meant in the Seattle context.

CONCLUSION

This chapter has explored critical sites of political activity for Filipina/o Americans during the 1930s, particularly in terms of unionization. My goal has been to address the role of unionism during this period and also to consider the union movement within the context of the various possibilities available to Filipina/o Americans in Seattle. I have emphasized the need to look at both public and private spaces, not only to discern the contributions of women in what are often considered "male" activities but also to more fully assess the costs and benefits of unionization for the community as a whole.

As a popular port, as a regional center for the CWFLU, and as the home of the University of Washington, Seattle offered a specific configuration of players in the battle for communal authority. Thus, local politics took on a unique form in the city. Communal politics often were personality-driven and built around charismatic leaders, patriarchal in orientation, and extremely factionalized. However, while recognizing the power plays that foreground community politics, it is also crucial to note broader shifts that go beyond the individual styles of leadership. Migratory male workers gained an alternative base of power in the union, even though the leadership over this base was still contested.

It is also important to point out that while the unionists occupied a different space than the more conservative business interests in the community, they were also integrally tied to these interests, particularly because of bonds related to ethnic solidarity and male identity. Furthermore, their gains did not necessarily bring political power to other parts of the community that also may have been politically marginalized. A few women held leadership positions in community organizations, but women were typically constrained in their political power. For example, they were largely barred from participating in the CWFLU, one of the most influential organizations at the time. The position of women, however, was also tempered by class and race, and by the men they were connected to, particularly if those men were community leaders.

Hence, although the union movement was a pivotal part of Filipina/o Seattle history, it offers only part of the story of the community's formation. Analyzing the insiders and outsiders to this narrative provides much insight into the workings of Filipina/o Seattle. The fact that the union was able to claim considerable political space suggests both the power of the movement and the male privilege and resources of the labor movement in Seattle as a whole. It also leads us to consider how colonialism, race, and ethnicity shaped and constrained political activity not only because of the restrictions, whether implied or actual, that community members faced in engaging in other kinds of political labor, but also because union leadership became a high-status position. It was one way to counter the existing economic and social privilege of the contractors, as well as another avenue for achieving higher rank in the community. Given the intense rivalries in community politics and the regular jockeying for power, these issues become quite significant. On another level, examining the union in a wider framework enables us to better see how men's history is also shaped by women's history, and vice versa. Margaret Duyungan Mislang's and Matilde Simon's cases illustrate the limits of worker solidarity and where the boundaries were drawn as "union men" claimed a space for themselves, even as "union women" challenged this space.

The resulting story is thus not a simple one of the rise of the working class, or the increasing democracy of the Filipina/o American community in Seattle, although these elements were part of the development of community politics. Becoming part of the American labor movement could also be considered an extension of the growth in political movements in the Philippines, as well as the securing of an alternate base from which to challenge, though not to ultimately unseat, power hierarchies within Filipina/o Seattle. In fact, there were more radical elements within the community, as well as those working outside of the AFL and CIO context, such as the Filipina/o Communists. However tempting it might be to identify a vision of "progress" and increasing democracy, the reality was a far more complicated and contradictory reflection of larger developments in the United States and the Philippines as a whole.

This story helps us to see that the CWFLU's history is contested space in which competing narratives articulate different versions of this story. In order to more fully understand the union's history, it is important to contextualize it within the formation of the community as a whole and to listen carefully to the stories of community members, not only to what is said but also to what is left out.

The Past and the Future

Adjacent to the Immaculate Conception Church on Capitol Hill in Seattle is a converted elementary school building, which houses several community organizations. On any given day, the building is alive with activity—preschool kids going off to recess, young people hanging outside Filipino Youth Activities before dance practice, adults reading bulletin boards as they wait to pick up family members. On the second floor is the office of Dorothy Laigo Cordova, the executive director of the Demonstration Project for Asian Americans. She is likely to be on the phone long-distance, patiently helping a researcher from the East Coast who is trying to find information about her grandfather for an assignment for school, or writing the paperwork and applying for a grant for an exhibition, or directing a high school student in an administrative task. She is there almost every day of the week, and often late into the evening, particularly if there is a gathering in one of the meeting rooms. Typically, during those times, her husband, Fred Cordova, is buried in papers in the National Pinoy Archives room, methodically going through articles for filing or writing yet another piece about community history to commemorate an organization's anniversary, perhaps, or yet another speech for a college students' organization in the Midwest that has invited him to come to speak.

Whereas Fred Cordova is from a farming family in Stockton and first came to Seattle in 1948 as a student, Dorothy Laigo Cordova was born and raised in Seattle. Her history is intertwined with the story of Filipina/o

Seattle. Her father was an early cannery contractor who brought many other relatives to the area. Her mother was also a community pioneer, and her story has been documented in this book. The eldest daughter in a large family, Dorothy Laigo Cordova went to elementary school in the building where she now works; when she was growing up, she was familiar with many of the pioneers in the community and with many Filipina/o community activities—in fact, she was a queen in a community contest during the 1950s. Later she would attend college and become involved in the social movements of the time. In addition to raising an expanding family that now numbers several children and grandchildren, she began to document the community. Her work as a researcher in the Washington State Oral/Aural History project led her to begin the Demonstration Project for Asian Americans, an early research organization, as well as to cofound the Filipino Youth Activities and to found the Filipino American National Historical Society. In 1997, both she and Fred Cordova received honorary doctorates at Seattle University, a result of their patient and pathbreaking labor in the community.

In the course of Dorothy Laigo Cordova's lifetime, there have been several changes in the "community." The former "small-town" atmosphere of pre–World War II Seattle has been transformed not only because of the city's growth as the urban center of the Pacific Northwest but also because of new demographic trends. In the past thirty-five years or so, immigration laws radically transformed Filipina/o America, as thousands of new immigrants came to various sites throughout the United States. The Filipina/o community, always complex, became even more so in the recent era. Most notably, with the anti–martial law movement, political differences between organizations split the community. Debates over whether it was more important to focus on the political oppression at home in the Philippines or on the domestic struggles here challenged community coalitions, exacerbated by ethnic divides as the formerly predominantly Ilocano-speaking community became outnumbered by Tagalog speakers. Among the major events to divide the community were the murders of Silme Domingo and Gene Viernes, two young leaders killed in what turned out to be an assassination influenced by then-president Ferdinand Marcos. Later, some community leaders were indicted and convicted for their involvement.[1] Meanwhile, the economic base of the community also shifted as new immigrants, many from urban and professional backgrounds, filled jobs in the Seattle economy.

In another community pattern that Dorothy Laigo Cordova has characterized as "late family formation," many older men married and had children with much younger women from the Philippines, a reflection of the delay in marriages often characteristic of transpacific communities, gender hierarchies, and the difficult economic conditions faced by the communities involved. Some of these families' children attend the University of Washington, which, like the pre–World War II community, has a sizable representation of Filipina/o—in this case mostly Filipina/o American—students.

Other women come through different channels. One famous case was that of Susanna Blackwell, who, along with a friend, was tragically gunned down in front of a Seattle courtroom by her husband, whom she had originally met as a mail-order bride, drawing the community's attention to domestic violence and the unequal power relations involved in many of these marriages.[2] In Chinatown, now the International District, where many community organizations are concentrated, there are senior centers such as the International Drop In Center, where I spent many hours while researching this book.

The glimpse that I have offered of Filipina/o Seattle illustrates the growth and vibrancy of a community that has long been an integral part of the city as a whole. I have aimed to show the role of Seattle as a colonial metropole in the expanded United States empire by charting the formation of Filipina/o Seattle in the period between World War I and World War II, and the transpacific culture that flowed between the American mainland and the Philippines in the first half of the twentieth century. I have done so primarily within the framework of American studies and Asian American studies, tracing the implications of the issues I have raised within the fields of American social history, immigration studies, and the history of the American West. As opposed to the popular emphasis on the migration and settlement of "immigrants" to the United States, this book strives to complicate the narrative by examining the role of colonialism in the movement of peoples between the United States and the Philippines, particularly because of militarism and political force. Transnationalism, this book demonstrates, is not a recent phenomenon in the history of the relationship of the United States to the Philippines. My study thus indicates how imperialism and colonization were important factors in shaping how Filipina/os occupied a space in Seattle and other parts of the American West.

Kay Anderson argues in her study of Vancouver Chinatown that the place and space of "Chinatown" was a creation of white imagination and political maneuvering, even as Chinese members of that community negotiated the various boundaries and restrictions that constrained them.[3] Similarly, to understand Filipina/o Seattle, it is essential to examine how it was influenced by American culture, whether through imperialist or military activities, through racial and legislative definition, or through the structure of industries that regularly confined Filipina/o American workers to marginalized positions. Although my study privileges the voices of community members in Filipina/o Seattle, it is fundamentally interested in the workings of American culture as a whole. Typically, studies that focus on people of color are considered community studies in a very narrow sense and, because of political hierarchies, are perceived as being more "specialized" or "specific."[4] This perspective on community studies is further emphasized by the assimilationist framework in which many of these works are read, again because of the dominant ideology in which various groups are viewed as being absorbed into an "American" identity.[5] The experience of groups considered marginal in "mainstream" culture thus becomes contained. From the outset, as I began conceptualizing this study in New Haven, Connecticut, roughly a decade ago, on the far side of the continent from Seattle, Washington, I wanted to contest this process. Rather, I wanted to determine how a study of Filipina/o Seattle opened up questions for scholars of American culture, beyond even Filipina/o American and Asian American contexts.

In contrast to the closed enclaves often depicted in the discussion of Asian American communities, the lives of Filipina/o Americans reveal an expansive community migration, both within the Philippines and abroad to the United States. Indeed, the very structure of movement to the Port of Seattle and the attraction of educational institutions such as the University of Washington were very much a function of colonialism. Seattle was a pivotal metropole, one of a number of major cities in the United States, as well as in the rest of the world, that drew colonials from thousands of miles away. Through these connections developed due to the American empire, people formed the "imagined communities" that linked colony to metropole, as described by Benedict Anderson.[6] My work thus emphasizes the political connections between Filipina/os in Seattle and Filipina/os back in the Philippines, as well as other sites in the extended diaspora. I also indicate how Filipina/o Americans on the American mainland and in Hawai'i actively strove to assert their presence and rights in the United States, whether through political legislation or unionization. Because of their experience with colonialism, Filipina/os considered both the United States and the Philippines "home" during the era I have documented.

In developing this project, I have sought to emphasize what was unique

about the Filipina/o American experience. While indicating the many historical similarities that Filipina/o Americans share with other groups,
such as Chinese Americans and Japanese Americans, I have also tried to
explain the contrasts. This is important because "Asian American" in
American culture typically refers to the Chinese American and Japanese
American experiences, and hence explaining Filipina/o American history
becomes especially challenging. Because of their status as "nationals,"
Filipina/o Americans had dramatically different options than Chinese
Americans and Japanese Americans during the first decades of the twentieth century. For example, because of the influence of the American
regime in the Philippines, Filipina/os who came to the mainland usually
had previous exposure to American education and culture and were not
"immigrants" in the same sense as newcomers from other parts of Asia.

I have also sought to underscore the integral position of the Filipina/o
American community within local and regional arenas and to indicate its
role in the formation of Seattle, Washington State, the Pacific Northwest,
and the American West. For example, in characterizing Filpina/o Seattle, I have emphasized the close connection between the rural and urban
experiences of Filipina/o Americans, and the impact these experiences had
on each other. In addition, I was interested in charting Seattle's racialized space and how these issues took shape in comparison with developments in other sites such as California. Unlike in many other parts of
the country, the dominant groups of people of color in the region were
Asian Americans and Native Americans, which contributed to the city's
unique politics. Furthermore, the integration of European Americans,
Native Americans, and others into the Filipina/o American community
reshaped ideas about race and ethnicity while also demonstrating the connections between Filipina/o Americans and many other groups.

The opportunities and limits of public education for Filipina/o Americans as colonized subjects provide another topic for this book, particularly as they related to American colonialism in the Philippines and the
United States. Education not only was a longed-for resource for many
people arriving in the United States but also affected people's sense of
self and their perceptions of others, particularly because education represented an unfulfilled dream for many in this generational cohort. In
addition, even those who achieved their educational goals were rarely
able to get jobs that were commensurate with their educational training,
particularly during the Great Depression. Whether realized or not, education thus profoundly shaped class formation and class identities.

Other issues also became more prominent in the course of research-

ing and writing this book. When I began, I focused primarily on the Filipino male migratory laborers who dominated the community in the
pre–World War II era and on the story of unionization that forms such
a fundamental part of Filipina/o American history. As I began to chart
this history, though, I realized that it encompassed both competing voices
and competing claims. The union history actually reflects factionaliza-
tion within the community, as evidenced by the turbulence of the 1930s,
and when the unions are placed alongside other organizations within
Filipina/o Seattle, these disputes become even more evident. The disjuncture between the male-oriented history of unionization and other
forms of political activity, particularly activity within the "private
sphere," indicates how important it is to understand the multiple spaces
of community formation. When "students" and permanent urban workers are placed alongside migratory male workers, many of whom had
membership in more than one of these groups, our understanding of the
role of city and the formation of class is transformed. If women in the
Filipina/o community—from all the different represented backgrounds—
are positioned as central players, the stories shift as well. The focus on
unionization widens to include contested stories of the union's exclusion
and separatism, and we also learn about household labor and reproductive labor, which typically take place outside of the public workplace.
Exploring both private and public spaces is thus essential because it provides both a fuller sense of community life and a better understanding
of how gender identities are created and shaped. Similarly, analyzing how
race and ethnicity shaped Filipina/o Seattle enabled me to better see how
Filipina/os were positioned within the ethnic and racial hierarchies that
formed Seattle and the American West.

The story of Filipina/o Seattle thus becomes more complicated, and
certainly more confusing, when one considers all these different parts.
The shifting of this story enables the inclusion of several more voices and
the recognition of a different constellation of themes. Instead of the typical focus on the community's male unionists that characterizes many
studies of Filipina/o Americans, my broader approach yielded different
insights, particularly about race, class, and gender, in which relations of
unequal power were regularly maintained within the community as often as they were contested within and without Filipina/o Seattle.

Ultimately, my goal in this project was to provide one contribution,
among many that are made in Filipina/o Seattle, to telling the history of
this community as I saw it based on observations, interviews, and research.
There are many more stories that need to be told. In the course of doing

this research, I often was struck not just by the narratives that are commonly repeated about immigrant sacrifice for the American-born children or the pivotal role of "The Union," as the CWFLU was regularly referred to by my informants, but also by the parts that are less discussed. I would have liked to learn more about the range of political organization in the community, especially about participation in leftist organizations or the impact of communism, and how that affected the community as a whole. Unfortunately, the people who probably could have told me more were largely gone, and the people whom I spoke with were often silent in this regard. This is not surprising, given the harassment leftist activists might have faced during the cold war period in the United States, or the tense political controversies that divided the Filipina/o American community during the martial law era of the Philippines.

There were other silences as well. For instance, I had hoped to find more information about the expression of sexuality in the community. The emphasis on heterosexual marriage, not only by the American and Philippine cultures but also by the state, led me to wonder about other forms of relationships in which people engaged. I wanted to investigate more about what companionship meant in terms of sexuality, and particularly about the histories of sexuality outside the carefully formulated heterosexual center. I found little discussion of lesbian, gay, bisexual, and transgender community members. I also found minimal information about domestic violence as a whole. Given the general level of violence and death that was present in the various realms of community life, I wondered how these issues manifested themselves in both private and public spaces. But the fact that there were palpable silences on these topics does not mean that they were not important, although it does mean that I found relatively little evidence in my investigation of these areas.

All these issues underscore how our role as researchers in the community has implications for what we look for and what we find. Certainly, many scholars have discussed the relationship of positionality to research. Some of the stories that I considered most interesting did not make it into these pages, primarily because they were told to me "in trust" or because I wanted to protect a family's privacy. As a scholar, I think about the tension between wanting to preserve that sense of trust and wanting to encourage discussion, especially when withholding a story perpetuates certain silences in the community. My feeling, though, is that our response to this tension is rooted in the moment and is contingent upon our relationship to the community. Is there a conversation unfolding in which these issues can fit? Is the time to speak them now, or would a later time be better? Or is it more appropriate for someone else to voice these issues? Certainly, the story I have told here is very different in some key respects from the dissertation I completed years ago. Over the course of my research, I became more interested in highlighting how different forms of power, such as class identity, male privilege, or ethnic nationalism, shaped the community. I also wanted to investigate how these forms of power, in turn, influenced how the community's history was narrated and remembered. I thus hoped to share alternate ways of seeing the development of pre–World War II Filipina/o Seattle, to analyze who gained from the community's relationships and movements, and who paid the costs for these changes and struggles. They were not necessarily the same people.

I have already noted the importance of understanding the experience of Filipina/o Americans as an integral part of the American whole, and of challenging the implicit power relations that relegate many works on people of color to being "community studies." Although the term *community studies* is often used in a problematic way in academia, I see this as a very different issue from the role and contributions that community history projects make to our studies of American culture. I thus want to acknowledge the large debt that I, as well as other writers, have to community history projects that undertake the monumental task of preserving people's stories and artifacts, particularly through oral history interviews. For example, interviews collected through the Washington State Oral/Aural History Program and the Demonstration Project for Asian Americans in the mid-1970s and early 1980s formed one of the foundations for this study. The resources available to us are far greater because of the contributions and efforts of both the interviewers and the interviewees. In particular, because Dorothy Cordova and others insisted that women's memories be part of these interviews, including those of women who were Filipina American community members although not of Filipina descent, writers like myself are able to draw from a much richer array of sources.

These kinds of studies are important not only because they often privilege how community residents themselves might have understood and interpreted events but also because they provide insights that otherwise might have been overlooked. While they might emphasize narratives of "progress," they often convey very human details about the complexity of emotion and experience, providing us with a glimpse of people's experience as a whole. I recognize, though, that even if these efforts might be forms of resistance to marginalization in the mainstream culture, the often relentless march to progress and assimilation that many community history projects convey can be deeply problematic, if not oppressive as well.[7]

At the same time, however, it is ultimately our responsibility to decide how we use these stories. Perhaps most important, they tell us that many "truths" must be considered in establishing a community's history. Just as we piece together different recollections within a family to gain a better understanding of the past, we must use these various community memories to forge our own sense of what has gone before. It is our job as researchers and listeners to understand the frameworks and narratives within which people discuss the past, and the ways that these frameworks and narratives shape how stories are told and remembered. Even as we retell the story in our own present, we must be aware of the range of power relations that shape our interaction with the past and of how that informs our use of history as a resource.

In closing, I hope that this book will both provide documentation about a crucial community in American culture and also suggest how American culture, in turn, has been shaped by the United States' colonization of the Philippines. I also hope it will be helpful in charting how history about this community is made and understood, since one of my goals has been to challenge the different narratives that constrain how the history of Filipina/o Americans has been perceived. Rather than adhering to the dominant assimilationist narrative of Filipina/o Americans becoming "incorporated" into the United States, I have sought to show that this process was highly contested, particularly because of the resistance, and sometimes conformity, of community members to race, class, and gender oppression. Instead of relying on the ideology of American exceptionalism, I stress the emergence of a fluid transpacific economy and culture, in which Filipina/o American community members, including many who were not of Filipina/o descent, made active choices regarding whether to pursue their options in the United States or the Philippines. Unlike analyses of Asian American history, which fit Filipina/o Americans within models that privilege the Japanese American and Chinese American experience, I strive to show the unique nature of the Filipina/o American experience, even as I underscore the many commonalities between Filipina/o Americans and other groups. In contrast to the many studies that focus only on the urban experience of Asian Americans, I have sought to include rural arenas in people's spheres of activity in the American West, thus emphasizing the impact of region on the formation of Filipina/o America. And although many of the people I present in this book are men, I have endeavored not just to include women's voices but also to demonstrate how their experience radically reshapes conventional understandings of community history.

I have tried to write a history that does justice to the complexity of people's lives and dreams, as well as one that addresses larger themes about the formation of American culture as a whole. I hope that my efforts will contribute to our understanding of the power of human agency in the struggle for social justice, even as we fight for those issues of social justice in our own time. I believe that ultimately it is through this kind of labor that we best honor the memory of those who made Filipina/o Seattle possible.

Notes

NOTE ON TERMINOLOGY

1. Jesse G. Quinsaat, ed., *Letters in Exile: An Introductory Reader on the History of the Pilipinos in America* (Los Angeles: UCLA Asian American Studies Center, 1976), preface, 1 [no page numbers].

2. Editors, "To Our Readers," *Amerasia Journal* 13, no. 1 (1986–1987), viii–ix.

3. I began using *Filipina/o American* in 1994 while writing the dissertation that formed the basis of this book. Other scholars who use *Filipina/o* include Teresa Amott and Julie Matthaei in *Race, Gender, and Work: A Multicultural Economic History of Women in the United States* (Boston: South End Press, 1991), 239–249; Joan May Cordova; and Theodore S. Gonzalves.

INTRODUCTION: THE ROLE OF COLONIALISM

1. Margaret M. Mislang, interview by Carolina Koslosky, FIL-KNG75-12ck, 16 June 1975, Washington State Oral/Aural History Program, 6. Hereafter, the Washington State Oral/Aural History Program will be abbreviated as WSOAHP.

2. Ibid., 7.

3. Ibid., 9.

4. For more on this division within the Filipina/o American community, see Chris Friday's discussion in *Organizing Asian American Labor: The Pacific Coast Canned-Salmon Industry, 1870–1942* (Philadelphia: Temple University Press, 1994), 156–158.

5. Mislang, interview, 10.

6. Ibid., 9–11.

7. In the court transcript, the figure is $1,768.06. Mislang, interview, 16; No. 310203, 1938–1939, "In the Superior Court of the State of Washington in and for King County, Margaret Duyungan, Plaintiff vs. Cannery Workers and Farm Laborers Union, Local 18257, a voluntary, unincorporated association, and I. R. Cabatit, Amado Logan, Antonio Rodrigo, John Doe Abella, and Vicente Navia [sic], Defendants, Complaint," 1.

8. Mislang, interview, 16.

9. Ibid., 6, 19–20.

10. Ibid., 1–2.

11. David Montgomery, *Worker's Control in America: Studies in the History of Work, Technology, and Labor Struggles* (Cambridge: Cambridge University Press, 1979); Herbert G. Gutman, *Work, Culture, and Society in Industrializing America: Essays in American Working-Class and Social History* (New York: Knopf, 1976). Examining the everyday lives of workers became an important component of the "new labor history." In her study of cigar workers in the first two decades of the century, for example, Patricia Cooper explores the rich "work culture" that she found, "a coherent system of ideas and practices, forged in the context of the work process itself, through which workers modified, mediated, and resisted the limits of their jobs." Patricia A. Cooper, *Once a Cigar Maker: Men, Women, and Work Culture in American Cigar Factories, 1900–1919* (Urbana: University of Illinois Press, 1987), 2.

12. See Gutman's critique of the "old" labor history in "Work, Culture, and Society in Industrializing America," in his *Work, Culture, and Society in Industrializing America.* On page 10, referring to how labor history was traditionally formulated by earlier historians, Gutman writes, "Together with able disciples, they studied the development of the trade union as an institution and explained its place in a changing labor market. But they gave attention primarily to those few workers who belonged to trade unions and neglected much else of importance about the American working population." The American Social History Project was founded by Herbert Gutman and Stephen Brier in 1981 to tell American history from the vantage point of "ordinary" people through productions for a wide range of academic and popular audiences. See, for example, the American Social History Project, City University of New York, under the direction of Herbert G. Gutman, *Who Built America? Working People and the Nation's Economy, Politics, Culture, and Society,* vol. 1, *From Conquest and Colonization through Reconstruction and the Great Uprising of 1877* (New York: Pantheon, 1989). The book's preface contains a discussion of the origins of the American Social History Project on page xii.

13. Christine Stansell, *City of Women: Sex and Class in New York, 1789–1860* (Urbana: University of Illinois Press, 1987).

14. Stuart M. Blumin, *The Emergence of the Middle Class: Social Experience in the American City, 1760–1900* (Cambridge: Cambridge University Press, 1989).

15. See Dana Frank, *Purchasing Power: Consumer Organizing, Gender, and the Seattle Labor Movement, 1919–1929* (New York: Cambridge University Press, 1994), 249.

16. In *Labor Immigration under Capitalism,* Lucie Cheng and Edna Bonacich

describe the United States' search overseas for exploitable labor to mitigate economic crises at home and the unequal incorporation of these overseas colonial workers in the American economy. Cheng and Bonacich also discuss the responses of others to this labor migration—for example, the resistance of local workers and monopoly sector workers to the competition posed by these entering laborers. See Edna Bonacich and Lucie Cheng, "Introduction: A Theoretical Orientation to International Labor Migration," in *Labor Immigration under Capitalism: Asian Workers in the United States before World War II*, ed. Lucie Cheng and Edna Bonacich (Berkeley and Los Angeles: University of California Press, 1984), 1–56, especially 39–46. Historian William Cronon's masterful study of Chicago, which portrays the economic landscape of the city, is another example of a work that has de-emphasized the social history of the individuals who built the city, in favor of other forces. William Cronon, *Nature's Metropolis: Chicago and the Great West* (New York: Norton, 1991).

17. See Him Mark Lai, Genny Lim, and Judy Yung, *Island: Poetry and History of Chinese Immigrants on Angel Island, 1910–1940* (San Francisco: HOC DOI [History of Chinese Detained on Island], distributed by San Francisco Study Center, 1980). Genny Lim also wrote an important play based on this immigration experience called *Paper Angels*, further promoting knowledge and discussion about this heretofore little-discussed aspect of American history. The play would later be dramatized through PBS's *American Playhouse* series, thus ensuring that people around the country would learn of the importance of this historical site. See *Paper Angels and Bitter Cane: Two Plays by Genny Lim* (Honolulu: Kalamaku Press, 1991), 1–52. A related work, John Kuo Wei Tchen and Arnold Genthe's *Genthe's Photographs of San Francisco's Old Chinatown*, represents another effort of reclamation in Tchen's careful recontextualization of photographs taken by the German photographer of San Francisco Chinatown at the turn of the century. Tchen demonstrates how Genthe's selective portrayal of scenic Chinatown figures and his alteration of photographs to delete white figures or replace English lettering with Chinese characters contributed to a stereotyped image of Chinatown as a strange, exotic, and "Oriental" place. See John Kuo Wei Tchen and Arnold Genthe, *Genthe's Photographs of San Francisco's Old Chinatown* (New York: Dover, 1984), especially Tchen's opening essay on pages 3–23. Marlon K. Hom's *Songs of Gold Mountain: Cantonese Rhymes from San Francisco Chinatown* (Berkeley and Los Angeles: University of California Press, 1987) also features poetry by immigrants from community newspapers. The strength of these sources and careful labor in the community is realized in Judy Yung's books on the experience of Chinese American women in San Francisco, *Unbound Feet: A Social History of Chinese Women in San Francisco* (Berkeley and Los Angeles: University of California Press, 1995), and the companion volume, *Unbound Voices: A Documentary History of Chinese Women in San Francisco* (Berkeley and Los Angeles: University of California Press, 1999). Yung, who grew up in San Francisco Chinatown and then became a librarian in its local library, was a researcher and community activist long before she entered a doctoral program at the University of California, Berkeley. The shared philosophy of these scholars and others in developing critical analysis of community-based history has very much inspired my own work. For another early example

of the importance of oral history documentation, see Victor G. Nee and Brett de Bary Nee's anthology, *Longtime Californ': A Documentary Study of an American Chinatown* (1972; reprint, Stanford, Calif.: Stanford University Press, 1986). This foundational study of San Francisco Chinatown showcases oral histories from a range of community perspectives. Like other oral history anthologies of marginalized communities, this study attempted to provide a more accurate and less stereotyped portrayal of the Chinatown community and to privilege the voices and analyses of its residents.

18. Up until the 1990s, research on the pre–World War II era had been a major focus of the field. This scholarship, usually written by community "insiders," often explored the important task of reclaiming a "forgotten" history, such as Fred Cordova's *Filipinos: Forgotten Asian Americans, A Pictorial Essay/1763-Circa-1963* (1983). Howard De Witt, who has published scholarship on laborers in the cannery industry and in agricultural fields, also made important contributions by documenting the struggles in those areas, while Barbara Posadas and Ronald Guyotte published a number of articles on the Filipina/o American experience in Chicago. There also has been increased documentation of the important history of women, with scholars such as Dorothy Cordova contributing work that charted this gendered history. Another important overall history is provided by the documentation of the Filipina/o American community in Hawai'i in Luis V. Teodoro Jr., ed., *Out of This Struggle: The Filipinos in Hawaii* (Honolulu: University Press of Hawaii, 1981; published for the Filipino Seventh-fifth Anniversary Commemoration Commission). For history documenting the pre–World War II era, see, for example, Barbara M. Posadas, "Crossed Boundaries in Interracial Chicago: Pilipino American Families since 1925," *Amerasia Journal* 8, no. 2 (1981): 31–52; Posadas, "The Hierarchy of Color and Psychological Adjustment in an Industrial Environment: Filipinos, the Pullman Company, and the Brotherhood of Sleeping Car Porters," *Labor History* 2, no. 3 (summer 1982): 349–373; and Posadas and Ronald Guyotte, "Unintentional Immigrants: Chicago's Filipino Foreign Students Become Settlers, 1941," *Journal of American Ethnic History* 9, no. 2 (spring 1990): 26–48; and Dorothy Cordova, "Voices from the Past: Why They Came," in *Making Waves: An Anthology of Writings by and about Asian American Women*, ed. Asian Women United of California (Boston: Beacon Press, 1989).

19. Michael Frisch, *A Shared Authority: Essays on the Craft and Meaning of Oral and Public History* (Albany: State University of New York Press, 1990), xv. In 1983, Fred Cordova's *Filipinos: Forgotten Asian Americans*, a pictorial history featuring oral history excerpts, was released. Community members organized the Filipino American National Historical Society in 1982 and instituted a national network of Filipina/o American history chapters throughout the country. The FANHS also set up the National Pinoy Archives in Seattle, a valuable repository for oral histories, articles, photographs, and other artifacts about the Filipina/o American experience in this country as a whole. It is no accident that these community-based history projects typically emerge in urban settings with large populations of Asian Americans, through the efforts of community-based scholars conducting documentation within and without the academy. Similar to the Museum of the Chinese in the Americas, both the Demonstration Project for

Asian Americans and the FANHS are housed in a converted school building, alongside other direct service community agencies, including Filipino Youth Activities, an organization focused on serving the community's youth, with activities ranging from a drill team to gang prevention.

20. The American colonial period is a rich source of information about Filipina/o Americans, particularly because so many Filipina/o students were studying at American universities at the time and documenting their experiences. The first wave of documentation about Filipina/o Americans encompasses the scholarship of Filipina/os studying in the United States such as Benicio Catapusan, who was a student of Emory Bogardus at the University of Southern California, and whose work employed the race relations cycle model. See Benicio T. Catapusan, "The Social Adjustment of Filipinos in the United States" (Ph.D. diss., University of Southern California, 1940). Another book, Bruno Lasker's *Filipino Immigration to Continental United States and to Hawaii* (Chicago: University of Chicago Press, 1931), a study produced by the Institute for Pacific Relations, an early Pacific Rim think tank, was written in response to pending legislation over Filipino independence and repatriation in the mid-1930s.

21. Michael Frisch, "The Memory of History," in his *Shared Authority*, 26–27.

22. Renato Rosaldo, *Culture and Truth: The Remaking of Social Analysis* (Boston: Beacon Press, 1989), 69. See the essays in Martin F. Manalansan IV's *Cultural Compass: Ethnographic Explorations of Asian America* (Philadelphia: Temple University Press, 2000) for a full exposition of the diverse issues that accompany the writing of Asian American community studies.

23. Of all the writings from the pre-1965 era, Bulosan's are the most discussed and accessible. Ronald Takaki, for example, features *America Is in the Heart* in his discussion of the Filipina/o American experience in *Strangers from a Different Shore: A History of Asian Americans* (Boston: Little, Brown, 1989), 343–354. Another well-known book from that period is Manuel Buaken, *I Have Lived with the American People* (Caldwell, Idaho: Caxton Printers, 1948). For examples of the interest in Bulosan's writings, see E. San Juan, *Carlos Bulosan and the Imagination of the Class Struggle* (Quezon City: University of the Philippines Press, 1972); and, more recently, Carlos Bulosan, *The Cry and the Dedication*, ed. E. San Juan (Philadelphia: Temple University Press, 1995); and E. San Juan, ed., *On Becoming Filipino: Selected Writings of Carlos Bulosan* (Philadelphia: Temple University Press, 1995). Another important work is Susan Evangelista's *Carlos Bulosan and His Poetry: A Biography and Anthology* (Seattle: University of Washington Press, 1985). See also Michael Denning's discussion of Carlos Bulosan in *The Cultural Front: The Laboring of American Culture in the Twentieth Century* (New York: Verso, 1996), 272–278.

24. In recent decades, a substantial body of literature has emerged on the relationship between memory and history, particularly because of the increased interest in oral history and public history in general. See, for example, Frisch, *Shared Authority*, and a special issue of the *Journal of American History* 75, no. 4 (March 1989). For a recent text that takes into account the role of memory and power, see Susan Lee Johnson, *Roaring Camp: The Social World of the California Gold Rush* (New York: Norton, 2000). See also Gary Y. Okihiro, "Oral History and the Writing of Ethnic History," in *Oral History: An Interdisciplinary Anthology*,

ed. David K. Dunaway and Willa K. Baum (Walnut Creek, Calif.: Altamira Press, 1996), 199–214.

Oral histories, like all historical sources, are produced out of particular contexts and are shaped by social and economic relations See, for example, Michael Frisch's chapter "The Memory of History," in *Shared Authority*, 15–27. Community histories, for instance, might be written to preserve the experience of a select sector of the community, to make sure that "our" history is maintained in the face of the growing strength of others, such as more recent immigrants. In recognition of the creative ways that memories acknowledge or present versions of the past, I often corroborate oral histories with materials I have found from other informants or other sources; at other times I indicate when the memories might be more problematic.

25. For more on Philip Vera Cruz, see my article "Rereading *Philip Vera Cruz*: Race, Labor, and Coalitions," *Journal of Asian American Studies* 3, no. 2 (June 2000): 139–162. Another wave of scholarship emerged in the 1970s and 1980s, influenced by the civil rights movement, which help to promote ethnic studies, the great demographic changes that took place following the landmark 1965–1968 immigration legislation in the United States, and the turmoil of the martial law period and the anti-Marcos movement in the Philippines and the United States. A famous UCLA anthology from that period provides a critical and illuminating portrait of that period, with articles ranging from the American oppression in the Philippines, to Filipina/o service in the navy, to political struggles in agricultural fields. See Jesse G. Quinsaat, ed., *Letters in Exile: An Introductory Reader on the History of the Pilipinos in America* (Los Angeles: UCLA Asian American Studies Center, 1976). Another early work that contains crucial memories about the Stockton community is *Voices: A Filipino American Oral History*, originally published in 1984. See Filipino Oral History Project, *Voices: A Filipino American Oral History* (Stockton, Calif.: Filipino Oral History Project, 2000). During this period, particularly because of the intense struggles in the Philippines, there was an increased focus on the U.S.-Philippines relationship, on what was happening "back home," and on the connections of these issues to Filipina/o Americans here. E. San Juan, for example, critiques assimilationist models that discount the internationalist struggle of Filipina/os around the world. The U.S.-Philippines relationship has always been a critical concern for scholars, as is apparent in E. San Juan's *The Philippine Temptation: Dialectics of Philippines-U.S. Literary Relations* (Philadelphia: Temple University Press, 1996). See Miriam Sharma, "The Philippines: A Case of Migration to Hawaii, 1906–1946," 337–358, and "Labor Migration and Class Formation among the Filipinos in Hawaii, 1906–1946," 579–615, in Cheng and Bonacich, *Labor Immigration under Capitalism;* Jack Masson and Donald Guimary, "Asian Labor Contractors in the Alaskan Canned Salmon Industry: 1880–1937," *Labor History* 22, no. 3 (summer 1981): 377–397; Gail Nomura, "Within the Law: The Establishment of Filipino Leasing Rights on the Yakima Indian Reservation," *Amerasia Journal* 13, no. 1 (1986–1987): 99–117; and Jon D. Cruz, "Filipino-American Community Organizations in Washington, 1900s–1930s," in *Peoples of Color in the American West*, ed. Sucheng Chan (Lexington, Mass.: Heath, 1994), 235–245, for other important studies of Filipina/o Americans. For a work in which religion is a cen-

tral theme, see Steffi San Buenaventura, "Nativism and Ethnicity in a Filipino-American Experience" (Ph.D. diss., University of Hawai'i, 1990; forthcoming from Stanford University Press). The era between World War II and 1965 remains less well documented, although there have been some important contributions to our understanding of this era. Arlene De Vera has conducted critical research on the Filipina/o American labor movement and has published "Without Parallel: The Local 7 Deportation Case, 1949–1955," *Amerasia Journal* 20, no. 2 (1994): 1–25. More recently, there has been an outpouring of new scholarship, long overdue, that focuses on dimensions of the post-1965 experience, such as Yen Le Espiritu's *Filipino American Lives* (Philadelphia: Temple University Press, 1995), a collection of oral histories from the San Diego community. Maria P. P. Root's *Filipino Americans: Transformation and Identity* (Thousand Oaks, Calif.: Sage, 1997), an anthology of different voices charting the contemporary terrain of Filipina/o Americans, is another example of this kind of scholarship. Barbara Posadas has also published a recent textbook on Filipina/o American history, *The Filipino Americans* (Westport, Conn.: Greenwood Press, 1999), which includes substantial information on the post-1965 era. These and other recent books are providing much fuller documentation on developments in Filipino America. For example, see Jonathan Y. Okamura, *Imagining the Filipino American Diaspora: Transnational Relations, Identities, and Communities* (New York: Garland Press, 1998). There is also another generational cohort emerging of scholars producing materials on diverse subjects in the Filipina/o American community, with particular attention to cultural studies. See, for example, Martin Manalansan, *Global Divas* (Durham, N.C.: Duke University Press, forthcoming); Charlene Tung, "The Social Reproductive Labor of Filipina Transmigrant Workers in Southern California: Caring for Those Who Provide Elderly Care" (Ph.D. diss., University of California, Irvine, 1999); and Rick Bonus, *Locating Filipino Americans: Ethnicity and the Cultural Politics of Space* (Philadelphia: Temple University Press, 2000).

26. Jennifer Ting, "Bachelor Society: Deviant Heterosexuality and Asian American Historiography," in *Privileging Positions: The Sites of Asian American Studies,* ed. Gary Y. Okihiro, Marilyn Alquizola, Dorothy Fujita Rony, and K. Scott Wong (Pullman: Washington State University Press, 1995), 278.

27. Chris Friday's book, for example, which offers an in-depth study of work culture and unionization in the Pacific Northwest, with particular attention to interethnic relations, focuses less on relations occurring outside of the workplace. See Friday, *Organizing Asian American Labor.* Howard De Witt's excellent studies of farm labor in California also need to be placed in the organizational context of the Filipina/o community as a whole. See Howard De Witt, *Violence in the Fields: California Filipino Farm Labor Unionization during the Great Depression* (Saratoga, N.Y.: Century Twenty One, 1980), 19–20; De Witt, "The Filipino Labor Union: The Salinas Lettuce Strike of 1934," *Amerasia Journal* 5, no. 2 (1978): 1–21.

28. See Frank, *Purchasing Power,* for an analysis of how integral consumerism and household labor are to the labor movement as a whole.

29. William I. Thomas and Florian Znaniecki, *The Polish Peasant in Europe*

and America, edited and abridged by Eli Zaretsky (Urbana: University of Illinois Press, 1984), 24–28.

30. Oscar Handlin, *The Uprooted: The Epic Story of the Great Migrations That Made the American People* (Boston: Little, Brown, 1951), 6.

31. For a further discussion of these issues, see Michael Omi and Howard Winant's chapter, "The Dominant Paradigm: Ethnicity-Based Theory," of which "assimilationism" is a major component. Michael Omi and Howard Winant, *Racial Formation in the United States: From the 1960s to the 1980s* (New York: Routledge, 1986), 14–24. Virginia Yans-McLaughlin's introduction to *Immigration Reconsidered: History, Sociology, and Politics* (New York: Oxford University Press, 1990), 3–18, offers a useful critique of immigration studies. She argues that the essays presented in the volume contest the role of American exceptionalism and conventional views of assimilation in American culture, and posit an international framework for migration.

32. See Henry Yu, "The 'Oriental Problem' in America, 1920–1960: Linking the Identities of Chinese American and Japanese American Intellectuals," in *Claiming America: Constructing Chinese American Identities during the Exclusion Era,* ed. K. Scott Wong and Sucheng Chan (Philadelphia: Temple University Press, 1998), 196–197.

33. S. Frank Miyamoto, *Social Solidarity among the Japanese in Seattle* (Seattle: University of Washington Press, 1984), 69.

34. Takaki, *Strangers from a Different Shore;* Sucheng Chan, *Asian Americans: An Interpretive History* (Boston: Twayne, 1991). See also Yans-McLaughlin's introduction in *Immigration Reconsidered,* especially pp. 5–8.

35. John Bodnar, *The Transplanted: A History of Immigrants in Urban America* (Bloomington: Indiana University Press, 1985), 207.

36. Ibid., 215–216.

37. In this regard, works such as Benedict J. Kerkvliet's *The Huk Rebellion: A Study of Peasant Revolt in the Philippines* (Berkeley and Los Angeles: University of California Press, 1977) present an important community study model by documenting an agrarian area in the Philippines that was the focus of political ferment and social upheaval. David R. Sturtevant's *Popular Uprisings in the Philippines, 1840–1940* (Ithaca, N.Y.: Cornell University Press, 1976), and Melinda Tria Kerkvliet's *Manila Workers' Unions, 1900–1950* (Quezon City: New Day Publishers, 1992) also provide insight about social change in the Philippines during the period under study by underscoring the pivotal role of working-class laborers in agitating for change.

38. Much work is still needed to make connections between what occurred in diverse sites of the Filipina/o diaspora and how the massive unrest of rural workers in the Philippines during the 1930s affected communities in the United States.

39. For example, more accurate portrayals of the role of culture are provided by George Sánchez in his book on Chicana/o culture in Los Angeles. Sánchez argues against "bipolar models that have stressed either cultural continuity or gradual acculturation." He demonstrates the complex relation of immigrants to their culture in terms of identity formation and adaptation, relying on a wide array of areas, from music and popular culture to unionization and political movements, to argue for the complexity of cultural formations in immigrant com-

munities. George J. Sánchez, *Becoming Mexican American: Ethnicity, Culture and Identity in Chicano Los Angeles, 1900–1945* (New York: Oxford University Press, 1993), 13. See also Robert Anthony Orsi, *The Madonna of 115th Street: Faith and Community in Italian Harlem, 1880–1950* (New Haven, Conn.: Yale University Press, 1985).

40. Sylvia Junko Yanagisako, *Transforming the Past: Tradition and Kinship among Japanese Americans* (Stanford, Calif.: Stanford University Press, 1985), 1–2; and Miyamoto, *Social Solidarity among the Japanese in Seattle.*

41. The Vincent Chin case, in which a Chinese American was beaten to death by two unemployed auto workers in Detroit, is often cited as an important example of the continued and deadly perception of Asian Americans as perpetual foreigners. For a further discussion, see chapter 3 of Helen Zia, *Asian American Dreams: The Emergence of an American People* (New York: Farrar, Straus and Giroux, 2000), 55–81.

42. Frank Thistlewaite, "Migration from Europe Overseas in the Nineteenth and Twentieth Centuries," in *Population Movements in Modern European History,* ed. Herbert Moller (New York: Macmillan, 1964), 73–92.

43. Mislang, interview, 9–16. More recently, another manifestation of this is the popular ideology of the American Dream, a product of the United States' military and economic dominance, particularly after World War II. According to this ideology, the reason that so many thousands of Asian immigrants have sought to come to this country was because of the promise of freedom—political, economic, and social—and the opportunities that they could then give to future generations. Despite hardship and discrimination, Asian Americans persevered to make a better place for themselves and their families. This narrative performs the important task of validating the experience of former generations and placing people at the center of the story. My concern is that it presents racism, sexism, and economic segregation as barriers that immigrants must overcome as part of the initiation process to the United States so that later generations might have a brighter future. Discrimination against immigrants then becomes naturalized and relegated to "part of the process."

44. See Linda Basch, Nina Glick Schiller, and Cristina Szanton Blanc, *Nations Unbound: Transnational Projects, Postcolonial Predicaments, and Deterritorialized Nation-States* (n.p.: Gordon and Breach, 1994), 7. The "transnational migrant circuit" that Rouse identifies in his research on Mexican migration is also useful for explaining the Filipina/o experience, particularly in the post-1965 era. See Roger Rouse, "Mexican Migration and the Social Space of Postmodernism," *Diaspora* 1, no. 1 (spring 1991): 10–15. Two studies that focus on the colonial and trans-Pacific experience are Stephen Griffiths's *Emigrants, Entrepreneurs, and Evil Spirits: Life in a Philippine Village* (Honolulu: University of Hawai'i Press, 1988), written in the field of anthropology, and geographer Daniel F. Doeppers's *Manila, 1900–1941: Social Change in a Late Colonial Metropolis,* Monograph Series no. 27 (New Haven, Conn.: Yale University Southeast Asia Studies, 1984). Griffiths's study demonstrates the impact of trans-Pacific migration on the local development of a Philippine community, for example, by looking at the impact of capital sent home by migrants to their families, primarily from Hawai'i. Doeppers's *Manila, 1900–1941,* provides an

extremely helpful model for studying the economic and social developments in a Philippine city and helped me to rethink the role of Seattle, particularly as a port city.

45. Key texts such as Miyamoto's *Social Solidarity among Japanese Americans in Seattle* and Yanagisako's *Transforming the Past* have provided vital information about the relationship of Asian Americans to Seattle and the rise of Asian American communities in the city. They further underscore the differential position of Filipina/o Americans in relation to other groups, such as Japanese Americans. Quintard Taylor's study of the African American community in Seattle's central district also provides us with a valuable recontextualization of Seattle's history by analyzing the connections of the African American and Asian American communities, despite a reliance on the "sojourner" model to explain Asian migration to the city. See Quintard Taylor, *The Forging of a Black Community: Seattle's Central District from 1870 through the Civil Rights Era* (Seattle: University of Washington Press, 1994), especially chapter 4, "Blacks and Asians in a White City, 1870–1942," 106–134. See pp. 109–110 and 133 for use of the "sojourner" model.

46. Dana Frank, "Race Relations and the Seattle Labor Movement, 1915–1929," *Pacific Northwest Quarterly* 86, no. 1 (winter 1994/1995): 35; Carlos A. Schwantes, "Unemployment, Disinheritance, and the Origins of Labor Militancy in the Pacific Northwest, 1885–86," in *Experiences in a Promised Land: Essays in Pacific Northwest History,* ed. G. Thomas Edwards and Carlos A. Schwantes (Seattle: University of Washington Press, 1986), 179–194.

47. See, for example, Takaki, *Strangers from a Different Shore.*

48. Chan, *Asian Americans,* 25. See Marina E. Espina, *Filipinos in Louisiana* (New Orleans, La.: A. F. Laborde, 1988), for the definitive discussion of this subject.

49. See, for example, Evelyn Hu-DeHart, "Coolies, Shopkeepers, Pioneers: The Chinese of Mexico and Peru (1849–1930)," *Amerasia Journal* 15, no. 2 (1989): 91–116.

50. Although several of the people I discuss in this book are men, I have sought to incorporate many women's voices as well, and even begin my chapters with discussions of several women's personal narratives. This framing of my materials is deliberate and is intended to counter the typically inevitable emphasis on the community's male history.

51. Ting, "Bachelor Society," 271–279. See also the important discussions in David L. Eng and Alice Y. Hom, eds., *Q & A: Queer in Asian America* (Philadelphia: Temple University Press, 1998).

52. One of the most extensive discussions of family and kinship in Asian America remains Yanagisako's account of the Seattle Japanese American community, *Transforming the Past.*

53. See Gary Okihiro's important discussion of the "tyranny of the city" in Asian American historiography in "The Fallow Field: The Rural Dimension of Asian American Studies," in *Frontiers of Asian American Studies: Writing, Research, and Commentary,* ed. Gail M. Nomura, Russell Endo, Stephen H. Sumida, and Russell C. Leong (Pullman: Washington State University Press, 1989), 6–13. For a brief discussion of the impact of "Chinatown," see Martin F. Ma-

nalansan IV's introduction to *Cultural Compass,* 6. Important books on rural Asian America include Sucheng Chan, *This Bittersweet Soil: The Chinese in California Agriculture, 1860–1910* (Berkeley and Los Angeles: University of California Press, 1986); Valerie J. Matsumoto, *Farming the Home Place: A Japanese American Community in California, 1919–1982* (Ithaca, N.Y.: Cornell University Press, 1993); Timothy J. Lukes and Gary Y. Okihiro, *Japanese Legacy: Farming and Community Life in California's Santa Clara Valley,* Local History Studies, vol. 31 (Cupertino: California History Center, 1985); and Karen Isaksen Leonard, *Making Ethnic Choices: California's Punjabi Mexican Americans* (Philadelphia: Temple University Press, 1992). Despite these important examples, there are still relatively few works on Asian American agricultural labor on the American mainland. Philip Vera Cruz's life history offers one important key, as do the essays and monographs by Howard De Witt. However, much work remains to be done. See Craig Scharlin and Lilia V. Villanueva, *Philip Vera Cruz: A Personal History of Filipino Immigrants and the Farmworkers Movement* (Los Angeles: UCLA Labor Center, Institute of Industrial Relations and UCLA Asian American Studies Center, 1992); De Witt, *Violence in the Fields,* as well as "Filipino Labor Union," 1–21. Fortunately, more works are available on the Filipina/o American community in Hawai'i, which have a strong emphasis on the rural experience because of the plantation system. See, for example, Robert N. Anderson with Richard Coller and Rebecca F. Pestano, *Filipinos in Rural Hawaii* (Honolulu: University of Hawai'i Press, 1984).

54. For a discussion of the origins of the "New Western history," see Patricia Nelson Limerick, Clyde A. Milner II, and Charles E. Rankin, *Trails: Toward a New Western History* (Lawrence: University Press of Kansas, 1991). Two of the most influential volumes regarding this reconceptualization of the history of the American West have been Richard White, *"It's Your Misfortune and None of My Own": A History of the American West* (Norman: University of Oklahoma Press, 1991); and Patricia Nelson Limerick, *The Legacy of Conquest: The Unbroken Past of the American West* (New York: Norton, 1987).

55. Richard Drinnon, *Facing West: The Metaphysics of Indian-Hating and Empire Building* (Minneapolis: University of Minnesota Press, 1980); Limerick, *Legacy of Conquest.* For an excellent discussion of these issues, see Steffi San Buenaventura, "The Colors of Manifest Destiny: Filipinos and the American Other(s)," *Amerasia Journal* 24, no. 3 (1998): 1–26. For students of Filipina/o American studies, scholarship on other groups encountering the forces of American expansionism is vital to understanding the wide scope of American conquest. Scholarship on Hawai'i—for example, Haunani Kay Trask's *From a Native Daughter: Colonialism and Sovereignty in Hawai'i* (Monroe, Maine: Common Courage Press, 1993) or Gary Okihiro's *Cane Fires: The Anti-Japanese Movement in Hawaii, 1865–1945* (Philadelphia: Temple University Press, 1991)—contributes to discussions of the United States' policy overseas, the results of its turn-of-the-century expansionism. Chicana/o studies literature, by underscoring the United States' takeover of Mexican territory and the consequent impact on community formation of Mexican peoples in what became the U.S. West, is also very important, particularly given the very real parallels between the Filipina/o American and the Chicana/o experience in the twentieth century. See, for instance,

Lisbeth Haas, *Conquests and Historical Identities in California, 1769–1936* (Berkeley and Los Angeles: University of California Press, 1995).

56. Richard C. Berner's volumes *Seattle, 1900–1920: From Boomtown, Urban Turbulence, to Restoration* (Seattle: Charles Press, 1991) and, even more important for my time period, *Seattle, 1921–1940: From Boom to Bust* (Seattle: Charles Press, 1992) provided crucial background for my study, particularly in terms of the city's politics and economy. Calvin F. Schmid, *Social Trends in Seattle*, University of Washington Publications in the Social Sciences, vol. 14 (Seattle: University of Washington Press, 1944), presents useful data and discussion about the various communities in the city. Also see Roger Sale, *Seattle: Past to Present* (Seattle: University of Washington Press, 1976). For regional histories of the Pacific Northwest, see Otis W. Freeman and Howard H. Martin, editorial committee, *The Pacific Northwest: A Regional, Human, and Economic Survey of Resources and Development* (New York: Wiley, 1942); Earl Pomeroy, *The Pacific Slope: A History of California, Oregon, Washington, Idaho, Utah, and Nevada* (Seattle: University of Washington Press, 1965); G. Thomas Edwards and Carlos A. Schwantes, eds., *Experiences in a Promised Land: Essays in Pacific Northwest History* (Seattle: University of Washington Press, 1986); and Carlos A. Schwantes, *The Pacific Northwest: An Interpretive History* (Lincoln: University of Nebraska Press, 1989). Quintard Taylor's *Forging of a Black Community* offers vital information about the growth of the African American community in the city. Another useful piece is Carl Abbott, "Regional City and Network City: Portland and Seattle in the Twentieth Century," *Western Historical Quarterly* 23, no. 3 (August 1992): 293–322. Ron Chew, ed., *Reflections of Seattle's Chinese Americans: The First 100 Years* (Seattle: University of Washington Press and Wing Luke Asian Museum, 1994), is a collection of memories by Chinese American community members. See also David A. Takami, *Divided Destiny: A History of Japanese Americans in Seattle* (Seattle: University of Washington Press and Wing Luke Asian Museum, 1998), for more documentation of the Asian American presence in the city.

57. See Sucheta Mazumdar's important argument about the need to evaluate Asian American studies' relation to Asian studies in "Asian American Studies and Asian Studies: Rethinking Roots," in *Asian Americans: Comparative and Global Perspectives*, ed. Shirley Hune, Hung-chan Kim, Stephen S. Fugita, and Amy Ling (Pullman: Washington State University Press, 1991), 29–44.

58. Howard A. Droker, "Seattle Race Relations during the Second World War," in *Experiences in a Promised Land: Essays in Pacific Northwest History*, ed. G. Thomas Edwards and Carlos A. Schwantes (Seattle: University of Washington Press, 1986), 353.

59. As Tomás Almaguer writes, "What resonates out most clearly in the racial histories that I have sociologically assessed is the primacy of race as the central organizing principle of hierarchical group relations in California. . . . White supremacist, capitalist, and patriarchal structures unfolded in a complex, historically contingent manner in which racialization fundamentally shaped the class- and gender-specific experiences of both the white and nonwhite populations." See Tomás Almaguer, *Racial Fault Lines: The Historical Origins of White Supremacy in California* (Berkeley and Los Angeles: University of California Press,

1994), 209. See also George Lipsitz's *The Possessive Investment in Whiteness: How White People Profit from Identity Politics* (Philadelphia: Temple University Press, 1998) for a discussion of how white racial privilege is institutionalized in the present day.

60. See Sarah Deutsch, *No Separate Refuge: Culture, Class, and Gender on an Anglo-Hispanic Frontier in the American Southwest, 1880–1940* (New York: Oxford University Press, 1987), 9.

Scholars of the history of the American West are extremely involved with the role of place, from concerns about the "frontier," to the very definition of their field as an area of regional study. In *Legacy of Conquest*, Patricia Limerick suggests a move away from Turner's frontier thesis to emphasize "place" over "process." She writes, "Reorganized, the history of the West is a study of a place undergoing conquest and never fully escaping its consequences" (26). Lisabeth Haas also employs categories of space and place in her study of Orange County, which is placed in a context that included "the Spanish colonial world, the culture of Greater Mexico, the U.S. Southwest as a region, and the Borderland." Haas, who argues that these concerns were integral to the formation of Chicana/o studies, writes, "Spatial dimensions of change, such as territorial conquest and the formation of the barrios, were among the first things studied by Chicano historians." By examining the social and political dramas enacted at different sites, from the San Juan Capistrano mission to the barrios in Santa Ana, she demonstrates how geography shapes power and identity, particularly in a multiracial context. See Haas, *Conquests and Historical Identities in California*, 5–8.

The American public's fascination with "Chinatown" and the vital nature of these communities for Asian Americans and other groups point to the role of space in shaping Asian American life. The forced removal and incarceration of Japanese Americans into concentration camps during World War II provides another important example of how the "place" of Asian American communities has always been contested and subject to dominant control. Space remains an important determinant in present-day Asian America, for example, in the focus on suburban areas, particularly with the exponential growth of Asian American communities in sites such as Monterey Park, California.

61. For more on the historical importance of Angel Island, see Lai, Lim, and Yung, *Island*.

62. Patricia Limerick, "Common Cause? Asian American History and Western American History," in *Privileging Positions: The Sites of Asian American Studies*, ed. Gary Y. Okihiro, Marilyn Alquizola, Dorothy Fujita Rony, and K. Scott Wong (Pullman: Washington State University Press, 1995), 97. Similarly, in his study of Chicago and its relationship to the American West, William Cronon articulates the importance of Chicago as a "gateway city" that served as "the principal colonizing agent of the western landscape." See Cronon, *Nature's Metropolis*, 307–308.

63. The nature of urban labor of Asian Americans in Seattle is still underaddressed, but Evelyn Nakano Glenn's *Issei, Nisei, Warbride: Three Generations of Japanese American Women in Domestic Service* (Philadelphia: Temple University Press, 1986) provides a critical counterpoint to the California example. The California agricultural industry is another central site for Filipina/o

American labor history. See Cletus E. Daniel, *Bitter Harvest: A History of California Farmworkers, 1870–1941* (Berkeley and Los Angeles: University of California Press, 1982). Devra Weber's *Dark Sweat, White Gold: California Farm Workers, Cotton, and the New Deal* (Berkeley and Los Angeles: University of California Press, 1994), 16, which examines California farm workers in the cotton industry during the New Deal, provides further documentation of the conditions encountered and addressed by agricultural laborers. Hawai'i represents another crucial site. For examples, see Anderson with Coller and Pestano, *Filipinos in Rural Hawaii;* and John E. Reinecke, *The Filipino Piecemeal Sugar Strike of 1924–1925* (Honolulu: Social Science Research Institute, University of Hawai'i, 1996).

64. See Amy Kaplan, "'Left Alone with America': The Absence of Empire in the Study of American Culture," in *Cultures of United States Imperialism*, ed. Amy Kaplan and Donald E. Pease (Durham, N.C.: Duke University Press, 1993), 14–18. The conversations posed in this anthology are an important intervention into debates about the United States and the role of imperialism.

65. In addressing these power relations, Said writes about "Orientalism as a Western style for dominating, restructuring, and having authority over the Orient." Edward W. Said, *Orientalism* (New York: Vintage, 1979), 3.

66. Susan Lee Johnson writes, "It is a commonplace of women's and ethnic studies that, in the U.S., women of all races and ethnicities and peoples of color, both women and men, constitute 'marked' and white men 'unmarked' categories of human experience—the unmarked category serving as the normative, the more inclusive, the less 'interested' and particular." See Susan Lee Johnson, "'A Memory Sweet to Soldiers': The Significance of Gender in the History of the 'American West,'" *Western Historical Quarterly* 24, no. 4 (November 1993): 495–517.

67. See also Lipsitz, *Possessive Investment in Whiteness:* "I argue that white Americans are encouraged to invest in whiteness, to remain true to an identity that provides them with resources, power, and opportunity" (vii).

68. Frederick Cooper and Ann Laura Stoler, "Between Metropole and Colony: Rethinking a Research Agenda," in *Tensions of Empire: Colonial Cultures in a Bourgeois World*, ed. Frederick Cooper and Ann Laura Stoler (Berkeley and Los Angeles: University of California Press, 1997), 1.

69. See, for example, Laura Tabili, *"We Ask for British Justice": Workers and Racial Difference in Late Imperial Britain* (Ithaca, N.Y.: Cornell University Press, 1994).

70. My thanks to David Montgomery for earlier comments on this draft that helped me to clarify these issues. For more on the shaping force of colonialism, see Benedict Anderson, *Imagined Communities: Reflections on the Origin and Spread of Nationalism* (London: Verso, 1985); and Cooper and Stoler, *Tensions of Empire.*

71. See James C. Scott, *Domination and the Arts of Resistance: Hidden Transcripts* (New Haven, Conn.: Yale University Press, 1990).

72. The resources and ideologies implemented by American education dramatically reshaped class positioning and opportunities, as well as, on a very basic level, the Filipinos' sense of self. For the most part, we have still to explore the historical implications of this education for class formation in the United States.

There have been a few works about the role of students in the earlier era, as well as documentation by contemporaries of that period such as Benicio Catapusan. The *Filipino Student Bulletin* and other periodicals and community newspapers often had "students" in leadership positions and thus offer key insights into the role of education. See Barbara M. Posadas, "Unintentional Immigrants: Chicago's Filipino Foreign Students Become Settlers, 1941," *Journal of American Ethnic History* 9, no. 2 (spring 1990): 26–48; Catapusan, "Social Adjustment of Filipinos in the United States"; and issues of the *Filipino Student Bulletin*.

73. Mislang, interview, 9–16.

74. Johnson, "'A Memory Sweet to Soldiers,'" 499.

CHAPTER 1. EMPIRE AND MIGRATION

1. Rufina Jenkins and Francesca Robinson, interview by Carolina Koslosky, 10 November 1975, WSOAHP, 1–12. See Quintard Taylor, *The Forging of a Black Community: Seattle's Central District from 1870 through the Civil Rights Era* (Seattle: University of Washington Press, 1994), 51, for more information on Frank Jenkins, referred to as Richard Jenkins in Taylor's book.

2. Anthony Pagden, *Lords of All the World: Ideologies of Empire in Spain, Britain and France c. 1500–c. 1800* (New Haven, Conn.: Yale University Press, 1995), 1.

3. David Joel Steinberg, *The Philippines: A Singular and a Plural Place,* 3d ed. (Boulder, Colo.: Westview Press, 1994), 39; Felix M. Keesing, *The Ethnohistory of Northern Luzon* (Stanford, Calif.: Stanford University Press, 1962), 1–3, 13–14; Samuel K. Tan, *A History of the Philippines* (Manila: Manila Studies Association; Quezon City: Philippine National Historical Society, 1997), 56–57. More information on local histories in the area can be found in the *Ilocos Review.* For example, see Manuel F. Aurelio, "The Birth of Ilocos Norte," *Ilocos Review* 20 (1988): 1–34, and vol. 21 (1989) of the journal for a special issue on Pangasinan.

4. Early trade had also been conducted with Peru but was halted because of its competition with the Porto Bello galleons from Spain. See William M. Schurz, *The Manila Galleon* (New York: Dutton, 1939), 366–367.

5. Schurz, *The Manila Galleon,* 375. See also Fred Cordova, *Filipinos: Forgotten Asian Americans, A Pictorial Essay/1763-Circa-1963* (Dubuque, Iowa: Kendall/Hunt, 1983), 1. In 1785, the Real Compania de Filipinas (the Royal Philippine Company) was chartered to stimulate trade between Spain and the Philippines. The company folded in 1834. See Schurz, *The Manila Galleon,* 412, 418.

6. Schurz, *The Manila Galleon,* 272. For a discussion of male sexual laborers, see Fr. Josemaria Luengo, *A History of the Manila-Acapulco Slave Trade (1565–1815)* (Tobigon, Bohol: Mater Dei Publications, 1996), 86–111.

7. Cordova, *Filipinos,* 1–2; Marina E. Espina, *Filipinos in Louisiana* (New Orleans, La.: A. F. Laborde, 1988), 79. Espina's book contains a full discussion of this community.

8. George I. Quimby, "Culture Contact on the Northwest Coast, 1785–1795," *American Anthropologist* 50 (April–June 1948): 252–253; "Northwest

Explorations" file, National Pinoy Archives. Hereafter, the National Pinoy Archives will be abbreviated as NPA.

9. Renato Constantino with the collaboration of Letizia R. Constantino, *A History of the Philippines: From the Spanish Colonization to the Second World War* (New York: Monthly Review Press, 1975), 120.

10. Ibid., 126–128.

11. D. D. Sar Desai, *Southeast Asia: Past and Present* (Boulder, Colo.: Westview Press, 1989), 143–144.

12. Daniel B. Schirmer and Stephen Rosskamm Shalom, eds., *The Philippines Reader: A History of Colonialism, Neocolonialism, Dictatorship, and Resistance* (Boston: South End Press, 1987), 5–6.

13. Eric Hobsbawm, *The Age of Empire, 1875–1914* (New York: Vintage, 1989), 51–52, 58–59; David Montgomery, *The Fall of the House of Labor: The Workplace, the State, and American Labor Activism, 1865–1925* (Cambridge: Cambridge University Press, 1987), 70–71; Nell Irvin Painter, *Standing at Armageddon: The United States, 1877–1919* (New York: Norton, 1987), xviii.

14. Sucheng Chan, *Asian Americans: An Interpretive History* (New York: Twayne, 1991), 9–13; Bonacich, "United States Capitalist Development," 106, 109; Painter, *Standing at Armageddon*, chap. 5, "The White Man's Burden," 141–169.

15. Edna Bonacich, "United States Capitalist Development: A Background to Asian Immigration," in *Labor Immigration under Capitalism: Asian Workers in the United States before World War II*, ed. Lucie Cheng and Edna Bonacich (Berkeley and Los Angeles: University of California Press, 1984), 106, 109; Lawrence H. Fuchs, *Hawaii Pono: A Social History* (San Diego: Harcourt Brace Jovanovich, 1961), 3, 36; Peter Hempenstall, "Imperial Manoeuvres," in *Tides of History: The Pacific Islands in the Twentieth Century*, ed. K. R. Howe, Robert C. Kiste, and Brij V. Lal (Honolulu: University of Hawai'i Press, 1994), 30–31.

16. Jenkins and Robinson, interview, 1–12.

17. In 1899, *McClure's Magazine* published Rudyard Kipling's famous ode to empire-building, "The White Man's Burden." For the text and discussion of that poem, see Painter, *Standing at Armageddon*, 153.

18. "Historical and Cultural Data of the Barrio of Anonag Mayor, Caoayan, Ilocos Sur," [no author listed]," in Philippines National Library, Historical Data Papers, Philippines National Library. I used a copy housed in the Carl A. Kroch Library, Division of Asia Collections, Cornell University.

19. Miriam Sharma, "The Philippines: A Case of Migration to Hawaii, 1906–1946," in *Labor Immigration under Capitalism: Asian Workers in the United States before World War II*, ed. Lucie Cheng and Edna Bonacich (Berkeley and Los Angeles: University of California Press, 1984), 342–343.

20. Florendo M. Pablo, Tomas R. Daradar, Juan C. Javier, Mariano N. Nalupta, Raymundo R. Sibucao, and Bablo C. Ayson, "A Chronological History of Batac, Province of Ilocos Norte, Commonwealth of the Philippines," 1939 [17–18], Historical Data Papers.

21. "Gathered and Compiled by": Fauso Bermio [?], Teresita A. Alconcel, Crescencia Llames, Maria Jimenez, and Serafina Velasco, "A Report on His-

torical Data of the Barrio of Pantay-Tamurong [Ilocos Sur]," Historical Data Papers.

22. Luzviminda Francisco, "The Philippine-American War," in *The Philippines Reader: A History of Colonialism, Neocolonialism, Dictatorship, and Resistance*, ed. Daniel B. Schirmer and Stephen Rosskamm Shalom (Boston: South End Press, 1987), 16–17.

23. Ibid., 17–18.

24. Painter, *Standing at Armageddon*, 155.

25. Schirmer and Shalom, *Philippines Reader*, 31–32. For example, in *Ilocano Responses to American Aggression, 1900–1901* (Quezon City: New Day Publishers, 1986), 37, William Henry Scott notes that one African American worked with Filipino troops.

26. Unsigned letter from the *Wisconsin Weekly Advocate*, 17 May 1900, in Willard B. Gatewood Jr., *"Smoked Yankees" and the Struggle for Empire: Letters from Negro Soldiers, 1898–1902* (Urbana: University of Illinois Press, 1971), 279. For a discussion of how different groups were viewed in the context of the American empire, see Steffi San Buenaventura, "The Colors of Manifest Destiny: Filipinos and the American Other(s)," *Amerasia Journal* 24, no. 3 (1998): 1–26.

27. Schirmer and Shalom, *Philippines Reader*, 32, original source, *Boston Post*, 18 July 1899.

28. Bonacich, "United States Capitalist Development," 120.

29. "Meet to Form Patriot Body," *Manila Times*, 7 June 1913, 19861/19 in RG350, Records of the Bureau of Insular Affairs, General Records Relating to More Than One Island Possession, General Classified Files, 1898–1945, 1914–1945, Entry 5, National Archives. Hereafter, RG350, Records of the Bureau of Insular Affairs, General Records Relating to More Than One Island Possession, General Classified Files, 1898–1945, 1914–1945, Entry 5, will be listed as RG350, and the National Archives will be identified as NA.

30. Francis Burton Harrison to Hon. Lindley M. Garrison, 8 July 1915, "1239–116 to 133, P.I. General Conditions Reports Part III," Box 285, RG350, NA.

31. David R. Sturtevant, *Popular Uprisings in the Philippines, 1840–1940* (Ithaca, N.Y.: Cornell University Press, 1976), 195.

32. Severo Fontanares Flores, excerpted in Cordova, *Filipinos*, 87.

33. See Lucie Cheng and Edna Bonacich, "Introduction: A Theoretical Orientation to International Migration," in Cheng and Bonacich, eds., *Labor Immigration under Capitalism*, 11, 20–21, for a discussion of the effects of imperialism.

34. Sharma, "The Philippines," 341–346. I thank David Montgomery for emphasizing to me the anomaly of the Philippines importing food into its economy in the context of general colony-colonizer relations.

35. Daniel F. Doeppers, *Manila, 1900–1941: Social Change in a Late Colonial Metropolis*, Monograph Series no. 17 (New Haven, Conn.: Yale University Press, 1984), 12. See John A. Larkin, *Sugar and the Origins of Modern Philippine Society* (Berkeley and Los Angeles: University of California Press, 1993), especially chaps. 5 and 6, pp. 147–236, for an important discussion about the economic primacy of sugar.

36. Sharma, "The Philippines," 344; Jose S. Reyes, *Legislative History of America's Economic Policy toward the Philippines*, Studies in History, Economics, and Public Law, edited by the Faculty of Political Science of Columbia University, CVI, no. 2, whole no. 240 (New York: AMS Press, 1967), 118–119.

37. Sharma, "The Philippines," 341–346.

38. Doeppers, *Manila, 1900–1941*, 4, 9–10, 18.

39. Mensalvas and Yambao, interview, 1.

40. Felicisimo E. Corsino, "Social Organization and Beliefs in Ilokos Sur," in *Ethnography of the Iloko People (A Collection of Original Sources)*, ed. H. Otley Beyer, vol. 1 (Manila, 1918), 2–3.

41. Josefina Tongson, "Ethnography of the Iloko People," in *Ethnography of the Iloko People (A Collection of Original Sources)*, ed. H. Otley Beyer, vol. 1 (Manila, 1918), 8.

42. For Turner's influential thesis, see Frederick Jackson Turner, "The Significance of the Frontier in American History" in *Major Problems in the History of the American West: Documents and Essays*, ed. Clyde A. Milner II (Lexington, Mass.: D. C. Heath, 1989), 2–21; and, for a critique, see William Cronon, "Revisiting Turner's Vanishing Frontier," in Milner, 668–681.

43. See Ronald T. Takaki, *Iron Cages: Race and Culture in Nineteenth-Century America* (Seattle: University of Washington Press, 1979), 253–279; and William Pomeroy, *American Neo-colonialism: Its Emergence in the Philippines and Asia* (New York: International Publishers, 1970), 13–15.

44. W. Kaye Lamb, *Empress to the Orient* (Vancouver: Vancouver Maritime Museum Society, 1991), 7.

45. Richard C. Berner, *Seattle, 1900–1920: From Boomtown, Urban Turbulence, to Restoration* (Seattle: Charles Press, 1991), 22.

46. "Vagrants and Immigrants," RG350, Box 522, File 8456, NA.

47. Thelma Buchholdt, *Filipinos in Alaska: 1788–1958* (Anchorage: Aboriginal Press, 1996).

48. See Karen Isaksen Leonard, *The South Asian Americans* (Westport, Conn.: Greenwood Press, 1997), 43–45.

49. Sammy R. Lopez, interview by Cyn. Mejia, FIL-KNG75-36cm, 24 November 1975, WSOAHP, 3–4.

50. Jesse G. Quinsaat, "An Exercise on How to Join the Navy and Still Not See the World," in *Letters in Exile: An Introductory Reader on the History of Pilipinos in America*, ed. Jesse G. Quinsaat (Los Angeles: UCLA Asian American Studies Center, 1976), 105; and H. Brett Melendy, *Asians in America: Filipinos, Koreans, and East Indians* (Boston: Twayne, 1977), 83–84.

51. See, for example, Port of Seattle, *The Port of Seattle Year Book, 1920–1921*, 6.

52. Walter A. Radius, *United States Shipping in Transpacific Trade*, issued in cooperation with the American Council, Institute of Pacific Relations (Stanford, Calif.: Stanford University Press, 1944), 161.

53. Ole Kay Moe, "An Analytical Study of the Foreign Trade through the Port of Seattle" (master's thesis, University of Washington, 1932), 30–33.

54. Radius, *United States Shipping in Transpacific Trade*, 132, 190–191.

55. Eliot Grinnel Mears, *Maritime Trade of Western United States* (Stanford, Calif.: Stanford University Press, 1935), 298.

56. Radius, *United States Shipping in Transpacific Trade*, 2.

57. Padraic Burke, *A History of the Port of Seattle* (Seattle: Port of Seattle, 1976), 30, 55, 72. Unlike in San Francisco, fees were charged on the cargo but not the ships. Hence, it cost five dollars less to use Seattle facilities than the San Francisco port when shipping a ton of cargo from Asia to the United States. See Burke, *History of the Port of Seattle*, 55–57.

58. Ibid., 8, 10.

59. Albert Lloyd Seeman, "The Port of Seattle: A Study in Urban Geography" (Ph.D. diss., University of Washington, 1930), 94–95, 103.

60. Felipe G. Dumlao, interview by Cynthia Mejia, FIL-KNG75-35cm, 21 November 1975, WSOAHP, 3.

61. Port of Seattle, *Port of Seattle Year Book, 1935*, 25.

62. Raymond Success Mathieson, "The Industrial Geography of Seattle, Washington" (master's thesis, University of Washington, 1954), 15; Seeman, "Port of Seattle," 49.

63. Mathieson, "Industrial Geography of Seattle, Washington," 17.

64. Mears, *Maritime Trade of Western United States*, 188–189. In 1868, the ship *Leo* commenced making occasional trips to Alaska, with regular passage beginning in 1882. In 1893, Seattle was the biggest supplier of goods to Alaska, with the Alaska Steamship Company organized for Alaska-Seattle trade by 1895. See Burke, *History of the Port of Seattle*, 10.

65. Mathieson, "Industrial Geography of Seattle, Washington," 28–30.

66. Margaret Catharine Rodman, "The Trend of Alaskan Commerce through the Port of Seattle" (master's thesis, University of Washington, 1930), 51.

67. Mears, *Maritime Trade of Western United States*, 190.

68. Lamb, *Empress to the Orient*, 33.

69. Moe, "An Analytical Study of the Foreign Trade through the Port of Seattle," 13.

70. Bruno Lasker, *Filipino Immigration to Continental United States and to Hawaii*, published for the American Council, Institute of Pacific Relations (Chicago: University of Chicago Press, 1931), 211–217.

71. John Mendoza, interview by Dorothy Cordova, FIL-KNG76-42dc, 6 April 1976, WSOAHP, 1.

72. Salvador Del Fierro, interview by Carolina D. Koslosky, FIL-KNG75-29ck, 15 September 1975, WSOAHP, 2–3. In another example, Ben Rinonos chose Seattle because he wanted to board the *Empress of Canada*, reportedly the biggest boat in the Pacific, which docked in Seattle. See Ben Rinonos, interview by Teresa Cronin, FIL-KNG-3tc, 27 March 1975, WSOAHP, 6.

73. Hobsbawm, *Age of Empire*, 50–51, 114; Sucheng Chan, *This Bittersweet Soil: The Chinese in California Agriculture, 1860–1910* (Berkeley and Los Angeles: University of California Press, 1986), 8; Henry Lewis, *Ilocano Rice Farmers: A Comparative Study of Two Philippine Barrios* (Honolulu: University of Hawai'i Press, 1971), 5.

74. E. V. "Vic" Bacho, *The Long Road: Memoirs of a Filipino Pioneer* (Seattle: self-published, 1992), 8.

75. Schirmer and Shalom, *Philippines Reader,* xx–xxi.

76. F. Landa Jocano, *The Ilocanos: An Ethnography of Family and Community Life in the Ilocos Region,* with the special assistance of Arnora Edrozo, Ernesto Cadiz, Thelma Beltran, and Milagros Dumlao (Diliman, Quezon City: Asian Center, University of the Philippines, 1982), 4, 27.

77. Sharma, "The Philippines," 351–352.

78. Sylvestre A. Tangalan, interview by Carolina D. Koslosky, FIL-KNG75-28ck, 27 August 1975, WSOAHP, 1.

79. Ceferíno Purísima, "Ethnography of the Iloko People of Luzon," in *Ethnography of the Iloko People (A Collection of Original Sources),* ed. H. Otley Beyer, vol. 1 (Manila, 1918), 6–7.

80. Henry Lewis, *Ilocano Irrigation: The Corporate Resolution,* Asian Studies at Hawaii, no. 37 (Honolulu: University of Hawai'i, 1991), 3.

81. Mercedes A. Vega, "The Social Customs of the Ilokos," in *Ethnography of the Iloko People (A Collection of Original Sources),* ed. H. Otley Beyer, vol. 1 (Manila, 1918), 3.

82. Lewis, *Ilocano Rice Farmers,* 24; Ricardo G. Abad and Benjamin V. Carino, with the assistance of Benilda Reyes-Escutin, *Micro-level Determinants of Migration Intentions in the Ilocos: A Preliminary Analysis* (Quezon City: Institute of Philippine Culture, Ateneo de Manila University, 1981), 53; Rosario Mendoza Cortes, *Pangasinan, 1901–1986: A Political, Socioeconomic and Cultural History* (Quezon City: New Day Publishers, 1990), 5.

83. Cortes, *Pangasinan,* 72.

84. Emerson Brewer Christie, "Notes on Iloko Ethnography and History," in *Ethnography of the Iloko People (A Collection of Original Sources),* collected, edited, and annotated by H. Otley Beyer, vol. 2 (Manila, 1919), 138.

85. Tongson, "Ethnography of the Iloko People," 9.

86. Christie, "Notes on Ilokano Ethnography and History," 143.

87. Tongson, "Ethnography of the Iloko People," 9.

88. Abad and Carino, *Micro-level Determinants of Migration Intentions in the Ilocos,* 44.

89. Sharma, "The Philippines," 345–346. See, for example, discussion of the interests of sugarcane businesses in developing a labor pool for the Philippine island of Negros in the Visayas in Larkin, *Sugar and the Origins of Modern Philippine Society,* 77–80.

90. Paul D. Simkins and Frederick L. Wernstedt, *Philippine Migration: The Settlement of the Digos-Padada Valley, Davao Province,* Monograph Series no. 16 (New Haven, Conn.: Yale University, Southeast Asia Studies, 1971), 68.

91. See Benedict J. Kerkvliet, *The Huk Rebellion: A Study of Peasant Revolt in the Philippines* (Berkeley and Los Angeles: University of California Press, 1977), 35–36, for a description of homesteading. Only a portion of the agricultural workers who applied for the lands were able to gain title to these lands. Kerkvliet focuses on Talavera, Nueva Ecija, as a site of study concerning the formation of the Huk Rebellion.

92. Al Bautista [pseud.], interview by author, Seattle, 19 July 1994.

93. Cortes, *Pangasinan,* 72.

94. Anastacio B. Gerardo, "The Present Status of Ilokos Norte," in *Ethnog-*

raphy of the Iloko People (A Collection of Original Sources), ed. H. Otley Beyer, vol. 1 (Manila, 1918), 2.

95. Jocano, *The Ilocanos*, 7–8.

96. Trinidad Soria and H. T. Pilar, "The History and Culture of Barrio Pilar," [47], Historical Data Papers.

97. Abad and Carino, *Micro-level Determinants of Migration Intentions in the Ilocos*, 53.

98. Bibiana Laigo Castillano, interview by Frederic A. Cordova, Jr., FIL-KNG75-19jr, 26 June 1975, WSOAHP, 1.

99. David Guerrero [pseud.], interview by author, Seattle, 10 September 1993.

100. Trinidad Rojo, interview by Carolina D. Koslosky, FIL-KNG75-17ck, 18 February 1975 and 19 February 1975, WSOAHP, 3.

101. Felipe Dumlao remembers how his brother, who had already gone to the United States, warned him against trying his fortune there: "It is very hard here he said and I did not believe it so I just proceed to come." See Dumlao, interview, 3.

102. Leo Aliwanag, interview by Cynthia Mejia, FIL-KNG76-50cm, 19 August 1976, WSOAHP, 5.

103. Juan V. Mina, interview by Carolina Apostol, FIL-KNG76-47cma, 30 May 1976, WSOAHP, 6; Aliwanag, interview, 7.

104. Maria Abastilla Beltran, interview by Carolina Koslosky, FIL-KNG75-9ck, 5 May 1975, WSOAHP, 9.

105. John Castillo, interview by F. A. Cordova, Jr., FIL-KNG75-15jr, 29 July 1975, WSOAHP, 6–7.

106. Jose Acena, interview by Dorothy L. Cordova, FIL-KNG75-24dlc, 28 July 1975, WSOAHP, 18–19.

107. As Charles Tilly writes, "Migrant networks articulate neatly with subcontracting because they give the subcontractor access to flexible supplies of labor about which he or she can easily get information and over which she or he can easily exert control outside the workplace." See Charles Tilly, "Transplanted Networks," in *Immigration Reconsidered: History, Sociology, and Politics*, ed. Virginia Yans-McLaughlin (New York: Oxford University Press, 1990), 86.

108. Susan Evangelista, *Carlos Bulosan and His Poetry: A Biography and Anthology* (Seattle: University of Washington Press, 1985), 1–2.

109. The Central Teachers, "History and Cultural Life of the Barrio-Rancho," in "History and Cultural Life of Santa," [43], Historical Data Papers.

110. Bonacich, "Asian Labor in the Development of California and Hawaii," 166.

111. Cheng and Bonacich, "Introduction," 27.

112. Vincent Yolenato Mendoza and Rosario Rosell Mendoza [listed as Mr. and Mrs. Vincent Mendoza], interview by Cynthia Mejia, FIL-KNG76-40cm, 13 January 1976, WSOAHP, 16.

113. Cheng and Bonacich, "Introduction," 27.

114. Bautista, interview.

115. Acena, interview, 17.

116. Stephen Griffiths, *Emigrants, Entrepreneurs, and Evil Spirits: Life in a Philippine Village* (Honolulu: University of Hawai'i Press, 1988), 16. The name of the informant is fictional.

117. Ibid.
118. William F. Nydegger and Corinne Nydegger, *Tarong: An Ilocos Barrio in the Philippines,* Six Culture Series, vol. 6 (New York: Wiley, 1966), 42.
119. Griffiths, *Emigrants, Entrepreneurs, and Evil Spirits,* 28–29.
120. Dorothy Cordova, "Voices from the Past: Why They Came," in *Making Waves: An Anthology of Writings by and about Asian American Women,* ed. Asian Women United of California (Boston: Beacon Press, 1989), 42–45.
121. Teodolo Aguinaldo Ranjo, interview by Cynthia Mejia, FIL-KNG76-41cm, 14 January, 1976, WSOAHP, 16; Robert Fernando, interview by author, 28 September 1993, Seattle, tape recording.
122. The section of poems entitled "Lamentations of Estranged Wives" is published in Marlon K. Hom's *Songs of Gold Mountain: Cantonese Rhymes from San Francisco Chinatown* (Berkeley and Los Angeles: University of California Press, 1987), 111–147.
123. Nydegger and Nydegger, *Tarong.*
124. Zacarias M. Manangan, interview by Carolina D. Koslosky, FIL-KNG75-30ck, 30 September 1975, WSOAHP, 3.
125. Paula J. Nonacido, interview by Cynthia Mejia, FIL-KNG76-49cm, 7 July and 22 September 1976, WSOAHP, 4–5.
126. Toribio Madayag, interview by Teresa Cronin, FIL-KNG-22tc, WSOAHP, 2 July 1975, 2.
127. Teodolo Ranjo reported, "They have ambition but they didn't have any way of coming over so they stowaway." See Ranjo, interview, 9.
128. Mina, interview, 7.
129. Aliwanag, interview, 9.
130. Dumlao, interview, 9, 16–17. See also Manangan, interview, 5.
131. "80 Filipinos on President Boat Very Ill; One Jumps Overboard," *Philippine Herald,* 30 August 1930.
132. Dumlao, interview, 17.
133. Manangan, interview, 4–5.
134. Jenkins and Robinson, interview, 6, 11–18.
135. See Frank Thistlewaite, "Migration from Europe Overseas in the Nineteenth and Twentieth Centuries," in *Population Movements in Modern European History,* ed. Herbert Moller (New York: Macmillan, 1964), 74–77. For a full-length survey of the phenomenon of "re-emigration," to use Thistlewaite's term, see Mark Wyman, *Round-Trip to America: The Immigrants Return to Europe, 1880–1930* (Ithaca, N.Y.: Cornell University Press, 1993).
136. Carlos Bulosan, *America Is in the Heart: A Personal History* (Seattle: University of Washington Press, 1991), 99.
137. Ibid. According to Carey McWilliams's introduction, Carlos Bulosan actually landed in Seattle on 22 July 1930. See ibid., xv. As a city, Seattle was to hold special significance for Bulosan, the author. Bulosan initially landed in Seattle, and he regularly passed through and worked in the city. He would eventually be buried in Seattle.
138. Laura Tabili, *"We Ask for British Justice": Workers and Racial Difference in Late Imperial Britain* (Ithaca, N.Y.: Cornell University Press, 1994).

CHAPTER 2. EDUCATION IN THE METROPOLE

1. Belen Braganza, interview by Nancy Koslosky, PNW81-Fil-014nk, 26 June 1981, Demonstration Project for Asian Americans, 1–4. Hereafter, Demonstration Project for Asian Americans will be referred to as DPAA.

2. Ann Laura Stoler and Frederick Cooper, "Between Metropole and Colony: Rethinking a Research Agenda," in *Tensions of Empire: Colonial Cultures in a Bourgeois World*, ed. Frederick Cooper and Ann Laura Stoler (Berkeley and Los Angeles: University of California Press, 1997), 7.

3. Benedict Anderson, *Imagined Communities: Reflections on the Origin and Spread of Nationalism* (London: Verso, 1985), 127.

4. Karen Isaksen Leonard, *The South Asian Americans* (Westport, Conn.: Greenwood Press, 1997), 23–24.

5. E. V. "Vic" Bacho, *The Long Road: Memoirs of a Filipino Pioneer*, self-published, 1992, 9.

6. Renato Constantino, "The Miseducation of the Filipino," in *The Philippines Reader: A History of Colonialism, Neocolonialism, Dictatorship, and Resistance*, ed. Daniel B. Schirmer and Stephen Rosskamm Shalom (Boston: South End Press, 1987), 47. Although discussions of the impact of education on the Filipina/o American community usually concentrate on the post-1965 era, a few historians have examined the importance of education for the pre–World War II community. See, for example, Barbara Posadas and Ronald Guyotte, "Unintentional Immigrants: Chicago's Filipino Foreign Students Become Settlers, 1941," *Journal of American Ethnic History* 9, no. 2 (spring 1990): 26–48; Catherine Ceniza Pet, "Pioneers/Puppets: The Legacy of the *Pensionado* Program" (bachelor's thesis, Pomona College, 1991), in "Pensionados" File, NPA.

7. For a similar discussion of the relationship of education and social mobility in late nineteenth-century and early twentieth-century Europe, see Eric Hobsbawm, *The Age of Empire, 1875–1914* (New York: Vintage, 1989), 170–179.

8. See Daniel B. Schirmer and Stephen Rosskamm Shalom, eds., *The Philippines Reader: A History of Colonialism, Neocolonialism, Dictatorship, and Resistance* (Boston: South End Press, 1987), 5–6, for more on this period.

9. Daniel F. Doeppers, *Manila, 1900–1941: Social Change in a Late Colonial Metropolis*, Monograph Series no. 27 (New Haven, Conn.: Yale University Southeast Asian Studies, 1984), 2–5, 60.

10. Bonifacio S. Salamanca, *The Filipino Reaction to American Rule, 1901–1913* (n.p.: Shoe String Press, 1968), 76; Constantino, "Miseducation of the Filipino," 45; E. San Juan, "Configuring the Filipino Diaspora in the United States," *Diaspora* 3, no. 2 (1994): 121.

11. Doeppers, *Manila*, 60.

12. Leo Aliwanag, interview by Cynthia Mejia, FIL-KNG76-50cm, 19 August 1976, WSOAHP, 2.

13. Salamanca, *Filipino Reaction to American Rule*, 76.

14. William Alexander Sutherland, *Not by Might: The Epic of the Philippines* (Las Cruces, N.M.: Southwest Publishing Company, 1953), 18.

15. Doeppers, *Manila*, 65.

16. Salamanca, *Filipino Reaction to American Rule,* 91. See also Pet, "Pioneers/Puppets." I thank Cathy Pet Choy for her consultation about sources for this issue.

17. Sutherland, *Not by Might,* 28.

18. Salamanca, *Filipino Reaction to American Rule,* 91.

19. Sutherland, *Not by Might,* 31.

20. Doeppers, *Manila,* 63.

21. Sutherland, *Not by Might,* 8.

22. Bruno Lasker, *Filipino Immigration to Continental United States and to Hawaii,* published for the American Council, Institute of Pacific Relations (Chicago: University of Chicago Press, 1931), 150.

23. Ibid., 150–151.

24. In 1933, the *Philippine Herald* reported that eleven Filipina/os attending Jikeikei University in Japan "were arrested for immorality committed on the person of Japanese girls." See "Uchida Sends Report on Filipinos' Plight," *Philippine Herald,* 2 August 1933.

25. No title, 1st Indorsement, 14 February 1935, by G. B. Francisco, Colonel, P.C., Chief of Staff, for Chief of Constabulary, "Respectfully Returned to Acting Governor-General J. R. Hayden, Manila," RG 350, Box 1295, 28317 to 28342-20, Folder "28342-2 & With," 28342/36-A, 2, Bureau of Insular Affairs Records, NA.

26. Letter from Eustaquir Sugintan to Bureau of Insular Affairs, 12 October 1931, RG 350, Entry 5, Box 1295, 28317 to 28342-20, 28342/10, NA.

27. Juan Mina remembered that "the majority of the old timer[s] you see around here came from 1927 to 1934, those years. And I'm one of them." See Juan V. Mina, interview by Carolina Apostol, FIL-KNG76-47cma, 30 May 1976, WSOAHP, 2–3. Filipina/o students were also located in other schools in the Pacific Northwest. For example, for information on the Oregon experience, see Willie and Ruth Olandria, "Filipinos Who Studied in Oregon Schools from 1906 thru 1936 and Filipinos in Indian Reservations in Oregon," FANHS, Oregon Chapter, "Indian Reservations" file, NPA.

28. "Orosa Listed as Outstanding Islander," *University of Washington Daily,* 7 April 1936, 1; "Girl of Philippines Wins Right to M.S.," *University of Washington Daily,* 31 May 1921, 3; "Graduates to Return to Home in Philippines," *University of Washington Daily,* 9 December 1921, 1; "Scholarships Cease; Filipinos Return Home," *University of Washington Daily,* 28 February 1922, 4.

29. "Rufino Foronda Cacabelos," 1–5, in "Rufino Foronda Cacabelos" file, NPA.

30. Bibiana Laigo Castillano, interview by Frederic A. Cordova, Jr., FIL-KNG75-19jr, 26 June 1975, WSOAHP, 1–9.

31. In the case of these Chinese American women, despite the highlighting of education because of political policies in China and access to public education in the United States, economic and racial barriers, combined with gender discrimination, made it difficult for many women in Yung's study to pursue their education. See Judy Yung, *Unbound Feet: A Social History of Chinese Women in San Francisco* (Berkeley and Los Angeles: University of California Press, 1995), 126–130.

32. Stephan F. Brumberg, *Going to America, Going to School: The Jewish*

Immigrant Public School Encounter in Turn-of-the-Century New York City (New York: Praeger, 1986), 3, 12.

33. Gilbert G. Gónzalez, *Chicano Education in the Era of Segregation* (Philadelphia: Balch Institute Press, 1990), 16–17. For examples of resistance, see Gónzalez's history of segregation in Santa Ana, 141–142.

34. Ibid., 13–14.

35. Gary Y. Okihiro, *Cane Fires: The Anti-Japanese Movement in Hawaii, 1865–1945* (Philadelphia: Temple University Press, 1991), 134–159.

36. Sucheng Chan, *Asian Americans: An Interpretive History* (Boston: Twayne, 1991), 57–58; Yung, *Unbound Feet,* 126.

37. Sucheng Chan, "Race, Ethnic Culture, and Gender in the Construction of Identities among Second-Generation Chinese Americans, 1880s to 1930s," in *Claiming America: Constructing Chinese American Identities during the Exclusion Era,* ed. K. Scott Wong and Sucheng Chan (Philadelphia: Temple University Press, 1998), 132–133.

38. Yung, *Unbound Feet,* 127.

39. Okihiro, *Cane Fires,* 17–18; Chan, *Asian Americans,* 59; Yung, *Unbound Feet,* 127.

40. Chan, *Asian Americans,* 58–59.

41. Ibid., 54.

42. Teodolo Aguinaldo Ranjo, interview by Cynthia Mejia, FIL-KNG76-41cm, 14 January 1976, WSOAHP, 38.

43. The percentage cited is for 1930. Yung, *Unbound Feet,* 198.

44. Eugenio P. Resos, "The Philippines at Washington," *The Columns* 1, no. 4 (1921): 26; Julius Ruiz, "—A Bullsession," *University of Washington Daily,* 19 February 1937, 1–2.

45. Agustin P. Palacol, "University of Washington Filipino Club," *Filipino Student Bulletin* 2, no. 6 (April 1924): 1.

46. Resos, "Philippines at Washington," 26; Ruiz, "—A Bullsession," 1–2.

47. Ruiz, "—A Bullsession," 1–2.

48. Sylvestre A. Tangalan, interview by Carolina D. Koslosky, FIL-KNG75-28ck, 27 August 1975, WSOAHP, 5–6.

49. John Mendoza also recalled, "Oh, yeah, I took a post-graduate here in Broadway, I played football in there also, by the way." See John Mendoza, interview by Dorothy Cordova, FIL-KNG76-42dc, 6 April 1976, WSOAHP, 5.

50. Roman Simbc and Hazel Simbe, with Sinforoso Ordona, interview by DeeAnn Dixon and Nancy Koslosky, PNW82-Fil-030dad/nk, 18 January and 22 June 1982, 6.

51. *Sealth* 1922, XIX, Broadway High School yearbook, 184. Toribio Martin also indicated that there was a sense of community among high school and college students: "There was about seventy-five of us in there, university campus. Some goes to the university district and some of the boys are going to the high school." See Toribio Martin, interview by Dorothy Cordova, FIL-KNG76-44dc, 27 April 1976, WSOAHP, 3.

52. Braganza, interview, 4.

53. Maria Abastilla Beltran, interview by Carolina Koslosky, FIL-KNG75-9ck, 5 May 1975, WSOAHP, 3.

54. Jose Acena, interview by Dorothy Cordova, FIL-KNG75-24dlc, 28 July 1975, WSOAHP, 3.

55. Pete Filiarca, interview by Frederic A. Cordova, Jr., FIL-KNG75-13jr, 8 April 1975, WSOAHP, 3–5.

56. David Guerrero [pseud.], interview by author, Seattle, 10 September 1993.

57. Felipe G. Dumlao, interview by Cynthia Mejia, FIL-KNG75-35cm, 21 November 1975, WSOAHP, 38.

58. John Castillo, interview by F. A. Cordova, Jr., FIL-KNG75-15jr, 29 July 1975, WSOAHP, 7.

59. Chan, *Asian Americans,* 136.

60. The school's first Filipina/o graduate was F. B. Bautista in 1915. Trinidad A. Rojo, "Who Is Who among Filipino Alumni of the University of Washington and Their Associates," unpublished manuscript, 1, in "Rojo, Trinidad Anunciacion, University of Washington Filipino Alumni Association," FANHS Archives.

61. "University of Washington Filipino Club," *Filipino Student Bulletin* 2, no. 6 (April 1924): 1. According to records from the Registrar's Office, Manuscripts and Archives Division, University of Washington, the numbers of Filipina/os peaked at 121 in the 1925–1926 school year.

62. Richard C. Berner, *Seattle, 1900–1920: From Boomtown, Urban Turbulence, to Restoration* (Seattle: Charles Press, 1991), 82–83.

63. See "University War Work Is Reported," *University of Washington Daily,* 15 January 1919, 1; "'U' May Supply Trained Men for World Commerce," *University of Washington Daily,* 12 December, 1918, 1.

64. In 1919, for example, Pan Xenia, an "honorary commerce fraternity" whose purpose was "to promote foreign trade, international commercial relations, higher ideals, and improved ethics of business," was organized at the University of Washington. See "Pan Xenia Installed at Manila University," *University of Washington Daily,* 29 March 1923, 4. The fraternity later expanded to five chapters in the United States and, through the initiative of Professor M. M. Skinner from the College of Business Administration, to other chapters in Asia—six in China and one in the Philippines at the University of Manila. See "Pan Xenia Begun Here Now Has 12 Chapters," *University of Washington Daily,* 21 May 1926, 2; and "Foreign Trade a Big Problem," *University of Washington Daily,* 26 May 1919, 3.

65. Even two years before the United States' entrance into World War II, the new head of the Oriental studies department, George E. Taylor, summarized the university's position: "This is the logical place for study of the Pacific rim, Alaska, China and Japan," he said, "and there is no reason for us to gape at the east [coast], where most of the study is concentrated. We must develop here to take full advantage of the specific advantages of the west." See "New Oriental Studies Head Calls Seattle 'Key to East,'" *University of Washington Daily,* 6 December 1939, 1.

66. "Cosmopolitan Washington: How East Meets West in the Shadows of the University Is Related by the President of the Campus Cosmopolitan Club," *The Columns* 1, nos. 4, 5 (April 1921).

67. "Out into the Pacific," *University of Washington Daily*, 21 February 1928, 6.

68. For example, see "Foreign Students Discuss Problems," *University of Washington Daily*, 8 April 1927, 6; "Club to Discuss Filipino Question," *University of Washington Daily*, 31 January 1930, 4; "Pride and Prejudice, or I'll Take Manila," *University of Washington Daily*, 27 April 1938, 2.

69. See "Philippine Educator on Campus Tuesday," *University of Washington Daily*, 4 May 1921, 1.

70. See "Travels 7,000 Miles to Attend University," *University of Washington Daily*, 12 October 1937, 1.

71. See, for example, "America's Answer to Ten Thousand Students, Future Builders of a Hundred Nations," *Filipino Student Bulletin* 2, no. 1 (October 1923): 1.

72. Ibid., 1–2; "The F.S.C.M.," *Filipino Student* 13, no. 1 (October 1934): 1.

73. "University of Washington Filipino Club," *Filipino Student Bulletin* 2, no. 6 (April 1924): 1. See "Foreigners Form Y's," *University of Washington Daily*, 3 December 1924, 1. As a worldwide organization, the YMCA was also active in Manila. In a 1931 address, Camilo Osias, resident commissioner from the Philippines, reported that the YMCA at that time had almost ten thousand members in Manila and had first arrived in the Philippines with the American military to attend to the needs of American soldiers. Osias ended his speech by speaking of the "great commission" that the letters "Y.M.C.A." should represent: "You Must Christianize All." See Camilo Osias, "The Y.M.C.A. in the Philippines," *Filipino Student* 9, no. 1 (15 October 1931): 4.

Ties between the University of Washington and the Philippines were also enhanced by regular visits from Philippine dignitaries and educational guests wishing to tour an American campus. Journalist and publisher Carlos P. Romulo came in to the university in 1935 to talk to students and alumni, as did Francisco Delgado, resident commissioner for the Philippines Commonwealth on his way to Washington, D.C. See "Manila Publisher to Speak at Club," *University of Washington Daily*, 17 October 1935, 1; "Philippine Students Will Hear Delgado," 13 October 1935, 1.

74. "Educational Advisor Talks to Filipino Club," *University of Washington Daily*, 6 December 1921, 1.

75. "Other Colleges Look to Washington for Foreign Student Problem Solution," *University of Washington Daily*, 10 December 1926, 4.

76. "Orientation Courses Here Aid Students from Abroad," *University of Washington Daily*, 19 January 1928, 1.

77. Rojo, "Who Is Who Among Filipino Alumni," 1–2.

78. "Our Cosmopolitan Friends," *University of Washington Daily*, 14 April 1919, 2.

79. Yung, *Unbound Feet*, 128.

80. "The Chosen Few," *University of Washington Daily*, 5 January 1922, 2.

81. Harold P. Levy, "Foreign Students on Campus Present Three-Sided Problem," *University of Washington Daily*, 10 November 1926, 4. In another article, reporter Harold P. Levy wrote, "One point made generally among the students interviewed is that there is more companionship among the foreign students

as a whole than between any part of the foreign student representation and American students." Harold P. Levy, "Oriental Students Not Admitted in Boarding Houses, Says Y. Tsang," *University of Washington Daily,* 15 November 1926, 1.

82. Harold Levy, "Foreign Students Take Steps to Break Down Social Barrier," *University of Washington Daily,* 2 December 1926, 1. Graduate student Shigeaki Ninomiya also criticized discrimination against foreign students in a speech to the freshman council of the YMCA in 1930. He cited not only their being barred from the Greek letter groups of the university but also name-calling, housing difficulties, and segregation from swimming pools and golf courses. See "Grad Speaks on Exclusion of Orientals," *University of Washington Daily,* 9 January 1930, 1.

83. Levy, "Oriental Students," 1–2.

84. "Filipinos Resent Exclusion from Student Affairs," *University of Washington Daily,* 12 March 1935, 2.

85. Velasco pointed out examples of inclusion such as being invited as dinner guests to organized houses seven years earlier; Filipino participation in the Pan Xenia honorary trade fraternity, the Stevens Debate club, the Badger Debate club, and the University YMCA; and the achievements of Andres Rivera, who won a minor "W" in boxing, and Victorio Edades, who received an honorable mention in a Northwest painting contest. V. Acosta Velasco, "Filipinos Get Square Deal," *University of Washington Daily,* 1 April 1935, 4.

86. Trinidad Rojo, interview by Carolina D. Koslosky, 18 February and 19 February 1975, FIL-KNG75-17ck, WSOAHP, 11–12. For more information on African American students during this period, see Quintard Taylor, *The Forging of a Black Community: Seattle's Central District from 1870 through the Civil Rights Era* (Seattle: University of Washington Press, 1994), 142–146.

87. Ranjo, interview, 38.

88. Simbe and Simbe, with Ordona, interview, 7.

89. Benicio T. Catapusan, "Filipino Repatriates in the Philippines," *Sociology and Social Research* 21 (September–October 1936): 75.

90. Doeppers, *Manila,* 61–62.

91. Ibid., 53, 63–64.

92. "Filipinos' Future Work Aim of College Careers," *University of Washington Daily,* 31 January 1928, 1.

93. Ruiz, "—A Bullsession," 1–2.

94. "To Those Returning Home," *Filipino Student Bulletin* 2, no. 7 (May 1924): 3.

95. "Filipino Is Awarded Educational Position," *University of Washington Daily,* 4 April 1923, 4.

96. "Forestry Grads Win Places in Philippines," *University of Washington Daily,* 8 March 1926, 1; "Filipino Graduates Win Promotion," *University of Washington Daily,* 2 February 1937, 1.

97. "U. Graduates Make Name in Islands," *University of Washington Daily,* 17 January 1936, 1; "Art Grad in Manila Operates Studio," *University of Washington Daily,* 11 February 1937, 1; "UW 'Pinoy' Grad Represents Islands at World's Fair," *University of Washington Daily,* 27 April 1937, 2.

98. Rojo, "Who Is Who among Filipino Alumni," 3.

99. Benedict J. Kerkvliet, *The Huk Rebellion: A Study of Peasant Revolt in the Philippines* (Berkeley and Los Angeles: University of California Press, 1977), 17–25.

100. Doeppers, *Manila*, 72.

101. "Schools Stormed by Degreed Boys Looking for Jobs," *Philippines Herald*, 11 June 1930.

102. Lasker, *Filipino Immigration to Continental United States and to Canada*, 224–225.

103. A 1936 article warned returning students of a saturation in jobs requiring "white-collar education" as many returnees had not found employment. See "Adjusting to Home Conditions," *Filipino Student Bulletin* 15, no. 1 (October 1936): 4.

104. Maximo C. Manson, L.L.M., "Are the Filipinos in the U.S. in as Good a Position as Aliens?" *Filipino Student Bulletin* 7, no. 2 (November 1929): 1.

105. Mina, interview, 3.

106. Tangalan, interview, 7.

107. Ruiz, "—A Bullsession," 1–2. See also "Filipinos Interested in University Affairs," *University of Washington Daily*, 21 November 1929, 1.

108. Rojo, interview, 14, 21.

109. Ranjo, interview, 22–23.

110. Evelyn Nakano Glenn, *Issei, Nisei, Warbride: Three Generations of Japanese American Women in Domestic Service* (Philadelphia: Temple University Press, 1986), 105–109.

111. Ibid., 124–127.

112. Filiarca, interview, 2.

113. Simbe and Simbe, with Ordona, interview, 8.

114. Mendoza, interview, 8.

115. While Felipe Dumlao earned ten dollars a month as a houseboy, he remembered, "You go to the country[,] you work from dark to dark" for a dollar a day. See Dumlao, interview, 6.

116. Ranjo, interview, 47.

117. Ben Rinonos, interview by Teresa Cronin, FIL-KNG-3tc, 27 March 1975, WSOAHP, 17.

118. See Dumlao, interview, 5–6, 36; Martin, interview, 20; Ponce Torres, interview by Carolina Koslosky, FIL-KNG75-14ck, 25 August 1975, WSOAHP, 2.

119. Gloria H. Chun, "'Go West . . . to China': Chinese American Identity in the 1930s," in Wong and Chan, *Claiming America*, 167.

120. Gary Y. Okihiro, *Storied Lives: Japanese American Students and World War II* (Seattle: University of Washington Press, 1999), 17–18.

121. Lorenzo Pimental, interview by Cynthia Mejia, FIL-KNG75-34cm, 14 November 1975, WSOAHP, 19.

122. Eddie Acena, interview by Bob Flor, FIL-KNG75-18bf, 26 June 1975, WSOAHP, 4. Felipe Bigornia also began at the University of Washington after graduating from Broadway High School but was unable to attend for more than two years "because of economic problems." See Felipe Bigornia, interview by Bob Antolin, PNW80-Fil-000ba, 22 May 1980, DPAA, 2–3.

123. "Filipino Student Admits Stealing Four Overcoats," *University of Washington Daily*, 26 February 1929, 1. The jail sentence was later suspended.

124. Rojo, "Who Is Who among Filipino Alumni," 4.

125. Felix Narte, interview by Teresa Cronin, FIL-KNG75-8tc, 21 April 1975, WSOAHP, 8.

126. Ray Edralin Corpuz, interview by Bob Antolin, PNW81-Fil-028ba, 22 September 1981, DPAA, 1.

127. Fred Floresca, interview by Carolina Koslosky, FIL-KNG76-2ck, 2 May 1975, WSOAHP, 16.

128. Chris Mensalvas and Jesus R. Yambao, interview by Carolina Koslosky, FIL-KNG75-1ck, 10 February and 11 February 1975, WSOAHP, 3.

129. Robert F. Flor, "The Development of the Filipino Community in Seattle, Washington," unpublished paper, NPA, 12–13.

130. Sergio Aguinaldo [pseud.], interview by author, Seattle, 22 February 1994.

131. Braganza, interview, 5, 9.

132. Ibid., 9.

133. Okihiro, *Storied Lives*, 159.

CHAPTER 3. REGION AND LABOR

1. Paula Nonacido, interview by Cynthia Mejia, FIL-KNG76-49cm, 7 July and 22 September 1976, WSOAHP, 1–12.

2. Ibid., 14–18.

3. Ibid., 3, 14, 23–25.

4. Virginia Scharff, "Mobility, Women, and the West," in *Over the Edge: Remapping the American West*, ed. Valerie J. Matsumoto and Blake Allmendinger (Berkeley and Los Angeles: University of California Press, 1999), 161.

5. Carlos Bulosan, *America Is in the Heart: A Personal History* (Seattle: University of Washington Press, 1991).

6. See Sarah Deutsch, *No Separate Refuge: Culture, Class, and Gender on an Anglo-Hispanic Frontier in the American Southwest, 1880–1940* (New York: Oxford University Press, 1987), 9.

7. For more on the 1930s dust bowl migration, see James N. Gregory, *American Exodus: The Dust Bowl Migration and Okie Culture in California* (New York: Oxford University Press, 1989).

8. David Montgomery, *The Fall of the House of Labor: The Workplace, the State, and American Labor Activism, 1865–1925* (Cambridge: Cambridge University Press, 1987), 59.

9. See Eric H. Monkkonen, "Afterword," in *Walking to Work: Tramps in America, 1790–1935*, ed. Eric H. Monkkonen (Lincoln: University of Nebraska Press, 1984), 242.

10. See Dennis Nodín Valdés, *Al Norte: Agricultural Workers in the Great Lakes Region, 1917–1970* (Austin: University of Texas Press, 1991), 25.

11. For more on the attractions of Chicago for immigrant and second-generation American workers, see Lizabeth Cohen, *Making a New Deal: Industrial Workers in Chicago, 1919–1939* (New York: Cambridge University Press,

1990). For the pivotal site of Los Angeles, see George J. Sánchez, *Becoming Mexican American: Ethnicity, Culture, and Identity in Chicano Los Angeles, 1900–1945* (New York: Oxford University Press, 1993), 64. See pages 63–70 for a further discussion of the migration of Mexicans to Los Angeles during this period.

12. Ray Edralin Corpuz, interview by Bob Antolin, PNW81-Fil-028ba, 22 September 1981, DPAA, 2.

13. Bibiana Laigo Castillano, interview by Frederic A. Cordova, Jr., FIL-KNG75-19jr, 26 June 1975, WSOAHP, 6–7.

14. Excerpt from "Jane Kwong Lee, Community Worker," in Judy Yung, *Unbound Voices: A Documentary History of Chinese Women in San Francisco* (Berkeley and Los Angeles: University of California Press, 1999), 233. Also quoted in Judy Yung, *Unbound Feet: A Social History of Chinese Women in San Francisco* (Berkeley and Los Angeles: University of California Press, 1995), 87.

15. See Louis Bloch, "Facts about Filipino Immigration into California," Special Bulletin No. 3, State of California, Department of Industrial California, San Francisco, April 1930, reprinted by R and E Research Associates, San Francisco, 1972.

16. Felix Narte, interview by Teresa Cronin, FIL-KNG75-8tc, 21 April 1975, WSOAHP, 2–3.

17. Zacarias Manangan, interview by Carolina D. Koslosky, FIL-KNG75-30ck, 30 September 1975, WSOAHP, 4.

18. Miriam Sharma, "Labor Migration and Class Formation among the Filipinos in Hawaii, 1906–1946," in *Labor Immigration under Capitalism: Asian Workers in the United States before World War II,* ed. Lucie Cheng and Edna Bonacich (Berkeley and Los Angeles: University of California Press, 1984), 586.

19. Leo Aliwanag, interview by Cynthia Mejia, FIL-KNG76-50cm, 19 August 1976, WSOAHP, 5–6.

20. Dean T. Alegado, "The Filipino Community in Hawaii: Development and Change," *Social Process in Hawaii* 33 (1991): 4; Sharma, "Labor Migration and Class Formation," 582–583.

21. Alegado, "The Filipino Community in Hawaii," 14–15; Sharma, "Labor Migration and Class Formation," 582.

22. "6,000 Filipino Laborers Thrown Out of Work in Hawaiian Islands," *Philippine Herald,* 1 February 1932.

23. See Haunani Kay Trask's *From a Native Daughter: Colonialism and Sovereignty in Hawai'i* (Monroe, Maine: Common Courage Press, 1993); and Robert H. Mast and Anne B. Mast, *Autobiography of Protest in Hawai'i* (Honolulu: University of Hawai'i Press, 1996), for more on the history of the Hawaiian people.

24. For more on the labor experience of Filipina/o Americans as Pullman porters, see Barbara M. Posadas, "The Hierarchy of Color and Psychological Adjustment in an Industrial Environment: Filipinos, the Pullman Company, and the Brotherhood of Sleeping Car Porters," *Labor History* 23, no. 3 (summer 1982): 349–373.

25. Narte, interview, 13–14. Zacarias Manangan remembers that a friend in Darrington, Washington, "called me up to come and work down there again." As soon as the work was done, the laborers were laid off. Ben Rinonos also worked

for a month changing rail ties, then returned to Seattle to get work in Alaska. See Manangan, interview, 7–8; Ben Rinonos, interview by Teresa Cronin, FIL-KNG-3tc, 15 September 1975, WSOAHP, 7.

26. Teodolo Aguinaldo Ranjo, interview by Cyn. Mejia, FIL-KNG76-41cm, 14 January 1976, WSOAHP, 12.

27. Antonio Rodrigo [listed as Tony Rodrigo,] interview by Dorothy Cordova, FIL-KNG76-53dc, WSOAHP, 30–35.

28. Sammy R. Lopez, interview by Cyn. Mejia, FIL-KNG75-36cm, 24 November 1975, WSOAHP, 3–4.

29. Jesse G. Quinsaat, "An Exercise on How to Join the Navy and Still Not See the World," in *Letters in Exile: An Introductory Reader on the History of Pilipinos in America*, ed. Jesse G. Quinsaat (Los Angeles: UCLA Asian American Studies Center, 1976), 105; and H. Brett Melendy, *Asians in America: Filipinos, Koreans, and East Indians* (Boston: Twayne, 1977), 83–84.

30. Fred C. Floresca, interview by Carolina Koslosky, FIL-KNG76-2ck, 2 May 1975, WSOAHP, 15.

31. Melendy, *Asians in America*, 83.

32. "9 Filipino Seamen Wanted in America," *Philippines Herald,* 16 October 1933.

33. Edna Bonacich, "Some Basic Facts: Patterns of Asian Immigration and Exclusion," in Cheng and Bonacich, *Labor Immigration under Capitalism,* 64–65; Edna Bonacich, "Asian Labor in the Development of California and Hawaii," in Cheng and Bonacich, *Labor Immigration under Capitalism,* 140, 167–168. For more on the California economy, see Karen Isaksen Leonard, *Making Ethnic Choices: California's Punjabi Mexican Americans* (Philadelphia: Temple University Press, 1992), 17–24. For an important discussion of the movement of Asian Americans into these different employment fields, see Sucheng Chan, *Asian Americans: An Interpretive History* (New York: Twayne, 1991), especially chap. 2, "Immigration and Livelihood, 1840s to 1930s," 25–42.

34. Bonacich, "Some Basic Facts," 68–69, 72; Chan, *Asian Americans,* 33–34. For an important study of Chinese American laundry workers in Chicago, see Paul C. P. Siu, *The Chinese Laundryman: A Study of Social Isolation,* edited by John Kuo Wei Tchen (New York: New York University Press, 1987). For a comparative discussion of the demographics of Asian Americans in the salmon canning industry, see Chris Friday, *Organizing Asian American Labor: The Pacific Coast Canned-Salmon Industry, 1870–1942* (Philadelphia: Temple University Press, 1994), 2–3. See also Evelyn Nakano Glenn's chapter 4, "The Labor Market," in her *Issei, Nisei, Warbride: Three Generations of Japanese American Women in Domestic Service* (Philadelphia: Temple University Press, 1986).

35. Chan, *Asian Americans,* 53–56; Leonard, *Making Ethnic Choices,* 19; Bonacich, "Asian Labor in the Development of California and Hawaii," 159, 161–165, 176; Bonacich, "Some Basic Facts," 74–75.

36. Chan, *Asian Americans,* 55–56; Bonacich, "Asian Labor in the Development of California and Hawaii," 165–166; Hyung-chan Kim and Cynthia C. Mejia, comps. and eds., *The Filipinos in America, 1898–1974: A Chronology and Fact Book,* Ethnic Chronology Series, no. 23 (Dobbs Ferry, N.Y.: Oceana Publications, 1976), 3, 15, 19.

37. Camille Guerin-Gonzales, *Mexican Workers and American Dreams: Immigration, Repatriation, and California Farm Labor, 1900–1939* (New Brunswick, N.J.: Rutgers University Press, 1994), 16.

38. De Cano was successful in challenging the 1921 alien land act that had been amended in 1937 to include Filipinos as aliens. See Gail Nomura, "Within the Law: The Establishment of Filipino Leasing Rights on the Yakima Indian Reservation," *Amerasia Journal* 13, no. 1 (1986–1987): 106, 108. See also Maria Abastilla Beltran, interview by Carolina Koslosky, FIL-KNG75-9ck, 5 May 1975, WSOAHP, 10; and Jose Acena, interview by Dorothy L. Cordova, FIL-KNG75-24dlc, 28 July 1975, WSOAHP, 7.

39. See "Anti-miscegenation Laws," in *Letters in Exile: An Introductory Reader on the History of the Pilipinos in America,* ed. Jesse Quinsaat (Los Angeles: UCLA Asian American Studies Center, 1976), 65, 69–70; Fred Cordova, *Filipinos: Forgotten Asian Americans, A Pictorial Essay/1763-Circa-1963* (Dubuque, Iowa: Kendall/Hunt, 1983), 117.

40. Alegado, "The Filipino Community in Hawai'i," 17–18.

41. Zacarias Manangan, interview, 11–12.

42. See Lauren W. Casaday, "Labor Unrest and the Labor Movement in the Salmon Industry in the Pacific Northwest" (Ph.D. diss., University of California, Berkeley, 1938), 103 n. 35. "Goo-goo" is probably a reference to the fact that Filipinos were often called "monkeys," "goo-goo" being an imitation of monkey sounds. For name-calling, see also Lopez, interview, 8–9.

43. Melendy, *Asians in America,* 55.

44. Bruno Lasker, *Filipino Immigration to Continental United States and to Hawaii,* published for the American Council, Institute of Pacific Relations (Chicago: University of Chicago Press, 1931), 358–365; Cordova, *Filipinos,* 116; Howard A. De Witt, *Anti-Filipino Movements in California: A History, Bibliography and Study Guide* (San Francisco: R and E Research Associates, 1976), 46–66. De Witt's monograph also contains a copy of E. S. Bogardus's contemporary research, "Anti-Filipino Race Riots: A Report Made to the Ingram Institute of Social Science, of San Diego, by E. S. Bogardus, University of Southern California, May 15, 1930," 88–111.

45. "U.S. Filipinos Ask Leniency for 8 Alleged Riot Leaders," *Philippines Herald,* 15 February 1930.

46. Essay by Fernando P. Bitanga, in "That Watsonville Incident," with pieces by Fernando Leano, Domingo H. Soriano, Fernando P. Bitanga, and Jose Esposo Evangelista, *Philippines Herald,* 2 February 1930; "Manifesto on U.S. Riots Sets Mourning Day," *Manila Bulletin,* 28 January 1930, "Tears Flow at Luneta," *Manila Bulletin,* 3 February 1930.

47. Lasker, *Filipino Immigration,* 358–365. See, for example, Abdon Llorente, "U.S. Filipinos Victims of Hate Others Inspire," *Philippines Herald,* 21 August 1930.

48. Ray Edralin Corpuz, interview, 2.

49. Montgomery, *Fall of the House of Labor,* 63; Bonacich, "U.S. Capitalist Development," 115–117.

50. See State of California, Department of Industrial Relations, Special Bulletin No. 3, "Facts about Filipino Immigration into California," State Building,

San Francisco, California, April 1930, 37–40. See also Edna Bonacich and Lucie Cheng, "Introduction: A Theoretical Orientation to International Labor Migration," in *Labor Immigration under Capitalism: Asian Workers in the United States before World War II* (Berkeley and Los Angeles: University of California Press, 1984), 27–29.

51. Toribio Martin, interview by Dorothy Cordova, FIL-KNG76-44dc, 27 April 1976, WSOAHP, 1.

52. Honorato Rapada, interview by Teresa Cronin, FIL-KNG75-11tc, 24 May 1975, WSOAHP, 21.

53. For a discussion of the alien land laws, see Chan, *Asian Americans*, 46–47.

54. Acena, interview, 6.

55. Ben Rinonos, interview by Teresa Cronin, FIL-KNG75-3tc, 27 March 1975, WSOAHP, 14.

56. Martin, interview, 14.

57. Lopez, interview, 8.

58. Al Bautista [pseud.], interview by author, Seattle, 30 September 1993.

59. Juan V. Mina, interview by Carolina Apostol, FIL-KNG76-47cma, 30 May 1976, WSOAHP, 13.

60. See Martin, interview, 13; Mina, interview, 13; Manangan, interview, 8.

61. Rapada, interview, 10.

62. Bautista, interview.

63. "Two Filipinos Crushed by Train at Crossing," *Philippines Herald,* 11 October 1930.

64. United Press, "American Killed, 3 Filipinos Injured in Automobile Crash," *Philippines Herald,* 1 October 1930.

65. Corpuz, interview, 3.

66. John Mendoza, interview by Dorothy Cordova, FIL-KNG76-42dc, 6 April 1976, WSOAHP, 3–3a. [Page 3 occurs twice in the transcript, and hence I have listed the second page "3" as "3a."]

67. F. Landa Jocano, "Elements of Filipino Social Organization," in *Philippine Kinship and Society,* ed. Yasushi Kikuchi (Quezon City: New Day Publishers, 1989), 2–3, 5–6.

68. Ibid., 4, 8–9.

69. Ibid., 21.

70. Frank Lynch, "Social Acceptance Reconsidered," in *Philippine Society and the Individual: Selected Essays of Frank Lynch, 1949–1976,* ed. Aram A. Yengoyan and Perla Q. Makil, Michigan Papers on South and Southeast Asia, no. 24 (Ann Arbor: Center for South and Southeast Asian Studies, University of Michigan, 1984), 35–36. Lynch's work focuses on lowland Filipina/os.

71. Don Velasco [pseud.], interview by author, Seattle, 9 February 1994.

72. Jocano, "Elements of Filipino Social Organization," 15–19.

73. Vincent Yolenato Mendoza and Rosario Rosell Mendoza [listed as Mr. and Mrs. Vincent Mendoza], interview by Cynthia Mejia, FIL-KNG76-40cm, 13 January 1976, WSOAHP, 7.

74. Lorenzo Pimental, interview by Cynthia Mejia, FIL-KNG75-34cm, 14 November 1975, WSOAHP, 17–18.

75. At this time, whites constituted the largest proportion at 37.3 percent, Na-

tive Americans counted 12.8 percent, and the remainder was formed by Japanese (8.6 percent), Chinese (5.4 percent), Mexicans (5 percent), and "Others" (1.2 percent). The numbers of Filipino fishermen in Alaska remained minimal. See Casaday, "Labor Unrest and the Labor Movement in the Salmon Industry," 79–84, 109. For the early history of the salmon canning industry, see Casaday's dissertation and Chris Friday's *Organizing Asian American Labor*. See also Thelma Buchholdt, *Filipinos in Alaska: 1788–1958* (Anchorage: Aboriginal Press, 1996), 42–60.

76. Buchholdt, *Filipinos in Alaska*, 61.

77. Ibid., 85–86.

78. Narte, interview, 8–9.

79. Manangan, interview, 20.

80. Casaday, "Labor Unrest and the Labor Movement in the Salmon Industry," 93–95.

81. Ibid., 93–94, 99–102.

82. Jack Masson and Donald Guimary, "Asian Labor Contractors in the Alaskan Canned Salmon Industry: 1880–1937," *Labor History* 22, no. 3 (summer 1981): 377, 381–382; see also Montgomery, *Fall of the House of Labor*, 73–81, for a description of the padrone system and other forms of labor recruiting. For a comparative discussion of the role of contractors in the Greek American community, see Gunther Peck's description of the relationship of workers to padrone Leonidas Skliris in "Padrones and Protest: 'Old' Radicals and 'New' Immigrants in Bingham, Utah, 1905–1912," *Western Historical Quarterly* 24, no. 2 (May 1993): 165–177.

83. John Castillo, interview by F. A. Cordova, Jr., FIL-KNG75-15jr, 29 July 1975, WSOAHP, 13; Friday, *Organizing Asian American Labor*, 104–112, for a discussion of Chinese and Japanese involvement in contracting and subcontracting. In the early 1920s, the main Chinese contractor in Seattle was Goon Dip and Company, later run by Lew Kay. The L.V.M. Trading Company (reportedly standing for the initials of the three Philippine regions, Luzon, Visayas, and Mindanao) was also prominent, although the specifics are unclear. According to Casaday's research, almost all of the Filipino cannery workers had contact with the L.V.M. Trading Company while being hired. Casaday speculates that Goon Dip or the L.V.M. Trading Company made deals with Filipino subcontractors, who were directly responsible for employing workers. The vice president of the L.V.M. Trading Company was Pio de Cano, who would emerge as one of the largest Filipino contractors in the city. In 1930, however, the company closed down after stockholders levied a suit "against the directors for misappropriation of funds." See Casaday, "Labor Unrest and the Labor Movement in the Salmon Industry," 156–157; Gerald Gold, "The Development of Local Number 7 of the Food, Tobacco, Agricultural and Allied Workers of America-C.I.O." (master's thesis, University of Washington, 1949), 11.

84. Casaday, "Labor Unrest and the Labor Movement in the Salmon Industry," 158–159.

85. Bibiana Laigo Castillano, interview, 13–15, 17–21; and Sergio Aguinaldo [pseud.], interview by author, Seattle, 22 February 1994.

86. Sebastian Abella, "How Filipinos Help Can Salmon," *Philippine Review*, July 1931.

87. Gold, "Development of Local Number 7," 9–10.

88. Carlos Toribio [pseud.], interview by author, Seattle, 18 July 1994.

89. Trinidad A. Rojo, "Canta Ti Alaskero," *Philippine-American Chronicle*, 1 December 1934. Rojo published the poem in the Ilocano language, and the original lines read: "Mauram combat canariam / Wenno mapeste amin aya kan / Ta agawid cam a padapada / A Di malpas contrata." I am using an excerpt from a translated version that appears in Casaday's dissertation, "Labor Unrest and the Labor Movement in the Salmon Industry," 137–138.

90. In addition, workers had to stay at the same kind of work unless a foreman or another "person in authority" changed them to another job, and they would not have any changes in wages. If workers did not follow orders, or became sick or hurt, they would be levied a fine of fifty cents for each hour not worked and fifty cents for every meal that the worker had during this period. After the fish began to run, the worker had to go to sleep at ten o'clock at the latest if there was no other work, and "gambling, carousing, brawling, shouting or loud noises" would result in a fine of five dollars. A worker who gave or sold liquor to Native Americans or other workers lost all right to wages and claims. If the worker got into a fight, became drunk, or exhibited raucous behavior during the fishing season, the employer could take away the contract and keep fifty cents for each hour from the beginning of the contract until the end of the season. All wages would be paid at Seattle, within the first week of returning to the city, and workers were told specifically to "waive the provisions of an Act of the Legislature of Alaska" concerning wages made in 1923. Money and merchandise loaned to the worker would be deducted from the worker's wages. See Casaday, "Labor Unrest and the Labor Movement in the Salmon Industry," appendix, 6–11.

91. Gold, "Development of Local Number 7," 12–13.

92. Narte, interview, 9; Gold, "Development of Local Number 7," 9–10; Masson and Guimary, "Asian Labor Contractors," 389–390.

93. Ponce Torres, interview by Carolina Koslosky, FIL-KNG75-14ck, 25 August 1975, WSOAHP, 3.

94. Narte, interview, 9.

95. Castillo, interview, 14.

96. Castillo, interview, 14; Casaday, "Labor Unrest and the Labor Movement in the Salmon Industry," 341.

97. Teodolo Aguinaldo Ranjo, interview by Cynthia Mejia, FIL-KNG76-41cm, 14 January 1976, WSOAHP, 45–46.

98. The trade-off for engaging in these activities, however, was that workers might seek other contractors for employment. See Masson and Guimary, "Asian Labor Contractors," 387.

99. Evidence here is sketchy, but Melendy, *Asians in America*, 81–82, speaks of white prostitutes; Masson and Guimary, "Asian Labor Contractors," 391, refer to Chinese, African American, and Portuguese prostitutes. See also National Industrial Recovery Administration Hearing on Code of Fair Practices and Competition Presented by the Canned Salmon Industry, Hearing Held at San Francisco, California, February 27, 1934, 246–264. More information needs to be gathered about female prostitution and the extent of this business practice as a whole.

100. Masson and Guimary, "Asian Labor Contractors," 390.

101. Manangan, interview, 20–21.

102. Cordova, *Filipinos*, 69.

103. See, for example, chapter 3, "Bulls, Bears, and Dancing Boys," in Susan Lee Johnson, *Roaring Camp: The Social World of the California Gold Rush* (New York: Norton, 2000), 141–183.

104. National Industrial Recovery Administration Hearing on Code of Fair Practices and Competition Presented by the Canned Salmon Industry, San Francisco, California, February 27, 1934, 247.

105. Ibid., 252–254.

106. Ylanan also remembered two families in which Filipinos were married to "[white] American women." See Mateo Ylanan, interview by unknown, date unknown, PNW81-Fil-101PA, DPAA, 15, 20, 21.

107. Salvador Del Fierro, interview by Carolina D. Koslosky, FIL-KNG75-29ck, 15 September 1975, WSOAHP, 4.

108. Buchholdt, *Filipinos in Alaska*, 65.

109. Ibid., 68–69.

110. Casaday, "Labor Unrest and the Labor Movement in the Salmon Industry," 344.

111. Pete Filiarca, interview by Frederic A. Cordova, Jr., FIL-KNG75-13jr, 8 April 1975, WSOAHP, 11.

112. Masson and Guimary, "Asian Labor Contractors," 393–394; Castillo, interview, 4; Casaday, "Labor Unrest and the Labor Movement in the Salmon Industry," 98.

113. Rinonos, interview, 10. Zacarias Manangan remembered how one boss made money by charging workers for housing in Seattle that was supposed to be free. See Manangan, interview, 20.

114. Guerin-Gonzales, *Mexican Workers and American Dreams*, 13; Carey McWilliams, *Factories in the Field: The Story of Migratory Farm Labor in California* (Santa Barbara and Salt Lake City: Peregrine Smith, 1971), 11–65. In 1939, both John Steinbeck's *Grapes of Wrath* and Carey McWilliams's *Factories in the Field* focused national attention on the plight of migratory workers in the West.

115. Donald Worster, *Rivers of Empire: Water, Aridity, and the Growth of the American West* (New York: Pantheon, 1985), 4–5.

116. Paul Taylor, "The Migrants and California's Future," in Paul Taylor, *On the Ground in the Thirties* (Salt Lake City: Gibbs M. Smith, 1983), 178.

117. Cletus E. Daniel, *Bitter Harvest: A History of California Farmworkers, 1870–1941* (Ithaca, N.Y.: Cornell University Press, 1981), 108.

118. Carey McWilliams, *Ill Fares the Land: Migrants and Migratory Labor in the United States* (New York: Barnes and Noble, 1967), 13, 16.

119. Guerin-Gonzales, *Mexican Workers and American Dreams*, 16–24; see also "Our Oriental Agriculture," chapter 7 in Carey McWilliams, *Factories in the Field*, 103–133.

120. McWilliams, *Factories in the Field*, 130–131.

121. Cordova, *Filipinos*, 149. Photograph is on page 38 of Fred Cordova, and description of Frank Mancao is on page x.

122. Mina, interview, 12–13.

123. Melendy, *Asians in America,* 74–75; Casaday, "Labor Unrest and the Labor Movement in the Salmon Industry," 96–97.

124. Garciano Garo, interview by Pearl Ancheta, PNW-Fil-009PA, 18 March 1981, DPAA, 4.

125. Martin, interview, 13.

126. McWilliams, *Factories in the Field,* 131; Melendy, *Asians in America,* 76; Rapada, interview, 7.

127. Aliwanag, interview, 7–8.

128. McWilliams, *Factories in the Field,* 131.

129. Mendoza and Mendoza, interview, 8.

130. Ibid., 9.

131. Daniel, *Bitter Harvest,* 108–109.

132. Mexican laborers were told to discontinue contact with Filipino strikers, menaced with the specter of deportation, and misled by a repatriation campaign that erroneously promised the availability of free land in Mexico if they went back home. See Daniel, *Bitter Harvest,* 110–117.

133. Cordova, *Filipinos,* 148.

134. See "Pair Celebrate 55 Years of Love," *San Jose Mercury,* 14 February 1995, in file in National Pinoy Archives. For a comparative study on Punjabi Mexican American families in California, see Leonard, *Making Ethnic Choices.*

135. Kim and Mejia, *Filipinos in America,* 19; McWilliams, *Factories in the Field,* 133.

136. Felipe G. Dumlao, interview by Cynthia Mejia, FIL-KNG75-35cm, 21 November 1975, WSOAHP, 49.

137. Mendoza and Mendoza, interview, 10–11.

138. Gordon Elwood Morton, "Farm Wage Workers in Washington" (master's thesis, University of Washington, 1943), 27.

139. See Nomura, "Within the Law," 99–117; also Joyce Benjamin Kuhler, "A History of Agriculture in the Yakima Valley Washington from 1880 to 1900" (master's thesis, University of Washington, 1940); Joseph Campbell Scroggs, "Labor Problems in the Fruit Industry of the Yakima Valley" (master's thesis, University of Washington, 1937); Grace Edith Miner, "A Century of Washington Fruit" (master's thesis, University of Washington, 1926).

140. By the time of the Great Depression, the Filipinos who thronged to the Pacific Northwest were part of a flood of new peoples arriving in the Pacific Northwest. Carey McWilliams notes that some 465,000 migrants came into the area between 1930 and 1940. Many of the people who migrated through the Northwest were white families who fled the devastation of drought and unemployment farther east from the Northern Great Plains, contributing to a larger pool of available casual labor and greater economic competition. See McWilliams, *Ill Fares the Land,* 51–60.

141. Rapada, interview, 19–20.

142. Anacleto Corpuz, interview by Teresa Cronin, FIL-KNG75-16tc, 23 June 1975, WSOAHP, 13–14.

143. Garo, interview, 3–4, 6.

144. Nomura, "Within the Law," 99–117; Mina, interview, 11.

145. Acena, interview, 3.

146. Bautista, interview.

147. Craig Scharlin and Lilia V. Villanueva, *Philip Vera Cruz: A Personal History of Filipino Immigrants and the Farmworkers Movement* (Los Angeles: UCLA Labor Center, Institute of Industrial Relations and UCLA Asian American Studies Center, 1992), 54–55.

148. Mike Castillano, interview by Frederic A. Cordova, Jr., FIL-KNG75-23jr, 2 July 1975, WSOAHP, 3–4, 6.

149. In 1929, Dionicio Cristobal attended school during the day and worked in a sawmill at night. John Castillo also remembered how college students worked summers in Hoquiam, Aberdeen, and Cosmopolis to support themselves. See Dionicio (Denny) Cristobal, interview by Carolina M. Apostol, FIL-KNG76-43cma, 10 March 1976, WSOAHP, 4–5, and John Castillo, 1, 8–9.

150. Mike Castillano, interview, 4.

151. Roman Simbe and Hazel Simbe, with Sinforoso Ordona, interview by DeeAnn Dixon and Nancy Koslosky, 18 January and 22 June 1982, PNW82-Fil-030dad/nk, 9–10.

152. Scharlin and Villanueva, *Philip Vera Cruz,* 55.

153. Simbe and Simbe, with Ordona, interview, 13–14.

154. Mike Castillano, interview, 4–5.

155. Narte, interview, 7.

156. See Lasker, *Filipino Immigration,* 365–368; Kim and Mejia, *The Filipinos in America,* 3, 14.

157. Acena, interview, 8.

158. Martin, interview, 9–10.

159. Acena, interview, 5.

160. "Many Filipinos Still in Hiding," *Manila Bulletin,* 10 May 1930.

161. "Filipino Tragedy Continues," 3, and "Filipinos Are Raided Again Near Kent, Washington," 5, *Philippine Review,* February 1931. For more on violence in Kent, see also "Scared Filipinos Still Unlocated," *Philippines Herald,* 9 May 1930.

162. Dumlao, interview, 18–19.

163. Castillo, interview, 1–2.

164. Rapada, interview, 21.

165. For important documentation on the Stockton community, see Filipino Oral History Project, *Voices: A Filipino American Oral History* (Stockton: Filipino Oral History Project, 2000).

166. Patricia Limerick, "Common Cause? Asian American History and Western American History," in *Privileging Positions: The Sites of Asian American Studies,* ed. Gary Y. Okihiro, Marilyn Alquizola, Dorothy Fujita Rony, and K. Scott Wong (Pullman: Washington State University Press, 1995), 97.

167. Two excellent studies that reflect the field's emphasis on Chinatowns as a site for community study are Yung, *Unbound Feet;* and Renqiu Yu, *To Save China, to Save Ourselves: The Chinese Hand Laundry Alliance of New York* (Philadelphia: Temple University Press, 1992).

CHAPTER 4. CROSSINGS AND CONNECTIONS

1. For more on the role of the phrase *bachelor society,* see Jennifer Ting, "Bachelor Society: Deviant Heterosexuality and Asian American Historiography," in *Privileging Positions: The Sites of Asian American Studies,* ed. Gary Y. Okihiro, Marilyn Alquizola, Dorothy Fujita Rony, and K. Scott Wong (Pullman: Washington State University Press, 1995), 271–279. As I have argued in my introduction, the phrase *bachelor society* originated with descriptions of the Chinese American community but has been used to characterize the Filipina/o American community during the pre–World War II era as well.

2. Honorato Rapada, interview by Teresa Cronin, FIL-KNG75-11tc, 24 May 1975, WSOAHP, 12.

3. Dorothy Almonjuela, interview by Teresa Cronin, FIL-KNG75-2tc, 9 April 1975, WSOAHP, 5–9.

4. Alexander Saxton, *The Indispensable Enemy: Labor and the Anti-Chinese Movement in California* (Berkeley and Los Angeles: University of California Press, 1971). See also Gunther Barth, *Bitter Strength: A History of the Chinese in the United States, 1850–1870* (Cambridge, Mass.: Harvard University Press, 1964), 212–213, for a discussion of the "sojourner," and Sucheng Chan, "European and Asian Immigration into the United States in Comparative Perspective, 1820s to 1920s," in *Immigration Reconsidered: History, Sociology, and Politics,* ed. Virginia Yans-McLaughlin (New York: Oxford University Press, 1990), 68, for a critique of that term.

5. Carlos A. Schwantes, "Unemployment, Disinheritance, and the Origins of Labor Militancy in the Pacific Northwest, 1885–86," in *Experiences in a Promised Land: Essays in Pacific Northwest History,* ed. G. Thomas Edwards and Carlos A. Schwantes (Seattle: University of Washington Press, 1986), 179–194; Dana Frank, "Race Relations and the Seattle Labor Movement, 1915–1929," *Pacific Northwest Quarterly* 86, no. 1 (winter 1994/1995): 35–44.

6. For further information on these communities, see Ron Chew, ed., *Reflections of Seattle's Chinese Americans: The First 100 Years* (Seattle: University of Washington Press and Wing Luke Asian Museum, 1994), and David A. Takami, *Divided Destiny: A History of Japanese Americans in Seattle* (Seattle: University of Washington Press and Wing Luke Asian Museum, 1998). See also Sucheng Chan, *Asian Americans: An Interpretive History* (New York: Twayne, 1991), 136, for more on Hirabayashi.

7. See U.S. Department of Commerce, Bureau of the Census, *Fifteenth Census of the United States: 1930,* Vol. 3, pt. 2 (Washington, D.C.: Government Printing Office, 1932), 1209; U.S. Department of Commerce, Bureau of the Census, *Sixteenth Census of the United States: 1940,* Vol. 2, pt. 7 (Washington, D.C.: United States Government Printing Office, 1943), 401.

8. See Carey McWilliams, *Ill Fares the Land: Migrants and Migratory Labor in the United States* (New York: Barnes and Noble, 1967), 3–10, for a graphic description of the constructed "invisibility" of migratory labor.

9. As Walter Licht demonstrates in his study of Philadelphia workers from 1840 to 1950, finding employment was a consuming part of people's lives, par-

ticularly before the Second World War. See Walter Licht, *Getting Work: Philadelphia, 1840–1950* (Cambridge, Mass.: Harvard University Press, 1993), 220–240.

10. Juan V. Mina, interview by Carolina Apostol, FIL-KNG76-47cma, 30 May 1976, WSOAHP, 11.

11. Roger Sale, *Seattle: Past to Present* (Seattle: University of Washington Press, 1976), 136–138; Dana Frank, *Purchasing Power: Consumer Organizing, Gender, and the Seattle Labor Movement, 1919–1929* (Cambridge: Cambridge University Press, 1994), 15–16.

12. Roy Rosenzweig, *Eight Hours for What We Will: Workers and Leisure in an Industrial City, 1870–1920* (Cambridge: Cambridge University Press, 1989 Reprint), 12–13.

13. Limited economic options also affected the number of African Americans drawn to the city. Howard A. Droker, "Seattle Race Relations during the Second World War," in *Experiences in a Promised Land: Essays in Pacific Northwest History*, ed. G. Thomas Edwards and Carlos A. Schwantes (Seattle: University of Washington Press, 1986), 353.

14. Sale, *Seattle*, 4–5.

15. Frank, *Purchasing Power*, 16.

16. Calvin F. Schmid, *Social Trends in Seattle*, University of Washington Publications in the Social Sciences, vol. 14 (Seattle: University of Washington Press, 1944), 99.

17. Quintard Taylor, *The Forging of a Black Community: Seattle's Central District from 1870 through the Civil Rights Era* (Seattle: University of Washington Press, 1994), 5.

18. George J. Sánchez, *Becoming Mexican American: Ethnicity, Culture and Identity in Chicano Los Angeles, 1900–1945* (New York: Oxford University Press, 1993), 137.

19. Schmid, *Social Trends in Seattle*, 149. For a recent publication about Seattle Chinatown that features short oral histories about the community, see Chew, *Reflections of Seattle's Chinese Americans*.

20. Schmid, *Social Trends in Seattle*, 97.

21. Ray Edralin Corpuz, interview by Bob Antolin, 22 September 1981, PNW81-Fil-028ba, 2.

22. Eddie Acena, interview by Bob Flor, FIL-KNG75-18bf, 26 June 1975, WSOAHP, 9; Schmid, *Social Trends in Seattle*, 131, 135. See also Monica Sone, *Nisei Daughter* (Seattle: University of Washington Press, 1953), for a detailed description of Japanese American community life.

23. Schmid, *Social Trends in Seattle*, 149.

24. Marco Aquino, "Little Manila," *Philippine Advocate*, January 1936.

25. Taylor, *Forging of a Black Community*, 86–87.

26. Ibid., 86.

27. Felipe G. Dumlao, interview by Cynthia Mejia, FIL-KNG75-35cm, 21 November 1975, WSOAHP, 24.

28. See Sone, *Nisei Daughter*.

29. Fred C. Floresca, interview by Carolina Koslosky, FIL-KNG76-2ck, 2 May 1975, WSOAHP, 17–18.

30. *Filipino Forum*, 30 January 1930.

31. *Philippine Review,* February 1931.

32. Dumlao, interview, 23.

33. Schmid, *Social Trends in Seattle,* 137–141. For more information on the African American community in Seattle during this era, see Taylor, *Forging of a Black Community,* especially chaps. 2–5. Pages 82–87 contain a discussion of African American community housing patterns.

34. Mariano Angeles, interview by Cynthia Mejia, FIL-KNG75-32cm, 6 November 1975, WSOAHP, 17. Quintard Taylor reports that African Americans were relegated to balconies in the Strand and Palomar movie houses: "Downtown department stores, such as MacDougall and Southwick, discouraged African American patronage," and "White (and occasionally Asian) restaurants and lunch counters turned away African American customers." See Taylor, *Forging of a Black Community,* 80.

35. Al Bautista [pseudonym], interview by author, Seattle, 30 September 1993. Rudy Romero also recalled segregation: "Sometimes I cannot sit here in the big theaters, or something like that." See Rudy C. Romero, interview by Teresa Cronin, FIL-KNG75-4tc, 20 March 1975, WSOAHP, 8.

36. Dumlao, interview, 67.

37. Hyung-chan Kim and Cynthia C. Mejia, comps. and eds., *The Filipinos in America, 1898–1974: A Chronology and Fact Book,* Ethnic Chronology Series, no. 23 (Dobbs Ferry, N.Y.: Oceana Publications, 1976), 12; "Not Typical American Justice," *Filipino Forum,* 30 March 1930.

38. Felix Narte, interview by Teresa Cronin, FIL-KNG75-8tc, 21 April 1975, WSOAHP, 16.

39. Dumlao, interview, 19, 67.

40. Bruno Lasker, *Filipino Immigration to Continental United States and to Hawaii,* published for the American Council, Institute of Pacific Relations (Chicago: University of Chicago Press, 1931), 103.

41. H. Brett Melendy, *Asians in America: Filipinos, Koreans, and East Indians* (Boston: Twayne, 1977), 53.

42. "Letter to the Editor," *Cosmopolitan Courier,* September 1938.

43. "Kikoy," "In the Spring Cafes Pop Up Like Mushrooms in Chinatown," *Cosmopolitan Courier,* March 1939.

44. Eddie Acena, interview, 11.

45. Pedro T. Antolin, interview by Bob Antolin, PNW81-Fil-022ba, 1 September 1981, 6.

46. John Castillo, interview by F. A. Cordova, Jr., FIL-KNG75-15jr, 29 July 1975, WSOAHP, 11–12. Felipe Dumlao remembered that a worker could take advantage of this system and, after Alaska, leave for California instead of paying debts in Seattle. The next year, the worker could claim that he had no money. See Dumlao, interview, 23.

47. Toribio Madayag, interview by Teresa Cronin, FIL-KNG75-22tc, 2 July 1975, WSOAHP, 4–5.

48. Vincent Yolenato Mendoza and Rosario Rosell Mendoza [listed as Mr. and Mrs. Vincent Mendoza], interview by Cynthia Mejia, FIL-KNG76-40cm, 13 January 1976, WSOAHP, 6–7.

49. Bautista, interview; Eddie Acena, interview, 11.

50. Sammy R. Lopez, interview by Cyn. Mejia, FIL-KNG75-36cm, 24 November 1975, WSOAHP, 11.

51. Bautista, interview.

52. Madayag, interview, 5.

53. Zacarias M. Manangan, interview by Carolina D. Koslosky, FIL-KNG75-30ck, 30 September 1975, WSOAHP, 18.

54. Toribio Martin, interview by Dorothy Cordova, 27 April 1976, FIL-KNG76-44dc, WSOAHP, 6.

55. Ray Edralin Corpuz, interview, 3.

56. Castillo, interview, 10–11.

57. Eddie Acena, interview, 12.

58. "$1,000,000 Pay-Roll Goes to Chinese Gambling Syndicate," *Philippine American Chronicle* 1, no. 1 (15 September 1934). The article also claimed that more than two thousand Filipina/os were farmworkers, the bulk of whom were students, and they lost 55 percent of their wages in gambling places. The percentage of students seems overly high and may have included Filipina/os who expressed a desire to go to school but were presently working.

59. Castillo, interview, 13.

60. Jose Acena, interview by Dorothy Cordova, FIL-KNG75-24dlc, 28 July 1975, WSOAHP, 12.

61. Trinidad Rojo, "Social Maladjustment among Filipinos in the United States," *Sociology and Social Research* 21, no. 5 (May–June 1937): 454. In one incident, Charles C. Clark, "merchant police" who was employed by a Chinatown dance hall, went to the Alps Hotel to question Fidel Molino "about extorting some money from Filipinos." Clark was seriously hurt by shots from an "unknown assailant" at 2 A.M. on January 9. See "Officer Hurt in Local Gun Battle," *Philippine American Chronicle*, 14 January 1936.

62. Peter Bacho, "A Manong's Heart," *Seattle Times*, 17 January 1982, in "Marino Guiang" file, National Pinoy Archives.

63. Marino Guiang, interview by Dorothy Cordova, FIL-KNG76-52dc, 24 September 1976, WSOAHP, 2.

64. Pete Filiarca, interview by Frederic A. Cordova, Jr., FIL-KNG75-13jr, 8 April 1975, WSOAHP, 10–11.

65. Lorenzo Pimental, interview by Cynthia Mejia, FIL-KNG75-34cm, 14 November 1975, WSOAHP, 20–21.

66. Floresca, interview, 10–13.

67. Vincent Yolenato Mendoza and Rosario Rosell Mendoza, interview, 7.

68. Sinforoso L. Ordona, interview by unknown, date unknown, PNW81-Fil, DPAA, 1–2, 9.

69. Carlos Toribio [pseud.], interview by author, Seattle, 18 July 1994.

70. Martin, interview, 1.

71. Taylor, *Forging of a Black Community*, 57.

72. Belen Braganza, interview by Nancy Koslosky, PNW81-Fil-014nk, 26 June 1981, DPAA, 3.

73. Manangan, interview, 18.

74. Dumlao, interview, 41.

75. Jesse Jackson, "Mayor" of Hooverville, "The Story of Seattle's Hoover-

ville," in Schmid, *Social Trends in Seattle,* 287. The article is reprinted in Schmid, *Social Trends in Seattle,* 286–293.

76. "The Meddler," "Tattle Tales" column, *Cosmopolitan Courier,* August 1938.

77. Dumlao, interview, 40–41.

78. Bibiana Laigo Castillano, interview by Frederic A. Cordova, Jr., FIL-KNG75-19jr, 26 June 1975, WSOAHP, 13–15, 17–21; and Sergio Aguinaldo [pseud.], interview by author, Seattle, 22 February 1994.

79. Bibiana Laigo Castillano, interview, 21.

80. Gordon Elwood Morton, "Farm Wage Earners in Washington" (master's thesis, University of Washington, 1943), 27–29.

81. Lauren W. Casaday, "Labor Unrest and the Labor Movement in the Salmon Industry of the Pacific Coast" (Ph.D. diss., University of California, Berkeley, 1938), 96; Morton, "Farm Wage Earners in Washington," 58–59.

82. Ben Rinonos, interview by Teresa Cronin, FIL-KNG-3tc, 15 September 1975, WSOAHP, 10; Rapada, interview, 13.

83. Sylvestre Tangalan, interview by Carolina D. Koslosky, FIL-KNG75-28ck, 27 August 1975, WSOAHP, 5–6.

84. Narte, interview, 17–18.

85. Brian Roberts, ed., *They Cast a Long Shadow: A History of the Non-white Races on Bainbridge Island* (Bainbridge: Minority History Committee of Bainbridge Island School District No. 303, 1975), 58–60.

86. Madayag, interview, 6; Rapada, interview, 13.

87. See Peter Bacho story "First There Were the Men," set in Seattle in the 1950s, for a demonstration of this phenomenon. The story is found in *Amerasia Journal* 19, no. 3 (1993): 138.

88. Here I want to be careful about how I use these terms, because although relationships were often established in familial terms, the implication is that they were always nonsexual, which might or might not have been the case. However, I want to pose these terms because they do capture the ways in which these kinds of relationships were often conceptualized by community members, particularly because of the impact of Philippine cultural mores.

89. The literal translation of *manong,* the term of respect used to refer to males in the community older than the speaker, demonstrates the closeness of affinity. (*Manong* actually means "older brother," indicating the degree of felt ties among community members.)

90. John Mendoza, interview by Dorothy Cordova, FIL-KNG76-42dc, 6 April 1976, WSOAHP, 3.

91. Jack Masson and Donald Guimary, "Asian Labor Contractors in the Alaskan Canned Salmon Industry: 1880–1937," *Labor History* 22, no. 3 (summer 1981): 394–395; Jack K. Masson and Donald L. Guimary, "Pilipinos and Unionization of the Alaskan Canned Salmon Industry," *Amerasia Journal* 8, no. 2 (1981): 8.

92. Charles Tilly, "Transplanted Networks," in *Immigration Reconsidered: History, Sociology, and Politics,* ed. Virginia Yans-McLaughlin (New York: Oxford University Press, 1990), 84.

93. "Filipinos' Plight in Hawaii Is Sad: Mission Attache Relates Impressions," *Philippines Herald,* 3 February 1934.

94. Lopez, interview, 11.

95. Braganza, interview, 11. Ray Edralin Corpuz also noted, "We were all males at that time, from L.A. to Seattle, you were lucky if you saw a Filipinoa *[sic]*." See Ray Edralin Corpuz, interview, 3.

96. Dumlao, interview, 68. See also Rhacel Salazar Parrenas, "'White Trash' Meets the 'Little Brown Monkeys': The Taxi Dance Hall as a Site of Interracial and Gender Alliances between White Working Class Women and Filipino Immigrant Men in the 1920s and 1930s," *Amerasia Journal* 24, no. 2 (1998): 115–134.

97. Dumlao, interview, 21.

98. Bautista, interview.

99. Stephen Griffiths, *Emigrants, Entrepreneurs, and Evil Spirits: Life in a Philippine Village* (Honolulu: University of Hawai'i Press, 1988), 29; and William F. Nydegger and Corinne Nydegger, *Tarong: An Ilocos Barrio in the Philippines,* Six Cultures Series, vol. 6 (New York: Wiley, 1966), 42.

100. The prevalence of gay, lesbian, and bisexual relationships is underdocumented in the pre–World War II history of Filpina/o America. Although it would be historically incorrect to transpose present-day readings onto the social practices of the period under study, it is important to note that anthropologist Martin F. Manalansan IV calls *bakla,* the Tagalog inclusive term for homosexuals, "an enduring social category." See Martin F. Manalansan IV, "Speaking of AIDS: Language and the Filipino 'Gay' Experience in America," in *Discrepant Histories: Translocal Essays on Filipino Cultures,* ed. Vicente L. Rafael (Manila: Anvil Publishing, 1995), 195–201.

101. Manangan, interview, 15–16.

102. See "Anti-miscegenation Laws" in *Letters in Exile: An Introductory Reader on the History of the Pilipinos in America,* ed. Jesse G. Quinsaat (Los Angeles: UCLA Asian American Studies Center, 1976), 65, 69–70; Fred Cordova, *Filipinos: Forgotten Asian Americans, A Pictorial Essay/1763-Circa-1963* (Dubuque, Iowa: Kendall/Hunt, 1983), 117.

103. Castillo, interview, 2.

104. Braganza, interview, 9–10.

105. Guiang, interview, 12.

106. Salvador Del Fierro, interview by Carolina D. Koslosky, FIL-KNG75-20ck, 15 September 1975, WSOAHP, 14.

107. Ibid., 15.

108. Martin, interview, 7.

109. Del Fierro, interview, 4.

110. Roman and Hazel Simbe, with Sinforoso Ordona, interview by Dee-Ann Dixon and Nancy Koslosky, 18 January and 22 June 1982, PNW82-Fil-030dad/nk, 12. Teodolo Ranjo also remembered the potential hostility from other people when he was with his white wife, and how his wife would respond. "She would say, 'You better look your best, honey, everybody is looking at you.' This would alarm these people, you know, so I didn't feel any, sometime when somebody get smart, you know, meet us, you know, when we are walking down, down-

town, I just curse them off." To avoid harassment, he would only go with his spouse to "high class hotel[s] or high class restaurants" where there was a lesser chance of discrimination. Teodolo Aguinaldo Ranjo, interview by Cyn. Mejia, FIL-KNG76-41cm, 14 January 1976, WSOAHP, 27.

111. Cordova, *Filipinos*, 7. See Carlos Bulosan, *America Is in the Heart: A Personal History* (Seattle: University of Washington Press, 1991), 103. In contrast to his negative characterization of a Native American woman, Bulosan tended to portray a number of white women in a more idealized manner. See, for example, his portrayal of "Marian," in *America Is in the Heart*, 209–218.

112. See Thelma Buchholdt, *Filipinos in Alaska: 1788–1958* (Anchorage: Aboriginal Press, 1996), 101.

CHAPTER 5. RESISTANCE, RETURN, AND ORGANIZATION

1. Mary Elizabeth Cronin, "Scooter-Riding Centenarian Glad to Be 'Still Living This Life,'" *Seattle Times*, 16 February 1988, in Josefa Barrazona file, National Pinoy Archives.

2. See Renato Constantino, with the collaboration of Letizia R. Constantino, *A History of the Philippines: From the Spanish Colonization to the Second World War* (New York: Monthly Review Press, 1975), 241, for the Constabulary. For more on Julian, see "Death Count Filed against Knife Wielder," *Seattle Post-Intelligencer*, 26 November 1932; "Slayer Says He Was 'Funny in the Head,'" *Seattle Post-Intelligencer*, 25 November 1932.

3. "'Grocer's Jibe Begins It All' Says Slayer," *Seattle Daily Times*, 25 November 1932; "Killer's Victim Tells Own Story," *Seattle Post Intelligencer*, 25 November 1932.

4. "Slayer Says He Was 'Funny in the Head,'" *Seattle Post-Intelligencer*, 25 November 1932; "Murderer of 6 'Feels Fine,' But Is Sorry," *Seattle Daily Times*, 25 November 1932; "6 Killed, 12 Wounded as Crazed Filipino Runs Amuck with Knife in South End," *Seattle Post-Intelligencer*, 25 November 1932.

5. "'Grocer's Jibe Begins It All.'"

6. "Slayer Says He Was 'Funny in the Head'"; "'Grocer's Jibe Begins It All'"; "Trail of Dead and Wounded Marks Killer's Mad Flight," *Seattle Post-Intelligencer*, 25 November 1932; Felipe G. Dumlao, interview by Cynthia Mejia, FIL-KNG75-35cm, 21 November 1975, WSOAHP, 34–35; Teodolo Aguinaldo Ranjo, interview by Cyn Mejia, FIL-KNG76-41cm, 14 January 1976, WSOAHP, 57–58.

7. "6 Killed, 12 Wounded."

8. "Running Amok Is Malay Way to Kill Self," *Seattle Post-Intelligencer*, 26 November 1932.

9. United Press, "Filipino, Doomed to Life Sentence, Starving Self," *Philippines Herald*, 18 April 1933; United Press, "Succumbs to Ham," *Philippines Herald*, 18 April 1933; "'Ham and ———' Ends Hunger Strike of Filipino Killer," *Seattle Post-Intelligencer*, 17 April 1933; "Slayer Goes on Hunger Strike," *Seattle Post-Intelligencer*, 16 April 1933; "Julian Breaks Hunger Strike after 3 Days," *Seattle Daily Times*, 17 April 1933; "Slayer of Six Rejects Food, Wants to Die," *Seattle Sunday Times*, 16 April 1933; "Attorneys for Julian May Ask Second Trial," *Seattle Daily Times*, 15 April 1933; "Julian Jurors Still at Odds after

48 Hours," *Seattle Daily Times,* 14 April 1933; "Julian Death Jury Blocked on Verdict," *Seattle Daily Times,* 13 April 1933; "Julian Trial Is Nearing Its End," *Seattle Daily Times,* 12 April 1933; "Both Sides Rest in Julian Case; Court Recessed," *Seattle Daily Times,* 11 April 1933; "Julian Given Life Sentence," *Seattle Post-Intelligencer,* 15 April 1933; "Jury Still at Odds in Julian Frenzy Killing," *Seattle Post-Intelligencer,* 14 April 1933; "Julian Jury in Deadlock," *Seattle Post-Intelligencer,* 13 April 1933; "State Battles Insanity Plea," *Seattle Post-Intelligencer,* 11 April 1933; "U.S. Jury Recommends against Death Penalty, Action Means Life Term; Court to Act Soon," *Philippines Herald,* 15 April 1933, "Julian Receives Life Sentence," *Seattle Daily Times,* 18 April 1933; "Julian Given Life in Prison," *Seattle Post-Intelligencer,* 19 April 1933; United Press, "Filipino, Doomed to Life Sentence, Starving Self," *Philippines Herald,* 18 April 1933; United Press, "Succumbs to Ham," *Philippines Herald,* 18 April 1933.

10. As Paul Gilroy argues regarding British discourse about blacks and criminality, "Explanations of criminal behavior are probably as old as the modern juridical system itself." See Gilroy, *"There Ain't No Black in the Union Jack": The Cultural Politics of Race and Nation* (London: Hutchinson, 1987), 77.

11. Chinese immigrants earned the dubious distinction of being the first group excluded from the United States because of race. The Chinese Exclusion Acts, the Gentleman's Agreement between the United States and Japan, and the *U.S. vs. Bhagat Singh Thind* case, in which Asian Indians were prevented from becoming naturalized citizens, were all examples of the systematic exclusion of Asians from the United States. For a concise summary of exclusionary legislation affecting Asian immigrants in the late nineteenth and early twentieth centuries, along with immigrants' resistance to these acts, see Sucheng Chan, *Asian Americans: An Interpretive History* (Boston: Twayne, 1991), chapter 5, "Resistance to Oppression," 80–100. See pp. 90–96 for a summary of legislation affecting the status of Asian Americans.

12. Jose Acena, interview by Dorothy L. Cordova, FIL-KNG75-24dlc, 28 July 1975, WSOAHP, 12–13.

13. Carlos Bulosan, *America Is in the Heart: A Personal History* (Seattle: University of Washington Press, 1991), 176.

14. Carlos Toribio [pseud.], interview by author, Seattle, 18 July 1994.

15. For more on the repatriation legislation, see Camille Guerin-Gonzales, *Mexican Workers and American Dreams: Immigration, Repatriation, and California Farm Labor, 1900–1939* (New Brunswick, N.J.: Rutgers University Press, 1994), 77, 94.

16. Karen Isaksen Leonard, *Making Ethnic Choices: California's Punjabi Mexican Americans* (Philadelphia: Temple University Press, 1992), 29, 52.

17. For a detailed discussion of Filipina/o organization strategies, see, for example, John E. Reinecke, *The Filipino Piecemeal Sugar Strike of 1924–1925* (Honolulu: Social Science Research Institute, University of Hawai'i, 1996).

18. "Filipinos Are Abused," *Washington Post,* 26 August 1911, reprint from *Seattle Times,* in RG350, 19861, NA.

19. Letter from Teodor R. Yangco to Brig. Gen. Chas. E. Walcutt, Chief, Bureau of Insular Affairs, 26671/9, "Filipino Laborers for U.S.," part 1. Yangco

also sent a cable to Osmena, apprising him of the plan. Cable, 21 August 1918, to Osmena from Yangco, RG350, Box 1103, File 26671, NA.

20. See 29 July 1919 letter from Charles M. Baxter to Frank L. Crone, 2667113A; 4 March 1920 letter from Charles M. Baxter to Charles Walcutt, 26671/16; 6 April 1920 letter from Charles M. Baxter to Charles Walcutt, 26671/19; and correspondence and other materials included in "Memorandum for the Secretary of Commerce and Communications," 26671/22A, all in RG350, Box 1103, NA.

21. War Department telegram from McIntyre, Insular Bureau, to Francisco Varona, 22 March 1921, 26671/33, RG350, Box 1103, NA.

22. "Lukban Labor Probe Bill Filed in House," *Philippines Herald,* 8 August 1930; "The Filipino Laborer in U.S.," editorial, *Philippines Herald,* 6 September 1930.

23. "Villamin Touring Filipinos' Camps," *Philippines Herald,* 26 September 1930.

24. United Press, "Villamin Warns against Immigration to America," *Philippines Herald,* October 1930.

25. "Sumulong Is Helping California Filipinos," *Philippines Herald,* 18 November 1930.

26. "Filipino Jobless in Hawaii Stage Mammoth Parade," *Philippines Herald,* 9 April 1932.

27. Reports of the extent of the unemployment varied. The secretary of war received statistics that indicated "not more than 200" were without work in Honolulu, whereas leader E. A. Toak was less optimistic, saying that more than a thousand Filipina/os were unemployed. See "Unemployed Hawaii Filipinos Demand Work or Return Fare," *Philippines Herald,* 18 April 1933. Ligot, the commissioner of labor in Hawai'i, had been controversial for a long time; he had been accused of being less responsible to Filipina/o workers and of having possibly received bribes from the Hawaii Sugar Planters' Association. Even after Ligot's position was abolished following the formation of the new position of labor inspector general, he was still under investigation, although he did have support from Masonic lodge members. Later, Ligot was replaced by Jose Figueras. See "Masons Urge Retention of C. Ligot in Hawaii," *Philippines Herald,* 5 January 1933; "Ligot Case Endorsed to Governor Halliday," *Philippines Herald,* 22 April 1933; "Decision of Ligot Case Up Soon, Sison Believes," *Philippines Herald,* 11 May 1933; "Post of Labor Commissioner in Hawaii Abolished," *Philippines Herald,* 3 August 1933; and "Murphy Orders Ligot Case Looked Into," *Philippines Herald,* 4 August 1933. See also "G. G. Advised of Figueras' Trip," *Philippines Herald,* 14 November 1933; "Hawaii Labor Leader Active," *Philippines Herald,* 19 December 1933; "Figueras to Go to Sacramento to Probe Riot," *Philippines Herald,* 4 January 1934; "Filipino Workers Hail Figueras as Labor Leader," *Philippines Herald,* 22 January 1934.

28. "Repatriation of Filipinos Now in Hawaii Is Urged," *Philippines Herald,* 21 October 1933.

29. "P.I. Workmen Respectfully Hear Leader," 24 November 1933, *Philippines Herald.* See also editorial, "Our Laborers in Hawaii," *Philippines Herald,* 24 November 1933.

30. "Our Laborers in Hawaii."

31. "Davis Is against Barring Filipinos," *Philippines Herald,* 18 September 1930.

32. Gilbert G. González, *Mexican Consuls and Labor Organizing: Imperial Politics in the American Southwest* (Austin: University of Texas Press, 1999), 101.

33. "Unemployed Farm Hands Placed at 40 Thousand," *Philippines Herald,* 1 February 1932.

34. See the records of the Bureau of Insular Affairs in Record Group 350 in the National Archives.

35. "800 Families Sent to Mindanao Last Year," *Philippines Herald,* 5 January 1933.

36. "Tenants in N. Ecija Reported Getting Bolder," *Philippines Herald,* 6 June 1932.

37. Constantino, *History of the Philippines,* 351–356. See also David R. Sturtevant, *Popular Uprisings in the Philippines, 1840–1940* (Ithaca, N.Y.: Cornell University Press, 1976), 158–192.

38. Constantino, *History of the Philippines,* 363–364; Daniel F. Doeppers, *Manila, 1900–1941: Social Change in a Late Colonial Metropolis,* Monograph Series no. 27 (New Haven, Conn.: Yale University Southeast Asia Studies, 1984), 123–133. For analysis of workers' organizations in Manila during the first half of the twentieth century, see Melinda Tria Kerkvliet, *Manila Workers' Unions, 1900–1950* (Quezon City: New Day Publishers, 1992). Kerkvliet has also documented the organization of labor federations in Manila during 1902, 1913, 1929, and 1945. Her research further explores the growth of the tobacco factory workers' union, a highly visible pre–World War II union that served the majority of Manila's income earners. The tobacco workers engaged in the majority of strikes in Manila from 1910 until the latter part of the 1930s. See Kerkvliet, *Manila Workers' Unions,* 1, 62. See also John A. Larkin, *Sugar and the Origins of Modern Philippine Society* (Berkeley and Los Angeles: University of California Press, 1993), 218–226, for more discussion of protests by workers in the sugar industry during the 1930s.

39. Constantino, *History of the Philippines,* 367–370; Sturtevant, *Popular Uprisings in the Philippines,* 215–248.

40. "Red Activities Traced by P.C.," *Philippines Herald,* 8 June 1932.

41. "Struggles of the 1930s, Luis Taruc," in *The Philippines Reader: A History of Colonialism, Neocolonialism, Dictatorship, and Resistance,* ed. Daniel B. Schirmer and Stephen Rosskamm Shalom (Boston: South End Press, 1987), 62–66. See also Luis Taruc, *Born of the People* (New York: International Publishers, 1953).

42. Constantino, *History of the Philippines,* 356–379.

43. Shirley Jenkins, "The Independence Lobby," in *The Philippines Reader: A History of Colonialism, Neocolonialism, Dictatorship, and Resistance,* ed. Daniel B. Schirmer and Stephen Rosskamm Shalom (Boston: South End Press, 1987), 55–58. For a description of resistance and protest, see Constantino, *History of the Philippines,* 364–387.

44. "Director H. Cruz Has Relief Plan," *Philippines Herald,* 1 March 1932.

45. "Filipinos Returning," *Philippines Herald,* 2 May 1932.

46. "300 Laborers Return on Pierce from Hawaii," *Philippines Herald,* 24 July 1933.

47. See Stephen Griffiths, *Emigrants, Entrepreneurs, and Evil Spirits: Life in a Philippine Village* (Honolulu: University of Hawai'i Press, 1988), 17.

48. Paula Nonacido also came back to the United States in 1940 and then returned to the Philippines in 1941. See Paula J. Nonacido, interview by Cynthia Mejia, FIL-KNG76-49cm, 7 July 1976 and 22 September 1976, WSOAHP, 3, 14, 23–25.

49. Dumlao, interview, 2.

50. Jose Acena, interview, 7, 10.

51. Bibiana Laigo Castillano, interview by Frederic A. Cordova, Jr., FIL-KNG75-19jr, 26 June 1975, WSOAHP, 10–11.

52. "Three Filipinos, Demented by Joblessness, Arrive," *Philippines Herald,* 27 September 1932.

53. "Seventy Lunatics Coming Feb. 9," *Philippines Herald,* 5 January 1933.

54. "Two 'Insane' Filipinos Arrive on Jefferson," *Philippines Herald,* 29 May 1933.

55. Correspondence from F. A. Delgado, Philippine Resident Commissioner to the United States, to Brig. Gen. Creed F. Cox, Chief, Bureau of Insular Affairs, 11 January 1935, 28342/10, NA. There is little documentation on the "forced labor camps" to which Delgado refers, although Arlene de Vera discusses the construction of a concentration camp close to Salinas built to hold Filipina/o strikers following the aftermath of the strike activity in 1934. See de Vera, "Without Parallel: The Local 7 Deportation Cases, 1949–1955," *Amerasia Journal* 20, no. 2 (1994): 1.

56. H. Brett Melendy, *Asians in America: Filipinos, Koreans, and East Indians* (Boston: Twayne, 1977), 55–57; Fred Cordova, *Filipinos: Forgotten Asian Americans, A Pictorial Essay/1763-Circa-1963* (Dubuque, Iowa: Kendall/Hunt, 1983), 118–120; Bruno Lasker, *Filipino Immigration to Continental United States and to Hawaii,* published for the American Council, Institute of Pacific Relations (Chicago: University of Chicago Press, 1931), 34–38; Benicio T. Catapusan, "The Social Adjustment of Filipinos in the United States" (Ph.D. diss., University of Southern California, 1940), 90–96. See also Emory S. Bogardus, "Filipino Repatriation," *Sociology and Social Research* 21 (1937): 67–71; Benicio T. Catapusan, "Filipino Repatriates in the Philippines," *Sociology and Social Research* 21 (September–October 1936): 72–77; J. M. Saniel, ed., *The Filipino Exclusion Movement, 1927–1935,* Occasional Papers, no. 1 (Quezon City: Institute of Asian Studies, University of the Philippines, 1967); Casiano Pagdilao Coloma, "A Study of the Filipino Repatriation Movement" (thesis, University of Southern California, 1939; reprint, San Francisco: R and E Research Associates, 1974). For a comparative analysis of Mexican repatriation programs during this period, see Guerin-Gonzales, *Mexican Workers and American Dreams,* especially pp. 77–109.

57. Bogardus, "Filipino Repatriation," 69–70.

58. See Guerin-Gonzales, *Mexican Workers and American Dreams,* 77, 94.

59. See David Takami, *Executive Order 9066: 50 Years before and 50 Years*

after, *A History of Japanese Americans in Seattle* (Seattle: Wing Luke Asian Museum, 1992).

60. Toribio Martin, interview by Dorothy Cordova, FIL-KNG76-44dc, 27 April 1976, WSOAHP, 3–4.

61. Juan V. Mina, interview by Carolina Apostol, FIL-KNG76-44cma, 30 May 1976, WSOAHP, 9.

62. Bibiana Laigo Castillano, interview, 26.

63. Catapusan, "Filipino Repatriates in the Philippines," 74–75.

64. Ibid., 75–77.

65. George J. Sánchez, *Becoming Mexican American: Ethnicity, Culture, and Identity in Chicano Los Angeles, 1900–1945* (New York: Oxford University Press, 1993), 218.

66. Catapusan, "Filipino Repatriates in the Philippines," 73–74.

67. Ibid.

68. Sánchez, *Becoming Mexican American,* 218–219.

69. See Sturtevant, *Popular Uprisings in the Philippines,* 183–192; Melinda Tria Kerkvliet, "Pablo Manlapit's Fight for Justice," *Social Process in Hawaii* 33 (1991): 153–154, 161–163.

70. Griffiths, *Emigrants, Entrepreneurs, and Evil Spirits,* 55–56.

71. C. L. R. James, *Beyond a Boundary,* with an introduction by Robert Lipsyte (New York: Pantheon Books, 1983), 72.

72. Don Velasco [pseud.], interview by author, Seattle, 9 February 1994.

73. John Mendoza, interview by Dorothy Cordova, FIL-KNG76-42dc, 6 April 1975, WSOAHP, 3.

74. Jose Acena, interview, 2; John Mendoza, interview, 2.

75. Velasco, interview.

76. Lawrence H. Fuchs, *Hawaii Pono: A Social History* (San Diego: Harcourt Brace Jovanovich, 1961), 235.

77. Andra Marhefka, "Filipino native insists on independence," [no publication information], Josefa Barrazona file, NPA; Carole Beers, "Josefa Barrazona, 106, Pioneer of Philippine Methodist Church," *Seattle Times,* 5 November 1994, Josefa Barrazona file, NPA.

78. Fred Cordova, "Maryknoll 75th Anniversary," news release, 14 October 1995, from "Maryknoll" file, NPA.

79. Fred Floresca, interview by Carolina Koslosky, FIL-KNG75-2ck, 2 May 1975, WSOAHP, 20; Mike B. Castillano, PNW81-Fil-004dc, DPAA, 12.

80. Eddie Acena, interview by Bob Flor, FIL-KNG75-18bf, 26 June 1975, WSOAHP, 1.

81. Belen Braganza, interview by Nancy Koslosky, PNW81-Fil-014nk, DPAA, 11–12, 15.

82. John Castillo, interview by F. A. Cordova, Jr., FIL-KNG75-15jr, 29 July 1975, WSOAHP, 2.

83. See Steffi San Buenaventura, "The Master and the Federation: A Filipino-American Social Movement in California and Hawaii," *Social Process in Hawaii* 33 (1991): 1969

84. Velasco, interview.

85. John Mendoza, interview, 16.

86. Velasco, interview.

87. John Mendoza, interview, 31.

88. Castillo, interview, 23–24, 26.

89. Floresca, interview, 20–21.

90. Pete Filiarca, interview by Frederic A. Cordova, Jr., FIL-KNG75-13jr, 8 April 1975, WSOAHP, 12–13.

91. Braganza, interview, 11–12.

92. Ranjo, interview, 28–29.

93. See Renqiu Yu, *To Save China, to Save Ourselves: The Chinese Hand Laundry Alliance of New York* (Philadelphia: Temple University Press, 1992).

94. Mary Paik Lee, *Quiet Odyssey: A Pioneer Korean Woman in America,* edited and with an introduction by Sucheng Chan (Seattle: University of Washington Press, 1990), 1, 72–73. See also Chan's discussion of these events in the introduction, xxvi–xxxii, and her description of the role of Korean American nationalism, l–lvi.

95. Leonard, *Making Ethnic Choices,* 82–83.

96. "Balagtas Society Makes Its Bow in Seattle April 18," *Philippine Advocate,* March 1937. See also "The National Language Problem," debating the pros and cons of English vs. Tagalog, *Philippine Advocate,* March 1937.

97. "Seattle Filipino Colony Celebrates Commonwealth Day," *Philippine Advocate,* October 1935; and "Big Celebration of New P.I. Government Is Launched by Seattle Filipinos," *Philippine-American Chronicle,* 22 October 1935; "Commonwealth Inauguration Nov. 15," *Philippine Advocate,* November 1935; "Birth of a New Nation Hailed; Quezon Gets 21-Gun Salute," *Philippine-American Chronicle,* 15 November 1935.

98. Ranjo, interview, 29–33; "C.D.A. Fraternity Fosters Industry, Love of Country," *Philippine Advocate,* February 1936.

99. See, for example, "Pres. Quezon Is Optimistic of Concession," *Philippine-American Chronicle,* 1 December 1934; and "Retention of P.I. Trade Is Favored by Murphy: Bar Japanese Imports," *Philippine-American Chronicle,* 15 March 1935.

100. *Philippine Advocate,* September 1935.

101. For example, upon the return of Raymundo Manuel to the Philippines in 1934 "to till the soil of his native land and at the same time be active in the political circles," the *Philippine-American Chronicle* named him a "Special Philippine Correspondent." See "Homeward Bound," *Philippine-American Chronicle,* 15 October 1934.

102. "General Ricarte Thinks America Should Give Filipinos Freedom," *Philippine-American Review,* February 1928, 5. See also "Philippine Island Independence Leader Residing in Japan," *Philippine-American Chronicle,* 15 September 1934.

103. *Philippine-American Chronicle,* 15 September 1934.

104. "Japan Shows Influence in Philippines as Isles' Independence Day Nearr [sic]," *Philippine-American Chronicle,* 15 December 1934.

105. Leonard, *Making Ethnic Choices,* 83. See also Chan, *Asian Americans,* 98–99.

106. Chan, *Asian Americans,* 98–99.

107. See, for example, "65,000 Filipinos to Honor Hero," *Philippine-American Chronicle*, 24 December 1935; "Communities throughout Continental United States Will Celebrate Rizal Day," *Philippine News Letter*, 15 December 1938.

108. See *Philippine Seattle Colonist*, special issue, "Rizal Day Number," 7 January 1927.

109. C. O. Arcangel, "The Significance of December 30," *Filipino Forum*, 29 December 1929.

110. "Filipino Community Honors National Hero," *Filipino Forum*, 15 December 1929.

111. Roland L. Guyotte and Barbara M. Posadas, "Celebrating Rizal Day: The Emergence of a Filipino Tradition in Twentieth-Century Chicago," in *Feasts and Celebrations in North American Ethnic Communities*, ed. Ramón A. Gutiérrez and Geneviève Fabre (Albuquerque: University of New Mexico Press, 1995), 120.

112. "No Communists in the Philippines," *Philippine-American Chronicle*, 15 September 1934.

113. "The Sakdalista Uprising," *Philippine Advocate*, May 1935.

114. "For a Philippine-American Society," *Philippine Advocate*, May 1935.

115. Trinidad Rojo, "The Philippine Uprising," *Philippine Advocate*, May 1935.

116. Enclosure to Letter Drafted ———— Addressed to the Honorable the Secretary of War, "Memorandum," 28 March 1933, 28342/10, NA.

117. De Vera, "Without Parallel," 1–25.

118. Yu, *To Save China, to Save Ourselves*, 191, 198.

119. David Takami, "Marcoses Found Liable for Seattle Cannery Workers Union Murders," *Amerasia Journal* 18, no. 1 (1992): 125–128; Cindy Domingo, ". . . Until We Have a True Democracy," *Amerasia Journal* 18, no. 1 (1992): 129–130.

120. Chris Friday, *Organizing Asian American Labor: The Pacific Coast Canned-Salmon Industry, 1870–1942* (Philadelphia: Temple University Press, 1994), 140.

121. Antonio Rodrigo [listed as Mr. Tony Rodrigo,] interview by Dorothy Cordova, FIL-KNG76-53dc, WSOAHP, 49. For an excellent discussion of the later harassment of Filipina/os in the union, see de Vera, "Without Parallel," 1–25.

122. See "First Report Un-American Activities in Washington State 1948," Report of the Joint Legislative Fact-Finding Committee on Un-American Activities, State of Washington.

123. Michael Denning, *The Cultural Front: The Laboring of American Culture in the Twentieth Century* (New York: Verso, 1996), 13, 66, 333–334. See Sánchez, *Becoming Mexican American*, 266–267, for more information on the Sleepy Lagoon case. Josephine Fowler's dissertation, "To Be Red and 'Oriental': The Experiences of Chinese and Japanese Immigrant Communists in the American Communist and International Communist Movements, 1920–WWII" (Program in American Studies, University of Minnesota, forthcoming), promises to be an important contribution to understanding the relationship of Asian Americans to the Communist Party in the United States.

124. Denning, *Cultural Front,* 16.

125. Members of the party included M. Manzon, who chaired the group, and Pedro R. Sajona, president of the Filipino Anti-Imperialist League of New York. See memorandum signed L. M. Pool, "Memorandum for Records: Subject: Call of Communists," 8 March 1934, 28342/10; "Statement of the Delegation for the Release of the Imprisoned Working Class and Peasant Leaders of the Philippines," 28342/10, NA; Memo to the Governor General of the Philippine Islands from Walter C. Short, "Subject: Statement of the Delegation for the Release of the Imprisoned Working Class and Peasant Leaders of the Philippines," 5 March 1934, 28342/10, NA. Communications in support of labor leaders in the Philippine Islands were also sent by a range of other organizations, including the Filipino Anti-Imperialist League; Angelo Herndon Branch, ILD (Brooklyn); M. Oreski Branch, ILD (South Brooklyn); Nathan Green Branch, ILD Fund (Brooklyn); Philippine Proletarian Labor Congress, Manila; Chinese Anti-Imperialist Alliance (New York City); and the Ella Reeve Bloor Branch, ILD (Santa Barbara, California), 28342/10, NA.

126. Letter from Filipino Anti-Imperialist League of New York by B. Schor, Secretary, to Franklin D. Roosevelt, 1 October 1934, 28342/10, NA.

127. (Translation) Telegram Received, The Secretary Alejando Benitez to Honorable Cordell Huyll, 19 May 1934; "Telegram Received, United Front Supporters to Secretary Cordell Hull, 21 May 1934," 28342/10, NA; Letter from the Asociacion Anti-Imperialista Puertoriqueña, Brooklyn, New York, 28342/10, NA.

CHAPTER 6. INSIDERS AND OUTSIDERS

1. Margaret M. Mislang, interview by Carolina Koslosky, FIL-KNG76-12ck, 16 June 1975, WSOAHP, 8.

2. Michael Denning, *The Cultural Front: The Laboring of American Culture in the Twentieth Century* (London: Verso, 1996), 6–7; George J. Sánchez, *Becoming Mexican American: Ethnicity, Culture and Identity in Chicano Los Angeles, 1900–1945* (New York: Oxford University Press, 1993), 240.

3. James R. Green, *The World of the Worker: Labor in Twentieth-Century America* (New York: Hill and Wang, 1980), 161.

4. Ibid., 160–162.

5. Ibid., 150.

6. Cletus Daniel, *Bitter Harvest: A History of California Farmworkers, 1870–1941* (Berkeley and Los Angeles: University of California Press, 1982), 258–262; Devra Weber, *Dark Sweat, White Gold: California Farm Workers, Cotton, and the New Deal* (Berkeley and Los Angeles: University of California Press, 1994), 123–126.

7. Weber, *Dark Sweat, White Gold,* 126.

8. Denning, *Cultural Front,* 4.

9. See, for example, Toribio Martin, interview by Dorothy Cordova, FIL-KNG76-44dc, 27 April 1976, WSOAHP, 1; George A. Valdez, "Brief History of Local 37," in International Longshoremen's & Warehousemen's Union, 1952 Yearbook, Local 37, ed. Carlos Bulosan, 12.

10. Howard De Witt, *Violence in the Fields: California Filipino Farm Labor*

Unionization during the Great Depression (Saratoga, N.Y.: Century Twenty One, 1980), 19–20.

11. See Miriam Sharma, "Labor Migration and Class Formation among the Filipinos in Hawaii, 1906–1946," in *Labor Immigration under Capitalism: Asian Workers in the United States before World War II,* ed. Lucie Cheng and Edna Bonacich (Berkeley and Los Angeles: University of California Press, 1984), 596–599; Ronald Takaki, *Strangers from a Different Shore: A History of Asian Americans* (Boston: Little, Brown, 1989), 152–155; Luis V. Teodoro Jr., ed., *Out of This Struggle: The Filipinos in Hawaii,* published for the Filipino Seventy-fifth Anniversary Commemoration Commission (Honolulu: University Press of Hawaii, 1981), 20–21.

12. Manlapit had a problematic reputation. While acknowledged as a key labor leader, he was also suspected as being in collusion with the planters in the 1920 strike and to have turned against the Japanese workers. Lawrence H. Fuchs, *Hawaii Pono: A Social History* (New York: Harcourt Brace Jovanovich, 1961), 214–225; Takaki, *Strangers from a Different Shore,* 152–155. See also Melinda Tria Kerkvliet, "Pablo Manlapit's Fight for Justice," *Social Process in Hawaii* 33 (1991): 153–168.

13. Records of the Bureau of Insular Affairs, General Records Relating to More Than One Island Possession, General Classified Files, 1898–1945, Entry 5, RG350, 3037–40 to 103, "Laborers from P.I. for Hawaii," Part 1, 3037/88–3037/90, NA; Sharma, "Labor Migration and Class Formation," 598.

14. United Press, *Philippines Herald,* 28 June 1933.

15. Sharma, "Labor Migration and Class Formation," 589, 596, 598, 600.

16. Sucheng Chan, *Asian Americans: An Interpretive History* (New York: Twayne, 1991), 87–88.

17. Howard A. De Witt, "The Filipino Labor Union: The Salinas Lettuce Strike of 1934," *Amerasia Journal* 5, no. 2 (1978): 1, 4; De Witt, *Violence in the Fields,* 13–14, 16–18.

18. De Witt, "Filipino Labor Union," 10–13; De Witt, *Violence in the Fields,* 56–110; Hyung-chan Kim and Cynthia C. Mejia, compilers and editors, *The Filipinos in America, 1898–1974: A Chronology and Fact Book* (Dobbs Ferry, N.Y.: Oceana Publications, 1976), 19; Carey McWilliams, *Factories in the Field: The Story of Migratory Farm Labor* (Santa Barbara, Calif.: Peregrine Smith, 1971), 133. For more on the organizing strategies of the CAWIU, see Devra Weber, *Dark Sweat, White Gold,* 79–83, 91–97, 204–206. For a general history of California farm labor prior to World War II, see Daniel, *Bitter Harvest.*

19. I am influenced here by William Cronon's study of the development of the metropolis of Chicago. Cronon stresses the great changes created by "the twin birth of city and hinterland" in the nineteenth century. As he writes, "The environmental dynamics of western places eventually had as much to do with their hinterland status as with their ecology." See William Cronon, *Nature's Metropolis: Chicago and the Great West* (New York: Norton, 1991), 264–265.

20. Valdez, "Brief History of Local 37," 12.

21. David Montgomery, *The Fall of the House of Labor: The Workplace, the State, and American Labor Activism, 1865–1925* (Cambridge: Cambridge University Press, 1987), 92–96.

22. Ponce Torres, interview by Carolina Koslosky, FIL-KNG75-14ck, 25 August 1975, WSOAHP, 6–7.

23. Ibid., 8.

24. Ibid., 7.

25. Cannery Workers and Farm Laborers' Union, "Minutes—Executive Board and Membership Meetings, bound together. 1933–1936. Folder No. 1/1," Manuscripts, Special Collections, University Archives, University of Washington. Hereafter, Manuscripts, Special Collections, University Archives, University of Washington, will be referred to as UW. Lauren Casaday provides a similar account of the organization of Local 18257, but perhaps because it relies heavily on Duyungan's testimony, it focuses on Duyungan's role in the founding of the union. See Lauren W. Casaday, "Labor Unrest and the Labor Movement in the Salmon Industry of the Pacific Coast" (Ph.D. diss., University of California, Berkeley, 1938), 357–361.

26. Julio Cortez [pseud.], interview by author, Seattle, 4 May 1993.

27. Diane Frank, *Purchasing Power: Consumer Organizing, Gender, and the Seattle Labor Movement, 1919–1929* (Cambridge: Cambridge University Press, 1994), 9, 233–234.

28. Valdez, "Brief History of Local 37," 12. For a detailed summary of the initial formation of Local 18257, CWFLU, see Chris Friday, *Organizing Asian American Labor: The Pacific Coast Canned-Salmon Industry, 1870–1942* (Philadelphia: Temple University Press, 1984), 136–145.

29. Jack Masson and Donald Guimary, "Asian Labor Contractors in the Alaskan Canned Salmon Industry: 1880–1937," *Labor History* 22, no. 3 (summer 1981): 396; Teodolo Ranjo, interview by Cyn Mejia, FIL-KNG76-41cm, 14 January 1976, WSOAHP, 46.

30. Mislang, interview, 9.

31. See Judy Yung, *Unbound Feet: A Social History of Chinese Women in San Francisco* (Berkeley and Los Angeles: University of California Press, 1995), 209–222, for a discussion of a strike by garment workers in San Francisco Chinatown in 1938.

32. By 1930, the Filipino Laborers' Association was organizing in Seattle, with Joe de Guzman as its president. See "The Filipino Laborers' Association," *Filipino Forum*, 15 May 1930; "Dean Bocobo Endorses Filipino Laborers' Association" and "Why We Should Join the Filipino Laborers' Association," *Filipino Forum*, 15 June 1930; advertisement, *Filipino Forum*, 30 June 1930. The Filipino Laborers' Association did not include cannery workers and, not surprisingly, was based on "ethnic exclusiveness," according to historian Chris Friday. See Friday, *Organizing Asian American Labor*, 136. A 1930 riot in Auburn, Washington, in the White River Valley area, led to a meeting organized by Joe de Guzman, the president of the Filipino Laborers' Association, representatives from the Japanese Growers' Association, and the police. As a result, the Japanese growers agreed to raise the salaries of Filipina/o workers. See Hyung-chan Kim and Cynthia C. Mejia, comps. and eds., *The Filipinos in America, 1898–1974: A Chronology and Fact Book*, Ethnic Chronology Series, no. 23 (Dobbs Ferry, N.Y.: Oceana Publications, 1976), 13. Bruno Lasker reports that in May 1930, white workers raided camps containing two hundred Filipina/os over the

alleged undercutting of wages. Filipina/os were being used to prepare vegetables for shipping, a job formerly occupied by whites, and the hourly pay had decreased from sixty cents to twenty-five cents. See Lasker, *Filipino Immigration to Continental United States and to Hawaii*, published for the American Council, Institute of Pacific Relations (Chicago: University of Chicago Press, 1931), 17. This kind of worker organization was countered with a response from the bosses. In 1931 the Philippine Commerce and Labor Council of America was organized by "Filipino business men and some prominent Seattle Filipina/o residents" to address labor issues—apparently from the viewpoint of the contractors. Leaders included major contractors such as Valeriano Sarusal, Pedro Santos, and Pio De Cano. See "F.C. & L.C. of America Elect Officers," *Philippine-American Review*, February 1928, 7; and "(Pangulong Tudling) Ang F.C. & L.C. of America," *Philippine-American Review*, February 1928, 9.

33. Antonio Manzano [pseud.], interview by author, Seattle, 4 October 1993.

34. Monroe was the site of labor unrest in 1932. C. H. Frye was a Seattle meat packer who ran a large lettuce farm in the Snohomish Valley. During the height of harvesting, up to 1,500 workers would be used to prepare the lettuce for sale elsewhere, largely in Chicago. Most of the workers consisted of casual help from the area and migratory workers, including 250 Filipina/os. These laborers earned eight to twelve cents per hour. Low wages and poor management contributed to worker discontent, leading to fights, property damage, and a three-day strike. During this time, two Filipina/os were killed, the result of a private quarrel among themselves. No changes were made, and the workers came back after this work stoppage.

The following year in Yakima Valley, an estimated 250 farmers harassed and beat up one hundred people meeting in Congdon's orchard to protest working conditions for peach and pear workers. The "so-called strikers" were arrested and locked in the city jail, while the National Guard was called in. To break up the crowd in Yakima, the National Guard used teargas bombs, resulting in more agitation. Despite an alleged influx of "Communists, IWW's and union leaders," there were apparently no formal consequences of this episode in 1933. See Gordon Elwood Morton, "Farm Wage Earners in Washington" (master's thesis, University of Washington, 1943), 91–94. In 1935, however, Filipina/os in Yakima Valley joined forces to create the Filipino Farmers' Market Co-operative, which eventually was declared illegal following changes in alien land laws. See Gail Nomura, "Within the Law: The Establishment of Filipino Leasing Rights on the Yakima Indian Reservation," *Amerasia Journal* 13, no. 1 (1986–1987): 116.

35. Manangan, interview, 12–14; see also Jesus R. Yambao, in Chris Mensalvas and Jesus R. Yambao, interview by Koslosky, FIL-KNG75-1ck, 10 February and 11 February 1975, WSOAHP, 18.

36. Sucheng Chan, "European and Asian Immigration into the United States," in *Immigration Reconsidered: History, Sociology, and Politics,* ed. Virginia Yans-McLaughlin (New York: Oxford University Press, 1990), 65–66.

37. Daniel, *Bitter Harvest*, 258–262.

38. Weber, *Dark Sweat, White Gold*, 164, 180–184.

39. The roster included Pio De Cano of the Manila Corporation, the lead-

ing contractor; contractor Valeriano Sarusal of Luzon Visayas Mindanao, Inc.; contractor Pedro Santos of the Philippine Investment Corporation; Vicente Agot from the Philippine Trading Co., Inc.; F. Urbano of the Urbano Electric Pencil Co.; other contractors Emiliano Sibonga, Valeriano Laigo, E. Seveilla, and Domingo Panis; and representatives from the *Philippine Digest*, the *Philippine-American Review*, and the University of Washington. See "F.C & L.C. of America Elect Officers," *Philippine-American Review*, February 1928, 7.

40. "Pio De Cano Offers Scholarship Prizes to U. of W. Filipino Students," *Philippine Advocate*, April 1936, 1.

41. "Filipinos Ask Canners' Aid," *Philippine-American Review*, February 1928; Friday, *Organizing Asian American Labor*, 130–131.

42. Ranjo, interview, 24; Emiliano Alfonzo Francisco, interview by Ms. Koslosky, FIL-KNG75-20k, 30 June 1975, WSOAHP, 13.

43. "U.F.C. Drives for Clubhouse," *Filipino Forum*, 13 October 1928; "Untitled," *Filipino Forum*, 30 October 1928; "University Filipino Clubhouse to Open in Near Future," *Filipino Forum*, 15 November 1928; "Clubhouse Movement Fails," *Filipino Forum*, 30 November 1928; "The Failure of the Clubhouse Movement," *Filipino Forum*, 15 December 1928.

44. "Editorial," *Filipino Forum*, 15 December 1928.

45. These board members were Vincent Agot, E. Azusanao, and Emiliano Sibonga, a contractor. With the departure of Leonard C. Galima, a University of Washington graduate, to the Philippines, the remaining members were Vincente Navea; P. Santos, a contractor; V. Sarusal, a contractor; V. M. Laigo, a contractor; E. Resos; P. De Cano, a contractor; U. Canesal; G. N. Perez; J. Dionisio; L. Zamora; and Placida De Cano, Pio De Cano's sister and one of the few women leaders involved in the contracting business. See editorial, *Filipino Forum*, 15 April 1930.

46. V. A. Velasco, "My Charges against the Administration of the University Filipino Clubhouse Fund," *Filipino Forum*, 15 June 1930. See also letter to the editor by J. Mendoza in the same issue, and "Filipino Clubhouse Campaign Is Losing Good Supporters," and "Announcement," *Filipino Forum*, 15 January 1930, 5; Ven M. Ysay, "What Is Wrong with the Clubhouse Fund," *Filipino Forum*, 30 January 1930.

47. Teodolo Aguinaldo Ranjo, interview by Cyn Mejia, FIL-KNG76-41cm, 14 January 1976, WSOAHP, 24; Sylvestre A. Tangalan, interview by Carolina D. Koslosky, FIL-KNG75-28ck, 27 August 1975, WSOAHP, 17–18.

48. "Chinatown Whispers" column, *Philippine-American Chronicle*, 1 November 1934.

49. For a detailed description of a queen contest in the Philippines, see Stephen Griffiths, *Emigrants, Entrepreneurs, and Evil Spirits: Life in a Philippine Village* (Honolulu: University of Hawai'i Press, 1988), 61–68. Griffiths documents a queen contest held in conjunction with the Bawang Progressive Club.

50. "1926 Rizal Day Biggest Ever"; "How Popularity Crown Was Won," 4; "More about Popularity Race," 11; *Philippine Seattle Colonist*, 7 January 1927.

51. *Philippine Advocate*, May 1936.

52. *Philippine Advocate*, July 1936.

53. *Philippine Advocate*, June 1936.

54. *Philippine Advocate,* July 1936.

55. A custom from the Philippines, a box social involved candidates' bringing a box of food to an event; the boxes were sold to the highest bidder. Typically, men competed to buy boxes prepared by young women, and to purchase dance time with them. The generated funds were donated to communal organizations. Constance "Connie" Ortega, interview by Dorothy L. Cordova and Nancy Koslosky, PNW81-Fil-017dc/nk, 20 July 1981, DPAA, 8–9.

56. Rita Camposano dropped inexplicably from 10,000 votes to 8,150, and Lorena Campo showed with 1,843 votes. Kathleen Darrah was not mentioned. See *Advocate-Tribune,* 14 November 1936. Peggy Nelson had previously left the contest because of health reasons, and Betty Woods also decided to make an early exit from the contestant pool. See *Philippine Advocate,* October 1936.

57. This point was also made by Dawn Mabalon, in a presentation at the 2001 Filipino American National Historical Society conference in Virginia Beach. Mabalon is conducting pivotal research on the Stockton Filipina/o American community for her dissertation at Stanford University.

58. "Janet Beers Leads in Queen Contest," *Advocate-Tribune,* 14 November 1936. I deduce that Kathleen Darrah, Peggy Nelson, and Betty Woods were European American because their ethnicity was not named in candidate profiles; candidates Rita Camposano, Angelica Floresca, and Lorena Campo were identified as Filipina. I suspect that if the first three were women of color, their ethnicity would have been identified. See "Popular Candidates Greet Alaskeros," *Philippine Advocate,* August 1936.

59. "Quotas Assigned the Different Filipino Organizations for the Commonwealth Celebration Fund," *Philippine Advocate,* October 1936.

60. Ponce Torres, interview, 8–9.

61. Ibid., 8.

62. Jack K. Masson and Donald L. Guimary, "Pilipinos and Unionization of the Alaskan Canned Salmon Industry," *Amerasia Journal* 8, no. 2 (1981): 24–25.

63. Ranjo, interview, 47.

64. Julio Cortez, interview, 4 May 1993.

65. The foremen included in the CWFLU were not supposed to have economic interests in firms through which they were employed. See Friday, *Organizing Asian American Labor,* 138; "Filipinos Reluctant to Pick Hops," *Philippine-American Chronicle,* 15 September 1934; "Constitution of the Cannery Workers' and Farm Laborers' Union," CWFLU Records, Box 7, Folder 7/1.

66. Casaday, "Labor Unrest," 363–366; Gold, "Development of Local Number 7," 45–46.

67. Ibid.

68. "Larceny Charge Dismissed," *Philippine-American Chronicle,* 3, no. 6 (10 September 1935): 1, 3.

69. According to Jack Masson and Donald Guimary, Duyungan later admitted his guilt in Seattle Superior Court and was sentenced to prison. However, despite Duyungan's misdeeds and consequent suspension from the union, he was reelected after he finished his sentence. See Masson and Guimary, "Pilipinos and Unionization," 15–16.

70. Friday, *Organizing Asian American Labor,* 158.

71. Ibid., 138–139.

72. National Industrial Recovery Administration Hearing on Code of Fair Practices and Competition Presented by the Canned Salmon Industry, San Francisco, California, 27 February 1934, 368.

73. Ibid., 369.

74. Ibid., 365–372.

75. Ibid., 382.

76. Casaday, "Labor Unrest," addendum, 22.

77. Friday, *Organizing Asian American Labor*, 140.

78. Ibid., 158.

79. Casaday, "Labor Unrest," 621; Masson and Guimary, "Pilipinos and Unionization," 16.

80. Casaday, "Labor Unrest," 367.

81. "Seattle Filipinos Form Strong Labor Protective Ass'n," *Philippine Advocate*, 1, no. 2 (April 1935): 1, Casaday, "Labor Unrest," 361.

82. "C.W. & F.L.U. Resents Intervention of the Filipino Protective Ass'n," *Philippine-American Chronicle*, 15 May 1935.

83. Ponce Torres, interview, 21.

84. Ibid.

85. Friday, *Organizing Asian American Labor*, 140.

86. Ibid., 141.

87. Casaday, "Labor Unrest," 370–373.

88. Ibid., 378.

89. Ponce Torres, interview, 10.

90. Julio Cortez, interview, 4 May 1993; Ranjo, interview, 46.

91. Julio Cortez, interview, 4 May 1993.

92. Ranjo, interview, 46–47.

93. Ponce Torres, interview, 14. Not surprisingly, the University Club members of University YMCA were unable to offer "material help" to the Duyungan-Simon Memorial Fund. See Minutes of the Regular Membership Meeting, Sailors' Union Hall, 30 March 1937, Box 1, Folder 1/4, CWFLU Records, UW.

94. Interview, 4 May 1993.

95. Reports of Negotiating Committee, April 13, 1937, Box 1, Folder 1/4, CWFLU Records, UW.

96. Regular Membership Meeting, January 10, 1937, Box 1, Folder 1/3, CWFLU Records, UW.

97. Even though Duyungan had brought cannery laborers through pickets set up by longshoremen in 1934 and 1935, the CWFLU had also given "several thousand dollars" to their strike fund, according to Masson and Guimary, "Pilipinos and Unionization," 19.

98. Regular Executive Board Meeting held on February 8, 1937, Box 1, Folder 1/4, CWFLU Records. Brother Woolf was likely George Woolf. See Friday, *Organizing Asian American Labor*, 169.

99. In February 1937, Leo Flynn told the CWFLU that the AFL was planning to initiate another Alaskan cannery workers union. The Japanese Cannery Workers Association was granted a charter as Alaska Cannery Workers Union Local 20454 at the beginning of April. Although Leo Flynn of the AFL demanded

that negotiations be held up so that the new local could be present, "[t]he Canned Salmon Industry did not wish to become embroiled in yet another workers' jurisdictional dispute," as Masson and Guimary write. The canners decided to support the CWFLU. See Masson and Guimary, "Pilipinos and Unionization," 19–20; "Minutes of Regular Membership Meeting Held at the Purse Seiners' Hall, April 20, 1937," Box 1, Folder 1/4, CWFLU Records, UW; "Minutes of Special Membership Meeting Held at the Sailors' Union Hall, April 26, 1937," Box 1, Folder 1/4, CWFLU Records, UW; Masson and Guimary, "Asian Labor Contractors," 396–397; Casaday, "Labor Unrest," 716; Friday, *Organizing Asian American Labor*, 158.

100. Masson and Guimary, "Pilipinos and Unionization," 22. Conrad Espe was one of the most important European American leftists to work with the union. A former organizer for the Fishermen and Cannery Workers' Industrial Union, Espe began working for the CWFLU before joining UCAPAWA, later returning to the CWFLU to encourage it to become an affiliate of the UCAPAWA. See Friday, *Organizing Asian American Labor*, 163.

101. "On the Court Proceedings," "Minutes of the Emergency Committee Meeting, September 13, 1937," Box 1, Folder 1/5, CWFLU Records, UW.

102. Another 169 votes were discarded by the NLRB.

103. Green, *World of the Worker*, 161.

104. Ponce Torres, interview, 15.

105. For example, Brother Olson, the secretary for District Number 1 of the UCAPAWA, argued at a 1938 membership meeting for the importance of a farm division to counter the "vigilante activities of the Associated Farmers of Kent, Auburn, Yakima." See Membership Meeting, 16 January 1938, Box 2, Folder 2/9, CWFLU Records, UW.

106. "Farm Policy Committee," "Minutes of the Regular Membership Meeting Held at the Sailors' Union Hall on March 30, 1937," Box 1, Folder 1/4, CWFLU Records, UW. According to a circular letter sponsored by the Agricultural Policy Committee of the union advocating for better conditions, farm laborers in Bainbridge Island earned "a starvation wage of Twenty Cents . . . an hour with no increase in pay for overtime work, and such wage is not paid until after three or four months or after the season is over." The letter further stated that laborers did not receive economic compensation for their work "in many cases." See letter from P. Torres, to the Secretary, Japanese Berry Growers Association, Bainbridge Island, 20 February 1937, Box 7, Folder 7/10, CWFLU Records, UW.

107. Letter from Ponce Torres, Secretary, Cannery Workers and Farm Laborers Union Local No. 18257 and Chairman, Farm Organizational Committee to Mayor R. E. Wooden, Kent, Washington, 15 April 1937, Box 7, Folder 7/10, CWFLU Records, UW.

108. "Farm Policy Committee," "Minutes of the Regular Membership Meeting Held at the Sailors' Union Hall April 13, 1937," Box 1, Folder 1/4, CWFLU Records, UW.

109. Executive Board Meeting 15 January 1938, Box 1, Folder 1/7, CWFLU Records; Membership Meeting, 16 January 1938, Box 2, Folder 2/9, CWFLU Records, UW.

110. In one 1940 hearing, second foreman Lorenzo C. Ompoc spoke of a difficult workday that lasted over sixteen hours in which some of these ethnic divisions were revealed: "The Visayans kept working; the Ilocanos were talking among themselves in dialect, and I couldn't understand what they were saying." Executive Board Meeting, 20 May 1940, Box 1, Folder 1/13, CWFLU Records, UW.

111. Pre-Election Rally Meeting, 2 May 1938, Box 2, Folder 2/10, CWFLU Records, UW.

112. "Special Executive Council Meeting," 28 June 1941, Box 2, Folder 2/3, CWFLU Records, UW.

113. Membership Meeting, 13 March 1938, Box 1, Folder 1/7, CWFLU Records, UW.

114. Executive Board Minutes, 8 March and 9 March 1938, Box 1, Folder 1/7, CWFLU Records; Executive Council Meeting, 20 December 1940, Box 1, Folder 1/14, CWFLU Records, UW.

115. In the meeting, Varona denied a newspaper article that claimed that Bellosillo suggested that Filipina/os not join the CIO upon Varona's words, and accepted an invitation by Espe "to attend the CIO industrial council." Membership Meeting, 13 March 1938, Box 2, Folder 2/10, CWFLU Records, UW.

116. Regular Membership Meeting, 20 January 1940, Box 2, Folder 2/12, CWFLU Records, UW.

117. Correspondence from C. O. Abella, President, to Clarence D. Martin, Governor of the State of Washington, 19 March 1937, Box 7, Folder 7/10, CWFLU Records, UW.

118. Trinidad Rojo, personal document lent to author [unpaged].

119. Masson and Guimary, "Pilipinos and Unionization," 25.

120. Bibiana Laigo Castillano, interview by Frederic A. Cordova, Jr., FIL-KNG 75-19jr, 26 June 1975, WSOAHP, 8–10, 13.

121. Ibid., 10–11, 13, 21, 22; "Prominent Filipino Businessman Murdered at Downtown Office," *Philippine-American Chronicle*, 26 February 1936.

122. Ibid., 13–14.

123. Ibid., 14, 18, 21.

124. Ibid., 14–15.

125. Ibid., 14.

126. Ibid., 21.

127. Ibid., 15, 20.

128. Ibid., 15.

129. "In the Superior Court of the State of Washington in and for King County, Matilde Simon, Plaintiff vs. Cannery Workers and Farm Laborers Union, Local 18257, a voluntary unincorporated association, and I. R. Cabatit, Amado Lugan, Antonio Rodrigo, John Doe Abella, and Vicente Navia [sic], Defendants," No. 303997, Filed 16 December 1937.

130. Simon case, Complaint, 1–3, "Application for Appointment of Guardian Ad Litem," 1.

131. Simon case, "Order Appointing Guardian Ad Litem," 1. See Friday, *Organizing Asian American Labor*, 140–141, for a discussion of Ayamo.

132. Simon case, "Stipulation," 1–2.

133. "In the Superior Court of the State of Washington in and for King County, Margaret Duyungan, Plaintiff vs. Cannery Workers and Farm Laborers Union, Local 18257, a voluntary, unincorporated association, and I. R. Cabatit, Amado Logan, Antonio Rodrigo, John Doe Abella, and Vicente Navia [sic], Defendants, Complaint," 1–3; "Duyungan-Simon Memorial Fund, Receipts and Disbursement for the Period December 2, 1936 to December 20, 1937," Duyungan case.

134. "In the Justice Court for Seattle Precinct of King County before Justice William Hoar, May 23, 1939, State of Washington vs. Ireno [sic] R. Cabatit, Antonio and Amado Logan, Defendants, 310203," 14.

135. Mislang, interview, 15.

136. Duyungan case, decree, 1.

137. Sucheng Chan, *Asian Americans: An Interpretive History* (Boston: Twayne, 1991), 84–85.

138. Vicki L. Ruiz, *Cannery Women, Cannery Lives: Mexican Women, Unionization, and the California Food Processing Industry, 1930–1950* (Albuquerque: University of New Mexico Press, 1987), xiii.

139. Lizabeth Cohen, *Making a New Deal: Industrial Workers in Chicago, 1919–1939* (New York: Cambridge University Press, 1990), 358–359.

140. See Thelma Buchholdt, *Filipinos in Alaska: 1788–1958* (Anchorage: Aboriginal Press, 1996), 105, for a description of a 1938 Rizal Day in Juneau.

141. Ibid., 80–82.

142. Ibid., 72.

143. See, for example, Carlos Bulosan's discussion of "Belle" in *America Is in the Heart: A Personal History* (Seattle: University of Washington Press, 1991).

CONCLUSION: THE PAST AND THE FUTURE

1. See David Takami, "Marcoses Found Liable for Seattle Cannery Workers Union Murders," *Amerasia Journal* 18, no. 1 (1992): 125–128; Cindy Domingo, ". . . Until We Have a True Democracy," *Amerasia Journal* 18, no. 1 (1992): 129–130.

2. Raquel Z. Ordoñez, "Mail-Order Brides: An Emerging Community," in *Filipino Americans: Transformation and Identity,* ed. Maria P. P. Root (Thousand Oaks, Calif.: Sage, 1997), 137–138.

3. Kay Anderson, *Vancouver's Chinatown: Racial Discourse in Canada, 1875–1980* (Montreal: McGill–Queen's University Press, 1991).

4. See Susan Lee Johnson, "'A Memory Sweet to Soldiers': The Significance of Gender in the History of the 'American West,'" *Western Historical Quarterly* 24, no. 4 (November 1993): 499, for a discussion of how the organization of these categories reflects relations of power around categories such as race and gender.

5. For a general overview, which includes a discussion of the longevity of the "assimilationist" framework, see Virginia Yans-McLaughlin's introduction to Virginia Yans-McLaughlin, ed., *Immigration Reconsidered: History, Sociology, and Politics* (New York: Oxford University Press, 1990), 3–18.

6. Benedict Anderson, *Imagined Communities: Reflections on the Origin and Spread of Nationalism* (London: Verso, 1985).

7. See Michael Frisch, *A Shared Authority: Essays on the Craft and Meaning of Oral and Public History* (Albany: State University of New York Press, 1990), especially his essays "The Memory of History," 15–27, and "Quality in History Programs: From Celebration to Exploration of Values," 183–190.

Bibliography

PRINTED SOURCES

Abad, Ricardo G., and Benjamin V. Carino, with the assistance of Benilda Reye-Escutir. *Micro-Level Determinants of Migration Intentions in the Ilocos: A Preliminary Analysis: Final Report.* Submitted to the Population Center Foundation by the Institute of Philippine Culture, 16 December 1981. Quezon City: Institute of Philippine Culture, Ateneo de Manila University, 1981.

Abbott, Carl. "Regional City and Network City: Portland and Seattle in the Twentieth Century." *Western Historical Quarterly* 23, no. 3 (August 1992): 293–332.

Alegado, Dean T. "The Filipino Community in Hawaii: Development and Change." *Social Process in Hawaii* 33 (1991): 12–38.

Almaguer, Tomás. *Racial Fault Lines: The Historical Origins of White Supremacy in California.* Berkeley and Los Angeles: University of California Press, 1994.

American Social History Project, City University of New York, under the direction of Herbert G. Gutman. *Who Built America? Working People and the Nation's Economy, Politics, Culture, and Society.* Vol. 1, *From Conquest and Colonization through Reconstruction and the Great Uprising of 1877.* New York: Pantheon, 1989.

Amott, Teresa, and Julie Mattaei. *Race, Gender, and Work: A Multicultural Economic History of Women in the United States.* Boston: South End Press, 1991.

Anderson, Benedict. *Imagined Communities: Reflections on the Origin and Spread of Nationalism.* London: Verso, 1985.

Anderson, Kay. *Vancouver's Chinatown: Racial Discourse in Canada, 1875–1980.* Montreal: McGill–Queen's University Press, 1991.

Anderson, Robert N., with Richard Coller and Rebecca F. Pestano. *Filipinos in Rural Hawaii*. Honolulu: University of Hawai'i Press, 1984.

Appadurai, Arjun. "Disjuncture and Difference in the Global Cultural Economy." *Public Culture* 2, no. 2 (spring 1990): 1–24.

Asian Women United of California, ed. *Making Waves: An Anthology of Writings by and about Asian American Women*. Boston: Beacon Press, 1989.

Aurelio, Manuel F. "The Birth of Ilocos Norte." *Ilocos Review* 20 (1988): 1–34.

Bacho, E. V. "Vic." *The Long Road: Memoirs of a Filipino Pioneer*. Self-published, 1992.

Bacho, Peter. "First There Were the Men." *Amerasia Journal* 19, no. 3 (1993): 135–141.

Barth, Gunther. *Bitter Strength: A History of the Chinese in the United States, 1850–1870*. Cambridge, Mass.: Harvard University Press, 1964.

Basch, Linda, Nina Glick Schiller, and Cristina Szanton Blanc. *Nations Unbound: Transnational Projects, Postcolonial Predicaments, and Deterritorialized Nation-States*. N.p.: Gordon and Breach, 1994.

Berner, Richard C. *Seattle, 1900–1920: From Boomtown, Urban Turbulence, to Restoration*. Seattle: Charles Press, 1991.

———. *Seattle, 1921–1940: From Boom to Bust*. Seattle: Charles Press, 1992.

Beyer, Henry Otley, ed. *Ethnography of the Iloko People (A Collection of Original Sources)*. Vols. 1–4. Manila, 1918–1922. Microform, Kroch Library, Cornell University.

Blumin, Stuart. *The Emergence of the Middle Class: Social Experience in the American City, 1760–1900*. Cambridge: Cambridge University Press, 1989.

Bodnar, John. *The Transplanted: A History of Immigrants in Urban America*. Bloomington: Indiana University Press, 1985.

Bogardus, Emory S. "Anti-Filipino Race Riots: A Report Made to the Ingram Institute of Social Science, of San Diego, by E. S. Bogardus, University of Southern California, May 15, 1930." In Howard A. De Witt, *Anti-Filipino Movements in California: A History, Bibliography and Study Guide*, 88–111. San Francisco: R and E Research Associates, 1976.

———. "Filipino Repatriation." *Sociology and Social Research* 21 (1937): 67–71.

Bonacich, Edna. "Asian Labor in the Development of California and Hawaii." In *Labor Immigration under Capitalism: Asian Workers in the United States before World War II*, edited by Lucie Cheng and Edna Bonacich, 130–185. Berkeley and Los Angeles: University of California Press, 1984.

———. "Some Basic Facts: Patterns of Asian Immigration and Exclusion." In *Labor Immigration under Capitalism: Asian Workers in the United States before World War II*, edited by Lucie Cheng and Edna Bonacich, 60–78. Berkeley and Los Angeles: University of California Press, 1984.

———. "U.S. Capitalist Development: A Background to Asian Immigration." In *Labor Immigration under Capitalism: Asian Workers in the United States before World War II*, edited by Lucie Cheng and Edna Bonacich, 79–129. Berkeley and Los Angeles: University of California Press, 1984.

Bonacich, Edna, and Lucie Cheng. "Introduction: A Theoretical Orientation to International Labor Migration." In *Labor Immigration under Capitalism:*

Asian Workers in the United States before World War II, edited by Lucie Cheng and Edna Bonacich, 1–56. Berkeley and Los Angeles: University of California Press, 1984.

Bonus, Rick. *Locating Filipino Americans: Ethnicity and the Cultural Politics of Space*. Philadelphia: Temple University Press, 2000.

Brands, H. W. *Bound to Empire: The United States and the Philippines*. New York: Oxford University Press, 1992.

Brumberg, Stephan F. *Going to America, Going to School: The Jewish Immigrant Public School Encounter in Turn-of-the-Century New York City*. New York: Praeger, 1986.

Buaken, Manuel. *I Have Lived with the American People*. Caldwell, Idaho: Caxton Printers, 1948.

Buchholdt, Thelma. *Filipinos in Alaska: 1788–1958*. Anchorage: Aboriginal Press, 1996.

Bulosan, Carlos. *America Is in the Heart: A Personal History*. Seattle: University of Washington Press, 1991.

———. *The Cry and the Dedication*. Edited by E. San Juan. Philadelphia: Temple University Press, 1995.

———, ed. *1952 Yearbook*. Local 37, International Longshoremen's and Warehousemen's Union.

Burke, Padraic. *A History of the Port of Seattle*. Seattle: Port of Seattle, 1976.

Catapusan, Benicio T. "Filipino Repatriates in the Philippines." *Sociology and Social Research* 21 (September–October 1936): 72–77.

Chan, Sucheng. *Asian Americans: An Interpretive History*. Boston: Twayne, 1991.

———. "European and Asian Immigration into the United States in Comparative Perspective, 1820s to 1920s." In *Immigration Reconsidered: History, Sociology, and Politics*, edited by Virginia Yans-McLaughlin, 37–75. New York: Oxford University Press, 1990.

———. "Race, Ethnic Culture, and Gender in the Construction of Identities among Second-Generation Chinese Americans, 1880s to 1930s." In *Claiming America: Constructing Chinese American Identities during the Exclusion Era*, edited by K. Scott Wong and Sucheng Chan, 127–164. Philadelphia: Temple University Press, 1998.

———. *This Bittersweet Soil: The Chinese in California Agriculture, 1860–1910*. Berkeley and Los Angeles: University of California Press, 1986.

Cheng, Lucie, and Edna Bonacich, eds. *Labor Immigration under Capitalism: Asian Workers in the United States before World War II*. Berkeley and Los Angeles: University of California Press, 1984.

Chew, Ron, ed. *Reflections of Seattle's Chinese Americans: The First 100 Years*. Seattle: University of Washington Press and the Wing Luke Asian Museum, 1994.

Christie, Emerson Brewer. "Notes on Iloko Ethnography and History." In *Ethnography of the Iloko People (A Collection of Original Sources)*, collected, edited, and annotated by H. Otley Beyer, 2:1–146. Manila, 1919.

Chun, Gloria H. "'Go West . . . to China': Chinese American Identity in the 1930s." In *Claiming America: Constructing Chinese American Identities dur-*

ing the Exclusion Era, edited by K. Scott Wong and Sucheng Chan, 165–190. Philadelphia: Temple University Press, 1998.

Cohen, Lizabeth. *Making a New Deal: Industrial Workers in Chicago, 1919–1939*. New York: Cambridge University Press, 1990.

Constantino, Renato. "The Miseducation of the Filipino." In *The Philippines Reader: A History of Colonialism, Neocolonialism, Dictatorship, and Resistance*, edited by Daniel B. Schirmer and Stephen Rosskamm Shalom, 45–49. Boston: South End Press, 1987.

Constantino, Renato, with the collaboration of Letizia R. Constantino. *A History of the Philippines: From the Spanish Colonization to the Second World War*. New York: Monthly Review Press, 1975.

Cooper, Frederick, and Ann Laura Stoler. "Between Metropole and Colony: Rethinking a Research Agenda." In *Tensions of Empire: Colonial Cultures in a Bourgeois World*, 1–56. Berkeley and Los Angeles: University of California Press, 1997.

———, eds. *Tensions of Empire: Colonial Cultures in a Bourgeois World*. Berkeley and Los Angeles: University of California Press, 1997.

Cooper, Patricia. *Once a Cigar Maker: Men, Women, and Work Culture in American Cigar Factories, 1900–1919*. Urbana: University of Illinois Press, 1987.

Cordova, Dorothy. "Voices from the Past: Why They Came." In *Making Waves: An Anthology of Writings by and about Asian American Women*, edited by Asian Women United of California, 42–49. Boston: Beacon Press, 1989.

Cordova, Fred. *Filipinos: Forgotten Asian Americans, A Pictorial Essay/1763-Circa-1963*. Dubuque, Iowa: Kendall/Hunt, 1983.

Corpuz, Onofre D. *The Bureaucracy in the Philippines*. Studies in Public Administration, no. 4. Institute of Public Administration, University of the Philippines, 1957.

Corsino, Felicisimo E. "Social Organization and Beliefs in Ilokos Sur." In *Ethnography of the Iloko People (A Collection of Original Sources)*, collected, edited, and annotated by H. Otley Beyer, 1:1–17. Manila, 1918.

Cortes, Rosario Mendoza. *Pangasinan, 1901–1986: A Political, Socioeconomic and Cultural History*. Quezon City: New Day Publishers, 1990.

Cronon, William. *Nature's Metropolis: Chicago and the Great West*. New York: Norton, 1991.

———. "Revisiting Turner's Vanishing Frontier." In *Major Problems in the History of the American West: Documents and Essays*, edited by Clyde A. Milner II, 668–681. Lexington, Mass.: Heath, 1989.

Cruz, Jon D. "Filipino-American Community Organizations in Washington, 1900s–1930s." In *Peoples of Color in the American West*, edited by Sucheng Chan, 235–245. Lexington, Mass.: Heath, 1994.

Daniel, Cletus E. *Bitter Harvest: A History of California Farmworkers, 1870–1941*. Berkeley and Los Angeles: University of California Press, 1982.

De Vera, Arlene. "Without Parallel: The Local 7 Deportation Case, 1949–1955." *Amerasia Journal* 20, no. 2 (1994): 1–25.

De Witt, Howard A. *Anti-Filipino Movements in California: A History, Bibliography and Study Guide*. San Francisco: R and E Research Associates, 1976.

———. "The Filipino Labor Union: The Salinas Lettuce Strike of 1934." *Amerasia Journal* 5, no. 2 (1978): 1–21.

———. *Violence in the Fields: California Filipino Farm Labor Unionization during the Great Depression.* Saratoga, N.Y.: Century Twenty One, 1980.

Denning, Michael. *The Cultural Front: The Laboring of American Culture in the Twentieth Century.* New York: Verso, 1996.

Deutsch, Sarah. *No Separate Refuge: Culture, Class, and Gender on an Anglo-Hispanic Frontier in the American Southwest, 1880–1940.* New York: Oxford University Press, 1987.

Doeppers, Daniel F. *Manila, 1900–1941: Social Change in a Late Colonial Metropolis.* Monograph Series no. 17. New Haven, Conn.: Yale University Southeast Asia Studies, 1984.

Domingo, Cindy. ". . . Until We Have a True Democracy." *Amerasia Journal* 18, no. 1 (1992): 129–130.

Drinnon, Richard. *Facing West: The Metaphysics of Indian-Hating and Empire Building.* Minneapolis: University of Minnesota Press, 1980.

Droker, Howard A. "Seattle Race Relations during the Second World War." In *Experiences in a Promised Land: Essays in Pacific Northwest History*, edited by G. Thomas Edwards and Carlos A. Schwantes, 353–368. Seattle: University of Washington Press, 1986.

Dudden, Arthur Power. *The American Pacific: From the Old China Trade to the Present.* New York: Oxford University Press, 1992.

Dunaway, David K., and Willa K. Baum, eds. *Oral History: An Interdisciplinary Anthology.* Walnut Creek, Calif.: Altamira Press, 1996.

East-West Population Institute. *Proceedings of Conference on International Migration from the Philippines, 10–14 June 1974.* Honolulu: East-West Center, 1975.

Edwards, G. Thomas, and Carlos A. Schwantes. *Experiences in a Promised Land: Essays in Pacific Northwest History.* Seattle: University of Washington Press, 1986.

Eng, David L., and Alice Y. Hom. *Q & A: Queer in Asian America.* Philadelphia: Temple University Press, 1998.

Espina, Marina E. *Filipinos in Louisiana.* New Orleans: A. F. Laborde, 1988.

Espiritu, Yen Le. *Filipino American Lives.* Philadelphia: Temple University Press, 1995.

Evangelista, Susan. *Carlos Bulosan and His Poetry: A Biography and Anthology.* Seattle: University of Washington Press, 1985.

Filipino Oral History Project. *Voices: A Filipino American Oral History.* Stockton, Calif.: Filipino Oral History Project, 2000.

Foronda, Marcelino A., Jr. "America Is in the Heart: Ilokano Immigration to the United States (1906–1930)." De La Salle University Occasional Paper no. 3, August 1976.

Francisco, Luzviminda. "The Philippine-American War." In *The Philippines Reader: A History of Colonialism, Neocolonialism, Dictatorship, and Resistance,* edited by Daniel B. Schirmer and Stephen Rosskamm Shalom, 8–19. Boston: South End Press, 1987.

Frank, Dana. *Purchasing Power: Consumer Organizing, Gender, and the Seat-*

tle Labor Movement, 1919–1929. Cambridge: Cambridge University Press, 1994.

———. "Race Relations and the Seattle Labor Movement, 1915–1929." *Pacific Northwest Quarterly* 86, no. 1 (winter 1994/1995): 35–44.

Freeman, Otis W., and Howard H. Martin, editorial committee. *The Pacific Northwest: A Regional, Human, and Economic Survey of Resources and Development.* New York: Wiley, 1942.

Friday, Chris. *Organizing Asian American Labor: The Pacific Coast Canned-Salmon Industry, 1870–1942.* Philadelphia: Temple University Press, 1994.

Frisch, Michael. *A Shared Authority: Essays on the Craft and Meaning of Oral and Public History.* Albany: State University of New York Press, 1990.

Fuchs, Lawrence H. *Hawaii Pono: A Social History.* San Diego: Harcourt Brace Jovanovich, 1961.

Fujita-Rony, Dorothy. "Rereading *Philip Vera Cruz:* Race, Labor, and Coalitions." *Journal of Asian American Studies* 3, no. 2 (June 2000): 139–162.

Gatewood, Willard B., Jr. *"Smoked Yankees" and the Struggle for Empire: Letters from Negro Soldiers, 1898–1902.* Urbana: University of Illinois Press, 1971.

Gerardo, Anastacio B. "The Present Status of Ilokos Norte." In *Ethnography of the Iloko People (A Collection of Original Sources),* collected, edited, and annotated by H. Otley Beyer, 1:1–7. Manila, 1918.

Gilroy, Paul. *"There Ain't No Black in the Union Jack": The Cultural Politics of Race and Nation.* London: Hutchinson, 1987.

Glenn, Evelyn Nakano. *Issei, Nisei, Warbride: Three Generations of Japanese American Women in Domestic Service.* Philadelphia: Temple University Press, 1986.

Gónzalez, Gilbert G. *Chicano Education in the Era of Segregation.* Philadelphia: Balch Institute Press, 1990.

———. *Mexican Consuls and Labor Organizing: Imperial Politics in the American Southwest.* Austin: University of Texas Press, 1999.

Green, James R. *The World of the Worker: Labor in Twentieth-Century America.* New York: Hill and Wang, 1980.

Gregory, James N. *American Exodus: The Dust Bowl Migration and Okie Culture in California.* New York: Oxford University Press, 1989.

Griffiths, Stephen. *Emigrants, Entrepreneurs, and Evil Spirits: Life in a Philippine Village.* Honolulu: University of Hawai'i Press, 1988.

Guerin-Gonzales, Camille. *Mexican Workers and American Dreams: Immigration, Repatriation, and California Farm Labor, 1900–1939.* New Brunswick, N.J.: Rutgers University Press, 1994.

Gutman, Herbert. *Work, Culture, and Society in Industrializing America: Essays in American Working-Class and Social History.* New York: Knopf, 1976.

Guyotte, Ronald L., and Barbara M. Posadas. "Celebrating Rizal Day: The Emergence of a Filipino Tradition in Twentieth-Century Chicago." In *Feasts and Celebrations in North American Ethnic Communities,* edited by Ramón A. Gutiérrez and Geneviève Fabre, 111–127. Albuquerque: University of New Mexico Press, 1995.

Haas, Lisbeth. *Conquests and Historical Identities in California, 1769–1936.* Berkeley and Los Angeles: University of California Press, 1995.

Handlin, Oscar. *The Uprooted: The Epic Story of the Great Migrations That Made the American People.* Boston: Little, Brown, 1951.

Hawaii Filipino News Specialty Publications. *Filipinos in Hawaii: The First 75 Years.* Honolulu: Hawaii Filipino News Specialty Publications, 1981.

Hayashi, Brian Masaru. *"For the Sake of Our Japanese Brethren": Assimilation, Nationalism, and Protestantism among the Japanese of Los Angeles, 1895–1942.* Stanford, Calif.: Stanford University Press, 1995.

Hempenstall, Peter. "Imperial Manoeuvres." In *Tides of History: The Pacific Islands in the Twentieth Century,* edited by K. R. Howe, Robert C. Kiste, and Brij V. Lal, 29–39. Honolulu: University of Hawai'i Press, 1994.

Hobsbawm, Eric. *The Age of Empire, 1875–1914.* New York: Vintage, 1989.

Hollnsteiner, Mary R. "Reciprocity in the Lowland Philippines." In *Four Readings on Philippine Values,* compiled by Frank Lynch, S.J. Institute of Philippine Culture Papers, no. 2. 2nd revised edition. Quezon City: Ateneo de Manila University Press, 1964.

Hom, Marlon K. *Songs of Gold Mountain: Cantonese Rhymes from San Francisco Chinatown.* Berkeley and Los Angeles: University of California Press, 1987.

Howe, K. R., Robert C. Kiste, and Brij V. Lal. *Tides of History: The Pacific Islands in the Twentieth Century.* Honolulu: University of Hawai'i Press, 1994.

Hu-Dehart, Evelyn. "Coolies, Shopkeepers, Pioneers: The Chinese of Mexico and Peru (1849–1930)." *Amerasia Journal* 15, no. 2 (1989): 91–116.

Jackson, Jesse. "The Story of Seattle's Hooverville." In *Social Trends in Seattle,* 286–293. University of Washington Publications in the Social Sciences, vol. 14. Seattle: University of Washington Press, 1994.

James, C. L. R. *Beyond a Boundary,* with an introduction by Robert Lipsyte. New York: Pantheon, 1983.

Jocano, F. Landa. "Elements of Filipino Social Organization." In *Philippine Kinship and Society,* edited by Yasushi Kikuchi, 1–26. Quezon City: New Day Publishers, 1989.

———. *The Ilocanos: An Ethnography of Family and Community Life in the Ilocos Region,* with the special assistance of Arnora Edrozo, Ernesto Cadiz, Thelma Beltran, and Milagros Dumlao. Diliman, Quezon City: Asian Center, University of the Philippines, 1982.

Johansen, Dorothy O., and Charles M. Gates. *Empire of the Columbia: A History of the Pacific Northwest.* New York: Harper and Brothers, 1957.

Johnson, Susan Lee. "'A Memory Sweet to Soldiers': The Significance of Gender in the History of the 'American West.'" *Western Historical Quarterly* 24 (November 1993): 495–517.

———. *Roaring Camp: The Social World of the California Gold Rush.* New York: Norton, 2000.

Kaplan, Amy. "'Left Alone with America': The Absence of Empire in the Study of American Culture." In *Cultures of United States Imperialism,* edited by Amy Kaplan and Donald E. Pease, 3–21. Durham, N.C.: Duke University Press, 1993.

Kaplan, Amy, and Donald E. Pease, eds. *Cultures of United States Imperialism.* Durham, N.C.: Duke University Press, 1993.

Karnow, Stanley. *In Our Image: America's Empire in the Philippines.* New York: Random House, 1989.

Keesing, Felix M. *The Ethnohistory of Northern Luzon.* Stanford, Calif.: Stanford University Press, 1962.

Kerkvliet, Benedict J. *The Huk Rebellion: A Study of Peasant Revolt in the Philippines.* Berkeley and Los Angeles: University of California Press, 1977.

Kerkvliet, Melinda Tria. *Manila Workers' Unions, 1900–1950.* Quezon City: New Day Publishers, 1992.

———. "Pablo Manlapit's Fight for Justice." *Social Process in Hawaii* 33 (1991): 153–168.

Kim, Hyung-chan, and Cynthia C. Mejia, comps. and eds. *The Filipinos in America, 1898–1974: A Chronology and Fact Book.* Ethnic Chronology Series, no. 23. Dobbs Ferry, N.Y.: Oceana Publications, 1976.

Lai, Him Mark, Genny Lim, and Judy Yung. *Island: Poetry and History of Chinese Immigrants on Angel Island, 1910–1940.* San Francisco: History of Chinese Detained on the Island, 1980.

Lamb, W. Kaye. *Empress to the Orient.* Vancouver: Vancouver Maritime Museum Society, 1991.

Larkin, John. *Sugar and the Origins of Modern Philippine Society.* Berkeley and Los Angeles: University of California Press, 1993.

Lasker, Bruno. *Filipino Immigration to Continental United States and to Hawaii.* Published for the American Council, Institute of Pacific Relations. Chicago: University of Chicago Press, 1931.

Lee, Mary Paik. *Quiet Odyssey: A Pioneer Korean Woman in America.* Edited and with an introduction by Sucheng Chan. Seattle: University of Washington Press, 1990.

Leonard, Karen Isaksen. *Making Ethnic Choices: California's Punjabi Mexican Americans.* Philadelphia: Temple University Press, 1992.

———. *The South Asian Americans.* Westport, Conn.: Greenwood Press, 1997.

Lewis, Henry T. *Ilocano Irrigation: The Corporate Resolution.* Asian Studies at Hawaii, no. 37. Honolulu: University of Hawai'i Press, 1991.

———. *Ilocano Rice Farmers: A Comparative Study of Two Philippine Barrios.* Honolulu: University of Hawai'i Press, 1971.

Licht, Walter. *Getting Work: Philadelphia, 1840–1950.* Cambridge, Mass.: Harvard University Press, 1993.

Lim, Genny. *Paper Angels and Bitter Cane: Two Plays by Genny Lim.* Honolulu: Kalamaku Press, 1991.

Limerick, Patricia Nelson. "Common Cause: Asian American History and Western American History." In *Privileging Positions: The Sites of Asian American Studies,* edited by Gary Okihiro, Marilyn Alquizola, Dorothy Fujita Rony, and K. Scott Wong, 83–99. Pullman: Washington State University Press, 1995.

———. *The Legacy of Conquest: The Unbroken Past of the American West.* New York: Norton, 1987.

Limerick, Patricia Nelson, Clyde A. Milner II, and Charles E. Rankin. *Trails: Toward a New Western History.* Lawrence: University Press of Kansas, 1991.

Lipsitz, George. *The Possessive Investment in Whiteness: How White People Profit from Identity Politics.* Philadelphia: Temple University Press, 1998.

Liu, John M. "Race, Ethnicity, and the Sugar Plantation System: Asian Labor in Hawaii, 1850–1900." In *Labor Immigration under Capitalism: Asian Workers in the United States before World War II*, edited by Lucie Cheng and Edna Bonacich, 186–210. Berkeley and Los Angeles: University of California Press, 1984.

Luengo, Fr. Josemaria. *A History of the Manila-Acapulco Slave Trade (1565–1815)*. Tobigon, Bohol: Mater Dei Publications, 1996.

Lukes, Timothy J., and Gary Y. Okihiro. *Japanese Legacy: Farming and Community Life in California's Santa Clara Valley*. Local History Studies, vol. 31. Cupertino: California History Center, 1985.

Lynch, Frank. "Social Acceptance Reconsidered." In *Philippine Society and the Individual: Selected Essays of Frank Lynch, 1949–1976*, edited by Aram A. Yengoyan and Perla Q. Makil. Michigan Papers on South and Southeast Asia, no. 24. Ann Arbor: Center for South and Southeast Asian Studies, University of Michigan, 1984.

Manalansan, Martin, IV. "Searching for Community: Filipino Gay Men in New York City." *Amerasia Journal* 20, no. 1 (1994): 59–73.

———. "Speaking of AIDS: Language and the Filipino 'Gay' Experience in America." In *Discrepant Histories: Translocal Essays on Filipino Cultures*, edited by Vincente L. Rafael, 193–220. Manila: Anvil Publishing, 1995.

———, ed. *Cultural Compass: Ethnographic Explorations of Asian America*. Philadelphia: Temple University Press, 2000.

Masson, Jack, and Donald Guimary. "Asian Labor Contractors in the Alaskan Canned Salmon Industry: 1880–1937." *Labor History* 22, no. 3 (summer 1981): 377–397.

———. "Pilipinos and Unionization of the Alaskan Canned Salmon Industry." *Amerasia Journal* 8, no. 2 (1981): 1–30.

Mast, Robert H., and Anne B. Mast. *Autobiography of Protest in Hawai'i*. Honolulu: University of Hawai'i Press, 1996.

Matsumoto, Valerie J. *Farming the Home Place: A Japanese American Community in California, 1919–1982*. Ithaca, N.Y.: Cornell University Press, 1993.

Matsumoto, Valerie J., and Blake Allmendinger, eds. *Over the Edge: Remapping the American West*. Berkeley and Los Angeles: University of California Press, 1999.

Mazumdar, Sucheta. "Asian American Studies and Asian Studies: Rethinking Roots." In *Asian Americans: Comparative and Global Perspectives*, edited by Shirley Hune, Hung-chan Kim, Stephen S. Fugita, and Amy Ling, 29–44. Pullman: Washington State University Press, 1991.

McWilliams, Carey. *Factories in the Field: The Story of Migratory Farm Labor in California*. Santa Barbara, Calif., and Salt Lake City: Peregrine Smith, 1971.

———. *Ill Fares the Land: Migrants and Migratory Labor in the United States*. New York: Barnes and Noble, 1967.

Mears, Eliot Grinnel. *Maritime Trade of Western United States*. Stanford, Calif.: Stanford University Press, 1935.

Melendy, H. Brett. *Asians in America: Filipinos, Koreans, and East Indians*. Boston: Twayne, 1977.

Milner, Clyde A., II, ed. *Major Problems in the History of the American West: Documents and Essays.* Lexington, Mass.: Heath, 1989.

Miyamoto, S. Frank. *Social Solidarity among the Japanese in Seattle.* Publications in the Social Sciences II, no. 2. Seattle: University of Washington, 1984.

Monkkonen, Eric, ed. *Walking to Work: Tramps in America, 1790–1935.* Lincoln: University of Nebraska Press, 1984.

Montgomery, David. *The Fall of the House of Labor: The Workplace, the State, and American Labor Activism, 1865–1925.* Cambridge: Cambridge University Press, 1987.

———. *Worker's Control in America: Studies in the History of Work, Technology, and Labor Struggles.* Cambridge: Cambridge University Press, 1979.

Morgan, Murray. *Skid Row.* Sausalito, Calif.: Comstock Editions, 1978.

National Industrial Recovery Administration Hearing on Code of Fair Practices and Competition presented by the Canned Salmon Industry, San Francisco, California, 1934.

Nee, Victor G., and Brett de Bary Nee. *Longtime Californ': A Documentary Study of an American Chinatown.* 1972. Reprint, Stanford, Calif.: Stanford University Press, 1986.

Nomura, Gail. "Significant Lives: Asia and Asian Americans in the History of the U.S. West." *Western Historical Quarterly* 25, no. 1 (spring 1994): 69–88.

———. "Within the Law: The Establishment of Filipino Leasing Rights on the Yakima Indian Reservation." *Amerasia Journal* 13, no. 1 (1986–1987): 99–117.

Nomura, Gail M., Russell Endo, Stephen H. Sumida, and Russell C. Leong, eds. *Frontiers of Asian American Studies: Writing, Research, and Commentary.* Pullman: Washington State University Press, 1989.

Nydegger, William F., and Corinne Nydegger. *Tarong: An Ilocos Barrio in the Philippines.* Six Culture Series, vol. 6. New York: Wiley, 1966.

Okamura, Jonathan. *Imagining the Filipino American Diaspora: Transnational Relations, Identities, and Communities.* New York: Garland, 1998.

———. "Kinship and Community: Filipino Immigrants in Honolulu." *DLSU Dialogue* 20, no. 1 (October 1984): 27–43.

Okamura, Jonathan, Amefil R. Agbayani, and Melinda Tria Kerkvliet, guest editors. "The Filipino American Experience in Hawai'i: In Commemoration of the 85th Anniversary of Filipino Immigration to Hawai'i." Special issue, *Social Process in Hawaii* 33 (1991).

Okihiro, Gary. *Cane Fires: The Anti-Japanese Movement in Hawaii, 1865–1945.* Philadelphia: Temple University Press, 1991.

———. "The Fallow Field: The Rural Dimension of Asian American Studies." In *Frontiers of Asian American Studies: Writing, Research, and Commentary,* edited by Gail M. Nomura, Russell Endo, Stephen H. Sumida, and Russell C. Leong, 6–13. Pullman: Washington State University Press, 1989.

———. "Oral History and the Writing of Ethnic History." In *Oral History: An Interdisciplinary Anthology,* edited by David K. Dunaway and Willa K. Baum, 199–214. Walnut Creek, Calif.: Altamira Press, 1996.

———. *Storied Lives: Japanese American Students and World War II.* Seattle: University of Washington Press, 1999.

Okihiro, Gary, Marilyn Alquizola, Dorothy Fujita Rony, and K. Scott Wong, eds. *Privileging Positions: The Sites of Asian American Studies.* Pullman: Washington State University Press, 1995.

Omi, Michael, and Howard Winant. *Racial Formation in the United States: From the 1960s to the 1980s.* New York: Routledge, 1986.

Orsi, Robert Anthony. *The Madonna of 115th Street: Faith and Community in Italian Harlem, 1880–1950.* New Haven, Conn.: Yale University Press, 1985.

Pagden, Anthony. *Lords of All the World: Ideologies of Empire in Spain, Britain, and France c. 1500–c. 1800.* New Haven, Conn.: Yale University Press, 1995.

Painter, Nell Irvin. *Standing at Armageddon: The United States, 1877–1919.* New York: Norton, 1987.

Parrenas, Rhacel Salazar. "'White Trash' Meets the 'Little Brown Monkeys': The Taxi Dance Hall as a Site of Interracial and Gender Relations between White Working Class Women and Filipino Immigrant Men in the 1920s and 1930s." *Amerasia Journal* 24, no. 2 (1998): 115–134.

Peck, Gunther. "Padrones and Protest: 'Old' Radicals and 'New' Immigrants in Bingham, Utah, 1905–1912." *Western Historical Quarterly* 24, no. 2 (May 1993): 165–177.

Pomeroy, Earl. *The Pacific Slope: A History of California, Oregon, Washington, Idaho, Utah, and Nevada.* Seattle: University of Washington Press, 1965.

Pomeroy, William. *American Neo-Colonialism: Its Emergence in the Philippines and Asia.* New York: International Publishers, 1970.

Posadas, Barbara M. "Crossed Boundaries in Interracial Chicago: Pilipino American Families since 1925." *Amerasia Journal* 8, no. 2 (1981): 31–52.

———. *The Filipino Americans.* Westport, Conn.: Greenwood Press, 1999.

———. "The Hierarchy of Color and Psychological Adjustment in an Industrial Environment: Filipinos, the Pullman Company, and the Brotherhood of Sleeping Car Porters." *Labor History* 23, no. 3 (summer 1982): 349–373.

Posadas, Barbara M., and Ronald Guyotte. "Unintentional Immigrants: Chicago's Filipino Foreign Students Become Settlers, 1941." *Journal of American Ethnic History* 9, no. 2 (spring 1990): 26–48.

Purísima, Ceferíno. "Ethnography of the Iloko People of Luzon." In *Ethnography of the Iloko People (A Collection of Original Sources),* collected, edited, and annotated by H. Otley Beyer, 1:1–9. Manila, 1918.

Quimby, George I. "Culture Contact on the Northwest Coast, 1785–1795." *American Anthropologist* 50 (April–June 1948): 252–253.

Quinsaat, Jesse G. "How to Join the Navy and Still Not See the World." In *Letters in Exile: An Introductory Reader on the History of Pilipinos in America,* 96–111. Los Angeles: A Project of Resource Development and Publications, UCLA Asian American Studies Center, 1976.

———, ed. *Letters in Exile: An Introductory Reader on the History of the Pilipinos in America.* Los Angeles: UCLA Asian American Studies Center, 1976.

Radius, Walter A. *United States Shipping in Transpacific Trade.* Issued in cooperation with the American Council, Institute of Pacific Relations. Stanford, Calif.: Stanford University Press, 1944.

Rafael, Vicente L. *Discrepant Histories: Translocal Essays on Filipino Cultures.* Manila: Anvil, 1995.

Reinecke, John E. *The Filipino Piecemeal Sugar Strike of 1924–1925*. Honolulu: Social Science Research Institute, University of Hawai'i, 1996.

Reyes, Jose S. *Legislative History of America's Economic Policy toward the Philippines*. Studies in History, Economics, and Public Law, edited by the Faculty of Political Science of Columbia University, CVI, no. 2, whole no. 240. New York: AMS Press, 1967.

Roberts, Brian, ed. *They Cast a Long Shadow: A History of the Nonwhite Races on Bainbridge Island*. Bainbridge Island, Wash.: Minority History Committee of Bainbridge Island School District No. 303, 1975.

Rojo, Trinidad. "Social Maladjustment among Filipinos in the United States." *Sociology and Social Research* 21, no. 5 (May–June 1937): 447–457.

Root, Maria P. P. *Filipino Americans: Transformation and Identity*. Thousand Oaks, Calif.: Sage, 1997.

Rosaldo, Renato. *Culture and Truth: The Remaking of Social Analysis*. Boston: Beacon Press, 1989.

Rosenzweig, Roy. *Eight Hours for What We Will: Workers and Leisure in an Industrial City, 1870–1920*. Cambridge: Cambridge University Press, 1989.

Rouse, Roger. "Mexican Migration and the Social Space of Postmodernism." *Diaspora* 1, no. 1 (spring 1991): 8–23.

Ruiz, Vicki L. *Cannery Women, Cannery Lives: Mexican Women, Unionization, and the California Food Processing Industry, 1930–1950*. Albuquerque: University of New Mexico Press, 1987.

Said, Edward. *Orientalism*. New York: Vintage, 1979.

Salamanca, Bonifacio C. *The Filipino Reaction to American Rule, 1901–1913*. Hamden, Conn.: Shoe String Press, 1968.

Sale, Roger. *Seattle: Past to Present*. Seattle: University of Washington Press, 1976.

San Buenaventura, Steffi. "The Colors of Manifest Destiny: Filipinos and the American Other(s)." *Amerasia Journal* 24, no. 3 (1998): 1–26.

———. "The Master and the Federation: A Filipino-American Social Movement in California and Hawaii." *Social Process in Hawaii* 33 (1991): 169–193.

San Juan, E., Jr. "Beyond Identity Politics: The Predicament of the Asian American Writer in Late Capitalism." *American Literary History* 3 (fall 1991): 542–565.

———. *Carlos Bulosan and the Imagination of the Class Struggle*. Quezon City: University of the Philippines Press, 1972.

———. "Configuring the Filipino Diaspora in the United States." *Diaspora* 3, no. 2 (1994): 117–131.

———. *On Becoming Filipino: Selected Writings of Carlos Bulosan*. Philadelphia: Temple University Press, 1995.

———. *The Philippine Temptation: Dialectics of Philippines-U.S. Literary Relations*. Philadelphia: Temple University Press, 1996.

Sánchez, George J. *Becoming Mexican American: Ethnicity, Culture and Identity in Chicano Los Angeles, 1900–1945*. New York: Oxford University Press, 1993.

Saniel, Josefa M., ed. *The Filipino Exclusion Movement, 1927–1935*. Institute of Asian Studies Occasional Papers, no. 1. Quezon City: University of the Philippines Press, 1967.

Sar Desai, D. D. *Southeast Asia: Past and Present*. Boulder, Colo.: Westview Press, 1989.

Saxton, Alexander. *The Indispensable Enemy: Labor and the Anti-Chinese Movement in California*. Berkeley and Los Angeles: University of California Press, 1971.

Scharff, Virginia. "Mobility, Women, and the West." In *Over the Edge: Remapping the American West*, edited by Valerie J. Matsumoto and Blake Allmendinger, 160–171. Berkeley and Los Angeles: University of California Press, 1999.

Scharlin, Craig, and Lilia V. Villanueva. *Philip Vera Cruz: A Personal History of Filipino Immigrants and the Farmworkers Movement*. Los Angeles: UCLA Labor Center, Institute of Industrial Relations and UCLA Asian American Studies Center, 1992.

Schirmer, Daniel B., and Stephen Rosskamm Shalom. "Selection 1.1: The Philippine-American War, Luzviminda Francisco," from "The First Vietnam: The Philippine-American War, 1899–1902." In *The Philippines: End of an Illusion*, n.p. London: AREAS, 1973. Reprinted in *The Philippines Reader: A History of Colonialism, Neocolonialism, Dictatorship, and Resistance*, edited by Daniel B. Schirmer and Stephen Rosskamm Shalom, 8–19. Boston: South End Press, 1987.

———. "Selection 2.6: The Independency Lobby, Shirley Jenkins," from Shirley Jenkins, *American Economic Policy toward the Philippines*, 34–37. Stanford, Calif.: Stanford University Press, 1954. Reprinted in *The Philippines Reader: A History of Colonialism, Neocolonialism, Dictatorship, and Resistance*, edited by Daniel B. Schirmer and Stephen Rosskamm Shalom, 55–58. Boston: South End Press, 1987.

———. "Selection 2.8: Struggles of the 1930s, Luis Taruc," with excerpts from Luis Taruc, *Born of the People*, 26–51. New York: International Publishers, 1953. Reprinted in *The Philippines Reader: A History of Colonialism, Neocolonialism, Dictatorship, and Resistance*, edited by Daniel B. Schirmer and Stephen Rosskamm Shalom, 62–66. Boston: South End Press, 1987.

———, eds. *The Philippines Reader: A History of Colonialism, Neocolonialism, Dictatorship, and Resistance*. Boston: South End Press, 1987.

Schmid, Calvin F. *Social Trends in Seattle*. University of Washington Publications in the Social Sciences, vol. 14. Seattle: University of Washington Press, 1944.

Schurz, William M. *The Manila Galleon*. New York: Dutton, 1939.

Schwantes, Carlos A. *The Pacific Northwest: An Interpretive History*. Lincoln: University of Nebraska Press, 1989.

———. "Unemployment, Disinheritance, and the Origin of Labor Militancy in the Pacific Northwest, 1885–86." In *Labor Immigration under Capitalism: Asian Workers in the United States before World War II*, 179–194. Berkeley and Los Angeles: University of California Press, 1984.

Scott, James C. *Domination and the Arts of Resistance: Hidden Transcripts*. New Haven, Conn.: Yale University Press, 1990.

Scott, Joan Wallach. *Gender and the Politics of History*. New York: Columbia University Press, 1988.

Scott, William Henry. *Ilocano Responses to American Aggression, 1900–1901*. Quezon City: New Day Publishers, 1986.

Sharma, Miriam. "Labor Migration and Class Formation among the Filipinos in Hawaii, 1906–1946." In *Labor Immigration under Capitalism: Asian Workers in the United States before World War II*, edited by Lucie Cheng and Edna Bonacich, 579–615. Berkeley and Los Angeles: University of California Press, 1984.

———. "The Philippines: A Case of Migration to Hawaii, 1906–1946." In *Labor Immigration under Capitalism: Asian Workers in the United States before World War II*, edited by Lucie Cheng and Edna Bonacich, 337–358. Berkeley and Los Angeles: University of California Press, 1984.

Simkins, Paul D., and Frederick L. Wernstedt. *Philippine Migration: The Settlement of the Digos-Padada Valley, Davao Province*. Monograph Series no. 16. New Haven, Conn.: Yale University, Southeast Asia Studies, 1971.

Siu, Paul C. P. *The Chinese Laundryman: A Study of Social Isolation*. Edited by John Kuo Wei Tchen. New York: New York University Press, 1987.

Smith, Peter C. "The Social Demography of Filipino Migrations Abroad." *International Migration Review* 10, no. 3 (autumn 1976): 307–353.

Soja, Edward W. *Postmodern Geographies: The Reassertion of Space in Critical Social Theory*. London: Verso, 1989.

Sone, Monica. *Nisei Daughter*. Seattle: University of Washington Press, 1953.

The Staff, researched by Henry Empeno. "Anti-miscegenation Laws and the Pilipino." In *Letters in Exile: An Introductory Reader on the History of Pilipinos in America*, 63–71. Los Angeles: A Project of Resource Development and Publications, UCLA Asian American Studies Center, 1976.

Stansell, Christine. *City of Women: Sex and Class in New York, 1789–1860*. Urbana: University of Illinois Press, 1987.

Steinberg, David Joel. *The Philippines: A Singular and a Plural Place*. 3d ed. Boulder, Colo.: Westview Press, 1994.

———, ed. *In Search of Southeast Asia: A Modern History*. New York: Holt, Rinehart and Winston, 1971.

Sturtevant, David R. *Popular Uprisings in the Philippines, 1840–1940*. Ithaca, N.Y.: Cornell University Press, 1936.

Sutherland, William Alexander. *Not by Might: The Epic of the Philippines*. Las Cruces, N.M.: Southwest Publishing Company, 1953.

Tabili, Laura. *"We Ask for British Justice": Workers and Racial Difference in Late Imperial Britain*. Ithaca, N.Y.: Cornell University Press, 1994.

Takaki, Ronald T. *Iron Cages: Race and Culture in Nineteenth-Century America*. Seattle: University of Washington Press, 1979.

———. *Strangers from a Different Shore: A History of Asian Americans*. Boston: Little, Brown, 1989.

Takami, David A. *Divided Destiny: A History of Japanese Americans in Seattle*. Seattle: University of Washington Press and Wing Luke Asian Museum, 1998.

———. *Executive Order 9066: 50 Years before and 50 Years after, A History of Japanese Americans in Seattle*. Seattle: Wing Luke Asian Museum, 1992.

———. "Marcoses Found Liable for Seattle Cannery Workers Union Murders." *Amerasia Journal* 18, no. 1 (1992): 125–128.

Tan, Samuel K. *A History of the Philippines*. Manila: Manila Studies Association; Quezon City: Philippine National Historical Society, 1997.

Taruc, Luis. *Born of the People*. New York: International Publishers, 1953.

Taylor, Paul. *On the Ground in the Thirties*. Salt Lake City: Gibbs M. Smith, 1983.

Taylor, Quintard. *The Forging of a Black Community: Seattle's Central District from 1870 through the Civil Rights Era*. Seattle: University of Washington Press, 1994.

Tchen, John Kuo Wei. "Modernizing White Patriarchy: Re-viewing D. W. Griffiths' 'Broken Blossoms.'" In *Moving the Image: Independent Asian Pacific American Media Arts*, edited by Russell Leong, 133–143. Los Angeles: UCLA Asian American Studies Center and Visual Communications, 1991.

———. *New York before Chinatown: Orientalism and the Shaping of American Culture, 1776–1882*. Baltimore: Johns Hopkins University Press, 1999.

Tchen, John Kuo Wei, and Arnold Genthe. *Genthe's Photographs of San Francisco's Old Chinatown*. New York: Dover, 1984.

Teodoro, Luis V., Jr., ed. *Out of This Struggle: The Filipinos in Hawaii*. Published for the Filipino Seventy-fifth Anniversary Commemoration Commission. Honolulu: University Press of Hawaii, 1981.

Thistlewaite, Frank. "Migration from Europe Overseas in the Nineteenth and Twentieth Centuries." In *Population Movements in Modern European History*, edited by Herbert Moller, 73–92. New York: Macmillan, 1964.

Thomas, William I., and Florian Znaniecki. *The Polish Peasant in Europe and America*. Edited and abridged by Eli Zaretsky. Urbana: University of Illinois Press, 1984.

Thompson, E. P. *The Making of the English Working Class*. New York: Vintage, 1966.

Tilly, Charles. "Transplanted Networks." In *Immigration Reconsidered: History, Sociology, and Politics*, edited by Virginia Yans-McLaughlin, 79–95. New York: Oxford University Press, 1990.

Ting, Jennifer. "Bachelor Society: Deviant Heterosexuality and Asian American Historiography." In *Privileging Positions: The Sites of Asian American Studies*, edited by Gary Okihiro, Marilyn Alquizola, Dorothy Fujita Rony, and K. Scott Wong, 271–279. Pullman: Washington State University Press, 1995.

Tongson, Josefina. "Ethnography of the Iloko People." In *Ethnography of the Iloko People (A Collection of Original Sources)*, collected, edited, and annotated by H. Otley Beyer, 1:1–17. Manila, 1918.

Trager, Lillian. *The City Connection: Migration and Family Interdependence in the Philippines*. Ann Arbor: University of Michigan Press, 1988.

Trask, Haunani Kay. *From a Native Daughter: Colonialism and Sovereignty in Hawai'i*. Monroe, Maine: Common Courage Press, 1993.

Turner, Frederick Jackson. "The Significance of the Frontier in American History." In *Major Problems in the History of the American West: Documents and Essays*, edited by Clyde A. Milner II, 2–21. Lexington, Mass.: Heath, 1989.

Valdés, Dennis Nodín. *Al Norte: Agricultural Workers in the Great Lakes Region, 1917–1970*. Austin: University of Texas Press, 1991.

Vega, Mercedes A. "Social Customs of the Ilokos." In *Ethnography of the Iloko People (A Collection of Original Sources)*, collected, edited, and annotated by H. Otley Beyer, 1:1–6. Manila, 1918.

Weber, Devra. *Dark Sweat, White Gold: California Farm Workers, Cotton, and the New Deal.* Berkeley and Los Angeles: University of California Press, 1994.

White, Richard. *"It's Your Misfortune and None of My Own": A History of the American West.* Norman: University of Oklahoma Press, 1991.

Wong, K. Scott, and Sucheng Chan. *Claiming America: Constructing Chinese American Identities during the Exclusion Era.* Philadelphia: Temple University Press, 1998.

Worster, Donald. *Rivers of Empire: Water, Aridity, and the Growth of the American West.* New York: Pantheon, 1985.

Wyman, Mark. *Round-Trip to America: The Immigrants Return to Europe, 1880–1930.* Ithaca, N.Y.: Cornell University Press, 1993.

Yanigisako, Sylvia Junko. *Transforming the Past: Tradition and Kinship among Japanese Americans.* Stanford, Calif.: Stanford University Press, 1985.

Yans-McLaughlin, Virginia, ed. *Immigration Reconsidered: History, Sociology, and Politics.* New York: Oxford University Press, 1990.

Yu, Henry. "The 'Oriental Problem' in America, 1920–1960: Linking the Identities of Chinese American and Japanese American Intellectuals." In *Claiming America: Constructing Chinese American Identities during the Exclusion Era*, edited by K. Scott Wong and Sucheng Chan, 191–214. Philadelphia: Temple University Press, 1998.

Yu, Renqiu. *To Save China, to Save Ourselves: The Chinese Hand Laundry Alliance of New York.* Philadelphia: Temple University Press, 1992.

Yung, Judy. *Unbound Feet: A Social History of Chinese Women in San Francisco.* Berkeley and Los Angeles: University of California Press, 1995.

———. *Unbound Voices: A Documentary History of Chinese Women in San Francisco.* Berkeley and Los Angeles: University of California Press, 1999.

Zia, Helen. *Asian American Dreams: The Emergence of an American People.* New York: Farrar, Straus and Giroux, 2000.

MASTER'S THESES, DISSERTATIONS, UNPUBLISHED PAPERS, AND OTHER WORKS

Casaday, Lauren W. "Labor Unrest and the Labor Movement in the Salmon Industry of the Pacific Coast." Ph.D. diss., University of California, Berkeley, 1938.

Catapusan, Benicio. "The Filipino Occupational and Recreational Activities in Los Angeles." Thesis, University of Southern California, 1934. Reprint, San Francisco: R and E Research Associates.

———. "The Social Adjustment of Filipinos in the United States." Ph.D. diss., University of Southern California, 1940.

Chu, Marilyn. "Metamorphosis of a Chinatown, International District, Seattle." Master's thesis, University of Washington, 1977.

Coloma, Casiano Pagdilao. "A Study of the Filipino Repatriation Movement." Thesis, University of Southern California, 1939. Reprint, San Francisco: R. and E. Research Associates, 1974.

Cordova, Dorothy L., and Damian Cordova. "Historic Account of the Filipinos in Seattle." Seattle: Filipino Youth Activities, 1976.

Cordova, Timoteo. "Across Oceans of Dreams." Script provided to author, Seattle, 1992.

Flor, Robert F. "The Development of the Filipino Community in Seattle, Washington." Unpublished paper.

Fowler, Josephine. "To Be Red and 'Oriental': The Experience of Chinese and Japanese Immigrant Communists in the American Communist and International Communist Movements, 1920–WWII." Ph.D. diss., University of Minnesota, forthcoming.

Gold, Gerald. "The Development of Local Number 7 of the Food, Tobacco, Agricultural and Allied Workers of America–C.I.O." Master's thesis, University of Washington, 1949.

Gonzalves, Theodore. "When the Lights Go Down: Performing in the Filipina/o Diaspora, 1934–1998." Ph.D. diss., University of California, Irvine, 2001.

Kuhler, Joyce Benjamin. "A History of Agriculture in the Yakima Valley, Washington, from 1880 to 1900." Master's thesis, University of Washington, 1940.

Manalansan, Martin Fajardo, IV. "Remapping Frontiers: The Lives of Filipino Gay Men in New York." Ph.D. diss., University of Rochester, 1997.

Mariano, Honorante. "The Filipino Immigrants in the United States." Master's thesis, University of Oregon, 1933. Reprint, San Francisco: R and E Research Associates, 1972.

Marquardt, Steve. "The Alaska Cannery Workers after World War II: Communism, Anti-Communism and Unionism." Unpublished paper, 1991.

———. "The Labor Activist as Labor Historian: Reforming the Alaska Cannery Workers Union." Paper presented at the annual meeting of the American Historical Association, Pacific Coast Branch, 1992.

Mathieson, Raymond Success. "The Industrial Geography of Seattle, Washington." Master's thesis, University of Washington, 1954.

Miner, Grace Edith. "A Century of Washington Fruit." Master's thesis, University of Washington, 1926.

Moe, Ole Kay. "An Analytical Study of the Foreign Trade through the Port of Seattle." Master's thesis, University of Washington, 1932.

Morton, Gordon Elwood. "Farm Wage Earners in Washington." Master's thesis, University of Washington, 1943.

Pet, Catherine Ceniza. "Pioneers/Puppets: The Legacy of the *Pensionado* Program." Bachelor's thesis, Pomona College, 1991.

Pitts, Robert Bedford. "Organized Labor and the Negro in Seattle." Master's thesis, University of Washington, 1941.

Port of Seattle. Port of Seattle Yearbooks, 1919–1941.

Provido, Generoso Pacificar. "Oriental Immigration from an American Dependency." Thesis [level unknown], University of California, 1931. Reprint, San Francisco and Saratoga: R and E Research Associates, 1974.

Raquel, Marciano Reborozo. "A Study of Guidance for Filipino Prospective Teachers in the University of Washington." Master's thesis, University of Washington, 1936.

Rodman, Margaret Catharine. "The Trend of Alaskan Commerce through the Port of Seattle." Master's thesis, University of Washington, 1930.

San Buenaventura, Steffi. "Nativism and Ethnicity in a Filipino-American Experience." Ph.D. diss., University of Hawai'i, 1990.

Scroggs, Joseph Campbell. "Labor Problems in the Fruit Industry of the Yakima Valley." Master's thesis, University of Washington, 1937.

Seeman, Albert Lloyd. "The Port of Seattle: A Study in Urban Geography." Ph.D. diss., University of Washington, 1930.

Tanaka, Stefan Akio. "The Nikkei on Bainbridge Island, 1883–1942: A Study of Migration and Community Development." Master's thesis, University of Washington, 1977.

Tung, Charlene. "The Social Reproductive Labor of Filipina Transmigrant Workers in Southern California: Caring for Those Who Provide Elderly Care." Ph.D. diss., University of California, Irvine, 1999.

United Cannery Agricultural Packing and Allied Workers of America. "Excerpts on Alaska Congressional Fisheries Hearings with Special Reference to the Salmon Cannery Industry, Traps, Non-resident Workers, Whites, Filipinos, Others, Etc." Seattle, 1939. Manuscript provided to author by Trinidad Rojo.

Woolston, Katharine Dally. "Japanese Standard of Living in Seattle." Master's thesis, University of Washington, 1927.

GOVERNMENT DOCUMENTS

State of California, Department of Industrial Relations. "Facts about Filipino Immigration into California." Special Bulletin, no. 3. San Francisco: State of California, Department of Industrial Relations, 1930. Reprint, San Francisco: R and E Research Associates, 1972.

State of Washington. "First Report Un-American Activities in Washington State 1948." Report of the Joint Legislative Fact-Finding Committee on Un-American Activities, State of Washington.

U.S. Department of Commerce, Bureau of the Census. *Fifteenth Census of the United States: 1930.* Vol. 3, pt. 2. Washington, D.C.: Government Printing Office, 1932.

————. *Sixteenth Census of the United States: 1940.* Vol. 2, pt. 7. Washington, D.C.: Government Printing Office, 1943.

SPECIAL COLLECTIONS AND ARCHIVES

Demonstration Project for Asian Americans, Seattle.

Kroch Library, Cornell University, Ithaca, N.Y.

Library of Congress, Washington, D.C.

Manuscripts, Special Collections, University Archives, University of Washington, Seattle.

Museum of History and Industry, Seattle.

National Pinoy Archives, Filipino American National Historical Society, Seattle.

Pacific Northwest Regional Branch, National Archives, Seattle.

Records of the Bureau of Insular Affairs, General Records Relating to More Than One Island Possession, General Classified Files, 1898–1945, National Archives.
Seattle City Archives, Seattle.
Seattle Public School Archives, Seattle.
Superior Court Records, King County Superior Court, Seattle.

INTERVIEWS

Note: The interviews listed here are from the Washington State Oral/Aural History Program, the Demonstration Project for Asian Americans, and the National Pinoy Archives of the Filipino American National Historical Society, as well as others that I conducted myself. I have changed the names of the people whom I interviewed directly. Five of the individuals with whom I spoke were also interviewed through other programs, and hence they are listed twice here.

Abastilla, Josefina [pseud.]. Interview by author, Seattle, 10 May 1993, 17 May 1993.
Acena, Eddie. Interview by Bob Flor, FIL-KNG75-18bf, Washington State Oral/Aural History Program, 26 June 1975.
Acena, Jose. Interview by Dorothy L. Cordova, FIL-KNG75-24dlc, Washington State Oral/Aural History Program, 28 July 1975.
Aguinaldo, Sergio [pseud.]. Interview by author, Seattle, 13 May 1993, 22 February 1994.
Aliwanag, Leo. Interview by Cynthia Mejia, FIL-KNG76-50cm, Washington State Oral/Aural History Program, 19 August 1976.
Almaguer, Henry [pseud.]. Interview by author, Seattle, 27 January 1993.
Almonjuela, Dorothy. Interview by Teresa Cronin, FIL-KNG75-2tc, Washington State Oral/Aural History Program, 9 April 1975.
Angeles, Carlos [pseud.]. Interview by author, Seattle, 14 September 1993.
Angeles, Mariano. Interview by Cynthia Mejia, FIL-KNG75-32cm, Washington State Oral/Aural History Program, 6 November 1975.
Antolin, Pedro T. Interview by Bob Antolin, PNW81-Fil-022ba, Demonstration Project for Asian Americans, 1 September 1981.
Barrazona, Josefa. Interview by unknown, Demonstration Project for Asian Americans, date unknown.
Bautista, Al [pseud.]. Interview by author, Seattle, 30 September 1993, 19 July 1994.
Beltran, Maria Abastilla. Interview by Carolina Koslosky, FIL-KNG75-9ck, Washington State Oral/Aural History Program, 5 May 1975.
Bigornia, Felipe. Interview by Bob Antolin, PNW80-Fil-000ba, Demonstration Project for Asian Americans, 22 May 1980.
Braganza, Belen. Interview by Nancy Koslosky, PNW81-Fil-014nk, Demonstration Project for Asian Americans, 26 June 1981.
Carlos, Donald [pseud.]. Interview by author, Seattle, 14 September 1993.
Castillano, Bibiana Laigo. Interview by Frederic A. Cordova, Jr., FIL-KNG75-19jr, Washington State Oral/Aural History Program, 26 June 1975.
Castillano, Mike. Interview by Frederic A. Cordova, Jr., FIL-KNG75-23jr, Washington State Oral/Aural History Program, 2 July 1975.

Castillano, Mike B. Interview by Dorothy Cordova, PNW81-Fil-0004dc, Demonstration Project for Asian Americans, August 1981.

Castillo, John. Interview by F. A. Cordova, Jr., FIL-KNG75-15jr, Washington State Oral/Aural History Program, 29 July 1975.

Cordova, Frederic. Interview by Dominic Cordova, PNW-81-Fil-018dc, Demonstration Project for Asian Americans, July 1981.

Corpuz, Alfred [pseud.]. Interview by author, Seattle, 4 October 1993.

Corpuz, Anacleto. Interview by Teresa Cronin, FIL-KNG75-16tc, Washington State Oral/Aural History Program, 23 June 1975.

Corpuz, Ray Edralin. Interview by Bob Antolin, PNW81-Fil-028ba, Demonstration Project for Asian Americans, 22 September 1981.

Cortez, Cesar [pseud.]. Interview by author, Seattle, 1 October 1993.

Cortez, Julio [pseud.]. Interview by author, Seattle, 4 May 1993, 11 May 1993.

Cristobal, Dionicio (Denny). Interview by Carolina M. Apostol, FIL-KNG76-43cma, Washington State Oral/Aural History Program, 10 March 1976.

Del Fierro, Salvador. Interview by Carolina D. Koslosky, FIL-KNG75-29ck, Washington State Oral/Aural History Program, 15 September 1975.

Diaz, Sam [pseud.]. Interview by author, Seattle, 28 November 1992.

Domingo, Zacarias [pseud.]. Interview by author, Seattle, 29 September 1993, 17 July 1994.

Dumlao, Felipe G. Interview by Cynthia Mejia, FIL-KNG75-35cm, Washington State Oral/Aural History Program, 21 November 1975.

Fernando, Robert [pseud.]. Interview by author, Seattle, 28 September 1993.

Ferrera, Paulo [pseud.]. Interview by author, Seattle, 7 October 1993.

Filiarca, Pete. Interview by Frederic A. Cordova, Jr., FIL-KNG75-13jr, Washington State Oral/Aural History Program, 8 April 1975.

Floresca, Fred C. Interview by Carolina Koslosky, FIL-KNG76-2ck, Washington State Oral/Aural History Program, 2 May 1975.

Francisco, Emiliano Alfonzo. Interview by Ms. Koslosky, FIL-KNG75-20k, Washington State Oral/Aural History Program, 30 June 1975.

Gamido, Antonio [pseud.]. Interview by author, Seattle, 15 September 1993.

Garcia, Luis [pseud.]. Interview by author, Seattle, 27 September 1993.

Garo, Garciano. Interview by Pearl Ancheta, PNW-Fil-009PA, Demonstration Project for Asian Americans, 18 March 1981.

Gonong, Amado [pseud.]. Interview by author, Seattle, 18 May 1993.

Guerrero, David [pseud.]. Interview by author, Seattle, 10 September 1993.

Guiang, Marino. Interview by Dorothy Cordova, FIL-KNG76-52dc, Washington State Oral/Aural History Program, 24 September 1976.

Jenkins, Rufina, and Francesca Robinson. Interview by Carolina Koslosky, FIL-KNG75-ck, Washington State Oral/Aural History Program, 10 November 1975.

Johnson, Nancy [pseud.]. Interview by author, Seattle, 21 September 1993.

Lopez, Sammy R. Interview by Cynthia Mejia, FIL-KNG75-36cm, Washington State Oral/Aural History Program, 24 November 1975.

Madayag, Toribio. Interview by Teresa Cronin, FIL-KNG75-22tc, Washington State Oral/Aural History Program, 2 July 1975.

Manangan, Zacarias M. Interview by Carolina D. Koslosky, FIL-KNG75-30ck, Washington State Oral/Aural History Program, 30 September 1975.

Manzano, Antonio [pseud.]. Interview by author, Seattle, 4 October 1993, 15 February 1994.

Martin, Toribio. Interview by Dorothy Cordova, FIL-KNG76-44dc, Washington State Oral/Aural History Program, 27 April 1976.

Mendoza, Arsenio [pseud.]. Interview by author, Seattle, 16 September 1993.

Mendoza, John. Interview by Dorothy Cordova, FIL-KNG76-42dc, Washington State Oral/Aural History Program, 6 April 1976.

Mendoza, Vincent Yolenato, and Rosario Rosell Mendoza [listed as Mr. and Mrs. Vincent Mendoza]. Interview by Cynthia Mejia, FIL-KNG76-40cm, Washington State Oral/Aural History Program, 13 January 1976.

Mensalvas, Chris, and Jesus R. Yambao. Interview by Carolina Koslosky, FIL-KNG75-1ck, Washington State Oral/Aural History Program, 10 February and 11 February 1975.

Mina, Juan V. Interview by Carolina Apostol, FIL-KNG76-47cma, Washington State Oral/Aural History Program, 30 May 1976.

Mislang, Margaret M. Interview by Carolina Koslosky, FIL-KNG75-12ck, Washington State Oral/Aural History Program, 16 June 1975.

Narte, Felix. Interview by Teresa Cronin, FIL-KNG75-8tc, Washington State Oral/Aural History Program, 21 April 1975.

Navarette, Ignacio. Interview by Dorothy Cordova, Washington State Oral/Aural History Program, 17 September 1976.

Nonacido, Paula J. Interview by Cynthia Mejia, FIL-KNG76-49cm, Washington State Oral/Aural History Program, 7 July 1976, 22 September 1976.

Nonog, Victorio. Interview by Cynthia Mejia, FIL-KNG76-38cm, Washington State Oral/Aural History Program, 2 January 1976.

Ordona, Sinforoso L. Interview by unknown, PNW81-Fil, Demonstration Project for Asian Americans, date unknown.

Ortega, Con[s]tance "Connie." Interview by Dorothy L. Cordova and Nancy Koslosky, PNW81-Fil-017dc/nk, Demonstration Project for Asian Americans, 20 July 1981.

Ortega, Mark [pseud.]. Interview by author, Seattle, 28 November 1992.

Pimental, Lorenzo. Interview by Cynthia Mejia, FIL-KNG75-34cm, Washington State Oral/Aural History Program, 14 November 1975.

Ramos, Vicky [pseud.]. Interview by author, Seattle, 28 November 1992.

Ranjo, Teodolo Aguinaldo. Interview by Cynthia Mejia, FIL-KNG76-41cm, Washington State Oral/Aural History Program, 14 January 1976.

Rapada, Honorato. Interview by Teresa Cronin, FIL-KNG75-11tc, Washington State Oral/Aural History Program, 24 May 1975.

Rapada, Mary Louise, and Honorato Rapada. Interview by Christina Corpuz, Independent Study Project—Spring Semester 1993, Oral History of Filipino American and Native American Elders of Bainbridge Island, National Pinoy Archives, 7 March 1993.

Rinonos, Bcn. Interview by Teresa Cronin, FIL-KNG75-3tc, Washington State Oral/Aural History Program, 27 March 1975.

Rodrigo, Antonio [listed as Mr. Tony Rodrigo]. Interview by Dorothy Cordova, FIL-KNG76-53dc, Washington State Oral/Aural History Program, 15 October 1976.

Rojo, Trinidad. Interview by Carolina D. Koslosky, FIL-KNG75-17ck, Washington State Oral/Aural History Program, 18 February 1975, 19 February 1975.

Romero, Rudy C. Interview by Teresa Cronin, FIL-KNG75-4tc, Washington State Oral/Aural History Program, 20 March 1975.

Simbe, Roman, and Hazel Simbe with Sinforoso Ordona. Interview by DeeAnn Dixon and Nancy Koslosky, PNW82-Fil-030dad/nk, Demonstration Project for Asian Americans, 18 January 1982, June 22 1982.

Tanaka, L. [pseud.], M. Hasegawa [pseud.], and C. Fugita [pseud.]. Interview by author, Seattle, 22 September 1993.

Tangalan, Sylvestre A. Interview by Carolina D. Koslosky, FIL-KNG75-28ck, Washington State Oral/Aural History Program, 27 August 1975.

Tapang, Bruno. Interview by unknown, PNW 81-FIL-007, Demonstration Project for Asian Americans, date unknown.

Toribio, Carlos [pseud.]. Interview by author, Seattle, 18 July 1994.

Torres, Ponce. Interview by Carolina Koslosky, FIL-KNG75-14ck, Washington State Oral/Aural History Program, 25 August 1975.

Torres, Virginia [pseud.]. Interview by author, Seattle, 14 September 1993.

Valdez, Sinforoso [pseud.]. Interview by author, Seattle, 9 September 1993.

Velasco, Don [pseud.]. Interview by author, Seattle, 9 February 1994.

Ylanan, Mateo. Interview by unknown, PNW81-Fil-010PA, Demonstration Project for Asian Americans, date unknown.

Index

Page numbers in italics indicate maps.